THE WORLD WE KNEW

A PERSONAL SOCIAL HISTORY OF NZ FROM THE 1930'S TO 1960's

Vonney Allan

Copyright Vonney Allan 2021

Dedicated to the women of NZ

ISBN: 9798459044911

Social history, New Zealand, memoirs, 1930s, 1940s, 1950s, 1960s.

Preface

I have dreams that come true. Many that are just day-to-day occurrences and seem akin to déjà vu but some that are more portentous. I have identified around 11 types of dreams but these ones are very specific. I understand immediately now even when dreaming them – they will happen – no matter what steps I may take to avoid them, even desperate ones. Every path will always lead there.

When I had been married several years with two children, had our own home built and found a regular part-time job, I had a dream in the form of a still photo of myself, my husband and two young children – only not the then present ones.

We were standing near the top of a hill looking out over a long view of a valley and rolling green countryside of farms with animals and trees and indistinct fences, no power poles or dwellings apparent, to distant bush set on higher ground at least 30 miles into the distance. It was a serene and beautiful scene.

Only my eyes seemed to have the option of moving. To my right was a house and although it appeared reasonably large, the angle showing was indirect so there were few details. The coloured panorama we were admiring would have been seen from its windows though and there was already a sense of it belonging to us.

Because my then children were not those in the picture, I realised with immediate certainty I had lost them. I never spoke of this dream to anyone for a long time, but quietly grieved to myself for what I knew I was really going to have to face. Imagining their loss and what had become of us became the thing uppermost in my mind. I wanted to believe I had dreamed for another person.

That dreamed scene is still as clear to me currently as it was to actually become some 12 years later when my new family had been looking for a 10-acre block within the radius of reasonable driving time to the city that we could afford. The day we walked up that sloping driveway, lined with trees obscuring the spectacular view at first, I stopped at the top in shock, the others with me, and said slowly in amazement, "We will be buying this place." Every dream detail matched the eventual reality.

Later, a clever friend, who believed in my experiences, puzzled about them until he decided that in my sleep I seem to be able to move through time, obviously not by choice. Although it may be an incredible hypothesis to some, it made sense to me, at least more than any other.

My Valley

My valley is a special place,
where hills dip down in curving grace,
and many greens combine to make
a soothing view, almost an ache.

The constant grass always covers
the brown of soil like a lover.
The hazy hills of hot horizon
blend with blue, a mirage liaison.

Even in the times of drought
the many trees contrasted doubt,
Their shape and height testament to,
a hidden lushness to renew.

Sunrise on surging fog from white
to sea of candy floss delight,
or creeping rain, feeling its way,
on up the slopes to blot the day.

A furious wind could whistle through
its folding curves with winter's brew.
The moody shadow of a cloud,
covering colour like a shroud.

But even in those darkest times,
there was a beauty in its lines.
A stunning sunset bronzed its light,
before the gloaming of the night.

Throughout its many moods it knows,
my love for it forever grows.
A foretold dream drew me to it,
where it grew part of my spirit.

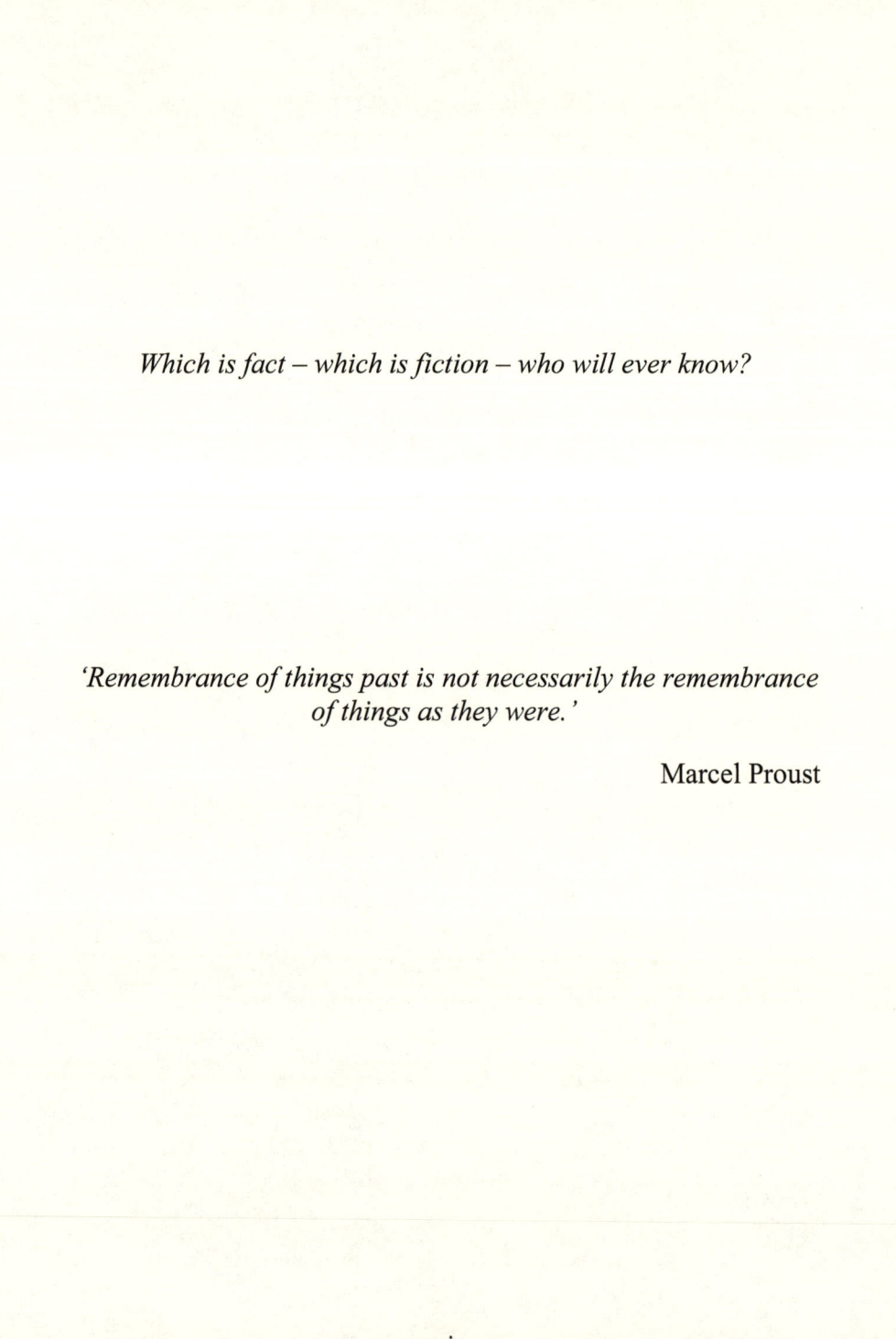

Which is fact – which is fiction – who will ever know?

'Remembrance of things past is not necessarily the remembrance of things as they were.'

Marcel Proust

My Valley v
A Brief Summary ix
Chapter 1 New Zealand 1930's to 1960's 1
Chapter 2 General 3
Chapter 3 Farming 15
Chapter 4 The 1930's Depression 23
Chapter 5 Depression Depths & Recovery. 46
Chapter 6 Communication/Radio/Wireless 53
Chapter 7 The Second World War 66
Chapter 8 The 1951 Watersiders' Strike 83
Chapter 9 Transport 87
Chapter 10 Housing 124
Chapter 11 Neighbours 138
Chapter 12 Health 143
Chapter 13 Education/Childhood Experiences 152
Chapter 14 Different Cultures 187
Chapter 15 Religion 192
Chapter 16 Country Living 1940's to 1950's. 195
Chapter 17 City Living 1940's to 1950's 217
Chapter 18 Events 232
Chapter 19 Teenagers 239
Chapter 20 Marriage & Social Expectations in the 40's & 50's
.... 245
Chapter 21 Working Women's Histories 275
Chapter 22 Hypocrisy / Divorce / Violence/ Murder 288
Chapter 23 Sexual Preferences & Experiences, Homosexuality
.... 312
Chapter 24 Fashion 342
Chapter 25 Entertainment & Leisure 361
Chapter 26 Food 385
Chapter 27 Our Summers 400
Chapter 28 Personal Pen Portraits 419

My thanks to:

The many people, including casual strangers, who encouraged me to continue with my book over the years when I was low, especially the young people when they heard about it, which had surprised me.

The friends who took a serious interest and did hours of proof reading, like Sheila Lee, and our North Shore Writers' Group that are the constant and patient ones who have hung in there through our regular meetings listening to anecdotes and commenting with insight. Our group grows ever smaller.

And my family who are so pleased for me to have finally officially become an author and probably even more pleased that my book is finally done!

A Brief Summary

These are the people written about and their relationship to the author.

Vonney	Vonney Allan. Author. Born 1937 in Auckland. Mary and Arnold's daughter. Married twice.
*Mary	Francis Mary Beal –Simpson –McDonald – Connolly. Born 10.06.06 in Rotorua. Vonney's mother. Mary was an only child. Married 3 times.
*Granddad	Dupair Edward Beal. Born 1867 in London. Moved to Sydney then NZ. Vonney's grandfather. Mary's father. Married twice. Widowed twice.
*Nana	Alice Maud Beal nee Hayter. Born 1870s -1880s in Australia. Died in 1944. Vonney's grandmother. Mary's mother. Second wife to Dupair.
Arnold	Simpson. A few years older than Mary. Born in Auckland. Mary's first husband. Vonney and Ralph's father. Present about 5 years. Marriage ended in divorce.
*John	John McDonald. A few years older than Mary. Born near Rotorua. Mary's second husband. Vonney's step-father. Veronica's father. Present about 5 years. Marriage ended in divorce.
Joe	Joseph Connolly. Mary's third husband when she was in her fifties, he in his sixties. Vonney's second step-father. Present 5 years. Separated for many years but never divorced.
Ralph	Ralph Dupair Simpson. Born 1934 in Auckland. Vonney's brother. Mary and Arnold's son. Married to Kay née Jones (Author's best friend). 5 sons. Moved to Australia in the 1960's.

Veronica	Veronica McDonald. Born 1943 in Auckland. Vonney and Ralph's half-sister. Mary and John's daughter.
Shanla	Vonney's first living daughter. Born 1958 in Auckland. Mentally retarded. Died 1985.
Bevan	Vonney's only son. Born 1959 in Auckland. Died 2014.
Kerry	Vonney's daughter. Born 1970 in Auckland to second husband Bruce Allan.
Jenny	Vonney's daughter. Born 1971 in Auckland to second husband Bruce Allan.
The Bevs	Bev Brown. A year older than Vonney, her neighbour in Grey Lynn, Auckland, Long-time friend. Bev Wildermoth. Same age from AGGS. Good friend.
*Colleen	The daughter of Aunt May and Uncle Charlie Aitken. Related through Veronica's family. A big part of Vonney and family's early lives
*Uncle Ross	Ross Turner and his children Mark (Ralph's age) and Carol (younger than Vonney). Family friends. Stayed in their old home many times and holidayed at Onetangi.
*Aunt Alice	Alice and Henry Tyson. Mary's older friends from Rotorua. Vonney and Ralph were cared for by them at different times.

*Fuller details for some people are in Chapter 28. Some names have been changed for various reasons.

Chapter 1 New Zealand 1930's to 1960's

Although the 1900's was a century of immense change, probably the most momentous we had ever experienced, when transport for instance developed from a man on his horse to a man on the moon, things went on evolving in their often subtle way and it is difficult at times to remember the exact time frame in which changes happened. They were accepted gradually, but not necessarily talked about much and it would sometimes take a comment from someone to think back to what used to be, to realise that they had even occurred.

Aside from the early Depression years and facts and figures researched to give a more accurate background, this whole piece is a personal take, complemented by information from conversations with others of a similar age or observations from reading. It reflects society as I or our family, friends, and acquaintances experienced it and limiting for that reason. It was a different time when, with the general adversities that had to be faced by everyone, family was really important and friends were friends for life, and usually partners too, whatever their shortcomings, idiosyncrasies and sometimes unforgivable behaviour – which would possibly have been kept secret. (There were few options for women at least.)

It was also partly because we didn't have the modern communication and travel options we have today so people settled into a community for the long haul. The unified community spirit is not easily imaginable when trying to relate it to our current world. Perhaps those who experienced the Christchurch earthquake or similar, could understand but it may only really be appreciated in the memory of those who were there, like every generation's ethos. Covid-19 has taken me back to the kindness of that time. Perhaps we identified with each other because we were predominantly workers and with lockdown we could relate to each other again because we were living in the same circumstances regardless of lifestyles.

The space and words allocated to the Depression, the Second World War and the 1951 Water-siders' Strike seem necessary to me as they had such an enormous influence on the whole community with the hard lessons learned and then reinforced. NZ is what it is today because of the direct, indirect and often subtle ongoing affects from those three major events. Radio also played a huge part in social and political change and deserves its place with the other three.

Chapter 2 General

The good thing about living in NZ in the 1930's to the 1960's period was the relatively simple, safe, and assuring attitudes of its people. It would be unusual not to trust anyone as we often had to rely on each other for various reasons. There were no such things as counsellors so support for men was unheard of except perhaps a pat on the back from a local doctor and maybe a mate. For women there were over-the-fence chats that often relieved tensions (since confirmed by those who would know) and if family were not available, neighbours and work mates were the first we went to in an emergency as we were definitely pragmatic. This reliance was enhanced during the Depression and the war, so for the most part, people were decent and dealt with each other with integrity. A hand shake would seal a deal. We followed the protocols of Western countries and Christianity and were proper, civil, and polite. Chivalry was still around, men opened doors to allow a woman to go through first, walking on the outside of a footpath to protect her, taking her arm under the elbow. It was the 'done thing'.

A polite hello, smile, or nod passing someone in the street was normal, the person known or unknown. We seemed to have an air of justifiable complacency and predictability about us, down-to-earth reasoning along with common moral values of thrift, honesty, integrity and devotion to family and friends, (usually) trusting the wisdom of those we saw as our betters along with regular church attendance. Older adults were often more formal and dignified and there was anyway a communal respect for them and by and large for the authorities as well. (These same values can be seen now as naive and old fashioned, contributing to people born in that era losing their life savings believing in hoax phone calls, email online contacts and friendly offers of help, sucked in by slick, scurrilous, conscienceless and covetous predators. Not that they, or other criminals, were not around then, but they were recognised more easily and shunned. As were alcoholics.)

House doors were not locked nor cars, if you were lucky enough to have one. Bicycles – people rode them everywhere, especially kids. Motorbikes and horses could be left anywhere and would remain there till picked up. This was accepted as the NZ way and confirmed years later by a German millionaire friend who had visited here not long after the war (he was a child during it) who told me he was so impressed with NZ, he made it his choice of country to live in when he married and had his own children.

Being conscious of other people's needs was part of society as a whole, compassion and kindness were common as was common sense, and we were 'for the underdog' in general. There was also a sense of equality ('a greater socio-economic equity') perhaps 'egalitarianism', although that may be too strong a word to have been used then or accepted. There were very few millionaires (billionaires not thought of) that ordinary people were conscious of anyway, except perhaps for the ones with what was referred to as 'new money'. Their spending was often more obvious and seen as inappropriate or flashy and sometimes ill-mannered – experienced by my sister-in-law Kay in a Newmarket shoe-shop where she worked. The older moneyed people there were polite. It was probably partly dependant on the area where you lived. (Given I have shifted 53 times, 3 times from choice, my experience is not necessarily typical.)

So envy on the whole was not a large factor, although there was a sense of wanting to get ahead and achieve. Nor did greed appear to be the dominating motivator, although it always would be for some. 'Value for money' was a generally accepted philosophy with the expectation that even if a product wasn't expensive, it would last for years. Rip-off merchants were seen off pretty quickly.

A woman a bit older than me I chatted to once, told me her little son always bizarrely said he was going to be a millionaire one day. She said she would constantly bring him back to the reality of their lives and tell him not to be so silly. He confounded her by becoming a millionaire in America very young. Children then did know that money was not to be squandered and often grew up to be good savers and aware of the value of everything – further education, low wages and apprenticeships in their teens controlling factors anyway.

The concept of there being rich and poor people is more difficult to assess. To me no-one felt any better than us. There were probably extremes of both but not so obvious and not the numbers there are now. Poor now and poor then seems so different too. (Dr. Clare Achmen, TV 1 2020, stated currently the wealth in NZ is incredibly unequal.)

There would have been degrees of poor as well, which because I was born near the end of the Depression and those awful years, I may not have recognised. No-one around me commented on anyone's situation. The only time that I remember as a child was when a temporary neighbour in one of the bush settlements we lived in briefly, noted Mary (our mother) used pieces of old blankets to wrap her inherited solid oak furniture in to protect it. We moved an average of six times a year in those days. She asked Mary if she could have the bits to sew together to keep her six children warm. I don't actually know what Mary's response was it being our last shift with our stepfather. I have since worked out she may not have left the blanket bits behind. It is often a final trivial argument that can trigger a separation, even with regular violence involved, and that perhaps was one of those times. We never lived with my stepfather again. I may have been nine.

Middle class, if there was one, was not that obvious either. We had no friends with a car. Before the war, people went on a holiday, not as we know them now though. Radios were an indication of perhaps having a little more than others, but it was often shared with neighbours and friends, especially for important news. (The TV of the day.) Clothes were passed on and down. First up, best dressed in big families. Food given, shared or swapped, bikes borrowed, useful things lent, free haircuts offered, newspapers and magazines like the National Geographic passed on. Perhaps because there were fewer choices then, there were fewer expectations.

None of us wore shoes to school in the summer. If a child was forced to leave home with them on they were soon removed and tucked into the large, heavy leather satchel bags we all used. Neither were they worn by some in winter in many parts of Auckland at least, regardless of chilblains. A friend in Otahuhu however said she had cardboard insoles and dreaded the rain. There was not an expectation of clothing being particularly special for school until intermediate or secondary level when uniforms were worn, although not usually in the country.

Mary sewed well (sometimes cutting a child's pattern from adult sized clothes) so we always looked acceptable and even if others didn't, it was not commented on nor were children teased/bullied about their clothes that I recall. Our family were seldom in other people's homes (some relations the exception) so there were few comparisons to make about furnishings and sizes of houses. The odd times we were, there were some obvious differences, coloured patterned toilet paper for me, quality of furniture and fittings and bigger houses – more obvious to adults – but the people themselves spoke and behaved similarly to us. They made us feel at home and did not rate themselves particularly. Our family always had good manners which were no doubt handed down from Mary's parents who, had we thought in 'class' terms, were probably at least used to having money around. 'Class' wasn't a word that seemed to be used much, probably deliberately by those who had experienced it.

Although there was always the races, Lotto hope was unknown. There were the Art Unions, the first national lottery in 1933 established after the Otago Art Society, and others had also used them as a way to raise funds but the early prizes of alluvial gold were relatively small. The 'Golden Treasure' of 1935 sold 200,000 tickets, with a top prize of 2000 pounds, and the lowest 400 prizes of 2 pounds. A review of Lotteries was done by the Second Labour Government in the late 1950's and in 1961 the National Govt. introduced the 'Golden Kiwi', a pale affair compared to today's Lotto hoopla and prizes.

NZ men generally thought of themselves with an earnest and humble pride as strong, resilient, conscientious hard working blokes in a self-reliant, sturdy, independent community. The biggest percentage of our population was working class and most Kiwis believed they were as good as their bosses. 'Jack is as good as his master' and 'We won't be bossed about' were common sayings.

On the whole there was probably loyalty both ways between a boss and workers and I think the security of the work relationship was a steadying influence on the marriage one. Men dreamed their dreams, hopeful of the future, some even aspiring to becoming prime minister, which was within the realms of possibility for anyone, educated and rich or not, but most dreams were much simpler then. The good old Scottish Presbyterian and Methodist hard work ethic was always encouraged, expecting it to lead to deservedly-earned pay rises and promotion, the reward for long term stickability and predictability. There was not so much a sense of striving, more an accepting settled staunchness and sometimes bloody-mindedness about getting on with it, innovation applied when necessary.

And at times there was a laid-back gravitas about things although it was also our penchant for irreverently 'taking the Mickey' and laughing at ourselves that often made the difference between a reasonable level of survival and not and we made our own fun. Men better at relieving tension with a joke. Light-hearted women could be considered 'away with the fairies'.

Although I can only speak from my own observations and experience, I don't think people we knew were particularly unhappy with their status by the late forties, regardless of the previous scarcity, hardship, and privation of the Great Depression and the losses and fears from the Second World War and the deprivation from its restrictions. The scars and limitations, mental and physical, were still there to be coped with. Men would have also missed the strong male supportive comradeship the war brought. Feelings were not discussed by men openly anyway. Only they knew how they felt, each having to find their own way to recovery.

Quote from the *New Zealand Herald*

> It seemed 'Our sense of nation was forged on the shores of Gallipoli' and we were still forming 'a real sense of it which the forties war contributed to. We recognised our individuality as a nation as did the eventual forced reduction of our export products by England, seen at the time as a betrayal to our loyalty, particularly our war losses. The reaction to that

weaning was a definite spur to self-reliance though and more independence.'

Quote from John Roughan, *NZ Herald*; 'We are a practical, liberal, reserved people who generally do not rush to judgement on those in a situation we don't face. We give them the benefit of the doubt.'

Farmers particularly were affected and dairy farms halved in five years. The English still called us 'Colonials' in those years but I didn't personally experience anyone who took offence. For aware people, they may have felt an underlying fear from the speculated scenarios that were written about over the years around being invaded by various countries, not without good reason at times, the thinking being that NZ was in a strategically useful position globally. Latterly it had been the horrors of repercussions from an atomic bomb spreading into the South Pacific. However, day-to-day the world felt about as safe as it was ever going to be for us and we mainly lived circled by our secure bubble of complacency.

Not that the radio news wasn't listened to or papers read regularly, when they were affordable, but we seem to have always been reasonably insular. In general most did not want to be bothered with any more disconcerting international problems and unless things impacted on us in some way, like it had from the overseas repercussions of 1929 Wall Street meltdown, the war, influenza or a Royal Family visit or celebrations, we were not particularly aware of or interested in what went on in the rest of the world.

The strong sense of detachment and isolation by our physical remoteness meant a token impact only, except for travellers or those directly affected by having relatives in other countries or needing to be aware of overseas prices.

It was usually enough dealing with our own personal everyday mini disasters. No-one seemed to have the stamina to take on anything else. Life was about returning to a new normality, with unemployment and food no longer big issues, and everyone wanted to shut out the previous deprivations of the Depression and the terrible thoughts of war. There was an underlying, unspoken community understanding that we all carried on with life as best we could, or at least were expected to, some probably better than others. Our welfare state was accepted as environmentally clean, we had free education and health care and so although society was regulated and constrained, people wanted to be left alone to get on with their own lives again with just everyday things. There was a need to embrace a sense of security, safety, and stability which lay in conformity. 'Getting back to normal' meant a caring, decent society and everyone being entitled to a 'fair go' with choices of jobs for the men. The acceptance for who you were – as long as no awkward questions were asked – a beer after work, some sport to watch and being as good as the next bloke with the wife and family safe at home.

Women were to be thrifty homemakers as money was precious. They were expected to be cheerful and house proud, look after the children and be accepting and contented with 'their lot'. A period of consolidation.

Our carefully nurtured constricting scenario of the tight little New Zealand world was all most of us knew although discontent in some quarters was to be expected, which the 1951 Waterfront Dispute highlighted, but at that time there had been no obvious sense of unrest from people around us.

The reality for some who wanted to 'spread their wings' living in this entrenched puritanical, parochial community and the often smothering social snobbery of colonial conformity, was especially stifling when conservative types dictated lives. Our mother Mary was brought up in that lifestyle from the twenties, so to her age group it was more familiar, and like then, deception and hypocrisy are still important to save face.

Unfortunately these attitudes were taken to extremes by some. Known criminals, or potential ones, 'were beyond the pale'. People were discriminated against for their mistakes so for those who crossed the unmercifully pious line, they stayed there. Whole families were often ostracised in the street, at the shops, public functions (especially men should they attend), gatherings and even church. Bias no doubt affected the men when they were looking for work.

There was always a gossip in towns and city communities (their populations small then too) who would pass on warnings when certain people went by, so moving on was not necessarily helpful or possible for the victims and the hassling would continue, justifiably or not, and sometimes of course with only rumour as the basis. They could be spoken about in a vicious or sarcastic way and spoken to in a deliberately provoking manner, especially when alcohol was involved. Sometimes nothing particularly nasty was said – just a look or a warning to be aware and not make friendly overtures to some families – what was left unsaid was often the most damning (also for me another puzzling part of life).

Children were punished as well as their parents for perceived or real misdeeds which was quite cruel and especially petty at school. The children were considered 'bad blood' and were often physically bullied or spoken to in self-righteous spite or just ignored, so youngsters were the ones who copped the most from hurting jibes when sanctimonious judgemental elders lacked the moral and/or physical courage to speak out directly to the parents.

Generally it seemed to me, men were the ones who held grudges and seemed more vengeful (which has not gone away with the 2012 admitted case of Ewen Macdonald) but devastatingly malicious women's tongues were the main reporting system and they could use more subtle but still hurtful remarks. The women were the ones who were victims of a male-oriented society, including violence and, unlike today, there was no recognition or help from the community except the Presbyterian Social Services and the Salvation Army, which was all I belatedly found. Constantly being at home with children, little mixed adult company and perhaps a husband without much to say and so little to distract or interest them, could result in women being bored (especially intelligent and/or educated ones) and overly fussing and in some cases to narrowmindedness and bigotry. The small things we can move on from now with all our distractions, sometimes led to perceived wrongs that could smoulder on for years and split friends and families.

But any family awash with secrets often imploded anyway, destroying them for things that could be seen as trivial at a later time. (Our current internet grapevine supersedes anything that has ever gone before.) Families were more important during the Depression, the war and down times as they were usually the real support when things went badly wrong, so if that happened and a church or friends did not fill the gap, life could have been pretty bad for some. Our family was the recipient of some biased attitudes at different times, nevertheless 'not to mix with undesirables' was the message we were also given from Mary. For women especially, it was important to be aware of how it was to behave like a lady. Appearances were everything – no matter what, and that had been Mary's standard for herself and our family – however inappropriate to our situation sometimes. Children, by contrast to later in the century, had much more freedom, boundaries wider without the concern about any great danger from strangers in cars or fear of being assaulted, sexually abused or murdered (except unfortunately by our own, maybe). Our parents did not need to be paranoid about our safety and we often amused ourselves for hours away from home in the city and the country, sometimes with the forbidden children as well, and no-one would be concerned we were up to mischief. 'We were to be seen and not heard' so we looked after ourselves. Beyond personal fears I think generally we all experienced fear of death by illness and for boys particularly, a call up for war, like previous generations. Although others I know would have been proud to go.

A younger friend from a large family who lived in an isolated beach area up north said his mum would pack their lunches for the day in the holidays and they would go off together or split up in pairs or like him, be on his own, and would swim and run along exploring the shoreline for unusual things or wander in the bush until dark or when hunger bit. Perhaps with warnings of what to be careful of, but none of the family came to harm and that freedom is in his memory as an ideal childhood.

Parents would expect children to contribute to the family and also include them in activities keeping them busy on a project like raising money for a scout den or school swimming pool by collecting soft drink bottles to claim a refund on and also help in the physical work of building. Farm kids didn't have much playtime, but that wouldn't have necessarily worried them. Only the privileged intelligent few made it to University, the rest of us were working by 15 or 16, some in a trade with an apprenticeship.

Four Cities

Each city was different. Scottish Dunedin was established in 1848 by a lay group of the Free Church of Scotland and was the most pre-eminent city in NZ by 1865, its layout influenced by Edinburgh 'planned with geometric precision'. It had a booming development whose population grew very fast especially after the gold rush in Otago in 1860's. Potential miners, made up of Chinese, Irish, English, Italians, French and Germans, would land from the many ships berthing at Port Chalmers, the primary port for the South Island, and pass through Dunedin, both on their way inland on the long and arduous Dunstan Trail as well as on their return. Some successful, some not. The remains of primitive schist huts used by miners at the end of the trail in rugged country are still there to this day.

There was a Christian (including Scottish Presbyterian) and cultural mix and as the city expanded they remained a steady society without the extremes of wealth we have today, although the eventual huge land-owners were in a category of their own. Rich cosmopolitan values and vibrant intellectualism and publishing encouraged discussions on world affairs and education was seen by the Scots as 'the salvation of society'. Their University, medical and dental schools were the first in NZ. It had firsts for businesses too and it was accepted the citizens were slightly dour and could be tight although they were trusted to be fair.

The NZ Steamship Co. developed and remained dominant till the end of the 19th century as did many big businesses in the commercial hub and the city's grand Scottish heritage was admired for its architecture – including the Otago University. The restored opulent old NZR Railway Station and Otago University reflect the proud history of its achievements. Today even more so since it has the highest density of historic Gothic and Edwardian and Victorian buildings left in NZ. It is admired as much by tourists now as it was originally. It remains an academic drawcard.

Christchurch seemed to have few coloured people, so seeing a Maori there in the city once in 1967 was a shock although they had settled there. The city was deemed conservative and very English with class awareness and the usual nepotism and the 'old boy/school tie' thing, our perception being it was stronger there than in other places. There were big land-holders in the South Island who would have had more influence on society along with perhaps a greater consciousness of people's background and money. 'Class' probably more appreciated although that was not a word that was much used there either.

The colder Christchurch weather wasn't to my liking when I lived there for a year once in the sixties with a partner, with snow in the city and often fog till lunchtime. Our first day there in the summer I had wondered why lunchtime women office workers walked around in winter skirts with light tops in 90 degree temperatures. At about 3pm we sat in the car near the evening paper building to buy one to look for jobs. A city high rise in our sight had a large square on its roof, 4 sides alternating the time and temperature. Between 3 and 3:30 the temperature dropped down to 60 degrees Fahrenheit so we quickly got the message.

I have not visited Christchurch since the earthquakes and don't really want to see the devastation in reality. All those lovely buildings gone just seemed too much. I wish everyone well and hope that their creative endeavours will once again make it a beautiful city for the 21st century.

On one of the few times I visited windy Wellington, rounding the corner of a building near the harbour, a gust blew me back again to my astonishment. A later visit proved it can also have amazing days – ones out of the box. I didn't envy the, by then, not-to-be trusted politicians who lived there or people with government jobs either who were in general considered 'government lackeys'. This attitude would be even more derogative at times when they were the ones who did have employment when thousands didn't. Envy and jealousy is always about although levels differ.

Of the four main cities, Auckland was always the largest in my youth with a more varied population (currently in 2018 with 220 different nations) and I think considered itself superior to the others, many feeling it should replace Wellington as the capital.

Our NZ Identity 2018

Our own unique NZ identity that eventually emerged and which we finally accepted and became known for, born from the hardship, loss, determination and the creativity of our forebears, seems to slowly be eroding and dissolving into a new more multicultural and diverse nation. The background values of my childhood based on religion, solid Scottish stringency and a generally accepted, 'all men are equal' philosophy, are no longer obvious in our everyday lives or expected to be honoured. Not something that would ever have been envisaged once.

Chapter 3 Farming

Farm Stint

My stepfather, John, primarily a bushman, also took jobs on dairy farms for short periods in the forties and we had often been around cows at different places in the country when people had their own one on spare ground near their house, especially if they had large families. Sometimes the children would let us hand milk if we asked.

A lone cow wasn't encouraged unless it had been tested for TB, not that people necessarily adhered to the rules. I doubt some parents would have been able to afford to have it done anyway, even if they knew to. Probably the 'she'll be right' attitude would have prevailed.

The worker's house was usually set away from the farm owners and was a reasonable size with 3 bedrooms, but we were more isolated then and for my half-sister Veronica and I there were no other children to play with. Shopping was difficult when there was no public transport. At times we did have more access to the shops if they were in reasonable walking distance (say two or three miles) or the farm was on or near a main highway with buses.

The rhythm of the day began with an early start in the lantern and candle-lit dark and we would vaguely hear Mary preparing porridge for a pre-breakfast for my stepfather, which included at least two cups of tea often with four teaspoons of sugar to get him going before he went down to the cowshed, coming back later in the morning for the main cooked meal.

Although there were milking machines there were no rotary ones in the places we stayed and stripping was still done by hand afterward on an average of between 50 and 100 cows. Plenty of milk and cream for the taking although it was raw and unpasteurised. The pigs were content with their skim milk and the bacon tasted better too. (Pork taste reflects what pigs have been fed on.)

When we were allowed in the shed while milking was in progress, we would try and slurp a mouthful of cream from where the separator's spout hung over its container, without being caught, and often the family cat did too. I was much more able to than Veronica. Silver cans of cream would be carted down to the gate pick-up point and left on stands for the big trucks and their usually cheerful, cheeky drivers to take to the dairy factories dotted all over the country. Different dairy factories produced various things – treated milk, dried milk, butter & sometimes cheese and casein. The sad sight today of the big indestructible-looking concrete buildings and loading bays, paint flaking off their neglected and exposed walls, set on the side of busy highways, represents the abandoned way of life that many will have mourned.

Aside from sometimes taking John his morning or afternoon tea when he was fencing further from the house than normal, we mostly played in the house grounds. Cows would sometimes be in a paddock near us and we would talk to them like the farmers did, although we didn't know their names. They would stand in clusters watching us over the fence, their doleful, stolid brown eyes gazing at us in a detached way from under long straight lashes, chewing their cud and evacuating at the same time, the pads steaming in the cool air. If I patted them, they would often lift their heads for more when I stopped, saliva slopping from their mouths. Veronica was too small to reach them and would just touch them quickly when I lifted her up.

On one farm for some evening emergency in winter when I was about seven, Mary unusually sent me to bring John back during milking. It was drizzling lightly at the end of several days of heavy rain and I had to open three gates around boggy ground to reach him. The last one nearest to the milking shed was in a hollow that had been churned more deeply than the others to a thick slurry of mud and droppings. I struggled along the fence line at first but found I had to step into the sucking mess at the actual gate to open it. I tried to find the most useful way through, but it swung away from me once I had. The instruction –'Never leave a gate open' was stuck in my head. I wobbled and slithered after it until I eventually somehow became totally stuck right in the deepest part of the smelly muck up past my thighs. I stood there trying to think of a way to get myself out of the situation, knowing that after milking someone would come, but found it hard to balance upright. Dreading falling over as I may not be able to get up again, in desperation and knowing Mary was impatiently waiting; I finally screamed and yelled as loud as I could for help. I didn't think there was much hope really as the throbbing sounds from the milking machine were quite loud even from where I stood swaying and shivering.

My wet straggly hair stuck to my face but when I pushed it away to be able to see I got a taste of the brew I was standing in and began dry-retching and crying. My tired body had nearly given up and fallen but over the sound of the cows mooing their complaints I yelled a bit louder again in desperation, thinking in the back of my mind I was lucky this farmer did not believe in 'music for more milk' (usually the radio). I was surprised, relieved and really happy a minute or so later when John appeared out of the gloom at the top gate. He took a short cut and came sliding fast down the slippery wet hill, past the pig pen, his lanky frame bent over, yelling like a long legged bellowing banshee. 'I'm coming. I'm coming. Hold on.'

I wished I could. I could feel my legs shaking and the tears bumping down my cheeks making tracks over the drying mud and sticky hair. John slid to a halt, and balancing by holding the gate post with one huge hand, he quickly reached over with his long powerful arm and plucked my tired body from the muck like a pliant plant from its squelchy hole, my gumboots left behind lost in the brown ooze. John's old black singlet was wet and dirty, his gumboots covered in smeared cow manure and he smelled but I didn't care. It was just such a relief not to have to stay still any more.

Carrying me tightly under one arm so that breathing became difficult he took me back up the hill to the cowshed with powerful strides, digging his heels into the ridged clumps of greasy wet grass until we reached concrete, and there he hosed me off in the yard like the cows – except with less water pressure. John's face *had been screwed up and I thought he looked quite frightened. It occurred to me I had never seen him look like that before and I wasn't so worried then about getting a clip round the ear for being useless. (It wasn't until the next day when John described me to Mary as looking like a 'bedraggled doll' that I even thought about what I must have looked like to him.) Mary's emergency may have been over by the time we got back. I don't remember anything about it as I was stripped and dried off quickly then plonked straight into bed with a hot water bottle, already half asleep from residual fear and exhausted relief.*

Farmers

Farming sustained us as usual, though not in the more industrial, sophisticated and diversified business-like way it does today nor with many millionaires probably. Farmers often lived from pay-out to pay-out on loans from the bank to cover outgoings. Wives and children were often their only labourers. I always think of them as big gamblers as fickle weather is what dictates their choice of living on the land which always seemed so important to them. The stakes are so high. I really admire their dedication and tenacity. Having since run a small business, I appreciate the responsibility of what that entails, but also enjoyed the heady freedom of being my own boss.

There was little variety in the farming area of the middle of the North Island our family moved in – it was mainly sheep and cows although there was cropping in some viable areas we came across. A few farmer friends we knew who were nearer retirement in the Bay of Plenty ran cattle, enjoying the trips to different towns for auctions, meeting up with similar folk. Although NZ was probably more progressive than some other nations, with improvements after the harsh lessons learned about exporting from the Depression, getting people to change their ways was much more difficult. Our doctor once asked me in the 1960's what my experience had been with farmers in general regarding diversifying, as he was investing in land. It was such an unexpected question from a doctor all I could think of to say was they were 'stick-in-the-mud types'. At least the ones we had contact with.

There were clever, creative entrepreneurial people around too, often with a rural and/or engineering background, who were familiar with the 'no. 8 wire' of 'do-it-yourself' ingenuity although they would particularly play down their achievements by understatement and deflection. Like William Gallagher Sr. in the 1930's with the electric fence and in the 1950's Bill Hamilton, a capable farmer/engineer, who with his ingenuity and amongst his other inventions, designed the jet propulsion speed boat, now known world-wide as the 'Hamilton jet'. He was motivated by his need to have a useful boat for the shallow waters of the South Island Rivers. We knew his son Jon and family from a marriage connection.

All farmers, successful or otherwise, had to be innovative really because of our country's isolation and the Depression and war years, when we could not always afford or were not permitted to import things that were needed. There has consistently been this underlying belief that we could create something ourselves and perhaps better than what was available elsewhere. A great country for inventors with their 'quintessential, irrepressible spirit of entrepreneurship', which I read somewhere. 'New Zealanders seem to have very deeply rooted cultural traits too, much more individual than collective, as in most other countries'.

Perhaps it was because our frontier ancestors had come such a long way to own land and be independent and individualistic, wanting a better life for themselves and their children even at the high cost to them, including the isolation. Their children appreciating that, felt they were justified in defending what the family land represented, especially on farms where the farmer is usually very much his own person. Proud of ownership and possessive, they would emotionally defend any move, legally or otherwise, against intruders – their response coming from a sense of being wronged and perhaps losing control of what they considered their own bit of dirt. Our family experienced the fuss about a legally approved oil pipeline across an unused part of a corner of a field on the home farm. It seemed to me as the in-law, that it was as much about a threat to individuality and rights as the actual ugly pipe, when being told there was no option.

The most passive and non-judgemental friend I have ever made, was an absolute stickler for the boundaries on her property, which quite shocked me. The land had been in her family for years and was split amongst them when their parents died. We had bought one of the surveyed sections from a brother and the real estate agent had outright lied to us over our boundary with her property. Once we built and shifted in, I erected a temporary fence along it to keep the children safe. My neighbour took the intrusion so personally, I thought at first it was because our section had been an area where she had played as a child, but her outrage was about her side of the boundary. She considered the land her own and was proud of her large acreage with her garden and fruit trees. I think it gave her a sense of self-worth and independence. Once I moved the fence to the right place and she got that it was not an intentional aggravation, we became close friends.

One hundred years ago around the turn of the 20th century, 50% of people lived on the land but only 1 out of 10 does now at the time of writing. Nevertheless, when people grew up on a farm or their grandparents had one, they seemed to always have that hankering to return to having land around them. This was especially the case if they ended up in a city or a town. Even today's distant dreamers abroad, as they age and have families of their own, still think about throwing their lives up to buy their own 10-acre block. That happened to my second husband and dictated our lives.

Land was a part of the deal for Second World War returned service men and 12,000 settled on farms through a ballot system. (From the 'Discharged Soldiers Settlement Act of 1915' formed for the First World War returned soldiers.) By 1956 holdings had grown to their peak of 92,000. There had been situations where land for farming was simply unworkable and many others were borderline, so only the determination and hard work of the whole family made survival possible. Women understood multi-tasking better than most in those days. The lucky families became part of the boom years when half our export income was from wool.

Mechanisation had continued to increase in the thirties and between 1936 and 1940 the use of tractors had doubled and the number of electric motors on farms had increased by 60%. By

1941 the use of milking machines meant hand stripping died out without any noticeable production loss, the mechanisation making a huge difference toward increased production. Compared with many countries in Europe we were revolutionary although fertilizer still had to be spread over large areas of farmland by intensive, time-consuming labour. To achieve the same cover done in minutes by flying, NZ developed the world's first, fast, revolutionary aerial topdressing in the small Tiger Moths, although the fertiliser flew back into the pilots' faces when the biplane took off as the superphosphate was in the converted front passenger seat. The first public demonstration of experimental top-dressing by plane in a large-scale field trial was in 1946. Robert Gummer, a 1950's aerial top-dressing pilot, was later given the job of testing the first Fletcher with its open cockpit, a purpose-built aircraft made in America, flying it over the rugged terrain of King Country farms and forests for a month. It later became the favourite for the few experienced and capable ex-Air Force pilots who were to work for Robertson Air Services Ltd. often having to take off from primitive airstrips bulldozed on the slope of a hill farm.

Top-dressing

We were on the last morning of a holiday in the early 1960's at a friend's beach bach in the Bay of Plenty, lazing outside on canvas loungers, enjoying the warmth before the temperature reached its zenith. We casually watched a small plane in the distance, its windows glinting in the sun as it swooped over a nearby farm on the flats below a set of rolling hills. With amazing skill the pilot released the finely drifting spray, judging the plane angle, wind force and height, settling it precisely within the farm boundaries, crop dusting the ground with death only feet below. It was like watching a precarious sweeping winged ballet, the repeated coils of white twirling out at the end of each beautifully executed run. A fitting finish to our stay.

(We had no idea of what the suggested repercussions would be later from those dainty coils. 2,4,5-T was widely used for spraying and contained the deadly dioxin used to form Agent Orange. It was banned in 1989 but in many areas, like New Plymouth, families still suffer the consequences.)

Progressive farming and the Minimum Wage Act of 1944 would have helped recovery along with the weekly five pounds five shillings for men for a 40 hour week although women were still paid less, three pounds three shillings, sometimes for the same work and hours. That didn't change too much as three pounds ten shillings is what I received when starting work in 1953.

In 1944 Britain accepted our entire exportable surplus for four years. In 1952 we made another deal that ensured duty-free entry of our meat till 1967 as well as one in 1957 for unrestricted access to the U.K. for dairy products for ten years. From 1949 to 1965 we went from 33 million to 54 million sheep and we were probably best defined in the world by them. Helped by wool becoming so valuable (it was picked off fences when the prices trebled), everything seemed to move forward from the fifties, the boom making many farmers wealthy, giving the economy a boost. Godfrey Bowen was world shearing champion and we were seen as the 'land of peace and plenty' which seemed borne out by the golden weather as well.

We didn't know EEC was looming in 1958. It was just as well in 1959 the old brown furry Chinese gooseberries were renamed 'Kiwi fruit' and multiplied like the origins of their name. Their export returns were a huge boost to our economy. People made fortunes on their success and some eventually lost them too. Britain joined the Common Market in 1982 and subsidies came in.

Chapter 4 The 1930's Depression

Although NZ did well with her exports in the First World War with a dramatic increase in 1919, prices fluctuated afterwards and there was a steep drop in 1926 with a short recovery in 1928-29 but with a longer fall in 1930, ending in a 40% loss over a short period of years. So our Depression really started earlier than the 1929 Wall Street crash in the USA that triggered the world wide calamity of the 'Great Depression'. That compounded the most serious depression in NZ history. We were so vulnerable because our economic security was always uncertain, relying on exporting primary produce – 80% of our national income was from wool, butter, cheese and meat – and we depended on imported goods for many things unavailable here. We had no conception then of a joint marketing venture or a 'guaranteed price scheme' to protect farmers and the country – a disastrous way to learn a lesson – and farmers' drop in income had a domino effect on the whole economy. Along with the USA and Great Britain, conservative entrenchment was the Coalition Government answer: balance the budget and wait for better things to come. The reality of that was we, the public, would just have to starve our way through it.

By 1934 it wasn't worth the effort to farm as there was so little if any profit, regardless of the priority based policies for farmers by the Government, made up predominantly of MPs from rural constituencies, policies that were often to the detriment of urban businesses and resented. The farmers in their turn felt it was 'too little too late' and many were critical of those that survived well and were living the easy life at their expense. I remember knowing very young how important farming was to our economy, understanding about the farmers' earnings and that they were supported at our expense 'because they were the backbone of the country'. However there was a reluctance about forgiving them because not everyone believed they deserved the support and there were mutterings around the adult table that there were better ways of dealing with the situation. MP Gordon Coates, younger and a war veteran, was the one with some enlightenment who took a wider view, and may have been able to save the day, but was unable to implement anything useful partly because of resistance within his own party.

It didn't help incomes either that much of farm work was becoming mechanised and able-bodied men left for the towns and cities where jobs were few in shrinking businesses and secondary industries were in their embryo stage. By 1932, two men out of five did not have permanent employment and were on relief work. That was also the year that old age, widows' and miners' pensions were cut by 10% for three years. The effects of the Depression peaked in NZ around 1933-4 and it was once described as 'the most shattering economic experience ever recorded' and at the time the general public felt that the politicians had no idea of the reality of the working man's situation. There was envy for workers who kept their jobs. They were thought to be in clover if they brought home four pounds ($8) per week.

At first the unemployed were abhorred along with the slackers, layabouts, homosexuals, conscientious objectors (sometimes a white feather would be dropped in their letter boxes or worse) and imported union reps (branded trouble makers) who were looked down upon. Poverty was often seen as a sin and having no job had to be a punishment for something 'these Dole Bludgers' had done, and it was felt generally, as it was overseas, that 'they only had themselves to blame'.

Respectable people saw safety and stability in the comfort and conformity of the familiar and on the whole would have been brought up simply, so it must have been shocking to face the reality of the Depression when they lost their incomes. Those with businesses or private means may have had no idea the unemployed included respectable citizens, like professionals, the well-educated and qualified workers, or understood the shame and humiliation they suffered. Those who were caught in the tailspin found themselves in mortifying sessions with mortgagees and bankers. Pretentiousness was stripped away and eventually, 'keeping up appearances' became impossible, although sometimes a husband would dress for work as normal for his family's sake and his own pride, leaving at his regular time but to go looking for work instead of to a job. Eventually however, so many people were out of work that it became obvious and any social distinctions that were harboured were largely discarded.

People became defiant and bitter. Men drank and sometimes left their families, relinquishing responsibility, if they weren't already separated by work. Women coped with the aftermath of the 6 o'clock closing swill, which lasted 50 years, the so-called temporary wartime measure because of the 1914-18 war.

Everyone had heard the stories about men jumping from New York buildings, but it seemed unreal and unlikely to happen here and I think our family were appalled and shocked when it did. For women, it was seen as a sign of weakness not to cope when they had breakdowns and lived with the fear of 'men in white coats coming for them' to take them to asylums. If there were children, they were also put into orphanages, which would have added hugely to their mothers' already guilty feelings of letting everyone down. Being punished instead of supported seems an anathema now.

They, especially women who had received shock treatment, often suffered in various ways for the rest of their lives and were also haunted by having to overcome that mental illness stigma. I have a friend who, into her seventies, still won't talk about her own experience. She said the fear of not being believed because of the judgement from others around her diagnosis had kept her mouth shut. She did once describe sneaking along to watch someone else have shock treatment at Kingseat and forever wished she hadn't.

Psychologists and psychiatrists were in fact very powerful people at the time. On their say-so life as you knew it could be over. Anyone forced by two doctors or the courts to be interviewed by one would be very circumspect if they did have any sense. Asylums were often impressive buildings, as we imagined expensive English country homes to be, often with locked gates, down long, sealed driveways in tranquil country settings of expansive lawns and trees with seats strategically placed – in dreadful contrast to the usually Dickensian treatment people received inside during confinement. This may have been for a person's lifetime, with the horrors of shock treatment and staff that could be kind or cruel, physically, emotionally, mentally and sometimes sexually.

Just the names of these places being mentioned colloquially – like the Wau Creek one in Auckland – 'You'll end up in the Wau' or 'The Nuthouse' and others 'the lunatic asylum', 'the loony bin' or just 'the bin'. Other well-known places were Kingseat, Oakley, Seacliffe, Porirua, Raventhorpe, Seaview, Sunnyside, Lake Alice, Ngawhatu, Cherry Farm and Tokanui: the government's answer to a mental problem which was often threat enough to keep most women struggling on. Children picked up on everyone's fear as well and would taunt some luckless victim, especially if a family member had already been incarcerated.

Asylums

One day in the 1950's when things would not have been quite so dreadful, Kay, my sister-in-law and I waited with our new babies in my brother's car, parked on the road outside Carrington Hospital in Pt. Chevalier, Auckland. Ralph had popped in to visit a workmate who had had a nervous breakdown. He must have been fitting the call in around driving me home. It was such a miserable day I imagine the cross town trip of an hour and a half and changing buses would have been a nightmare with my baby, especially trying to fit the pushchair into the outside carrier and hold onto her at the same time.

Kay and I sat and chatted and played with the babies in the muggy, breast-milk-laden air and only got a bit restless after about three quarters of an hour when the littlies were fretful and the noise of the storm had finally broken over us, straight from the windy Waitakeres. We had thought Ralph brave to even go into the asylum, never mind for that long. Kay turned the wipers on intermittently and cleared the inside of the small A40 windscreen with a nappy to watch for Ralph. We decided to amuse ourselves by making a game of identifying people as staff, visitors or escapees as they hurried out the big asylum gates hunched over in soaking coats under pummelled umbrellas which were trying to get away from them. There was one male in particular who came hurtling erratically along the wide path of the grounds, uncovered head down and a coat flapping everywhere seemingly disoriented, not sure where he was heading. We laughed nervously together and Kay said, 'He's definitely an escapee'.

When he hesitantly came our way we were glad the side windows were all fogged up and the doors locked and we didn't have to actually look at him as he passed – our teenage minds already imagining some gross and dangerous person. But he didn't go by. He stopped and tried the car door handle rattling it and yelling, 'Let me in! Let me in!' I don't know who squealed the loudest – us or the babies when we panicked. Out in the raging rain poor Ralph struggled to find his own keys in a drenched coat to eventually let himself in to the terrified but by then embarrassed occupants, as we had both now realised whom it was. We could hardly tell him what we had been thinking when his dripping hair and annoyed face appeared asking us what the hell the matter was. We said the storm had frightened us. There had been a loud bang and an immediate bolt of lightning around the time he had tried the door.

Kay and I spent the next few minutes trying to retrieve some equanimity and calm the babies down. A grumpy Ralph muttered to himself about 'Bloody hysterical women!' and immediately lumped us in with every other woman that screamed. As he would.

I doubt that Kay and I ever gave way to a repetition of that again although after a few miles we began to giggle, bordering on hysteria, but in relief this time, until Ralph threatened to stop the car and put us all out or at least tell him the joke so he could enjoy it too. But we couldn't speak for laughing.

We forgave ourselves later such was the fear we all had of being incarcerated. I was in fact locked in with a ward full of inmates when I was a bit more mature, visiting Carrington myself in the evening to see a friend. The patients started to tease me about the doors not being opened again till morning, no matter how often you knocked and yelled. How, they asked, did I think I would survive the night – males and females taunting. I said, 'Well, the first thing to do is to find the best mattress,' and made as if to rush around testing them. The immediate hilarious scramble by everyone to defend their territory had us all laughing and afterwards a shy female even offered to share. Luckily someone did come and open the door about an hour later.

Grief was just another burden to be borne, very familiar to the older generations for many reasons. Obvious distress was only acceptable in the proper place – a funeral. Any more tears to be shed in private so as not to embarrass others. Black was worn and continued for at least 2½ years for a widow (sometimes much longer or perhaps just a black armband) although three months was more acceptable for a widower in Victorian/Edwardian times as it was recognised that he would need someone to look after the children so he could go back to work. Outside of this accepted tolerable grief timeframe, women particularly became very good at denying their feelings (and no doubt men too) in the stoic silence of suppressed loss, especially when it was from a pregnancy that miscarried, or of stillbirths, young babies or children. Mourning that continued beyond a few weeks was considered unnecessarily sentimental and brought a judgement of being hysterical (or unhinged) and comments like 'foolish emotional woman' and being told to 'bear up' or 'toughen up', sometimes spoken about in these terms to others in the woman's presence, even by a doctor. The ultimate consensus could be some sort of treatment was required, again the dreaded possibility of incarceration in a mental institution.

Women in the workforce by 1931 paid taxes (like young men under 20) and yet could not receive assistance. This was sometimes exploited by employers and young girls and women could be forced to work 14 hour days, 7 days per week at a low rate: their alternative was no income at all. Women endured and were expected to know their place, which was whatever the community, dominated by men, perceived it to be, femininity often regarded as synonymous with triviality.

Unless things were really bad, children weren't usually as mentally affected as adults in hard times, although some children were very aware. Those ones could be counted on to take an adult role, looking out for younger siblings, especially when there were big families. Most kids would conscientiously gather up old soft drink bottles worth a ha'penny and beer ones worth one penny at a shop they were sold from, perhaps some keeping the proceeds for themselves but many understanding the family or community need. Ordinary people sold anything door to door and children did that too. I remember my Nana once buying soap from a boy of about 10 who said to make it, he and his dad boiled fat with caustic soda in an old kerosene drum over an outdoor fire. That was an exception – she didn't do it twice. The soap was such a poor quality.

The government did not really take proper responsibility for the unemployed until the 1930's and even then not well. After the Unemployment Act did come in, the Unemployment Board could make arrangements with local bodies and employers, including farmers, (who would be paid out for supplying work) which could mean men would be used in ways such as replacing horses on poorer farms for harrowing or pulling other machinery. Such work would have seemed inconceivable previously.

There was little initiative to do sensible work for achieving anything useful. Non-productive, soul-destroying Public Works Dept. schemes had men just shifting a pile of dirt to one place and back again. It was demeaning, degrading, and heart-breaking. They also had camps with huts or tents for single men (and sometimes married ones) with dirt floors often in barely survivable atrocious conditions without even the minimum of basic hygienic living or heating or drying in winter. They did physically stressful jobs (replacing machinery, like digging drains or doing roadworks with picks and shovels, sledge hammers and wheelbarrows and occasionally blasting rock) in what was a form of slavery and as wives usually lived vicariously through their partners, even though separated, their morale dropped too. The work was usually in isolated country areas, like construction of the East Coast Railway, where the men would have had no chance of finding anything better without transport. It was also a way to separate groups of dissatisfied men and help prevent unrest in the cities.

Others fossicked for gold in Central Otago living in sod huts they built themselves, some became 'swaggers', and many were 'just pushed down too far to ever come up again' and stayed like that, some their self-image so low, committing suicide. Our family didn't know anyone personally who did, but I remember Mary talking about a friend of a friend who had. He was a lawyer.

Although we had the 'best kept parks and streets in the world in the midst of poverty', local bodies seldom used their initiative either to capitalize on the 'Scheme 5' opportunity implemented in the 1920's to use this cheap labour. In the main centres even to get what relief work there was, it was necessary to stand with hundreds of others and hope to have your name called. 'Cash in hand' wages (the usual method of payment for transactions) for the unemployed were minimal and early on included a 1 week unpaid stand-down every 3 weeks, and payments were also eventually reduced as money ran out.

This scheme, like others, was revised regularly with an increase in taxes and reduced payments, till eventually it was abolished in 1933 and at last became the dole – a sustenance allowance which did not require work to receive. Unemployment figures remained at over 50,000 until 1936. All physically hard work was done for a pittance, although it was considered a better option than the dole by many.

Private enterprises were quicker to see the possibilities of the number 5 scheme and several large city edifices were built this way. 'God helps those that help themselves' was a common comment when someone scored. The Chamberlain Park Golf Course was a positive outcome and there was one eventually really useful scheme. It was the planting of exotic trees in the middle of the North Island which developed into the forestry products industry now worth millions of dollars.

When applying for anything, especially to do with a government agency, there were embarrassing questions on how previous money had been spent, whether anything else had been received (as little as an apple – which could have been stolen from an orchard), even about the minute details of life like whether underwear or a toothbrush had been bought (families should share the latter), and all forms were to be filled out and policed to make sure no-one got more than their fair share – as pitiful as it might be. There were always those who found ways around the system too and their faces were not forgotten years afterwards.

Law enforcers though like magistrates and the police could be very hard on men on the dole. At places there were policemen standing behind counters (which often had a form of protection above the grilles to the roof) to keep order. Just looking authoritative would be enough for those cowed by hunger and cold. There was often an air of pomposity about people in power, even minor officials, who may have felt overlooked otherwise. Some just enjoyed bullying people, passing denigrating remarks to those who had missed out, and even sometimes taking punitive pleasure in the pettiness and mindlessness of the situation, playing controlling games and making mean-minded rulings that could put a whole family out of food for a week. These people however once away from their protected areas, children at least would 'take the Mickey' whenever they could get away with it as a former lead protagonist told me with a grin on his old face, hinting at the sly enjoyment he experienced carrying out devious little deeds.

Charitable organisations and churches like the Salvation Army opened soup kitchens and aid/relief depots. Supplies were usually by donation as today. At first, many could not bear the shame of the queues that formed where order chits were given out after the correct answers to questions, and as often as not served up with moral judgements, and the chits were then taken to a grocery shop. There were other long queues for free bread. The government provided relief through Hospital Boards although their grants were cut as funds ran out, like every other Govt. department including the building industry, which created a housing shortage.

As the Depression worsened, condition of the sub-standard houses that existed in city slums was pretty shocking and described as 'deplorable'. People squeezed into unsuitable accommodation, with nine in one room and up to a dozen families under the same roof 'The sharing of 20 people for baths and conveniences was not rare.' Cheap accommodation meant camping grounds and beach baches became homes with no running water and sub-standard sanitary conveniences. It was common for children to stay living at home with their parents into adulthood. Clothes were hand-me-downs of hand-me-downs often and the cheapest footwear were light Japanese sand-shoes, a sort of uniform which many seemed to wear or otherwise make do with cardboard inside shoes for the holes in the soles. An older friend, living in the country, said she walked to school barefoot every day and in winter broke ice on puddles with her toes. The word poor then could mean little or no food, no shelter, no conveniences, no shoes, few clothes, no transport, being cold, wet, dirty, and miserable, with no certainty for the future and a blank level of hopelessness on their faces beneath the dipped heads that comes with deprivation and depression.

Swaggers of all types, often decent men down on their luck, were young and old, educated and not. They could walk hundreds of miles looking for work, some forced into being itinerant workers, becoming dispensable labourers for seasonal jobs like farm work, particularly shearing and mustering, harvesting and fruit picking. They carried their sugar-bag over their shoulder, usually at the end of a stick. (They could hold 70 pounds with all their possessions including clothing and perhaps some flour and a blanket although that may have been rolled and attached outside covered by an oilskin sheet – no such thing as a back-pack. Sometimes a blackened billy hung on it too.) Others were drifters who didn't actually want work. They could roam in groups, pairs or alone and those ones would be the closest our family came to that level of need. Nana called them 'Swagmen' or 'Swaggies' as in Ozzie.

There was not a great sense of desperation about the ones we saw though and some were known colourful eccentrics, mostly independent and light-hearted despite their circumstances or perhaps because of them. They would usually politely come around to the back door to knock referring to Nana as 'Missus', offering to do a job like fix something, weed in the vege garden, pick fruit or chop kindling in exchange for a meal and a cup of tea from the ever-hot kettle on the coal range. Everyone drank tea. They would be gone in a few hours and Nana would comment that in the city they would sleep rough under bridges or in parks or someone's outbuilding if they could. In the country it would be barns and haystacks in summer (proper ones, similar to a Vincent van Gogh painting). Swaggers had faded away by the 1950's, not necessarily found if they had died in isolated places which the loners who panned or dug for gold could do. Stories were sometimes shared by swaggers if they were asked, which Nana did sometimes. I think once they had found someone who was a soft touch they would return on their next trip around. I would have been under five to remember them so that would be in the early 1940's. In other times the men may have been different.

Objectified, hungry, and deprived people facing demeaning conditions, anger, frustration, desperation, and what was seen as a useless political response to a disastrous situation, can and do commit terrible acts. In NZ in 1932 over two nights of rioting in Auckland, unemployed men fought police, mounted and unmounted, special constables and sailors armed with batons. There were injuries and over 80 arrests. In April another crowd from the Unemployed Workers Movement and others who joined in with Jim Edwards their leader, were controlled so that a minor clash with the police did not escalate. Edwards had less success the following evening as students and professional men had been enrolled as special constables. They were resented by the protestors, who felt they were taunted, and they rampaged in the street looting and breaking windows. We were lucky it never became worse than that with the intolerable situation and their justified despairing, simmering resentment.

Disasters

In the middle of this was the 1931 Napier 7.8 earthquake lasting 2.5 minutes with 525 aftershocks. Everything collapsed under an avalanche of brick and mortar. Fires began straight away which were exacerbated by the increasing wind strength until the whole city was ablaze. It took a day and a half to extinguish. The airport, housing, industrial areas were all affected, only a few buildings in central Napier surviving. Hastings' retail area was also devastated. The main roads into both places were blocked by rubble and more damage was caused by landslides in the hilly parts as well. In the Hawkes Bay region 256 people died and 400 were hospitalised.

Although it was often referred to, I only spoke to one person who had actually been there and seen the devastation. It was my later father-in-law, a farmer from Waverley who had previously been a brick-layer. He'd driven across country to help with the aftermath, but had little to say about his role in it when I asked, or at any time really like many that worked alone on the land – reminiscent of the Second World War guys later, and the scene in his mind would probably not have been too different either. He did say some people were mute with shock still, even when he arrived a few days later. The absolute devastation was appalling and included his horror at all the brick chimneys that had fallen causing so much destruction resulting in people injured and killed by them in otherwise sometimes untouched houses. He guessed the lime mortar had crumbled and disintegrated so there was little but the weight of the bricks holding them together.

Everything was unrecognisable, especially in the downtown area, and the smell in some places was appalling. Partly sewerage, but bodies were not readily able to be got to either (no-one to help like the professionally trained people of today). There was dust mixed with ashes everywhere spreading from the burnt out areas where the fires had been and some still had drifting, persistent hazy smoke. The fire engines had been trapped in their destroyed fire station and water mains were broken. Power lines, possibly still dangerous, trailed amongst demolished buildings and on roads and there was land where sea had been previously. Some water was still able to be brought up from wells.

He briefly mentioned the weird feeling of waiting for the next shock, its repercussions obviously in his mind, and felt everything could have been much worse afterwards if the Royal Navy Ship HMS *Veronica* hadn't been there. Later more warships were sent. With other means of communication destroyed, the ship transmitted news to the rest of the country by radio and information on what help was required and set up soup kitchen type facilities to feed people. He had talked to friends later who lived through it and they commented that watching the sailors' disciplined response had helped calm them down and brought some order to a dire situation.

The landscape changed, the coastline lifting by two metres and 40 kilometres of seabed became dry land. Napier was top of the list of our natural disasters and it brought an unsettled feeling up for everyone.

My memory of Napier was from after the rebuild in the style of the 1930's Spanish Mission/Santa Barbara Style (called Art Deco in the sixties) and I loved it. The curves so graceful and different and the colours appealing.

There had been an earlier earthquake in Murchison in 1929, also a 7.8 one, that had killed 17 people. The fact is that we permanently live with, but seldom really think about earthquakes, unless prodded by Civil Defence. Christchurch is a huge ongoing wakeup call. At the time I lived in Christchurch (1967), what surprised me most was when people knew I was from Auckland, they invariably told me about the tragedy of the 1947 Ballantynes' store fire, the worst fire in NZ history at that time with 41 deaths. It was as if it had happened the day before to many, although it was by then 20 years later. It had obviously been horrifying. It was very much a part of local folk-lore but is now eclipsed by the earthquakes.

Lighter times

There must have been lighter moments during the Depression years. Art Union winners would have been ecstatic even with a few pounds. There were some great movie stars around and their lives would have been fascinating, as in another richer, happier world. I would think pictures with the child star Shirley Temple, the Marx Brothers, Charlie Chaplin, Fred Astaire and Ginger Rogers, and fantasies like *'The Wizard of Oz'*, with the loved Judy Garland and Johnny Weissmuller in *Tarzan* would have had a cheering effect on people's spirits, even if they couldn't afford to go and see for themselves. They would have heard about them from others and seen the posters. Perhaps not the distracting and consuming entertainment of today but a temporary lift and proof that the world did go on and there was hope for recovery.

The people we looked up to were not necessarily those that had done well internationally in areas such as science, singing, music, writing, poetry or legislation, but rugby as always had its heroes and George Nepia, who played his last All Black test in the 1930's, must have been a great solace to those who followed the game. Turning to Rugby League later would have pleased others.

His name is so familiar just hearing it brings up a grin and he was at his best well before my time.

In 1930 Phar Lap won the Melbourne Cup and I can just imagine the celebrating that would have caused – something to really drink to. His death in 1932 in California would have been a terrible downer. Partly as he was such a dream horse and so admired but also the mystery around the cause of his death and whether he was poisoned. That question hung around for years with all the innuendos and accusations going the Americans' way. 'It would be bloody typical of those bastards to kill something they couldn't beat!' Someone must have said that around me more than once when the subject ever came up.

NZ-born courageous, famous aviatrix Jean Batten, would have made New Zealanders proud in the 1930's with her daring, record breaking and internationally acclaimed first solo flight from England to NZ and her ten and a half hours from Australia to NZ.

In 1934 Jack Lovelock won the gold medal in the mile at the British Empire Games and another one in the 1500m at the 1936 Berlin Olympics his career highlight, setting a world record. Sport has always played a big part in our developing country pride and perception of a classless society, 'our social cement – anyone could play or watch regardless of wealth, class or education' as someone put it. A united front to the world we all identified with and winners would have seemed particularly wonderful people in the atmosphere of the day. Some good news.

Our Family

We were lucky as a family during the Depression (although Mary may only have agreed with that retrospectively when she had found out what happened to others) because I don't remember really starving and we always had a roof of some kind over our heads. While we were still living with Arnold, my father, till I was 18 months he had his own taxi and seemed to do as well as anyone – he at least had a job. Later, when we went to live with our Nana, (about 1939) I think it was mainly thanks to her careful nurturing of every penny that we survived as well as we did. Mary, being an only child, inherited all her English China tea sets with beautifully shaped rose cups as well as silver tea services, crystal pieces and lovely pots and figurines along with furniture and expensive rugs, so those things anyway had not been sold off.

Utilities and Utilising

In those stressed years, everything that was re-usable was adapted in some way if no longer suitable or needed for its original purpose including the ubiquitous 70 lb. jute sugar bags, which were useful for many things. Tony Simpson's book 'The Sugar Bag Years' describes 'ripping down one side of a sugar sack and leaving the bottom of the other seam sewn up then shoving your head into the corner' which form a peaked hat that would have helped to block the wind and slough off rain and hail. Perhaps because we didn't have a need for that sort of outdoor protection our family used them as aprons for gardening and heavy work and oven cloths, sometimes embroidered with a mixture of coloured wool.

Groceries were sold in bulk and our pantry was just off the kitchen facing south and was cooled by a small louvered opening covered with perforated metal for a fly-screen. Items such as salt, flour, sugar, oatmeal, split peas, lentils etc. were kept there and in one corner as well as baskets of fresh fruit there was bottled fruit, jam, chutney and tinned food. Meat, butter, milk, and other perishables were put in a fly proof safe too but hung just outside the back door in the shade and hopefully a breeze from the SW usually. The large cotton bags of flour were needed as some people baked home-made bread along with the usual pies, cakes etc. for those that could afford to. Once brand names were removed from the flour bags with kerosene or washing soda and they were boiled up in the copper's soapy water till they were white, the good quality material was useful for innovative women to think of something to make them into. The most common uses were bandages (safety-pinned into place) and cloths for all sorts of things, as well as linen replacements like tea-towels, aprons, pillow cases, and sometimes even sheets. Children's clothes too if families were really desperate, although usually night clothes or underwear, probably sewn on treadle machines or ones like my Nana's with a handle on the wheel. Also hand sewing.

Nana had a special day of the week when she would sew, darn and iron. There were a couple of power points in the kitchen and because of Granddad being an electrical engineer with access to British imports we were lucky and had an electric iron and an electric jug which was no doubt used for the numerous cups of tea drunk (we were one of the biggest tea drinking countries in the world – Mary making a cup frequently as she got older and when she couldn't always find the last cup she would just make another) but no other kitchen appliances that I remember. Toast was made on the coal range. No vacuum cleaner but the noise from the rhythm of a carpet sweeper is very familiar. No whiteware – a word unknown then – was available.

Washing was usually done weekly, probably on a Monday which was the accepted ritual day for housewives. Always white sheets, pillow cases, tablecloths, table napkins and any other whites including clothing that would survive the boil-up. Stains that may be stubborn were treated first with soap and a strong brush or rubbed on the washing board.

In our Levonia St. house, twin concrete tubs took up most of one wall in the utility room at the back of the house next to the kitchen. They sat by the copper which was set in concrete in the corner with a space underneath for a fire to boil up the soapy water. Fine pieces of yellow/gold Sunlight soap were flaked off the long bar into the copper and larger pieces cut to fit in a soap shaker for the kitchen sink. I don't particularly remember a chimney but there must have been one as I have since seen a square brick tub in a similar setup. Ours may have gone out through the wall and up (as a potbelly stove) past the roof outside. Luckily the utility room faced south too as summertime washing was a hot laborious job.

The copper had to be hand filled with buckets of water from the tap over the tubs and baled out later. I can remember Nana's sweaty wet face once the boiling time was up and she struggled with the large copper stick, a yard (1 metre) long and thicker than a broom handle, the wood whitish, slightly soft and feathered from use. Removing, rinsing and wringing the smaller articles was not so difficult but to get a proper hold in the boiling water pushing at a heavy linen or cotton sheet would have been difficult, Nana having to then heave it up and out from the rising clouds of steam. Holding it to rest a minute by balancing the stick on the concrete edge of the tub, letting the excess scalding water pour back into the copper, she would then twist the sheet around the wood and when enough water had run off, manoeuvre the sodden weight into the first rinsing water. All this at her stretched 4 foot 11 inches (1.5m) and in her sixties. (I get annoyed now if I have to spend time rearranging the sheets in the washing machine when it isn't spinning evenly.)

This tub-full needed poking and prodding until as much of the soapy water as possible could be removed. It was necessary to find and gather an end of the heavy but cooler wet sheet, to guide it into the rollers of the large wringer attached to the upright middle of the concrete tubs. If things weren't lined up correctly on the rollers they could catch at the sides, getting caught up in the turning mechanism and rip. Too bulky and they wouldn't go through. The tray underneath had to be adjusted each time so the squeezed water didn't run into the fresh tub. Turning the wringer handle and struggling with the hot wet clothes and making sure to have shirts and blouse buttons inside out before going through the wringer – all at the same time – was an art, and women like Nana would have it off pat from years of repetition, but it would not be a job they looked forward to.

The second rinse was much cooler to handle, going back through the wringer to the final one in the first tub, by then emptied and refilled with fresh blued water. The solid form of blue colouring (Reckitts Blue squares) came in little material bags tied with soft string at the top which slowly released the blue when swished in the cold water, the timing finely judged to get the perfect mix. Neighbours could be critical if there was too much colour but God forbid your wash wasn't blue-white! Coloured clothes were washed separately by hand, unless they were colour-fast enough for the boil up, and after being checked for the worst soiled parts, were rubbed up and down on a ridged wooden washing board set in a tub half full of hot soapy water from the copper. Starching was done in a wide bowl, usually males' shirts, at least their collars, and school blouse collars too. Woven wicker baskets with firm handles were used to take washing to the outdoor clothes line. These were made from a long special type of fine, light rope or wire and hung between posts about 20 to 30 feet (6 to 9 metres) apart. A cleft pole of tea-tree, or any slim strong branch of wood about 6 feet (about 2 metres), was used to hold the line up in the centre and washing was hung out with wooden pegs. (These were, sometimes, also used to make miniature dolls.)

The rest of our utility room had storage shelves and cupboards and was full of all sorts of useful and useless things. Basically anything that wouldn't fit anywhere else was kept there (as there were no garages for storage) like the older treadle sewing machine, and Granddad's wooden, foot-shaped shoe last that he repaired many a worn sole on. Mainly though there were cleaning materials like rags, brooms, mops (wet & dry), a carpet sweeper, buckets, gumboots, gardening tools and clothes, wooden toys old and new, although nothing like the quantity and variety now, mostly home-made or passed around ones (too early for plastic and no Buzzy Bee in our house). Ralph's Meccano set would have been kept in his room with his windup toy cars and marbles. I did get my hands on their little bag sometimes but he hid it usually. He had other much more interesting toys than mine but they were considered male only, like his precious shanghai (slingshot) which he got into trouble with himself anyway.

The chooks' mash (pollard) food was stored there too. An old four-gallon kerosene tin held food scraps, and hot water and mash were mixed in with them, and fed out each day. Nana would check the garden for any unusable greens on the way to opening the chicken wire gate to the run and call out, 'Here chook, chook, chook, here chook, chook, chook' and they would scramble to meet her while Ralph or I skirted around them to fetch the eggs from the hen house while they were occupied. They could be vicious and attack each other, and had chased Ralph once, cornering him. Nana had had to flap her pinny at them and call out until they were distracted so we took no chances. Once they were locked up again though after that, Ralph would tease them, pretending he had food and call out to them in his high child voice imitating Nana.

The toilet was also built into a corner of the utility room, an awkward place, but perhaps the only suitable space available. It was common for the time for it to be in an out of the way place *anyway and being the city with sewerage available, may have been built in with the original plans. I don't remember a septic tank with its air vent. (We had piped water as today as opposed to tank). Decorated china chamber pots were mainly used at night for adults and children, partly a hangover from when toilets (lavatories/lavs/dunnies/outhouses) were outside but also if they had been inconveniently placed when relocated inside away from bedrooms. The young and the old did not always have good control.*

A Visit from Uncle Ross

At Christmas, birthdays, and especially when our fruit was ripe, our Uncle Ross would visit us. He used to delight in coming over to do battle with our fruit trees, the plum mainly. Though in his late fifties he would soon be up the wobbly wooden ladder, onto the roof, leaning out agilely to get onto the laden branches, and he'd often aim fruit as much at us as the ground or baskets, so luckily it was usually ripe when he did get a human target. We'd be calling out from below, 'You've missed some big ones' and 'Shake that branch' or Mary saying 'Watch yourself Ross. Oh dear, don't stretch too far' and Ralph yelling 'There's one further out', egging him on to danger.

Uncle Ross was far too wily to fall, teetering like an acrobatic scarecrow; he'd stretch out his limited length and shake the final fruit off before swinging down swiftly from the four or five metre plum and fig trees. The Golden Queen peaches, Golden Delicious and Granny Smith apples weren't as high so no challenge to him. Our poor man's orange (grapefruit) tree wasn't used much but the ever-producing lemon tree was helpful for setting jam that wouldn't take and baking. We would all be sampling the fruit and though they may have been imperfect in shape (no sprays), nothing compares today to their unforgettable juicy, firm, delicious taste and the smell of sun on their ripened skins.

In the evening, to the heated fragrance of chutney making, pungent plopping plum jam and preserving peaches, we were allowed to stay up till that night's bottling was done – Granddad, Nana and Mary all working together sometimes needing to preserve without sugar – while we played games with Uncle. But he always won because he was so quick. His hands as fast as his tongue, he would give us a bowl of something and just before we took it, he would drop it and then deftly catch the bowl when we missed. As we got older, he would leave us to do the catching and when we weren't quick enough he'd say, 'Slow-coach'. A container of eggs was the scary one. A teasing trick that was to hone my reflexes, often saving me along with a bit of luck in bad situations and sometimes even my life when driving.

Somehow when I sat on his knee, Uncle would find a big copper penny behind my ear or in Ralph's pocket. If we were quick enough to find it before him, we could keep it, otherwise we had to make do with a lolly. Stories, dirty deeds, party tricks and a quick wit were all part of his forte. He would tease us with outrageous adventure tales and the adults with witty jokes until we were packed off unwillingly to bed, wanting more laughter and lies. His fast quips were often right on target, sometimes painfully so, but always good for a giggle and they helped us laugh at ourselves. Mark, his son, also remembered coming over to our place one evening with his mum and dad when he was quite young, probably for late-fruiting trees so not that much excitement. Rounding the corner to our street, he says he saw me for the first time, flying down the road in my pink nightie, curls in disarray, and his mother saying, 'My goodness me, isn't that Mary's daughter running away?' Obviously an escapee.

We often stayed with him and his family later. He was in our lives right up to my teens. There were only Carol and Mark left by then similar in age to Ralph and me – his elder daughters Dorothy and Jill married and gone. We stayed in the big front bedroom of their old Mt. Eden villa, between Mary's husbands or quick trips to the city. I boarded there several times and eventually was married from there too.

The Old Maids

Our Levonia St. house must have had a mortgage on it (although I only thought this out later as it is the one reason that made sense – I had always assumed Nana had owned it, given her family's wealth) because once when I was about four, Mary took me with her out for a walk, not far up the hill from our place. It seemed strange to be all dressed up in my best frock and shoes and not go into town so I was full of questions, but Mary warned me impatiently not to chatter and be on my best behaviour. We stopped shortly and went through a large fancy gate, up a path bordered by a fiery flounce of flowers to the front door of a big substantial old house, with a better view even than ours, right over to the western Waitakere hills.

I understood Mary's warning when we were welcomed by two severe old maids who would have related well to the characters in a Jane Eyre novel. They were sisters, not unalike, tall for that time and what is often described as horsey looking. Probably more pronounced as they'd got older and although I couldn't imagine them ever being on horses, they possibly would have had to learn to ride, as that would have been the only transportation when they were growing up. Perhaps they had had a buggy and a driver. Nana had told me about that and she would have only been a little younger.

The sisters were very ladylike, immaculately mannered and dressed in similar beautiful but old-fashioned clothes and the surroundings had a slightly musty atmosphere, as if the doors and windows weren't opened much. Disconcertingly, they did things in unison, like ushering us through to their 'parlour', each pulling out a high backed chair, one sister helping me to scramble up, pushing the exquisite lace tablecloth away from my legs. (We called our best room, that wasn't used much, the sitting room and sometimes the front room as it was in the front of the house.)

The tea was brought over to the table from the sideboard in an elaborate silver pot on a tray and left to steep. The sister who did the pouring and most of the chatting must have been the eldest as at times during the intense conversation, she would give her sister a look which must have meant, 'I will handle this'. The younger one would back her up with quiet humphs and an occasional 'Yes, yes' and then stop speaking and drop her eyes, looking my way and smiling politely.

I doubt they had had much to do with children. The younger one was fascinated by me as I was of her, urging me on to have more cakes, especially the pretty butterfly ones with the pink icing and the cream holding the wings of sponge up. They smelt and tasted delicious, and there were plenty of them on the three-tiered silver stand with doilies underneath them. In addition there were cucumber sandwiches and pikelets with jam and more cream. But Mary firmly said two cakes had been quite enough for me, so I spent the rest of what must have been in reality an interview, wriggly and restless on the high Victorian chair.

Their cluttered with bric-a-brac but shiny clean parlour, smelling faintly like Granddad's shoe polish mixed with something else, had heavy, full length dark drapes caught back with a gold cord blending with what would probably have been a patterned Axminster carpet. The little light seemed to be absorbed by the heavy soft furnishings. The fire place was very large and the wooden surround had elaborate carvings and beside the clock on the mantelpiece, there were photos of very old fashioned looking people and horses. Also a pair of large antlers which I had never seen before and had to ask what they were. They had a very dominant position so perhaps had belonged to their father. It did not look like much had changed in their family home for many years.

A fascinating domed glass held flowers that Mary commented afterward belonged at a cemetery. The velvet covered chairs had turned legs like the dressers, tables and couches. There were odd shapes covered by a heavy Damask drape just at my eye level which intrigued me enough to squirm down to investigate. Mary had forgotten me momentarily as I had moved behind her but before I could lift the folds of the cover the younger sister said to me, 'Your mother is going now dear.'

Mary had ducked her head down, her favourite smart blue hat partly covering her face, and I could see she was trying not to cry as she groped for my hand and held it tightly. The sisters were chatting brightly to each other and pretended not to notice, urging Mary and me toward the hallway full of huge frames of old family portraits, its ceiling high up in the dark, the decorative coloured glass in the doorway and side-panels the only light in the gloomy big entrance. Opening the door efficiently and politely the sisters ushered us out.

Mary didn't speak as we walked back down the hill and shushed me when I tried to talk to her. Nana didn't look very happy when we arrived home either, after Mary had described the atmosphere at the meeting which obviously had not been successful. Nana changed the subject when I started asking questions again and Mary chatted about the furnishings as it wasn't often by then that we were invited into such luxurious homes and I think both Nana and Mary missed what had once been everyday visits to similar places for them.

I had noticed everything too because the ladies were so alike (as twins intrigue) and very different from anyone or any home elsewhere in the neighbourhood that we knew of anyway.

The sisters, who probably had sold Nana the property and held the mortgage, may have relented on their terms later though, because Mary was happier one night not long after she had read a letter from the mail that day and talked about when we went to see the two funny ladies. Nana said, 'What would they need money for at their age anyway? They're not such a bad couple of old biddies after all,' which made me worry because I hadn't thought much about Nana being old, although I knew she was. Old people died. I thought of that every time we went past the sisters' place.

Much later, long after the war and our Nana had died, we came closer to being destitute than the Depression years when we were living on Waiheke.

Chapter 5 Depression Depths & Recovery.

1933-4 seemed to be the depth of the Depression after the initial years of shock and insecurity had greyed out into hopelessness and apathy, exacerbated by hunger, boredom with no work and exposure to the elements for some. The total invasiveness of that period of despair and despondency never really left many people and was often passed on, albeit diluted, to their children and succeeding generations, even if not openly discussed, then by osmosis, an informal and perhaps unintentional indoctrination. Everyone appeared to look back at what they had lost and could not imagine a better future or perhaps bear to hope for one in case it didn't happen. Part of this was also that there was a general acceptance that depressions always happened anyway so you rode them out and survived them as best you could. This perpetuated the negative acceptance of it having happened before so it might again, and perhaps worse.

Although most recovered once they had work again, the after-effects left many afraid with a deep insecurity that they could lose their independence at any time. It seemed to me that fear never really went away and perhaps led to the inability to appreciate the good time when it did come later. Happiness would have been so precious – 'it might be too good to be true'. It no doubt accounts for the generalised cautious attitude of many of the children who survived those years with hoarding and a respect for the value of money and a job. Children's reactions could also have been to rebel against such restrictive thinking.

I remember contemporaries who were often blasé and deliberately wasteful, much to their parents' horror, especially if they were by then reasonably well off. 'Buying on tick', 'time payment', 'hire purchase', 'pay-as-you-go' – whatever way it was referred to, eventually became more acceptable towards the fifties and my generation of worriers were able to carefully acquire goods (a washing machine justified it for me) that may have taken years to save for – the normal way for the older Depression survivors. Obviously that caution has well and truly bounced off the current generations. Some of those with an expectation of entitlement and instant gratification that has developed since then and the ungratefulness for when it is, is often unbelievable to older people.

Retrenchment policies of the Coalition Govt. were revolted against in the 1935 election, the rout a surprise to some. Not Mary or her family. I remember over the years her saying how marvellous it was listening to the election results come over the radio. We had our own radio, but for many there may only have been one in an area where people could gather. Mary, like many, remained faithful to Labour all her life. It was seen as the working man's party. She would refer back in an idolatry way people think about heroes and saviours, to the hope that Labour Party ministers brought when they came to power with names like Walter Nash, (Jack) John A. Lee Under Secretary to the Prime Minister, Peter Fraser Deputy Leader, Bob Semple (he was described as an 'unconventional and irrepressible politician') and especially Michael (Micky) Joseph Savage who was experienced by the public as a warm, kindly man trusted even outside his own party. He was given the title 'New Zealander of the Century' by the *New Zealand Herald* in 1999.

He had 'devotion lavished on him probably more than any other NZ Prime Minister' and 'felt the need to overcome pessimism' and 'build and not destroy' helping the 'little man' with policies like the 1936 Primary Products Act, a guaranteed price scheme to insulate farmers so NZ's standard of living would no longer be dependent on fluctuating earnings from primary exports. It helped that export prices were rising again and farming improved. A positive effect on the economy and confidence began to return.

NZ was referred to as the 'social laboratory of the world' as we were the first country to grant a vote to women in 1893 (Labour had the first woman MP, Elizabeth McCombs in 1933). Also the 1898 social legislation was said to be 'The measure the first of its kind in any British country and the foundation stone of the welfare state' and based on the Government taking some responsibility for the poor and the deserving aged. Our world of today began in a seemingly insignificant way when the 'Old Age Pensions Act' provided a small monthly pension for those who qualified. From there other social legislation was added over the years and payments regularly increased and so people felt 'protected from cradle to grave', although this was challenged during the Depression when allowances were reduced.

The comprehensive Social Security Act of 1938 brought in by Micky Savage's first Labour Government was an update and consolidation of the previous social legislation. Elderly people particularly were grateful at the 60-year-old standard age benefit being raised, including Nana and Granddad, along with the sickness benefit and deserted wives pension (which Mary and we were to eventually benefit from). In 1945 or '46 the Family Benefit became universal, every child under 16 eligible regardless of the family income and it was increased to £1 ($2) per week. Enlighteningly, it was paid out to the mother (from page 29 SS act 1938) and they were also authorised to make application for family allowances, instead of the right being restricted to the father – but one wonders if the women ever knew about that. Although politics were usually seen as being of interest for older people, particularly men, there may have been a few young women voters gained if they did. Often though wives followed their husband's guidance.

The new system of medical and hospital insurance fund was to be paid for by using 5% of our income and subsidised by general taxation. Everyone was entitled to free hospital treatment and prescribed medicine and to have ordinary medical fees refunded. For the workers, wages and salaries were increased, (the 40 hour week had been introduced in 1936 and by 1945-46 it had become nearly universal), factory conditions were improved, and provision for solving the housing shortage made (state housing). The State Advance Corporation was set up in 1936 for first mortgages too. There were still 10,000 of the 50,000 (a fifth of the work force) left unemployed and on relief by the time war broke out in 1939 but unlike earlier, men were being usefully occupied on public works projects. The Social Security Bill leading to the 'Welfare State' came into force on the 1st April 1939 and was seen by Labour as their 'Crowning Glory'.

When Michael Joseph Savage died in 1940 his funeral was huge. People were really upset, the train taking two days from Wellington to Auckland, stopping at every station for the public to view his flower-covered casket. He was buried at Bastion Point in Auckland and his memorial was "built on the site of a former gun emplacement dating from the 'Russian Scare' of the 1880s overlooking the Waitemata Harbour". It was officially opened in 1943 which is when Mary took us to see it.

She said, "If he had been a beloved king I don't think people could have been sadder and some people wore black for months". Officials were amazed at the interest people took in his monument, but the workers that had survived the Depression understood.

To some, any Labour policy that seemed innovative or extreme 'smacked of the Red Revolution' and was totally unpalatable. The reasoning was that Labour wanted to encourage Communism, which started activities here in the early 1920's. Their fears were not unwarranted as there were Communists in unions, but their active members were never enough to be really threatening. With its people's party ideology it appeared attractive to those disillusioned by our social system and had impressed some – like my stepfather John.

If it was ever going to become a real political force here, the Depression would have seemed the ideal time. Given the general unhappiness of the population, it is surprising Communism and the apparent hope it offered, didn't flourish, and catch fire in the fervent ashes of desperation and despair. Perhaps there was a learned caginess from our Depression losses and I remember a comment often heard later, "Send the buggers off to Russia and they can come back and tell us how wonderful things are there." John, my stepfather, used to get very defensive when he heard those sorts of criticisms. They would not be repeated in his presence after his often fast violent reaction. He, like others in the party, had defiantly clung to self-destructing beliefs and spoke in bitterness about what 'should' have been achieved. It was always someone else's fault, and like the organisation of unemployed workers, foretold doom.

Probably the mistrust of the ability for any government to understand, or really care about the basic needs of its more needy constituents from that time, lingers in the community memory and possibly still influences voting decisions in the elderly at least.

As much as it was the state of the world and the approximately 10 year length of the Depression (for us anyway), it was also our own singular lost way of life, our unique tentative identity as a country, that left us gutted. The possibility of anyone starving here where food so easily grew, or at least being undernourished on the scale it became – especially for children – must have seemed unimaginable before the Depression.

Our undeniably confident sense of freedom, being our own person, the preciousness of our individuality to us (that other countries don't obviously have in quite the same way, with the possible exception of Australia) seemed to dissipate. The dream of our young country had been about 'Independence and the land of boundless opportunity'. Our long recovery period from all this perceived loss, especially our self-identifying loss, permeated our thoughts for years to come and contributed to such a devastating period in our development.

The protest marches were not referred to and when I read about them, they seemed surreal and must have horrified our conservative community as we children were never told. We were often given dark predictions though and warnings of things to avoid and to save our money so that my/our future would be better than their generation.

Growing up in that time was in a way like living with a tribal affliction. I absorbed my own limited childish perspective, based on incidences with our family's, neighbours' and friends' lives or events and the everyday lack of things, while living in Auckland anyway.

However, it has been difficult to come to terms with dealing to what Veronica and I at least had felt was a nebulous hovering cloud that we didn't understand the origin or details of. We felt its unpredictable force though and were told it would one day descend on our generation – which it did too, much later, but not quite in the same way. Subsequently, it wasn't until my minor research and the various books I read about the Depression, that our experiences made sense. The collation of this informal information for writing this book has left me feeling much more settled and accepting about how we and others developed the way we did and feel the way that we still do (in some cases). Like unfortunately retaining the often compulsive need to keep everything, no matter how decrepit and useless it may be. Also why, in particular circumstances, we can lose our sense of humour. How could many of us not?

I have always been a good saver and the following quotes resonate with me;

> 'The fundamental insecurity that one bout of poverty can inflict for a lifetime, no amount of money can ever remedy.' Plus 'The devouring anxiety of the insecure.'

Last move as a whole family;

The last time we moved as a family in 1953 my boyfriend of the time came around to help and Veronica and I found him squatting by the under-sink cupboard busily disposing of rusting tins into a rubbish bag. They would have been mainly types of cleaning fluid, that had very little of anything useful in them, ones that I had packed innumerable times. We stood there in horrified silence. Not because we didn't want to get shut of them ourselves but because Mary's reaction would be so appalling it wasn't worth the trouble. Trying to explain Mary's desperate ingrained need to keep everything to someone who didn't understand what our lives were based on and the endless recriminating repercussions we would have to suffer afterwards, seemed pointless. I just carefully said to him that I would sort them later and diverted his attention to the more basic decisions of moving furniture. Veronica and I simply accepted that most of Mary's generation, that we came across anyway, just could not let go of the mindless hoarding. They felt they had good reason – they were cautious, they may need whatever it was again one day. To them, everything had value and things were made to last and were expected to. I thought that perhaps my boyfriend's family had survived the Depression quite well.

Ralph's response of always 'taking the Mickey' when packing (on the odd times he was there) was to treat it the same as with any of Mary's other foibles like 'never put your shoes on the table,' 'no umbrellas up inside' and 'always sit down and count to ten if you had already left the house on an outing and had to go back inside', and certainly 'don't walk under a ladder' – that was practical so not so bad. I can't remember the black cat one. All would bring you bad luck, to be sure. Ralph ignored them. I remember thinking I had broken a small hand-mirror when I was quite young, that was seven years bad luck, which seemed forever so I was already stuffed. I gave up and simply couldn't be bothered worrying. I remember Mary being horrified when she noticed.

Superstition for most was a way of life in those days, more pronounced in some families than others and perhaps also dictated by their country of origin. Everyone could quote you something until to a child it was often bewildering. Ignorance and fear would have been a big part of it. Most were not that well educated and there were so many things we didn't understand. Especially around illnesses, TB one of the most frightening. (No Google) When I asked different people, they all had their own interpretations, many conflicting.

Ralph had probably been the one who had gone without the least as, like in many a family; he had been the much-wanted son by parents and maternal grandparents. Also much of his young life from about 10 had been spent boarding with other more affluent people who may not have been too badly affected by the Depression and war years and had more knowledge. His basic attitude was a friendly, positive and cheerful one anyway and he remained that way all his life with the odd temporary suspensions when things went really wrong. His sense of humour would have been a saving grace.

Chapter 6 Communication/Radio/Wireless

There were scant forms of communication. In Auckland the daily newspapers that were delivered to the home were the *NZ Herald* in the morning and the *Auckland Star* in the evening or else they were picked up at a tobacconist or some other shop outlet. Colour was not used. In Auckland's CBD (and possibly smaller centres) young boys had stands on street corners with their own personalised high pitched call, usually unidentifiable, to attract the public. In the suburban neighbourhoods they had their bikes (no gears) with a split canvas hold-all slung over the cross bar (like my brother Ralph's) delivering to letter boxes. It was the evening '*Star*' for my family when I grew up. There were few landline phones, limited cars and some motorbikes (which may have had a trendy side-car).

Air travel was a dream for most when it did become available. Trams, trains, buses and ferries were mainly in towns and cities and relying on bikes, horses or Shanks' Pony (walking) meant most of us lived in our own very limited and staid, reasonably formal worlds.

There were ham-radio buffs who were interesting people who knew more than most about what went on outside our shores, and people who helped sailors in trouble were much admired.

Unlike our transient situation, most people tended to stay within the known area they were born in with family and familiar people around. In Christchurch where we lived for a year in the sixties, I made a lovely older friend there who told me she had never been further than 20 miles (32 km approx.) from her home. Following the War and the Depression, people may have moved after the purchase of a farm with Government support for war veterans, job offers or transfers or if other opportunities arose like large long term building projects (e.g. dams), but on the whole we were a reasonably stable nation. As today, older couples often stayed in their up to 4-bedroom homes until they died or became unable to do for themselves, and sometimes a spinster daughter would be around to take care of them. For the rest of the family there must have been much comfort derived from knowing mum and dad were always in the same place.

The few who could afford an overseas journey usually went by ocean liner or sometimes via a cargo ship with accommodation or later flew, but the closest most of us came to travel outside NZ, or feel what it was like to fly, was thanks to the movies themselves or sometimes the shorts before the main attraction (like advertising today). When newsreels also showed the resulting havoc after tragedies, it all seemed part of the entertainment we had come for and it was difficult to relate to their reality, although it could temporarily put us off our fanciful travel aspirations to that area.

Phones

Telephones eventually came into their own, large black Bakelite ones, and by 1939 NZ had more phones per head of population than any other country except the USA. They were nothing new to Mary as her parents had phones as part of their jobs in the early 20th century in her childhood (although that was unusual), but she herself never had one again until she was into her seventies. My first memory of a phone was on a farm as a child of around 8 years old just after the war. The farmer's phone was on a party line which meant if you picked up the phone to ring out and if others were using it, their conversations could be heard, so no privacy, and gossip was rife. Each household identified their own call in from the number of rings activated from the manual switchboard operator at the Post Office, usually a female, based on Morse code (i.e. 'A' was one short ring and one long). There could be up to 10 or more households on a line depending on the area serviced. When the phone rang, everyone listened to see if it was theirs. If you wanted to make a call out, you listened to check that the line was clear and rang for the operator. They would then connect the number through for you, or if that line was engaged or it was a toll or overseas call, they may ring you back. Charges were quite high so you didn't make toll calls lightly. (My Nana had been one of the first phone operators in NZ.)

When the dial-up phones first came in we still had to go to an operator for a toll call. The dial-up meant putting your finger in the hole over the number required and turning the clear plastic piece around until it wouldn't go any further, then removing your finger so that it would return to its original position. You could then dial the next numbers – usually seven in total. Direct toll dialling wasn't available until 1953 (subscriber toll dialling – STD) and the 111 emergency number was available from 1958 however our family did not have our first phone in the city until the early sixties. There were phone boxes strategically placed around the city and suburbs and sometimes there were groups of red and glass boxes in densely used areas like the main Post Office in Auckland city. By 1976 phones eventually became single lines, much more quickly in the city than in the country. After my second marriage, we shifted out to 10 acres in Albany and we went back to a 2-party line for a while – to our horror. I had been into the city looking for a new job as well and had applied to Telecom but when they said the equivalent of "Don't call us we'll call you" I said, "Don't bother, our lines are usually down".

A trig station was above our property and although our view was lovely, the wind was a problem. I eventually got the Telecom job and also our own phone line as I worked in their Engineering Department and spoke to the Engineer-in-charge. He was quite non-committal about it at first but when it became an inconvenience around my job, it changed his priorities and we eventually had an underground connection of a single line. He didn't know we had also only just been connected to mainstream power.

In 1964 77% of all phones were automated and by mid-1965, 35% of New Zealanders had a phone. We were rated the third highest in the world.

Given the preceding hundreds of years of slow evolution, when eventually things did begin to change and the technical revolution really began, it seemed to the older generations at least, to be proceeding at the pace of an out-of-control steam engine, about the most frightening man-made thing they could imagine aside from weaponry.

Television, cell phones, iPads, computers, the internet, social interaction like Facebook, Pinterest and electronic gaming, CD's & DVD's, paying bills online etc. were somewhat bewildering to many older people. (Luckily I had pushy children who nagged me until I 'got with it' and ended up running a NFP Organisation for 20 years and writing the content of a large website for it.)

Radio

Without the proliferation of today's means of communication the radio with a human voice was the most important way to receive the latest news stories, although we called it the 'wireless' then. During both the Depression and the war and until TV in 1960, radio was always a big part of our lives for the more immediate announcements, especially major national items like election results and world events. Although the sound could be scratchy, often with background noise, radio brought the controlled but emotionally charged voices with the outbreak and end of the war, Royal visits and speeches and any disasters like mountain eruptions, earthquakes and the Tangiwai Rail one. We heard it first over the radio waves.

Radio was first broadcast in NZ in 1921 at the University of Otago. Auckland's original radio broadcasts were from 1YA in 1925 and (later 1ZB) with others evolving in a radius of about 100 miles. Wellington 2YA & 2ZB, Christchurch 3YA & 3ZB, Dunedin 4YA & 4ZB. The ZB commercial stations in 1936. The Government were divided between choosing the contentious American model and the English. The former 'let's make money' all bets are off and advertising, or the latter, go for the BBC style and rigid control educating the public for their own good and controlling entertainment. The BBC style won. During the Second World War news was censored.

The public tuned in using expensive or cheap radio receivers. The personal, simple crystal set was the most basic and least expensive, often made by its owner with scrounged materials. The crystal arrangement was very crude, Ralph said, when he made one when he was around 13. Tuning into a station was achieved with a loud squeal.

The valve radios were housed in large, free-standing, often opulently decorated wooden cabinets, a piece of furniture in its own right, or similar ones in a variety of smaller sizes and less elaborate. These sat on a surface somewhere handy to family activity, usually the large kitchen and the warmest place with the stove going. Houses mainly had a separated lounge or living room. My Aunty Alice had one of the very large ornamentally carved cabinet radios in oak, that never gave up and I think she loved it for its tenacity as much as its looks, but when she and Uncle Henry aged, they shifted into a smaller place and it didn't fit in the lounge so they bought a more portable model. Aunty hung onto her old radio though, she was sure it would eventually become valuable again and it sat for years in the corner of the turn in the hall passageway, making passing it difficult when carrying anything. She covered it an elaborate white cloth and placed its own special vase on top, putting fresh flowers in it every day from her lovely garden. By the time it was an antique she had severe arthritis and had been in an old people's home for about 30 years, as she lived on into her nineties, so I don't know where her admired radio ended up.

There was not very much to send to air at first except for music programmes, the biggest percentage of which was light, but the other genres were covered as well. Clive Drummond was the first pioneer celebrity radio announcer of his kind in NZ. Aunt Gwen was a children's announcer and so popular her wedding was broadcast.

Music became the core of radio, a background to our days, a family affair. An amateur singer, the enthusiastic and gregarious English Daisy Basham, became involved with it early in her radio career, first as an arranger and then hosting a children's programme. She was forever after known by the name 'Aunt Daisy'. Referring to announcers in Aunt and Uncle terms was to overcome the formality of Mr. and Mrs. and was also in general use for friends of the family when they were not relations (like our Uncle Ross and Aunt Alice), for the same reason. When the Depression came and radio jobs went to men only, in 1933 Aunt Daisy joined Uncle Scrim (the Rev. Colin G. Scrimgeour) and Uncle Tom (Garland) at the private church radio station called the 'Friendly Road' in Auckland. Radio was under State monopoly and when the government really understood what a powerful medium radio was, they brought in the 1936 Broadcasting Act, and the 1ZB station was amalgamated into National Commercial Service 1ZB along with Aunt Daisy. It then changed from having only religious and music programmes to the more serious business to educate, inform, and entertain along with the allowance of products to be mentioned.

Aunt Daisy's career then really began. She gave her show a 'sense of personality', ignoring most of the broadcasting conventions and with no script, she simply spoke as herself, with a genuine concern for people and her programme went out to the entire country. Only products she approved of were advertised and endorsed and they flew off shop shelves. Her clear, cheerfully familiar, lilting greeting of "Good morning, good morning, good morning everybody," at 9am every day accompanied by 'Daisy, Daisy' music went for 30 (some say 45) minutes offering letters, stories, weather discussion, suggestions for conserving and 'the waste not want not ethic,' with homely and efficient hints for house-wives' problems thrown in with every day recipes that eventuated into several cook books. Aunt Daisy's and another English woman's book, *Mrs. Beeton's Household Management*, were what women often referred to when looking for hints in their daily lives. Her job supported her family and it made her a trusted and loved friend or companion to many women and often men as well. Although she was only four feet eleven and a half inches tall (1.520m), through the continuity of her chatty morning sessions the inimitable Aunt Daisy became the most successful saleswoman and popular broadcaster of her time. She greeted us nationally each morning for 25 years, lasting right through until her death in 1963, and must have had a reassuring effect on our nation with a comforting sense of security and practicality through the upheavals of the end of the thirties and on into the forties, fifties and early sixties.

Uncle Scrim, who had formed the 'Friendly Road Children's Choir' in the early thirties, was later taken over by the nearly as popular personality Uncle Tom. My sister was later accepted into his choir. The iconoclastic Uncle Scrim was not the controlled and anonymous figure the government envisaged. He felt radio should be more lively and controversial and upset the Coalition

Government by his sessions supporting 'the unemployed man in the street' that he saw as victims of the Government's ineptitude. He campaigned for the underdog from the point of view of social reform and Christian ethics. His comments were about the fact we had trees everywhere but couldn't shelter the poor, we had abundant food rotting yet our children were malnourished (farmers couldn't sell crops or meat) and there was a shortage of clothes with wool wasting after the closure of woollen mills. He was a much-loved figure and people felt that at least someone was on their side. He also commented that the newspapers felt threatened by him as he was often first with the news. They would have to get used to that.

Although the government denied it, the scandal of the New Zealand Post Office trying to jam Uncle Scrim's 1ZB radio broadcast on the eve of the 1935 election came out. He was 'such a formidable opponent' that he was eventually sacked in 1944 to the dismay of many.

During the war at 9pm Big Ben's dong could be heard striking the hour from London which was followed by a minute of silence for prayer and then the war news came on. Adults would shush any children around to listen carefully to what was being broadcast. I can still see Granddad's white hair and beard bent towards the radio in concentration. He was from London and although he never was one to look back or think of 'if onlys', I wondered if listening to the sound of Big Ben was precious to him.

Other perspectives.

> *'Radio was our connection to the world directly into our sitting rooms and we would hear the voices of important leaders, like Winston Churchill, who we trusted to help us and our boys survive, and even our own caring King spoke to us compassionately at approximately the same time as he did to the English people on the other side of the world, which for then was really amazing, and especially reassuring at those times of uncertainty and fear. The continuity of the usual BBC news, although grave, always gave us a sense of belonging that was meaningful and of having a place in the*

Commonwealth and the war. Both direct broadcasts that signalled the end of the war on VE and VJ days in 1945 came to us at the same time as everyone else. Radio was really significant in our lives.' (Loosely quoted from an acquaintance whose husband was overseas for 3 years.)

Uncle Ross

NZ's shortwave radio service was established in 1948 and after that Uncle Ross could be found in his big lounge where his large cabinet-sized radio was in a corner near the formal dining area. At night after the 9 o'clock 1YA news from London, Uncle Ross, sitting there till all hours, would tune in by shortwave to overseas stations, so close on the display numbers it took concentration, patience and tenacity to catch the separate voices. The static and waves of sound would rise and fade, so that every few words, one would be missed and have to be guessed at, which didn't seem to bother him. Sometimes too the blast of a foreign language would seem to leap out of the cabinet, making him jerk back as he quickly twisted the dial again while the rest of us jumped if we were near.

If he hadn't answered the door to our knock when visiting during the day, we would find him there, fingers hovering over the dials. He was deaf but seldom used his hearing aid and would be hunched up close, glued to the speaker in his comfortable armchair, listening to some interesting programme he'd found. He wouldn't break his concentration when he saw us but give a brief wave of acknowledgement at the same time shooing us out to wait in the kitchen where we would make a cup of tea and dip the ginger nuts we'd brought, until he came out and joined us. All we could ever really hear from the radio in passing were jumbled words.

The names of radio people famous for other reasons were Winston McCarthy, rugby commentator "It's a goal", Dr. Turbott known as the 'Radio Doc' was a temporary short series which began in 1943 and eventually lasted 40 years, Arthur Pearce "Rhythm on Record" (National radio), Selwyn Toogood "It's in the bag" and other quiz programmes he took over when popular John Maybury went to Australia.

Selwyn Toogood eventually became as well-known and admired as Aunt Daisy in his own entertaining way, his hearty, jovial voice paternalistic and cheering. He stayed around until TV came and his big frame dominated the stage in his shows, his enthusiasm catching.

There was Marina in the 'Women's Hour' and Merv Smith's breezy un-PC breakfast sessions. Phil Shone, also of breakfast show fame, was the one who in 1949 seriously warned mothers to protect their children and not let them outdoors to go to school because of the calamity of 'an invasion of a swarm of wasps' coming from Papatoetoe and crossing the city. He updated progress frequently with "The wasps are coming, the wasps are coming" refrain and finally mentioned offhand that the date was the 1st of April. Mary missed that but was not impressed anyway and sent us off regardless. I don't know if she believed the hoax or not. I biked to school with one eye on the road and one on the sky, comforted when shops were handy to duck into if necessary.

There were American serials for various ages in the evening originally when there had been fears about 'slang' and one thrilling one at 7:30pm (its name eludes me) that Ralph and I fought over in 1947 (the only year we spent together again as a family at Arnold's before our state house at Panmure much later) as he had something else he wanted to listen to at that time. Someone mentioned 'Night Beat' and it could have been that. I do remember 'Portia Faces Life' and 'Dr. Paul' in the fifties and 'Dr. Kildare' later, so medical entertainment has always had its followers even if not at today's level and there were the comedians from the BBC. Family shows like 'Dad & Dave' from the 1930's, 'Fred and Maggie Everybody', 'The Lone Ranger' for kids and the 'Lever Hit Parade' (top pops). Live sports broadcasts, like rugby, wrestling and racing were difficult because of cumbersome equipment required. Smaller portable transistor radios made their appearance at the end of the 1940's and I understand there was quite a bit of under-the-counter goings-on when they were brought in undeclared from overseas by sailors, so exempt from duty (on some things up to 150%), and sold at bargain rates often making normally honest NZ'ers feel like criminals.

We missed some of the songs of the 1950's 'Rock-'n'-Roll' era although if we had a turntable and the money when 78 RPM records were replaced by the 33's and 45's in the mid-fifties, we could purchase our own, especially the cheaper singles. Disc jockeys were invented around that time along with increased pop programmes on commercial radio. I feel really privileged to have been the age I was for the music, movies and entertainment of the 'Fifties' and the following decade. That era's prolific song writers, bands and singers made it such an incomparable period in pop music as today's radio stations specialising in nostalgia proves.

But we were short-changed again and there was discontent with the government's monopoly of radio dictating programmes especially after the portable radios became popular. For me it was also the conservative, humourless, very proper English tones of the news readers spoken in a country where it was not particularly appropriate, although the clear diction was appreciated.

Later, weekend radio had stations given over to racing and there was always someone's portable around and even if it was some distance away and the reception wasn't that good, the pitch of the announcer's voice rising to an excited crescendo and then dying away, followed by the radio owner's closer, clearer and louder swearing reaction when a bet was lost. That was very distinguishable.

Radio Hauraki

Eventually direct competition from Radio Hauraki, the private pirate radio station (the Good Guys), sorted that out. I happened to be down at the Auckland waterfront one evening in early December 1966, when the drawbridge over the narrow channel was being lowered to try and stop the ship *'Tiri'* gaining access to the harbour. It was going to broadcast offshore from a tiny triangle of inhospitable international water between the Hauraki Gulf Islands. To allow the *'Tiri'* to be cleared for sea, classed as either a ship or a small barge, was a big problem. However, once it was outside NZ territorial waters the government would lose control over the competition.

The Leaving

The prearranged time for sailing must have passed I think when I got there so I wasn't expecting much to be going on, but there were groups of people everywhere (estimated at around 2,000), the biggest clusters on both sides of the wharf close to where the drawbridge was, yelling their support and using abusive language and sometimes trying physical coercion. They must have been fought off by the law, Marine Dept. officials and a small group of police, although from where I was standing it was difficult to distinguish who was who.

There was an extra roar of encouragement from supporters as the 'Tiri' was spotted leaving its nearby moorings and motoring toward what seemed the jerkily closing gap of the lowering drawbridge. The crowd segments began to merge and moved forward and then back again in surges, the angry voices sometimes breaking into a chant, and the yelling and higher voices of screaming girls, unless they were close, were mostly lost in the frightening roar. One giggly girl hung upside-down briefly from the bridge structure after losing her balance and before friends could haul her back. She screamed senseless encouragement with her long hair, exposed underwear and swinging bare legs temporarily distracting the guys in the crowd.

With so much noise and the early evening light dissipating there was confusion in places as it was not always clear whose side some were on and there was an unnecessary skirmish near me until it was sorted – by back patting and strained but slightly euphoric laughter. It felt like anything could happen and there was a strong sense of restlessness and determined behaviour to come, some people more reckless than others.

When I could see again, the Tiri appeared stuck partway to the bridge (because of the lowering tide I found out later) and apparently some of the crowd were pulling it forward with a rope which someone had a dip in the water to achieve. It at least gave the crowd something practical and useful to do. To resounding crowd encouragement, a battle to protect the bridge mechanism from closing was going on between officials and three of the

Radio Hauraki staff who sat wedged beneath it and from the movement around that area, it seemed quite violently.

There was banging on the shack windows and yelling at the person controlling the bridge mechanism that he could kill someone if he kept lowering. The jeering and yahooing gradually lessened as the boat got closer and we all stared in petrified fascination as the distance between the bridge and the ship dwindled. Some had their hands clamped over their mouths, waiting for what looked like an inevitable crash – right up to the last few seconds when I was wishing someone from the crowd would call to the captain to stop the suddenly fragile-looking ship.

But they were determined, although I think there was a moment or two of hesitation (and maybe it was to line up the boat) as the speed drifted off just before they reached the point of no return. We couldn't see what was going on but heard really loud shouts of warning and official sounding threats and argumentative responses for a time, the people at the back becoming frustrated not knowing how things were going. We could see the Tiri's mast though and the top of it and the lip of the partly-closed bridge suddenly became entangled to the dismay of the crowd. Two of the Radio Hauraki team appeared (although we didn't know who they were till later) and clumsily climbed up the bridge. They tried pushing with their feet to cheers while others from the crowd pushed the boat from below. The crowd became enraged and roared its disapproval until after what seemed an age, the Tiri was suddenly through! Something had worked.

The stunned crowd were quiet for a few seconds then erupted into a whistling, cheering triumph mixed with hilarity and relief. The sound bounced out over the wake of the boat to where we belatedly realised the fight wasn't over as the Hauraki staff were seen on deck struggling with police who had jumped on board and were trying to break into the locked and barricaded wheelhouse. The resolute skipper grimly sped up and steered for the freedom of the open sea in the darkening night.

The hesitating crowd slowly dispersed. I think most of us were feeling we had done our best to support a good cause although *unsure of what the eventual outcome would be with the fighting on deck still pictured in our minds as the ship had rounded the wharves out of sight. We found out later that out in the harbour off Devonport, extra platoons of police had boarded and they had stopped the struggle and used their brains instead, and disconnected the fuel lines. They eventually broke into the wheelhouse and everyone was arrested, including the crew, and they were picked up by the police launch Deodar. However, 'The ensuing court case exonerated the "Hauraki pirates" and proved that several Government departments had conspired to prevent the Tiri from sailing.'*

The ship eventually left the harbour again, unmolested, and began regular transmissions in December 1966 after various problems were sorted. The tiresome ongoing struggle with the government to have their music station legalised with a private broadcasting licence and based onshore continued for 3½ years. The cost to the young guys in personal lifestyle, time, money, and mental stress would have probably been pretty desperate in themselves without the ongoing wild weather conditions at sea on both the Tiri and Tiri II, with physical peril as well, given the close shaves.

Their tenacity and determination has to be admired and I would think David Gapes and Derek Lowe and co., who had known the venture could be risky and dangerous, would have been pretty thankful when it was over. The sadness of their final voyage back to Auckland though would probably stay with them forever. Instead of their big celebration, unfortunately and shockingly, right at the end in June 1970, their colleague Rick Grant was lost overboard.

Chapter 7 The Second World War

Reflections on NZ's Cultural Identity formed at Anzac Cove, Gallipoli.

Commemorating 25th April, 1915

Honouring the lost – only the sea can be heard,
no fluttering or even the call of a bird.
Just the perpetual wash of waves in the air,
and the uncanny hush of the 10,000 there.

A sense of respect and grief, envelops the crowd,
creating a calm, hallowed, invisible shroud.
Subtle light diffused over the sacred scene,
commemorating spirits where once war had been.

The blood from their bodies now nourishes the earth,
symbolised by wreathed poppies, at the new day's birth.
Eerie spiritual reverence for those who were slain,
then a grateful voice speaks in the sudden soft rain.

To the commitment and courage of all those men,
the wounded and the dead that were sacrificed then.
Whose intrepid characters formed a camaraderie,
of loyal Kiwi mate-ship, assuaged by the sea.

Their rite of passage was forged on each steep, stark hill,
unimaginable now in this peaceful chill.
The site carefully preserved, an antithesis to
The hell of the battle, where the death bullets flew.

> Traditional devotion to country and king,
> that price, innocence lost and acceptance to bring
> a defining offensive of fire by our guns;
> A nation reborn from squandered lives of our sons.
>
> A pilgrimage of belonging evoked each year
> from 'the utmost ends of the earth', we will be there.
> A profound sacred summons to a 'country of mind',
> surpassing all logic, here where nations combined.
>
> That poignant sadness of the bugler's 'Last Post',
> encompasses all memories left on that coast.
> 'We will remember them' – all those lost, brave men,
> when the solemn stillness pervades once again.

This is how the war affected us and is probably a very limited experience by comparison to other NZ'ers.

When war was declared in 1939, England was still generally thought of as the 'Mother country' and 'Going home' always meant travelling to England, so most people were willing to respond to her call as part of that deal.

> *"Both with gratitude for the past and with confidence in the future, we range ourselves without fear beside Britain. Where she goes, we go; where she stands, we stand. We are only a small and young nation, but we are one and all, a band of brothers and we march forward with a union of hearts and wills to a common destiny."* Michael Joseph Savage N.Z. P.M.

Perhaps not those though who had experienced or knew about the real conditions in places like Gallipoli in the First World War and the arrogance of questionable decisions that were made then that had cost us New Zealanders so much. They would have had reservations about sending our brave young men and potential leaders off to fight for England and Europe. We were told about one family who lived in an isolated country area (they were actually Australians) with one long unsealed dead-end road in and out, heavy bush, and steep topography curbing more extension. The mother, father and daughters lived in the first house on the road and were the service providers to the sons living about a mile further on. Whenever anyone from the government appeared, for whatever reason, they had a system to let the boys know someone was coming (which may have been from firing a gun with a sequence of shots – no phones) and the sons would disappear into the attic or into the bush if necessary. This family secret was only revealed later when they had all died – not from a bullet. Their deaths were in the due course of time and natural.

No-one could have known how long the war would last or have envisaged the full price of the Government's decision. Many people thought it might be over before the troops even reached the other side of the world after their long boat journey. 'We'll be home by Christmas' was often heard. Young men would mostly never have been able to afford to travel and they were of an age when a challenge would appeal to them and New Zealanders like to win. There was not much to do here anyway for youth looking for some action so they wouldn't be missing anything and the forces at least treated them as adults. They had their health and innocent optimism and the war was generally thought about as an exciting adventure, a gateway for reaching other lands and cultures. (I'm sure it began the idea of us as world nomads.) Men and boys didn't think they would die – I was told – they were worried more about being thought yellow for not joining the 7,000 enlisting volunteers that were signed up within four days of the war declaration. They had no idea about how much courage may be needed and that it sometimes had a limit. The possibility of injury or death was more a parent's fear than theirs. Conscription came in June 1942 when volunteers were not enough and eventually around 130,000 men and 10,000 women were to serve in the forces.

Disillusionment would have set in by the time the Japanese entered the war in the Pacific in 1941 after Pearl Harbour and many men wanted to come back and fight from here. They were even keener when the letters they were receiving meant they also felt the need to protect their women from the Americans. 45,000 Americans had arrived in NZ in mid-1942 in response to the NZ and USA government agreement to leave our troops in the Middle East and eventually more than 100,000 spent various periods in NZ until 1944.

Previous Governments had always been aware back as far as a Russian scare in the 1880's that we were vulnerable, and had at times secretly built gun placements at various strategic points around NZ, many of them in isolated places and not necessarily known about by the general public for years. Auckland Harbour had them at Motutapu, Howick, Te Atatu and the concealed one in a State house at Kennedy Park, Castor Bay on the North Shore. (The house façade is still there at the time of writing – don't know about the gun). Stony Batter on Waiheke Island, (which we knew about as kids but it wasn't accessible to us overland from Onetangi) and Whangaparaoa's Army Bay were the other places with concrete gun emplacements. The Ponsonby PO had an anti-aircraft gun though it wasn't fired when the Japanese reconnaissance spotter plane flew up the Waitemata Harbour one peaceful pre-dawn. Coastguard watching stations were set up around the country for German raiders and WW1 veterans patrolled the coastline in Navy requisitioned private launches. Barbed wire entanglements were rolled out on North Shore beaches. Although vastly under-appreciated in the beginning, the first radar station was quickly erected on a cliff at Piha so men and women of the forces could scan for approaching aircraft and submerged submarines.

Another war-time building was the Musick Point Aeradio Station which is located beyond Bucklands Beach on the promontory at the end of the Tamaki River. It was once a fortified Maori Pa (village) and with the superb views of the Auckland Harbour, Tamaki Strait, and the offshore islands it is understandable why it would be a Maori Stronghold. The Aeradio Station was opened in 1942 at the same time the concrete bunker nearby was erected as an emergency radio station for air and shipping, in case of enemy action damaging the Aeradio Station itself. It has since been used by Telecom (Spark) and one of the engineers commented to me once how important that position had been in war time and also that the Aeradio Station building is named after Captain Edwin G. Musick, a 1937 trail-blazer of flying boat routes from North America to South America, China and New Zealand. Its cross shape also a memorial in itself to him as well as loosely depicting an aircraft.

Because nothing serious had eventuated from previous war threats over the years, we had settled back into our insular lives again, so I think here at home we would have been glad to at least have some able men around after the scares in the 1940's from the German raiders destroying our shipping off the Northland coast and the German cruiser *Orion* laying 228 contact mines, and who knew what the Japanese were capable of? Local gossips living in isolated harbour areas swore they had seen submarine turrets in their waters. Though it was not officially confirmed in 1940, after negotiating the bar, a Japanese submarine was seen entering and leaving the Manukau Harbour as well. It had shocked us and shattered our illusions that distance alone could protect us from an enemy attack. We had assumed and been reassured that the Naval Base at Singapore would protect us. It was horrifying to everyone when it fell to the Japanese.

In 1942 the Prime Minister Peter Fraser asked the Allies for help to bolster our defences when the Japanese Assault on the South Pacific became more threatening. It was responded to by Franklin D. Roosevelt. NZ was useful to the Americans as a staging post for a source of supplies, training, planning operations and for the injured and R&R on the way to and fro from the American battles in the Pacific War. They substituted for our own men, many who had already been away for up to three years.

A common saying was, the 50,000 Yanks 'were overpaid, over-sexed, and over here'. NZ women's moral code of 'no sex before marriage' would have been really tested with the virile American invasion. The appealing figures of clean-cut young men dressed in impressive uniforms were tempting and they really knew how to treat a girl with flowers, boxes of chocolates, nylon stockings, and cigarettes along with their impeccable manners, smart slang, and Hollywood accents. They were also in general more light-hearted than NZ boys so girls succumbing to their charms were inevitable. 1,500 Kiwi girls married them during and after the war.

Loss

A close friend, who would never talk about the details, was engaged to an American pilot when in her early twenties. He died in the Pacific Islands. She sewed beautifully and apparently he had been going to supply her with a silk parachute for the material to make her wedding frock. I think he actually did, as one of her daughters told me they had found all sorts of things after she died, including some carefully wrapped old silk (65m), tied with a ribbon and packed away carefully in a box. My friend hadn't married until her 30's, and although she stuck with her husband until he died, I don't think she was ever particularly happy.

The press release of their arrival 'The Yanks are here', was delayed for security reasons from 12th June to November but their appearance was an open secret as they marched smartly from the wharf to the railway station a short distance away, after disembarking from five transport ships, supported by a cruiser and destroyer anchored in the Hauraki Gulf. (Later there were American ships by the hundreds.) They also took part in the 'United Nations Day' parade the next week which most of Auckland must have attended given the enthusiastic numbers that turned out.

The Americans were camped in parks including in front of the Museum and seven or eight places around Auckland. There were huts and tents and they built temporary hospitals in Hobson Park, Avondale (eventually Avondale College) and part of Cornwall Park, the latter later used by us when it became Cornwall Hospital. It's where two of my children were born and my granddad ended his days. Their Western Springs rest camp on the corner of Motions Rd. and Great North Rd. was where our family also had short-stay accommodation (emergency housing) in their prefabs when I was 15, before our allocated Government state house became available, like many others over the years, until 1959. They still had the flat feel of temporary, surplus, ex-military housing. With the zoo nearby, during the day there were just the general animal noises, although the monkeys were probably the most persistent, but it was the lions roaring at night that often kept us awake until we adjusted. Curiously, as it was only a short walk away, we never went to the zoo. The flats have all gone now and that area is part of a lovely large park with a lake and picnic and playground areas. Restored trams go back and forth from where the old planes are stored and displayed at Keith Park Memorial Field, past the zoo and where we used to live, on the way back to their home at MOTAT.

Bombing Precautions

After the Japanese entered the war, Nana showed Ralph and me the small calico bags she had made for us that had our names embroidered on them (I presume now for identification) which held our war kits. They had a tape attached so they could be hung around our necks, like mini satchels, and although I know they contained cotton-wool for ear plugs and a cork on a string for biting down on, the other things elude me except for the smell of camphor for some reason (perhaps to help with breathing if we were bombed) and the exotic, to us, chewing gum added later when the Americans arrived. Other people have said they had things like scissors & sticking plaster as well.

The little bags were stored in a special place in our bedroom and Ralph and I were given strict instructions to run and crawl under our beds with these around our necks when we were told to by adults or if we ever heard a plane (planes were not common and seldom went overhead where we lived). We had to practise doing this weekly. Ralph did at school too although perhaps more often there. Bags hung on a nail on the side of desks. The children also had to go into shelters if there was time or duck under their desks.

Knowing how much my brother loved planes I doubted he would be hiding anywhere. He'd be out looking for them, probably even waving them our way from the front porch if he was home with no adult around. If it was at night, we were not to peep out of windows or doors for any reason. I'm sure Ralph would have found a way for that too if he had heard anything. I do remember later that it was very dark outside as street lights were not turned on and we had to close our curtains, as well as pull down our dark brown Holland blinds, keeping any lights from showing in case of 'the enemy'. Mary said road signs had been removed in country areas to confuse the Japs and people got lost if they didn't know the area (and sometimes when they did.) The farmer husband of a friend of Mary's on their way to hospital took a wrong turn and she had their baby in the car, a story always told about him but usually behind his back.

Around 5 kilometres of slit trenches were dug in parks and open spaces around the city and there were public air raid shelters in various places including the 3.5km of tunnels built under Albert Park, enough shelter for 58,000 city workers. Years later when looking at a property to buy near Three Kings, the old owner showed me quite large lava caves in his back yard, one with a strong door on, which he said he and other locals would have used if necessary. Others remembered their own home-built air-raid shelters.

Bomb Shelter

At first, John, our stepfather-to-be in his mid-thirties, used to turn up at intervals at Levonia St., between jobs I think. He would have probably been seconded to do Second World War related work once 1939 came. He had some health problem which must have prevented him from going overseas with the army as I can remember him coming home from work in a uniform. His disability, and I think it was flat feet, didn't stop him digging a huge hole though in our back yard between the fruit trees. That was to be our bomb shelter for use when the Japanese invaded. It had an old iron roof with an exposed end where the steps went down the side but I don't think there was much in it like furniture or food. We were never told to actually use it if planes did come.

As that danger from the Japanese passed and the Americans arrived, it became our play-house instead, the best in the neighbourhood until winter came and it filled up with water. The hole was the fore-runner of many future ones we were to discover. I think of it as a 'John fetish'. He was used to digging holes for every country shift, and there obviously had been many and were many more to come. His first self-elected job was to do a new 'bog-hole' for the outdoor toilet and a trench for waste. He would fairly quickly dig to his height and all anyone would see after that was flying earth from seemingly nowhere.

The Public

There were the few who anticipated war shortages and, perhaps spurred by the memory of the Depression, accumulated tea, sugar, flour, and reels of cotton in panic quantities. They perhaps hadn't thought of rubber being in short supply because of the Japanese, making men's braces and women's elastic unavailable for 'bloomers' or 'scanties' in particular, so men went without and used belts and women had to have a button on their underwear instead. Not very convenient when caught short and cold fingered.

The 'Regulation Emergency Act' was passed, and prices of all commodities were frozen but it also dismayingly gave the government powers to do almost anything.

As a nation we tried to do 'our bit for the war effort' at home and women especially came into their own. Single women were mobilised (man-powered) first into essential occupations and by 1944 all women from 18 up to age 44, without children, were expected to register for work so it became socially acceptable. Some work under certain conditions was at equal pay like Women's Teachers Assn., Federation of Business and Professional Women and the Public Services. Many of the jobs women did had been closed to them before the war especially in the public services and any drivers' jobs. They were let loose on trams, buses, Post Office vans, and trucks and rode posties' bikes with a special uniform of a split skirt, and became wireless telegraphers, assembled steel helmets and munitions and did engineering work.

Our Red Cross were always there as they had been in WWI and the 'Women's War Service Auxiliary' was set up in the early forties to co-ordinate the hundreds of women registering as volunteers for the war effort. As well as helping in the laundries at hospitals and as assistants, doing typing and clerical work, like the single women they also did men's work driving ambulances for the Transport Section, volunteering at fire stations and were trained in emergency skills from Morse code signalling and first aid to repairing trucks and cooking for camps. Staffing canteens that were run by the American Red Cross at their military camps with their own recreational hall would have been one of the more enjoyable jobs. It introduced our women to hamburgers, toasted sandwiches, maple syrup, doughnuts, Lamingtons, Coke, coffee, and ice-cream sodas as well as the latest dance and music crazes. Driving for senior officers of the American forces would have been another sort of dream job.

The Women's Land Service, (called the Women's Land Army until 1942 and formed from the WWSA), was a government initiative set up to keep agricultural production going, part of which was driving tractors. These 'Land Girls' were issued smart dress uniforms along with a working kit that included 3 working shirts, 3 pairs of overalls and gumboots. It makes you wonder what those who were city girls thought of that. Young women from both cities and towns were encouraged to enlist to bolster the rural workforce and they worked on farms and orchards around Auckland city's outskirts, some in specially created state gardens at Mangere, Patumahoe, Pukekohe and Waiuku – 'essential work' – where 38,000 tons of vegetables were produced as food for Britain and USA in the Pacific.

Other varied groups were also set up around NZ so that women could chat together while they knitted, some used knitting machines and looms, and they sewed and packed parcels for relatives or 'the boys overseas', fighting or imprisoned, with things like plum puddings, fruit cakes, Anzac biscuits, pyjamas, handkerchiefs, cigarettes, toothbrushes, razors and soap, socks, balaclavas and other knitted items. Around that time women were also accepted into the armed forces – WAAC's. (An offshoot of war was that women between 25 and 30 became eligible for jury duty.)

In 1940 the Cambridge RSA formed the National Military Reserve and was put on coast watch and booby traps were put into position. In 1941 blackout precautions were rigidly enforced by Air-raid Wardens, who wore tin hats, canvas shoulder bags, and armbands and who checked for lights, including car headlights which had to be painted blue. In 1942 the Government Emergency Precaution Scheme (EPS) came into being to supervise Civil Defence in blackout and air-raid shelters and sort supplies of sand buckets and stirrup pumps for fires.

The Home Guard, set up in 1940 in groups as civilian soldiers, eventually numbered 123,000 men and was made up of volunteers at first but in 1942 it became compulsory for men aged 35 to 51. Ineligible for service because of age or other reasons like manpower for essential industries, they were often unfairly resented by both others and the men themselves. The first year some were equipped with sporting guns, others used their own guns or wooden replicas they made themselves. These part-time infantry were not uniformed although they had various armbands to distinguish them, one was a red crown and an embroidered 'AG' with angled stripes on a cream calico background. The men were organised on an official basis in 1941, and after Japan entered the war they were uniformed, given any assorted weapons available and with only 40,000 regular troops at home were to be relied on to potentially hold off any invasion – although instructions on how they were to achieve this was not clear nor in any way feasible. They were lucky they were not needed and went into reserve in 1943.

I doubt our family or anyone else around us actually knew about that, although those with knowledge of war would have worked it out that any relief coming from 12,000 km away would have been a bit late. I think there was generally much unexpressed fear and uncertainty for many reasons and most people hoped for the best. It's what you did. It was years before any of what really went on became public.

We were out of Auckland by then too and I wondered latterly if part of the reason Mary married John, which I have tried to make sense of over the years, was to get away safely to the country, as there had been talk of women and children being evacuated. It could have accounted for the equanimity that she appeared to have dealing with the lack of conveniences and the hard work experienced on our rural sojourn at Mokai.

Because we were frequently so isolated with no electricity, our family at least had little idea of what was really going on at the fronts except for what people told us they had heard on the radio or had seen in the shorts at the movies.

The combination National Film Unit with their rousing theme music and marching NZ troops, established by the government in 1941, the British News and their magazine style pieces and Movietone News, all gave New Zealanders the only actual idea of war conditions and sometimes pictures of the terrible circumstances battles were fought under, but along with newspapers and mail, they were censored so no bodies were shown in close-up, nor the reality of the deaths and injuries suffered. Propaganda was as much about not showing something as about misleading information.

Parents, siblings and wives of fighting men lived with apprehension, always aware of the uniformed telegram boy (sometimes women later) on his bike and the dreaded and dreadful knock on the door when they would be handed the 'Urgent' marked telegram, short white strips of paper with their stilted, stark black symbols glued to a flimsy yellow form of fear from the Ministry of Defence – the government's terse, passionless form of communicating the death of a loved one at war. The heartbroken grieving families supported each other as best they could along with friends, many of whom would have experienced similar circumstances. In some cases, mothers and wives especially lost their minds and had to be institutionalised. In normal circumstances, their relation's death meant a body to bury in a local graveyard, somewhere it may have been a comfort to visit.

'Our boys' were left in the foreign soil of *'Egypt, Greece, Italy, Malta, Singapore, England and 57 other countries'* and ultimately, for NZ *'the casualty rate suffered by the military was the worst per capita of all Commonwealth nations, except for Great Britain'* (Wikipedia) and overall, Russia.

Aftermath

Our young nation's psyche evolved from many things, including both wars, and is unique to us in the world, as is each country, but there are few as isolated as us with no-one on our borders and that makes a difference. We may now have a mixture of nationalities but the European culture of mainly Scottish and English was our backbone supplemented by the Irish, Chinese and others – plus Maori, once they eventually recovered from their low birth stats, and came into towns and cities, and began to intermarry.

Another difference between us and other overseas countries was NZ's low population numbers, and luckily for us we were not in the end in the direct line of attack so hadn't been bombed or invaded (although the Americans did feel like they did benignly invade at the time) which made a huge difference to those of us at home. Our expectations were different as well and perhaps that was the shock about farms being lost, when country families couldn't manage any more. Farming was our backbone. Up to six sons were killed from some. Also everyone knew someone who had a relation that had been wounded or died. But grief was all around. It was horrific for everyone wherever they were in the world.

Adjusting back to any sort of normal family life would have been difficult everywhere. The changed power base would have been confusing and resented by some children, who may not have even remembered their fathers, and perhaps saw them as unwelcome strangers who took over their mother's time and someone who she would have to accede to. Others may have welcomed it and felt more secure.

Many men felt strongly that a woman's place was in the home, even if she had worked outside of it for the war effort, and they expected the marriage to return to the same status quo as before they had left. The wife may have been happy to welcome her husband back or could be resentful too after being used to coping on her own, making decisions that now would probably be taken out of her hands. On both sides, there could be guilt about relationships that may have been formed when apart, perhaps the men's more fleeting.

There would have been stigmas experienced from the community if a child had been conceived when the husband could not have been the father, which was not unusual with the Americans here. The aggrieved husband would have felt justified and supported in any action he took, sometimes a violent one. The situation may have been resolved with talking, but with no such idea as counselling as we know it today around till later, possibly only if a minister or priest were consulted. I think people probably floundered along unhappily for years and made the best they could of the situation – everyone part of a more accepting community. It was the done thing. Some marriages just eventually disintegrated anyway and possibly talking would have made no difference and in some cases was made worse according to Mary who knew such a couple who eventually separated.

For most men returning from war, (back to Civvy Street) the understanding and empathy that they needed, support which should have been theirs by right, was seldom offered or deemed necessary. These soldiers were real men, surviving as best they could (or not), adjusting back to a society that had no perception or understanding of what they had suffered and were often still suffering, physically and mentally with nightmares and flashbacks. Today they would probably have been diagnosed as being in post-traumatic shock (PTSD). Those underlying unresolved feelings hung around in some form probably all their lives and possibly accounted for the war generation of habitually holding their tongues.

You could feel it in them if you knew what to watch for and if anyone ever got to them they would close down and resort to humour and light heartedness. An uncle of a friend who I got to know quite well, evaded any questions with a teasing, "Don't you worry my dear! Everything will be fine. How's the boyfriend? Got him wrapped around your little finger have you? You young girls know how to catch a fella!" Only a couple of the men who had been away that I came across briefly, referred to the war and then obliquely. One said there were unwritten rules of 'Never give in' and 'Keep faith with your mates and don't let them down'.

RSA

It was 40 years on at the RSA (Returned & Services Association) a place where the men would have found tacit companionship. 'We are the boys from way down under' had been played earlier in the evening and we talked about that at first. He seemed a cheerful sort and said he'd actually enjoyed the war as a soldier, seeing it as an adventure, comparing it to the cowboys and Indians games he and his brothers and neighbours played as kids on their farm, honing their target skills with bows and arrows and, although sad for the mates he lost, he said he loved that time of challenge and comradeship and action. I wondered later if he'd been a sniper. He didn't say where he had fought and he didn't think of himself or others as heroes – they were all 'just doing their job'. As a parallel for something he couldn't perhaps put into words about himself, he referred to a navy mate who told him about the sense of pride he'd felt to be on a ship in a convoy, all with powerful military weapons and, although he understood the danger they were in, his mate somehow felt safe being part of this mighty armada of ships along with a strong sense of making history.

At war's end I doubt any of us really understood the destructive outcome from the power of those atomic bombs dropped on Japan and the subsequent fall-out. They would surely still be adding horror to the memory though of those who have since had to survive the 2011 Japanese catastrophe as well.

By comparison to the WWI and WWII soldiers, the following generations of young men may have seemed callow to the fighting men. They were probably pleased for them too though. Not many would choose war who had experienced it. Like other mothers, Mary was just grateful that she hadn't reared 'cannon fodder' and uneasiness about another 'world war to end all wars', probably stayed with her and other parents for years. However, I don't think it was passed onto the next generation like the effects of the Depression fears although perhaps it was worse in another way when the 'Cold War' tensions heightened and intensified between the Western Powers and the Soviet Union. The fear then was the 'Atomic Bomb' or the even more powerful fusion 'Hydrogen Bomb', both powers developing enough for world annihilation many times over. In 1954 the then PM Sid Holland said the Hydrogen bomb was 'the greatest' as it belonged to the United States and they were our protectors.

Eventually it was and is 'Nuclear Bombs' which when placed on rockets can reach targets anywhere in the world. That was such an extreme fear for many and in a way, because of that, limiting.

It was simply too overwhelming that the world as we knew it could end, although the movies may have depicted that. It was another nebulous fear that was ever-present, hanging over everyone, although this cloud, unlike the 'Great Depression' one, had been seen in the sky and was real enough. I remember being in a night class and looking around the walls at secondary school level children's art work and the images were from the nuclear testing in the Pacific. There were all these A4 size depictions of a mushroom cloud and nothing else. It was horrifying to think that the children walked around with that sort of 'end of the world' image in their heads at that age.

The assumption by some that we were too far away and hopefully nuclear missiles would not reach us, however, was not valid so we lived with our fears like every generation has to. There would have been local apprehension from the beginning of civilisation but unlike then, these bomb scares were extreme and global. It would have been easy to be sucked into an Armageddon mind-set, but useless.

Although WWII had given us back our sense of pride in ourselves, as we had performed as well as, if not better than some other countries, punching above our weight, it wasted our youth our possible young, progressive and fresh creative thinkers and leaders and our best opportunity to build on and surpass what we had already achieved. Many of our strong young 'Lochinvars' returned sucked dry (some feel even their souls), shell-shocked, (PTSD), depleted and disillusioned. They had to not only learn again how to just survive, but how to live back in a familiar but different world with hope and optimism for a fresh start. (You can see by the old faces at the ANZAC Day ceremonies that they never forgot.) Politically, we were left with the old guard, who continued with their limiting dictatorial policies. Our chance for a more innovative and open society was lost to the war and fear of 'reds under the bed'.

By the 1950's though it was apparent that NZ soldiers who had fought for a better world wanted the reality of that and were clear about it – they had pride in their achievement and had earned their right to have it. They had thought about what being a New Zealander really meant to them and welcomed becoming an official NZ citizen on the 1st January 1949. People were designated either NZ Citizens or 'aliens' requiring either NZ passports or those of another country. *See NZ Government Archives.*

Brother and Fiancé

Wars hadn't gone away though and like many of the previous young men, Ralph wasn't unhappy to do 'Compulsory Military Training', his duty as an 18-year-old. He joined the Royal NZ Air force, forging a career from that. Ralph didn't go to war but my fiancé was finally called up in 1953 not long after we became engaged. He had signed up for the Korean War before I met him. His has become part of 'The Forgotten War', which it wouldn't be by him and his mates.

Chapter 8 The 1951 Watersiders' Strike

To place the strike in a time perspective, it was when NZ obtained a commitment for its security with the USA by the ANZUS Treaty and the beginning of the wool boom.

> 'The waterfront dispute of 1951 was the biggest industrial confrontation in New Zealand's history. Although it was not as violent as the Great Strike of 1913, it lasted longer – 151 days, from February to July – and involved more workers. At its peak 22,000 waterside workers (wharfies) and other unionists were off the job, out of the country's population of just under 2 million.'

The passion that is associated with this pivotal part of NZ history is very strong in our folklore, continuing on for over 50 years to hold a central spot in the NZ labour movement – 'a bitter legacy'. Like the politicians and the split union movement, the ordinary community were polarised but also fearful and confused by ignorance. With the obvious committed and passionate strength of feelings on both sides, who were we to believe, and hadn't all this been about some overtime pay? Or maybe underpaid men working long shifts in unsafe conditions?

Why did the Government take such a strong stance with their 'Emergency regulations' giving them the ability to imprison ordinary New Zealanders for so much as an apple fed to a child of a unionist? What were they really frightened of? What did Nazis, traitors, terrorists and the 'Cold War' have to do with it? Would we be taken over by the sinister Communists (Commies) if the Unions won and would our whole lifestyle have to be given up? Why did the government call it a strike and wharfies call it a lock-out?

Why were the communist-led (and often overseas born) militant wharfies always major players in all our largest strikes? Was this strike just the flashpoint and culmination of their years of unrest? Did they have so much power because they controlled our exports or because Auckland Carpenters' Union, the divided Public Service Association, coal miners, freezing workers, seamen, hydroelectric power workers and some drivers and railwaymen, had joined them as well? Did the latter only join in because of the 'Emergency Regulations'? How and why had the strike become nationwide? They couldn't all be wrong could they? Was the real cause the post-war economic situation? After years of restrictions and shortages, with the economy booming and the cost of living soaring, weren't all workers entitled to a higher wage anyway? Was NZ a too highly regulated society?

None of the answers to these questions was clear to the public at the time and unless you were directly involved and impartial, which is unlikely, it was impossible to see the whole picture or understand what motivated the personalities involved and what the nuances were around the desperate situation. We knew very little about the real behind-the-scenes action or in front of the screen facts of this dismaying confrontation. Our naivety in hindsight was appalling. Depending on whom you spoke to, answers were often biased and usually second-hand and everything was always tainted by the threat of Communism, real or otherwise. Because newspapers and the radio (which only had the evening news once a day at 9pm) were censored by the controlling National Government, we were told by word of mouth and possibly flyers, 'not to trust anything we read or heard from a government source as it was all twisted by the manipulative and dictatorial Sid Holland and the Government's point of view. The workers deserved better conditions and wages with the upturn in the economy and were prepared to fight for them.'

The simplistic understanding in the general public afterwards seemed to be that unions could get out of control very easily, were run by militant communist sympathisers and power-hungry trouble-makers that were born in other countries, like Ireland and Scotland, and were men who did not understand our NZ ways. They were still fighting a class structure in their heads from another world that did not exist here, in the form they were used to anyway, and they threatened our way of life and should take their troublesome ways and go home again. They were not welcome here. No credit was given to those who actually envisaged a just society and were using the legitimacy of a union to achieve that.

We in fact had got used to the amount of authority the government had over the nation from the war period, probably recognised more quickly by an outsider than ourselves, but the horror was unprecedented when Prime Minister Holland took a hard line and confronted unionism head on, arguing that New Zealand's vital export trade was under threat and warned that New Zealand was "at war", declaring a state of emergency and sending troops onto the Auckland and Wellington wharves to replace the striking wharfies. This seemed a harsh over-reaction to the situation and the amount of power given to the police was frightening. Ultimately the government won the day because of the inability of the unions to communicate by normal means to fight for public approval, along with all the fear the situation generated generally, and the Prime Minister called a snap election.

On a personal level it was the first time I, like others, had heard the word 'scab', which sounded disgusting, but became part of our language very quickly, being used frequently in the following years over issues often unrelated to those considered to be union betrayers, but people got the message. Had we still been living with John, he would have been in his ranting element, but he had gone and I was still at school and boarding at 14, so there were no family discussions, even if it had been legal, to make sense of anything and plenty of confusion about whose side should be taken. Although the strike was to forever change our perceptions of ourselves once more, it was years before most of us could stand back and get a perspective on what it had all really been about. The main thing I remember is the secrecy and the guilt and whispering when ordinary people, not directly involved, felt sorry for the wives and children of the strikers, and surreptitiously gave donations of food and clothing, often left on a back doorstep after dark to remain anonymous. Being against the law, it was not an easy thing to do, perhaps not worrying waterside sympathisers so much, but it also brought up thoughts of the Depression for people I think and they were hurting from those old memories, and the fact it was happening all over again, albeit with a smaller group of sufferers. The watersiders and their families were still mostly New Zealanders, whatever the rights or wrongs of the case, and deserved to be fed and clothed. And talked to. How could our own government make it illegal to discuss the watersiders' point of view when 20,000 workers were striking nationwide to talk about a situation that affected New Zealander's nationally?

Chapter 9 Transport

The most common way to move around in Auckland city was by trams or train, later trolley and diesel buses, and motor bikes (side-cars were trendy when cars were a luxury). Trucks were for household deliveries of ice, wood and coal and other goods when they weren't moved by train – usually the cheapest transport – especially with petrol and other restrictions on private vehicles during the war and afterwards, until 1950, when the petrol ones ended. Shank's pony (walking) and bikes (no gears) were normal for shorter distances, saving the price of a tram fare in the city anyway. No need for gyms. Keeping fit was not a chore but part of living. Crash helmets or seat belts were unheard of.

To give an idea of progress in travel, l talked to a 95-year-old once in 1960, the great-great-grandmother of my children on their father's side. She said that when she was a girl and horses were the mode of travel, it took her two to three days to get from Waitemata Harbour to Manukau Harbour, depending on the weather and the state of the track meandering through the rough territory of streams, mud, and bush. Today in a car that trip would take about 20 minutes depending on the time of day.

Trains

The problem with freight in the early days was overcoming the various hazardous coastal shipping conditions including difficult port entries and the weather. The cargo boats in Auckland were unloaded at the wharves along the waterfront onto rail trucks. Rails, set in the middle of Quay St., led up to the railway station and complicated the roads where cars travelled, especially when cars became more popular. (The era before containers).

Initially built for freight distribution which peaked in 1950, most goods were eventually moved by train throughout NZ and the Railway Workshops were the biggest engineering plant in the country. This huge employee closed in 1975. Quote; 'Rail made NZ what it is today joining the country with its engineering marvels like one of the world's highest viaducts, the Mohakea Gorge and the Raurimu Spiral.'

City trains for passengers were useful when they were convenient to where you were coming from and going to. It was no help that due to the discord between two MPs when the decision was made for where Auckland's (Chief/Central) General Post Office was to be, the Postmaster General won. The railway station had been built on reclaimed land at the bottom of Queen St., and was behind what became the General Post Office with entrances to the railway station each side of it – *see Sir George Grey, Special Collection, Auckland Library.* (The present Britomart Railway Station (2003) is built approximately beneath this site.) However, ultimately the station building was replaced near the bottom of Parnell Rise off Beach Rd, causing inconvenience to millions and millions of people travelling over the years. To get to downtown Auckland and connecting trams and later buses, it was necessary to take a short journey by tram or taxi to complete the journey unless you had the time and patience to walk. Not so good with young children, handicapped people, carrying suitcases, or after shopping on the way home in inclement weather.

The impressive Railway Station building itself, designed like others around NZ considered 'Grand Urban Monuments' (like Dunedin), was completed in 1931. Above a spacious colourful garden set at a lower depth with a centre flagpole, there was a one way, half crescent road around the building's lower levels for commercial use and a matching one on a higher level above for passenger traffic with central tram lines and car and taxi access. All vehicles could stop right outside the upper entry where there were two big sets of doors off the wide covered pavement (the sheltering roof a bit like an overgrown fancy carport with pillars, that on inspection could have been an after-thought), and depending where the drop-off point was, either doors were used. Once through, the foyer opened up into an amazing height of about 2 storeys, with two spectacular columns at each side supporting the ceiling, and echoed the sound from trolleys of luggage and people on the move everywhere. The light from the grand chandelier was somewhat lost in the fantastically decorated surroundings. The noise was exacerbated by the floor that was laid in durable and expensive but clattering marble (terrazzo?) tiles that had huge patterns set out across them.

The next set of doors with their coloured decorative glass and extra windows above, led on into the main central hall with more pillars stretching the length of it, the lofty concourse making every sound even more clamorous as engine noises could also be distantly heard. There was an airy feeling from the curved ceiling of imported glass and metal letting light in from inset windows and tall supporting ones each side. Seating was around the walls and areas off it were for various facilities including toilets, a ticket counter, and a wider one for luggage to be passed over for storage. There was also a huge bustling dining room with tables and white cloths and further on a special 'Ladies Waiting Room'. At the end was access to platforms and the trains. All walls were enhanced by specifically made maroon and yellowy tiles up to about 3 feet (a metre) with NZR lettering on them, with the odd border depicting various old fashioned means of communication. There was 'symmetry, grandiosity and formality' and NZ Heritage describes it as 'one of the most self-consciously monumental buildings erected in early 20th century NZ.' It was certainly overwhelmingly spectacular to us kids especially on arrival at the end of our journey after living in the sticks.

Intercity trains, covering our main arteries, were the ones we were familiar with. Long distance travelling was done by rail, and the Rotorua Express, a steam engine with many carriages, ran daily, with restrictions from shortages during the war. Steam did not begin to give way to diesel until 1954 although it still lingered another 17 years to 1971. Sometimes there were oil conversions like the K900 at MOTAT. They all seemed just huge hulking black monsters to a child in the dark.

Rotorua, near the middle of the North Island, was the end of the line which always intrigued me as a youngster. What was beyond the big concrete block at the end and why didn't the rails go past there? (Probably the lake if I could have seen it.) Mary said the comfortable Auckland to Wellington train ended by the water in Wellington so that made sense. She talked about this 'spectacular main trunk line' with its unique and incredible 'Raurimu Spiral', as it had opened two years after she was born in 1908 and

Granddad had known some of the clever engineers involved in its construction. It was NZ's most important transport route down the centre of the North Island right through until the Second World War and the main connection to many small communities. Petrol was scarce after the war and it stayed that way until we were free of restrictions. Later diesel/electric rail was introduced. In 1962 the ship *Aramoana* was launched with roll-on, roll-off rail and car facilities on the Wellington to Picton run. Later with more choices of cars available and cheaper prices, roads came into their own. In the late 1960's there was also a drop in train passengers as planes became more affordable.

Train Travel

We often went on the Auckland to Wellington night limited express train when Veronica was old enough to walk, although we never ended up there. I remember the times of going to the King Country to one of the outback settlements, not necessarily even on a map then (these journeys to places with odd-sounding names had been repeated so often for us it had become normal). We recognised when we had reached the Auckland Station at the start of the journey from looking out the tram window and seeing the flag in the garden out the front. Veronica at 2½ was always overwhelmed by the railway building's size and its crowds, the noise and the underlying smell of soot mingling with body odours and she would obsessively cling to my hand or want to be carried. I was nine and she was getting a bit heavy for me. Mary meanwhile would be struggling with our luggage until some kind person gave her a hand or she found a porter. They and the uniformed guards looking purposeful and important added to the clamour, glamour, and sense of alluring destiny that seemed to hang around everything, enhancing the excitement of the journey.

A similar atmosphere is in airports today but was perhaps more intense then as travel wasn't so commonplace or as casually undertaken. Distance meant a certain amount of alienation from the known, perhaps tinged with apprehension, even if the destination was familiar and a welcome assured, which it wasn't with us. The possibilities, the unknown future, the adventure of the journey, however trivial it might be, seemed to gather us all in and take us along with it on an inevitable consuming wave with officious time keepers ready to leave us behind if we weren't aboard. Waiting was then for the guard's whistle clearing us to go and predicable last minute passengers who may or may not have been let on. The emotional farewelling, waving, blown kisses and tears were for other faces pressed up against the window but Veronica would join in too.

On one of our last trips, we had facing seats to ourselves at the end of the carriage. Veronica and I were entranced as usual with the rushing, changing scenery, first of the city and then the country and occasional little towns, their back fences and clothes lines a few feet away, some yards with junk, others orderly with vegetable gardens and at times, children waving to us from a porch or swing.

On this journey, eventually bored, with Veronica already over her new dragon book, we wandered the length of the carriage and peered briefly into other seats for anyone or anything of interest and when the door was opened by the conductor, stared out at the rattling rusty connections to the next carriage. The most fascinating but frightening features we found were the toilets at the end of the carriage. We were told by the stern conductor, 'You are not to use them at stations' as if Veronica was small enough to fall through the toilet hole, wagging his finger at her, 'you would drop down onto the rails with the pooh!' Veronica held onto me really tightly after that when she had to go.

There would be a temporary fluster of agitation when we knew a tunnel was coming up as windows needed closing to stop smoke and coal dust billowing in. We were always gritty though anyway as a layer of dust was inevitable. We stopped at either Mercer or Frankton and other stops later like Taihape or Taumaranui (closed in 1975) for a quick cuppa which meant me being propelled along with the adults onto the station platform and into the tearoom. There I would slither through the boisterous demanding crowd, about five deep, (8 minutes to serve 400–500 people) to jump up and down at the counter to be noticed. We couldn't afford a pie (just as well as I have since found they caused a severe reaction especially on holiday weekends because 60 dozen would have been left around in boxes un-chilled, often for three days) or sandwiches and scones or a rock or fruit cake. Just a cup of tea for Mary.

I could understand Mary not wanting to join the undignified scramble and listen to the swearing and roughness of some of the more aggressive men. It took me so long to be served with the now iconic thick, white cups with their NZR lettering, small crown and the heavy saucers (locally made at Crown Lynn), that the place was nearly empty. Listening to the train noises that sounded like the precursor to leaving, I would want to rush back to it empty handed. A picture of Mary's annoyed face was all that kept me there as I watched and listened in terror for any real train movement. What would happen if I was left behind? Where would I go? Would anyone even notice me? Had the whistle already gone and I hadn't heard it in the busy, echoing racket from loud voices while I waited?

Finally a white uniformed, unconcerned assistant would half-heartedly serve me and I would struggle back to the train, desperately counting the carriages to reach the right one, unable to run and finding it hard to balance the precious heavy cup and saucer and not spill the tea while negotiating the steps. Unperturbed, Mary would quickly rescue them from me as the train moved off, balancing them carefully against the jerky movements. She would sip intermittently until finished, complaining, 'It's more like dishwater', then place the cup and saucer on the floor under the seat, briefly checking for any message pattern in the tea leaves when she tipped it over. 'Tasseomancers' do a ritual reading and interpret messages in tea leaves left in the bottom of the cup (no teabags). However I doubt Mary took herself as seriously as that although her friends may have. She once saw a really recognisable map of Australia in her own cup and in fact was needed over there to sort out problems with sections her mother had left her when she died. This was a few years later. I remember us feeling reasonably well off for a little while after that happened as one was sold.

As uncollected china was picked up and returned by a later crew, that empty cup rattled on its saucer for the rest of our ride – along with others, reminding me of my unnerving little panics – not something to worry Mary about of course. The next refreshment stop was Taumaranui but thankfully we would probably have got off before then.

Meantime, when we became restless again, Mary pulled out her surprise for us. There was a new suitcase in the luggage rack above (they were normally put in the baggage car) and when she got it down and opened it, it was full of parcels. We scrabbled at the wrappings until there were clothes everywhere and it felt like all the Christmases we should have had. Mary said we needed new ones as where we were going it was very cold and would snow. There were warm undies, jumpers, skirts, thick stockings and winter hats – all in the latest styles. We thought we were in fashion heaven and busily tried everything on, wanting to wear some of the clothes straight away, but it wasn't really cold enough for that although she gave in to me wearing a skirt and Veronica a hat. (It must have been part of the Oz section windfall for her to be able to spend so frivolously. It did snow a few weeks later at night and Mary insisted we put layers of clothes on before going out to see it but of course once it had snowed it wasn't as cold as it had been before.)

After our excitement died down, we ate our snack for dinner which had been prepared before we left Auckland. An exhausted Veronica quickly went to sleep afterwards on Mary's lap, where she sat on one padded bench, and I lay down on the other. The daylight had dissipated by then and we only had brief glimpses of the lighter western sky when the train turned a bend.

The comforting thumping sing-song sound from the clickety-clack of the train on the track was mesmerising and I drifted off too until Mary shook me and said we were getting off soon. She had the suitcase and bags down in the passage, ready to go. We were next to the exit door and she said the conductor had agreed to give us a hand as our carriage would be away from the station platform and there was a high drop down to the ground. It was possibly Te Kuiti or it may have been Mangapehi.

Mary woke Veronica up. We put our coats and hats on, and I had to push the still drowsy Veronica ahead of me to wait in the cold, damp gangway between the carriages. Mary struggled out with our luggage. It was a dense cloudy country night, no city lights to show a horizon, the wind catching at us as we waited. I told Veronica to hold tight to the hand rail above the steps so she wouldn't fall. When the train chugged slowly to a rasping, hissing, squeaky stop we could just see to the last step below, glittering wetly in the carriage light. There was about a yard (metre) gap straight down onto the rough stones beside the rails. It was pretty scary as we could hear the steam engine ahead that seemed to be puffing and chortling impatiently to itself in readiness to leave.

We waited anxiously for the conductor but only heard a male voice call out to someone in the dark, 'Ready to go yet?' and 'Nearly' was the frightening answer. Mary had got our gear stacked handily and we were all cramped together on the small platform. We waited and still no-one came even after Mary peered along the carriage to where we had heard the voices and called out for help. There was a jerk that made us hold tighter to the hand rails and Mary began panicking, fearing she wouldn't get us and everything off before the train left again. She suddenly pushed past Veronica and me and frantically began throwing our case and bags out into space one after the other. They landed in what sounded like sliding shale as we heard them slithering down before bumping into each other. The light didn't reach that far.

I had already begun easing myself backwards onto the steps, and my new full woollen skirt kept getting in the way. Holding onto the hand rails with a deathlike grip, I couldn't fix it, and anyway was reluctant enough to loosen my fingers to slide them down when I found the next step. It seemed a long way for my short legs. I felt for another one and another but suddenly there was only space. I knew it wasn't far from the ground but couldn't really see to judge. I held onto the cold steel rail with my hands as low as I could take them and inhaling a desperate breath, stepped back into space with my knees bent like jumping from a tree, letting my hands go at the last minute. My skirt was useful this time, although I could already imagine hearing Mary's scolding voice saying, 'Couldn't you have protected it?' as it cushioned my knees from the stones, and I was grateful after falling forward onto my hands. I brushed the clinging debris off, wincing as the stones came unstuck and blood appeared. I quickly balanced myself, so aware of not wanting to slide down *the slope into the bags, that the pain seemed a minor discomfort. Mary was calling to me to hurry up so I reached back up to where she was urging and pushing at little Veronica to get down. I tried to coax her to let go of the hand rail too, but she'd only really been half awake and now she was terrified, crying and making a fuss. I'd said: 'hold tight', so she did. The ground below must have seemed like a black hole to her and the noise from the train like the dragon in her book, especially with the heat coming up from below.*

In the end, desperate, Mary just tore her hands off and grabbed her by the wrists. Bending over, she dropped her at me, by-passing the steps. There was a sighing noise that sounded to us like the train's brakes being released. Veronica's kicking feet were in my face and her startled scream should have brought some help, but it didn't. It would have been too late anyway. Veronica slid down me and luckily I caught her at the waist without falling over backwards and she had already transferred her tenacious grasp to around my neck instead, nearly choking me. I watched horrified, and just as well Veronica couldn't see, as the train jerked in its preliminary first move and Mary, still on the little platform, lost her balance.

The whistle blew and I had a quick vision of Mary still kneeling down with one hand forlornly stretched out to us as the last carriage and noise and lights of the train disappeared and took her away and we were left alone with just the taste and smell of the sooty, cindery dark. She probably had similar thoughts and, inelegantly for her, slid backward off the top step scrambling down awkwardly in her hat, high heels and bulky fur coat, forcing her right arm against her body tenaciously gripping her handbag which was hooked over her arm. She landed awkwardly to totter off-balance in her heels on the edge of the uneven ground, throwing her arm around Veronica and me where we all stood swaying until she managed to swing her handbag arm and catch at the carriage railing and regain balance, just before the train made its first real judder of movement.

We quickly took a step back and then cautiously felt our way down to our case and bags where Mary scrabbled about in the dark until she had them all together, counting to herself several times. Meanwhile Veronica still clung to me, looking up at what must have seemed to her an impatient monster, heavily panting and hissing its oily breath, straining to be off. I tried to get her to sit on our case but she was having none of it, her little body still shaking.

Sparks flared and noises increased until after another hesitating shudder, the train finally chugged off, its lit carriages rolling heedlessly past, the train rhythm picking up to speed quite quickly leaving a thick trail of smoke behind to encircle us, like a gesture of arrogance, although oblivious to our puny struggles and Veronica's last sobs. She was rubbing her eyes as she probably had smuts in them by then. Mary had sat down on our case and Veronica with her eventually and in the sudden peace, we brushed ourselves down and began 'pulling ourselves together' as our Nana would have said. Veronica was really attached to Mary this time – but we were all grateful to be in one piece with no real injuries, before facing anything else that might need to be negotiated.

With the distant last whoo-hoo of the train whistle, probably near the town's crossing, and the dissipating fumes and cinders wafting off into the night's stillness, we could smell familiar bush scents and hear a Morepork that sounded as lonely as we felt. It seemed a shock to be suddenly away from all that noise and in a place we were not very familiar with although the station could not be far ahead. There were lights but we realised we were looking through the beginning of fog.

We had vaguely begun thinking of moving toward them when we heard distant voices arguing and trudging footsteps coming toward us along the track, crunching alternatively on the loose stones and the sleepers, and quite suddenly nearby a torch shone and we heard a male voice calling, "Anyone there – anyone there?"

Mary answered, "We are."

The voice said, "My goodness – someone thought they heard a scream. Can we help? Are you okay?"

Mary calmly answered while adjusting her hat to its most becoming angle, "Of course. We just need a hand with our luggage please." This was 'par for the course' in our family.

What happened to us after that couldn't have been very dramatic by comparison, although it was probably difficult as we didn't know anyone in the area, and I have no idea where we ended up that night.

Harbour Bridge

Transport-wise, the North Shore was a separate issue. A rural backwater away from the then-popular beaches and also dependent on ferries that appealed in the summer, when people just liked the trip for itself, not always bothering to get off for the lovely empty beaches, and not in the winter. The alternative route, with no Harbour or Greenhithe Bridges, was the 50km long winding western highway which ran through Riverhead and Coatesville, the latter winding route still as dangerous as ever, even though sealed.

It wasn't until Mayor Sir John Allum, an electrical engineer from London, made it his 'cause' that progress was made toward a crossing for the Waitemata Harbour. He convincingly persuaded the government that a bridge was a necessity and he eventually became the Auckland Harbour Bridge Authority's inaugural chairman (along with other previous titles) and stayed in that position until the Harbour Bridge opened for traffic in 1960 (called 'Jack Allum's Bridge' by colleagues) albeit without all the lanes that had been originally planned or the rail or pedestrian access – cost the main limiting reason.

There was an open day so the public could walk the bridge before the official opening on 30/05/59 and my neighbours offered to drive me there, but I was unable to make it because one of my children was ill. It would have been great to have walked over with those 106,000 people – a big day for Auckland.

It still took a while for the Shore to develop. In Wairau Valley, Porana Rd. had brickworks in the middle of it for years and Hillside Rd. stopped within a few hundred metres of the motorway off-ramp too. When we had a business in Wairau

Valley, I met a man who remarked that his dad had owned a farm up by Hillside Rd. which he had been paid peanuts for when he sold it.

After Sir John Allum, D.M. Robinson, although referred to by his intriguing name, Sir Dove-Meyer Robinson (originally born Meyer Dove Robinson) or just Robbie, had an unequalled 18 year split term and with his cocky, ego-driven, booming voice, became the most affectionately remembered mayor. The fact that he was a short Pommie (his controversial bronze statue can be seen in Aotea Square in Auckland) and had been born a Jew (the latest revelations also suggest he was a communist) did not seem to faze him or the public. They voted him in. He was an achiever with his big personality and wide vision. His attention was on sewerage before travel. Robbie had fought to forestall the Drainage Board's controversial Brown's Island sewerage scheme (that would have allowed partly untreated sewage to be released off the Island into the Waitemata Harbour) a great political cause célèbre. Aucklanders always remembered and the people we knew were grateful to him when it was overturned in 1953 after he was elected as a councillor. Robbie was also appointed to the Drainage Board and subsequently elected chairman where he was in a prime position to support the early development of the Manukau sewage oxidation ponds – 'Robbie's ponds'. There must have been a few noses out of joint over that about-turn.

He was mayor from 1959 to 1965 and again from 1968 to 1980 and in this term he was frustrated by the much debated Auckland railway/transport issue. Robbie had visited London in 1970 with underground trains on his mind, and always seemed to see the future in a clear way many others in positions of power couldn't match. Although the money and the land were secured, the building of the world class transport infrastructure he sponsored, an electrified underground rapid rail with a loop in the CBD, was thwarted by the local and national leaders of the day, along with much of the public agreeing. Opportunity lost. They simply could not envision the need and the cost was so high. In addition, Robbie had crossed some lines. His critics had made ground, he had become a controversial figure, considered difficult, and he had behaved in odd ways at times as well as in his personal life he was divorced more than once. Also he was considered by some to be past it and still trying to hold on to his position. This did not help.

A decision was made to dismantle bus and ferry routes, encouraging people to drive and 'we need more motorways' was the answer to our problems. It was all about the car, and by the time those decisions were implemented here, partly based on American thinking, they had already gone out of favour over there. The emerging international trend toward rail systems was ignored and in 1983 the Auckland Regional Authority tried to shut down the rail system altogether.

The Southern motorway seemed to take a long time to finally reach the inner city in 1965 after the completion of the Newmarket Viaduct Bridge but once it did we ended up in the heart of the CBD. It was magic if driving a car. There were parking meters (about three pence for half an hour) but it wasn't difficult to get free parking near Queen St. so very convenient for shopping and the theatres. There were only six automated traffic lights in the city in 1947, two sets in Queen St., although there had been earlier mechanical traffic signals around from 1922. Britomart Place Bus Terminal in downtown Auckland had opened in 1937.

Birthday

I once took a station-wagon load of pre-school children (sitting on a mattress on the folded down back seat – no seat belts required) into Queen St. on my own in the early 1970s, and parked – no problem – near McDonalds (their first in NZ I think) for one of my daughter's birthday party lunch. They held hands and sang songs as they scampered along the footpath toward this new exciting place, to the slightly pop-eyed and laughing amazement of a group of Japanese tourists, clicking away on their cameras.

Other motorways were gradually added over time, mostly with some sort of controversy. At MOTAT, I remember seeing a model of the Auckland motorways to come and marvelling at how convenient travelling would be. The nearly completed complex motorway system as it is today could never really have been envisaged or imagined as being necessary in the 1950's.

Even Robbie would have been floored. Pity a glass ball hadn't been around for them all to see the number of vehicles on the road now and the disastrous effect their insular, flawed, and short-sighted decision has had on today's traffic chaos in Auckland.

For years I was annoyed every time I passed the motorway junction of three major arteries with the nine incomplete, wasted, square concrete sentinels with their protruding rusting reinforcing fingers pointing skyward, like a desperate appeal to be noticed. I thought they would at least be used when that area was finally completed (30-something years later) but most were destroyed as was part of the old massive concrete structure, B Ramp, the original link to Dominion Rd that never happened. A new separate structure on top of the old ramp carries the new link across now. As a friend, who married late to a reasonably useless provider, and unexpectedly had four children one after the other, commented to me when I mentioned the piers: "Put me in charge of one of their schemes and watch how carefully, thoughtfully and with well researched foresight I would spend their money – they could do worse". She lived in Otahuhu and I have often wondered how different our Auckland transport system would have been if they had gone ahead with the canal there at Portage Rd. It was the narrowest point of the isthmus and it seemed to me to be begging to open up the Tasman Sea to the Pacific Ocean.

Cars

The first cars around were Benz, referred to as 'horseless carriages' as they were odd-looking things very much like a buggy without the shafts to attach to a horse and were unreliable, appearing in NZ around the turn of the century. A suspicious public, who were used to horses, were likely to exclaim in a heated discussion, "Don't talk to me about those noisy, dangerous new-fangled things."

However, technology developed spectacularly fast and by 1905-06, cars began to look vaguely familiar, the most popular models being European until about 1908 (Benz, Peugeot, Renault, etc.), but there were a few American models too (Cadillac, Oldsmobile, Rambler and Essex – my stepfather and his father had one each in

World War II). They were often only bought initially by the affluent as a hobby or a toy until World War I, with doctors being the main group of people with a serious purpose for them.

Cars were assembled in NZ because the early 1930's tariff policy made it cheaper to import 'completely knocked down' cars and from 1934 Todd Motor Industries in Petone assembled Chrysler & Rootes vehicles and in 1936 (when the speed limit was 30 miles per hour) Seabrook Fowlds (amongst others like Ford and General Motors) assembled them from body shells at their Manukau Road factory.

New Zealanders began their spectacular climb to be one of the highest owners of cars per head of population in the world, though they were generally modest and staid models compared to the variety in other countries. We also had more second-hand ones. By 1938 there were approximately 200,000 cars on the road and around 27,000 new cars were registered. By 1942 when the Americans arrived they were proudly told that we had 12,000 miles of main highways and thousands more of local roads, not all sealed of course – which I can vouch for – including what are some of today's main arteries.

However imports had dropped right away because of the war and there was petrol rationing. Manufacturing was also suspended in 1942, assembly lines producing military vehicles and arms and munitions instead. 24,000 private vehicles were off the road by 1943 anyway with lack of spare parts and tyre shortages as well. Only 4,000 of the pre-war cars went back on the road again when the war ended.

By then technology had advanced dramatically and prices had come down, but laws basically forbade the purchase of new cars unless you had foreign currency to pay for them so it was still really only the rich and farmers who could afford them. Second-hand cars remained the norm. The government also used the importation of cars to control the flow of NZ currency overseas, favouring trade with British Commonwealth countries, so heavy tariffs pretty much eliminated US cars from the roads. Farmers, for example, sold their produce overseas, and could get paid in pounds sterling or US dollars. Since they didn't have to exchange

NZD for foreign money – the so-called 'no-remittance' – they were allowed to use their overseas currency but as the US tariffs were still in place, the car choice was usually British.

Austin A40 Devon & A70 Hampshire, Morris Minors & Oxfords, Standard, Hillman, L-series Vauxhall Velox and Wyvern, English Ford were the biggies, with the last two being the most popular and then Consul, Zodiac and Zephyr, these in the early 1950's. The more American-looking Humber Super Snipe name still rolls off the tongue as it did for those who dreamed of having one, usually by peering through a car showroom window.

I remember envious comments like 'trust those rich bloody farmers to be able to afford them – they're the ones that are subsidized'. However, for farmers it was a way to get their overseas funds back into the country and a vehicle was often one of the necessities when living in outlying areas not usually served by public transport, so they had more reason than city folk to need a car or maybe a work truck which could double as the family vehicle. Carrier trucks eventually carried their animals to the slaughter houses and beware following behind trucks that had pigs, sheep, or cows on board.

The posher models included Wolseley, Triumph, Jowett, Rover, Sunbeam, Humber etc. and anything American was seen as extravagant, although Chevrolets and Chryslers were assembled here too as the NZ economy struggled to get on its feet. Cars then were very identifiable by size, shape and often colour, as there were more choices, and also like now a particular name. Eventually there were more cars per head of population when imported petrol was no longer rationed in 1950. A relief, like many things after the war.

Work Vehicles

Men like my brother Ralph had work vehicles. His was a little Austin A40, while he worked part-time for an insurance company and did his accounting degree at Auckland University. He had earlier had a motorbike which he came off after dropping his girlfriend home one night. He'd lost control when forced into loose gravel on the side of the road and made a mess of his left leg. Mary wasn't having that and unusually 'put her foot down' and told Ralph to get rid of that 'dangerous machine'. He and a mate pulled a stunt outside Greenlane Hospital, making sure they were near help if it was needed, and managed to cause enough bike damage to claim an insurance 'write-off'. If they had hurt themselves, they didn't say. I don't know if Mary knew it had been a set-up.

It wasn't the first time Mary had had a hand in Ralph's bad choices. A car he had bought at a second hand yard slowly fell apart; the final insult happening in the middle of the city. Unusually, I was in the back seat between a couple of his mates at the time and after hearing a suspicious noise when we went over a bump, I turned around to see something square sitting in the road behind us. The only thing I knew about cars was that they had to have a battery to start, so I called out, "Ralph, you've just dropped your battery." As we were still rolling downhill in Wellesley Street and nothing appeared to be wrong I was the butt of much laughter and ridicule. Once through the Queen St. intersection at the bottom however and it was all uphill from there, Ralph suddenly started to swear and looked back. He wouldn't look at me.

Mary was horrified when she found out the extent of the problems the car had and took it upon herself to go and confront the salesmen at his car yard, a trip by bus that took her right across to the other side of the city. Not a good start for the guy. She spoke to him in her outraged voice (Mary in high dudgeon was a force to be reckoned with) and threatened legal action as Ralph was under the legal age for purchasing a car, which would have made the guy nervous. He capitulated and peace resumed at home and it was around then that Ralph took the job with a car.

Anyone that could afford to (sometimes even if they couldn't) would have had a car and hire purchase broke down the resistance of many to the previous 'save for everything first' advice. Leisurely weekend outings were reserved for the family and a Sunday jaunt with the man of the house driving, a generally accepted custom, helped along by instructions on direction quite often from either the passenger seat or possibly a mother-in-law in the back. Not for us though. Cars were for girlfriends.

When I was 17, in late 1954, I met my first husband and he had a small Austin Seven. (That was quite impressive for a 19-year-old.) It was the first car I had ever driven and from the Otahuhu on-ramp there were few other cars on the lovely, black, smooth new motorway that day in 1955. No intersections to worry about and at 45 miles per hour (speed limit 50 mph/80km, 55mph /90km in 1962) it felt very heady for a learner. Where the motorway ended near Penrose, we went via Great South Rd. into the city. I bought my own car 10 years later; a family-sized Vauxhall Wyvern, powerless but roomy and comfortable, not the spunky Mini I would have preferred.

A farmer friend around then advised me to never buy a car over five years old or a new one (dream on). The latest models he had discovered often had bugs that needed ironing out and around a two-year period he felt was needed to overcome that.

On The Water

New Zealand has always been a maritime nation. It was, and still is in undeveloped areas, such a wild and rugged country that sea transport, starting with the Maori, was the most practical answer to travel, continuing to dominate our development right through into the 20th Century. The thousands of shipwrecks on our coastline are evidence of the many sacrifices made to hostile seas and what it took for our country to become what it is today. To achieve land development, establish our country and overcome the terrain for road and rail links took tremendous innovation, dedication, imagination and a massive output from tenacious labourers. However, as an isolated island nation we still depend on our surrounding seas to survive, on many levels.

Ships

Our family did not have anyone close as seafarers, so aside from local transport we admired all kinds of boats but they were an unknown quantity. A Waitemata Harbour ferry was about the level of our experience as a family.

Watching the ships come and go in the Port of Auckland has always been fascinating. Thinking about where they had come from, what their cargoes were, their size, and the sailors speaking different languages all seemed very exotic and exciting. They came from a world we had no real conception of except it would be very different from ours, not least because we knew we lived in a young, only partially developed country.

Travelling to places as far away as Europe by ship depended on the type, the facilities available, the era, and the depths of your pockets. During the war of course, travel was not an option for most and liners were converted to troopships. After the war ships went back to their normal resplendent civilian mode. New Zealanders were eager to go to the Northern hemisphere by then too and refugees and migrants glad to escape from it. Visiting Australia was a more common route though and Mary regularly visited her mother's family there, as she had done since she was a child.

When we were adults, Mary would give the family maybe a day's notice and suddenly announce she was off and we would be obliged to pick her up with all her bits and pieces, lucky to fit them in the car with the family. "I may need them for emergencies dear." How she kept track of everything was beyond me. We would take her down to one of the big liners at Princes Wharf on the city waterfront, like the '*Wanganella*'. The most exciting one she left on was the overpowering (in those days) '*Oriana*', her proud lines and immense full size only really appreciated from a distance.

One of Mary's Australian Jaunts

Veronica and I had been on board for a while before departure time, admiring Mary's sumptuous cabin and the view. She had been double-booked so scored a luxury suite on the upper deck, the thrill of which I doubt she ever really recovered from, the story often told. Brought up as a lady she would have held her own with any of the passengers – it would be the temptation to spend that would be her problem. Mary was in a happy anticipatory mood, fussing about getting herself organised with Veronica half helping and talking excitedly, the animation in her face from wishing to be going too. I left them to it and wandered off to see what the entertainment and other facilities were like. I ended up in one of the lounges with a bar and was admiring the elegance and opulence when a guy sitting on a nearby stool caught my eye. He held up his drink in an inviting way but I shook my head. He wasn't satisfied with that and came along and persisted in buying me something. After refusing at first I thought well, why not? He was about my age and not bad looking. How often would I get the opportunity of saying I'd had a drink on the Oriana? We chatted away for a few minutes on a superficial, slightly titillating level till I got the message he was setting himself up for the voyage to come, and thought I was a passenger. They didn't waste any time on this level! Trying to keep a straight face I responded to his repeated question of what my cabin number was, with the one next to Mary's. He looked impressed and bragged away with some wit about various previous trips he'd had until I excused myself and vaguely intimated I might see him afterward.

Reaching Mary's cabin just as the call for visitors to leave came, with Veronica still on a dreamy/weepy high from just being on the ship and saying goodbye to Mary, we made our way back to the exit ramp. Mary watched down on us from the upper deck railing as we stepped ashore and we waved but eventually we could only see glimpses of her amongst the other crowding travellers, all dwarfed by the ship's size. We could identify her vaguely now and then by her facial features but more by her interesting glasses and ever-present hat, and her right hand clutching the trailing white scarf ready for signalling later. The smell of wet rope and the sound of dripping salt water became stronger and we were suddenly looking up at the steep retreating overhanging bow of the ship. There was some sobbing to be heard over the moving music at the reality of the poignant leaving and the empty feeling would have been a blow to some after the excitement.

Mary seemed already nearly gone as the huge majestic ship eased away from the wharf, imperceptibly at first, leaving the excited crowd cheering and yelling last minute messages to those on the lower decks who could hear. "Bon voyage", "Have a good trip", "Remember me to –," "Don't forget to write", "Let me know how you go", "Did you remember your –," and "See you when you get back", the tears eventually flowing down like the streamers thrown from the boat's decks. Caught by well-wishers, the streamers formed a long multi-coloured tenuous web along the ship's side and they were held onto for as long as possible at both ends, protracting the leaving. The stretched ribboned paper eventually snapped, drifting against the side of the ship in thin gay stripes till becoming caught up in its wake, while the band sentimentally played the sound of the soulful 'Now is the hour for us to say goodbye'. (According to some sources, that so NZ melody was first written and sung in Maori. The English version was picked up by Gracie Fields after WW II and was later a top single in America in 1948 for Bing Crosby)

We followed along to the end of the wharf but knew we wouldn't be able to see Mary again until the angle altered when the ship changed direction further out in the harbour. People lingered on long after the music stopped, waiting for the turn even though they probably knew individual passengers could not be identified on the crowded decks even if they could have seen them. I can't remember when we heard the final steady, breathy, heavy sound of her departure, but I imagine the booming of it whenever I think of that day.

The ship straightened gradually but all clothing had morphed into a collage of colour, except for some like experienced Mary with her white scarf or others' large light-coloured hankies, waving to show they were still looking back, the strong light picking up on the moving miniature silvery dazzles. Mary's flag of goodbye was very tiny and only recognised for about a minute before everything was finally lost in reflections and movement.

As the ship was manoeuvred by the tugs toward the channel and its speed picked up, we headed back for our car as did others, and quickly joined the exiting crowd, scooting along Quay St. as fast as we could, passing lower Queen St. to reach Tamaki Drive. We caught glimpses of the top of the ship intermittently until we had a brief clear view of her length before she turned away, easing toward Rangitoto and around North Head, into the channel proper. A queenly, dramatic, seemingly gliding passage, befitting her distinction above the smaller vessels which bobbed like tiny toys on an undulating, sparkling salt water playground, the Oriana's outline eventually fading into the slightly sun hazed distance.

The reality of Mary leaving was more wistful than sad to me although the emotional crowd had affected both of us, and Veronica was openly crying. It had only left me with an unsettled feeling. I hoped Mary enjoyed her trip but didn't wish to be in her place.

The thought of the potential lover came into my head and I laughed quietly to myself picturing him knocking on a cabin door that would not bring him the results he might expect. Perhaps he would get an even better deal though as his presumptuous behaviour could be more acceptable to others.

Local Boats

The downtown Auckland Ferries and Ferry Buildings were familiar to us as children and mostly we would take the boat across just for the trip to look at the shops at Devonport and Takapuna, a really useful hardware one at the latter on Hall's Corner, the main intersection, which seemed to survive longer than most. In the early days a steam train ran from Bayswater to Hall's Corner in Takapuna and several North Shore bays had their own wharves.

We'd have an ice-cream to take down to the beach while we paddled, Mary scolding if we went out too far with no towels to hand. Playing in the sand was a novelty and after eating a prepared lunch we'd go back on the ferry, embracing the sea air and view of the city as a special outing. Mary used to go on the ferry trip to Devonport when she was young herself, Granddad in his suit, high collar and hat and she and Nana all dolled up in their best, with hats and parasols (used for sun and rain) and stroll along the water's edge. (There is a surviving photo of them around.)

North Shore

We had friends and relations we would visit on the North Shore sometimes as well. A day would be set aside and confirmed ahead by mail and if it was to Torbay to an old aunt's place (I think my real father's relation), it was a major undertaking as a family, with the changes from tram, to ferry and a bus and return. We didn't go that often. After the ferry, the only public transport option was on the uncomfortable seats of a rattly old bus that took us along bumpy metalled roads with dust and exhaust fumes seeping into every part of the bus and us, especially in summer, through the doorway. If there had been a door, and I'm not sure there was, it was left open for a breeze to dispel the heat. On the interminable journey, the droning noisy engine, especially when it was stretched on some of the long steep hills, would sometimes bore or bump us to sleep.

We had a walk as well from the bus stop to Aunt's place when we reached Torbay but looked forward to the prepared lunch we knew would be on offer – the highlight of our day. Our aunt had an airy dining room where the waist-up windows could be folded back along the length of the wall with a view of the sea, Rangitoto in the distance. Aunt's lovely peaceful garden wafted scents in from flowers and fruit trees, where we would play later. Our food would be set out ready waiting with a handmade lace tablecloth on the extended table. There were dainty crustless sandwiches of cucumber and tomato, thin bread and butter to go with pickles, a silver cake stand of home-baked offerings including sponge butterfly cakes, their wings nestled in the thick cream, and crunchy peanut brownies she knew were our favourites. Her lovely English rose bone-china tea-set matched the colour of her own climbing roses on the archway framing the beach scene outside and the beautifully shined silver teapot, sugar bowl and milk jug were the same as our Nana's. Worth the journey.

On a wet day at the Ferry Buildings when there was a high tide it was necessary to be very careful accessing the ferry on the slippery, steep wooden gangplanks. I once watched two men take a pram on board and instead of turning it sideways and walking across from each other, they held it head and tail lengthwise. I followed them up holding my breath, my hands ready to catch the baby. The pram was tipped as high an angle as it could be without it falling out. The tightly tucked covers were probably what stopped a tragedy. Women did not question men's decisions that much, and were often 'pooh-poohed' if they did. Don't think a lot has changed sometimes.

Yachts

One summer weekend down at the Ostend wharf on Waiheke, several of us from the same class at the local school, where I went for one year, had been there swimming, the boys diving. I'd only ever jumped into a swimming pool before and never dived properly, especially into water that was deep enough for a ferry, but as it seemed to be nothing to the boys, I copied them and gave it a go. I didn't know it was necessary to change the angle of a dive once I hit the water so it wasn't until the sea floor was in my face that I realised what had looked simple from above needed some experience. Quickly putting my hands out to stop my momentum so that I slid along the bottom instead, I luckily came up again with only a few grazes.

Some good-hearted yachties off one of the big racing boats which was tied up at the wharf were offering any children who would like to try sailing a go on their boat. Thinking that a sail might be less dangerous than diving, I happily put up my hand. Two boys volunteered as well and when we were accepted we clambered aboard, crossing ropes and other sea-going paraphernalia to lie on a space on the deck. The crew good-naturedly instructed us where to hold on tight with fingers and toes to anything unmoving and stay there while they did their work. Once we went out past the points of the Ostend bay, the sou'westerly caught the sails, the yacht leaned over and seemed to be alive as it bucked and smacked across the sea surface. Our faces so close to the water enhanced what to us felt like an exhilarating and impossible speed that I at least thought might end with us under the waves. Perhaps no safer then than the diving.

Nothing I had experienced matched this combination of fear and elation at the same time. The crew were professionals and went about their jobs with such confidence and sureness, their voices yelling information above the noises which became louder when the taut sails flapped as the yacht tacked and then settled and they ballooned again. When there was the opportunity we strained to see past our immediate surroundings and caught the sight of distant shorelines, sometimes the emptier spaces of rugged Waiheke inlets and their framing steep points or white beaches and baches. Coming back the irregular skyline of the dense buildings of Auckland city seemed to waver in the heat, windows suddenly catching the sun, but were only brief flashes as we lost focus. The sailors chatted and teased us when they had a moment until we eventually relaxed and just enjoyed the adventure, revelling in every minute when we began to understand why they did things and what was going to happen next. The sweeping spray smelt clean and salty, cooling and refreshing us. The closely swishing sea and the blue and white of both it and the sky and clouds on that lovely hot day left impressions that I would always appreciate sailors for. Time out in total focus of an exalting trip. Love the America's Cup.

Titanic

Regardless of the distance we were away from it, the news of the '*Titanic*' disaster was part of our family's folklore, as I am sure it would have been for many others. Nana had a friend on board who had survived which made it more personal. I don't think they saw each other afterwards though they wrote for years. (Mary would have kept her mother's letters but I was not near her papers when the decision was made to dispose of them.)

Flying

In 1937 PanAm offered a flying boat service to San Francisco at a price. The trip was described as arduous and not particularly popular. Hobsonville, in the north-west of the city, opened in 1928, initially as a separate seaplane base because of its ideal position near Auckland in the Waitemata Harbour and continued in this role until the last of the thundering Sunderland Flying Boats retired in 1967. During the war it also served as a maintenance facility when the Sunderlands were hunting submarines and dropping depth charges. Later the Chathams were grateful for the Sunderland services. Whenuapai RNZAF Station, built as a base for bombers beginning in 1937, was one of three aerodromes in NZ with a sealed runway in the 1940's and at the end of the war the Government made it available, on a temporary basis, for civil airline operations. Although Whenuapai's runway apparently had problems it actually lasted for 20 years from 1945–65, the civil side eventually taking precedence. Flying was not common in the 1950's and 60's but one of the football trips my husband went on to Australia left from there in the late 1950's. Everyone wandered out onto the tarmac on their return, lots of family members of all ages as it was a 'happening place', and not a Customs man in sight.

Tasman Empire Airways Limited (TEAL), the forerunner of Air NZ, also operated seaplanes out of Mechanics Bay flying to Australia between 1940-54, 1952 the height of its service. If we were in the city when one was taking off, it was always worth stopping and admiring how the huge plane, with its slightly clumsy looking floats, spectacularly conquered the waves – especially on a rough water day. Once it was in its own element and wheeling gracefully up into the clouds, it was a sign of achievement, affluence and luxury to us and those lucky passengers on board were to be sighed over. We used to watch in envy from the Farmers' top floor dining room. The RNZAF operated many of the civil services post-war; while the National Airways Corporation (NAC) was being organised and was eventually based at Whenuapai. That had changed by 1960 with jet aircraft such as the DC-8 and the B707 being developed so it was clear that a new international airport would be needed.

Auckland Aero Club had leased land for an airfield from a dairy farmer in Mangere for their three De Havilland Gypsy Moths. The money had been raised in an 'Art Union' which the Government of the day was impressed by and began their own in 1932. The club's president noted; 'the site has many advantages of vital importance for an aerodrome and training ground. It has good approaches, is well drained, and is free from power lines, buildings, and fog'.

Flying in 1938 was equivalent to the scariest adventures of today (e.g. bungee jumping). There were no jobs on offer after WWI for pilots or their planes. 'Joy rides' were from suitable paddocks, usually owned by a handy-to-the-town farmer or from race courses. Stunt pilots ('Cowboys' who were mad enough to fly) would do air displays to draw a crowd – their money was in the quick spin rides afterwards. They were considered risky, dangerous, and exciting. It must have been such an amazing experience for anyone with vision and energy at that time as aviation was in its infancy.

1934 saw the first government licenced passenger service called 'Air Travel NZ' in the South Island flown by Capt. Bert Mercer, who delivered passengers, mail and freight, even animals on board his De Havilland Fox Moth plane to a limited West Coast area. There was no road from Hokitika to Haast there at the time, only bullock tracks and steamers to rely on. It was the first commercially operated plane in NZ.

In 1936 Union Airways ran the country's first trunk service to NZ cities and domestic services took off. Following WWII, all NZ air services were nationalised.

Ralph and Planes

In 1938, when my brother Ralph was five years old, he flew in a small bi-plane from the Rotorua Racecourse. (It would probably have been on someone's lap.) Mary was considered a reckless mother no doubt, but actually was brave as he was very precious after her long wait for children. Also knowing Ralph, he would have just kept persisting to go up till she gave in. He had always loved planes and their pilots were heroes to him. His life path was confirmed that day.

Written by Ralph;

'I was working as an Aeradio operator for the Civil Aviation in 1950-1 at the Aeradio Station at Mangere. (How I managed that job at 15½ I just don't know) You certainly needed earphones ... no speaker. The airport at Mangere was simply a long grass strip with the sea at both ends and a short cross runway. There was a private Club hangar and Clubhouse and not much else. They had no Gypsy Moths by the fifties as they were very old and long gone. I commenced flying with the Auckland Aero Club in late 1951 at 17 and my instructor was a very good pilot but a hopeless instructor. He later committed suicide at Papakura by driving an aircraft into a hill.

Conversely the Chief Flying Instructor was very good. I always cursed that I was with the wrong one. I went solo I think very early in 1952 and also did my National Service as an 18-year-old that year with the RNZAF plus refreshers till

1955. *(Compulsory Military Training was brought in after the Cold War tensions had heightened.)*

Most of my early flying was on Tiger Moths and the one I owned in the late 50's was ZKAIE. (It is now in the RNZAF Museum at Ohakea painted in RNZAF colours).

The Auckland Aero Club fleet then was roughly as follows:
1 Rearwin Speedster
1 Whitney Straight
1 Stagger Wing Beechcraft
1 Fox Moth
1 Ercoupe (which I flew in once) – one or two of these were lost due to accident between 1949-1951
5 DH82 Tiger Moths – they did have 6 but one disappeared into the Manukau

Some years later I was instructing on them and some other types (the Piper Cub gradually replaced the Tigers).

I later flew in the Islands as a commercial pilot for SPANZ (South Pacific Airlines of New Zealand), a short-lived 1960–65 company. I eventually became a First Officer on Electras with TEAL and flew around the new Mangere airport a month or so after it was opened. Compared with other airports it was a nice spot to learn to fly. More like a country club. When I look at Auckland Airport now it is hard to imagine what it was like back in the early 50's. Our old grass field has turned into acres of concrete and steel buildings. That's progress! [As far as I know none of our family ever flew with Ralph.]

After initially using grass runways for the city's domestic airport, these were closed off in 1947 to all but light aircraft, safety concerns cited, and then in 1960 work began on a new main airport for Auckland at Mangere and the runway area extended into the Manukau Harbour by reclamation.

Lost Flights

When there are air crashes in NZ it isn't always easy to find exactly where the plane has actually gone down, especially small ones. Over the years in certain isolated areas of both of our North and South NZ Islands, with rugged terrain and dense bush, some planes have never been traced.

On October 23rd 1948 an NAC Lockheed Electra ZK-AGK *Kaka,* en route from Palmerston North to Hamilton and flying in shocking weather, crashed onto the SW slopes of Mt. Ruapehu and it took seven days of intense searching to find. 11 passengers and 2 crew were killed. At that time it was the worst civil aviation accident in New Zealand history and the greatest search mounted.

In 1949 a Lockheed Lodestar airliner crashed near Waikanae on the Kapiti Coast en route from Auckland to Dunedin via Paraparaumu, and all 15 passengers and crew were killed. It was considered a major air disaster. Ralph was later to lose a boyhood friend along with 24 others in the 1963 NAC DC3 crash in the Kaimai ranges.

Trams

The tram guys at MOTAT tell me they had a saying which was 'There was always a tram in sight'. I guess that depends on what your line-of-sight was, and from my experience not necessarily true – and the tram may also have not been going the required direction anyway. They ended their run in 1956 after 54 years. There was nostalgia and celebration for the last trams – a coup to have been on the very last one especially. Electric buses replaced them. Their smoothness seemed a let-down after years of listening out for the forewarning rattling trundle of an approaching tram – often time to pick up the pace or even make a run for it when necessary.

1941

One of the few times I distinctly remember John, my then new step-father, in a mellow mood was while we still lived with my grandparents and it was only that one time I think. I was around 4½ years old. There had been an undefined sense of expectation around the family when he took me out with him on that Sunday evening not long after Pearl Harbour had been bombed. I was excited, as Ralph was the one who normally got to do interesting things. We went by tram and I clearly remember this special journey because it was in the early evening and unusual for me to be out at that time.

We walked down to the main highway about a quarter of a mile from home to where the tram stopped. I had been on trams before but this night I watched all the familiar things with relish. (The stops were about the same distance apart as bus-stops today and payment was for similar stages although trams did not travel as far away as buses from the city.)

It seemed a great adventure to rattle along the route from Western Springs through Grey Lynn to Karangahape Rd., and down to the Auckland CBD – although it was just 'The City' then – and I became enchanted by everything. The conductor collected our money after we sat down and John gave me the coloured ticket to hold. There were shiny buttons on the military looking dark navy uniform of the conductor, his shirt and tie formal and a peaked cap with its large badge above projecting over part of the brim and with his air of power, it all made him look very authoritative. He had a slight swagger too, possibly from the tram movement and the large leather pouch strapped around his waist that looked heavy, perhaps affecting his balance. This held a range of tickets on a clip, different colours for different distances and charges, and also several well-worn pockets that gaped open for change. Large heavy copper pennies and smaller half-pennies being part of the currency with travel relatively cheap; they would have been the bulk of the bag's weight.

Although passengers pulled the cords for their own stop, (and my ambition from the very first ride I remember was to grow tall enough to stand on the seat and pull it myself) when we were to start up again, the conductor would lean across passengers' seats to the high cord above the window and ring the bell attached at the end. It let the driver know everyone had alighted and boarded from the back platform steps. On some trams the cord ran along the more centrally placed metal rail that held hanging hand straps.

Outside on the tram platforms, removable chains hung across one opening on the non-exiting side, so no-one stepped from the wrong side into oncoming traffic. The driver could see *passengers on the front steps for himself as the narrow, closed-in area behind him where he stood holding the wheel was usually open each side. Some trams with doors also had a small viewing window.*

The seating was set out like those on trains but was made of slatted wood, unpadded, and the back-rest slid backwards or forward on a runner down the side or on some trams flipped over so passengers faced whichever way the tram was going. As the tram filled, many new passengers had to stand; holding onto the straps or the back of a seat for balance and the conductor took a while longer to reach them on his regular forays up and down the passageway. I think he would have to have been an astute person with a good memory for faces and ticket values he'd sold, as no doubt there would always have been the odd person not paying enough money and extending his ride past his section stop. Beware the inspector when he came on board in his special uniform, swinging along to each leather strap with confidence and panache.

The culmination of all routes and final destination, from as far away as Onehunga (the furthest), Avondale and Ellerslie, was the inner city hub at the crossroads of Queen and Custom Streets. The trams that came down Queen St. would need to manoeuvre through the complex pattern of extra changing tracks with curving and straight lines called the 'grand union tram tracks'. It would then park outside the Chief Post Office at the bottom of Queen St., overlooking the harbour and opposite the Ferry buildings. If it were going back up Queen St. the driver would stop and simply unlock the steering handle and taking it with him, leave his cab and walk down to the other end of the tram. The cab there would be facing the right way and all he would have to do was re-connect the handle.

If a tram's next route was a continuation in the same direction, as in crossing Custom St. East to West for instance, to go to Mt. Eden perhaps from Herne Bay, the driver would simply cross the Queen St. intersection to the downtown stop on the other side and be ready for the next trip. The most difficult and commonly watched manoeuvre was when a tram was turning into or out of Custom St. East or West. The combined weight of the tram's multiple wires in the centre of the junction of Queen and Custom streets was supported by an extra heavy centre pole, with Victorian decoration, where there was sure to be sparking and maybe something more interesting as when a pole dropped down, requiring attention and holding everything up.

Every tram changed their destination signs at this junction. They were set outside in the butterfly box shaped like a flat V (<) on the tram's roof and a canvas blind would be rolled backward or forward until the correct area's name came up. The curved front and backs of each tram had its own number and a large single headlight that was switched on, whichever end the driver was using.

There were also concrete platforms here called 'safety zones' set a step up from the tarsealed road on either side of the double tracks which ran down the road centre – they were long enough for two trams each side at this main intersection. These platforms were also at other major stops, although only the length of one tram, like the corner of Symonds St. and Grafton Bridge and several along Karangahape Rd. Further out from the city centre, unless it was a shopping centre, traffic had to stop along with the tram until passengers safely crossed the road.

It was all amazing to me being in downtown Auckland, where we had got off, watching the lights come on in the shops and streets and so many people being out in the night. No-one seemed to take any notice of the red phone boxes with their warning posters of "Careless talk costs lives," that Ralph teased me about when I chatted on. Everyone around us was talking.

The carnation-red trams (more a wine colour compared to the phone boxes) with a cream trim all had different coloured advertising set on the roof and along the panelled sides and sometimes the front. They were for things like tea, biscuits, butter, sugar, soap, and cigarettes. Some windows were pushed down from the top with heads hanging out of them for a better view, cutting out the ads. Warning clangs sounded as the trams began their new journeys, startling me, as did the shooting sparks from the overhead power lines when trams made right-angle turns.

There was the noise of a tram suddenly losing its pole connection, leaving it flaying around in the air with its line dangling, looking deliciously dangerous. I remember clinging tightly to my big stepfather, but the driver swung nonchalantly down from his curved cab to haul on the line, then sighting his aim, precisely reconnected the pole to the power cable above. This seemed an awe-inspiring ability to me.

When there were more serious problems like a detachment from a span wire, it would be reported by a passing tram driver and the tower wagons had to be called in to do repairs. We had seen one at Western Springs a few days before when shopping. They were scary things too if you didn't like climbing and heights, with their concertina platform that had to be raised on site, blocking the road sometimes.

We were right down by the waterfront and I knew the big Navy ships were out there in the dark as once when we went over to Birkenhead on the ferry, I heard people remark on their size. No-one had thought then that we would have to worry about the war at home although it must have been comforting to see them anyway as were the gun emplacements around the harbour.

My stepfather put me up on his high, bony shoulders above the crowd and at the top of the shop window and told me to focus on a moving light beam, tipping his own head back a little as well, to look up to the sky. The light had an oscillating pattern and went a long way up to the sparse clouds. It seemed impossible that anything could reach that high and I remember being fascinated at the sight. John said it was meant to catch sight of any planes. They were not seen often then even in the daytime and were new-fangled things for most people. John had been walking as I watched and suddenly we were at the light source. I saw a round silver monster with light coming from its centre that hurt my eyes. It was surrounded by intent excited people all concentrating on the sky. Some were in uniform but most were not and they just stared until the crowd moved them on. There seemed to be an underlying hum more than loud talking but I heard a man say, 'I can't see any damn planes.' Another answered him with, 'Well if the Germans have sunk ships off our coast – and that Jap sub had something to do with that spotter plane over the harbour – what's next? It happened in Wellington too. The big ones could be coming any time.' And further on, 'How much would a searchlight see anyway?' (The Japanese launched a small, spotter sea plane from a submarine in Auckland and Wellington's harbours)

It sounded a bit scary so I clamped my knees more securely on my stepfather's neck, careful not to knock his hat off, holding on to his head near his ears, his thick black stubble slippery and smelling of hair cream. I secretly felt safe up there though, taller than everyone else. It was probably the last time in my life I would ever have that illusion.

We hung around like everyone else until we became bored with nothing happening – just a false alarm. People moved off, others came to replace them in the constantly shifting crowd which we flowed along with until we reached our tram's platform. John lifted me down from my amazing viewing seat and we boarded our tram and set off for home. I was satiated by the novelty and strangeness of the evening and the earlier excitement and, with the soporific swaying of our tram, went to sleep against my stepfather's arm. He had to wake me at our stop and I think carried me home.

06/06/1945

My next strong memory of a tram was during the day this time and on my own with hardly anyone else on board. That felt good because at seven and a half and without Ralph to take charge, I was looking forward to finally being the one to pull the bell cord at my Aunt May's stop. We had just turned into Victoria St. West from Hobson St. when the tram came to a halt. It wasn't near the concrete platform for passengers to alight and the pole hadn't come off during the turn so I couldn't understand what was happening.

Suddenly the driver leapt out of his cab into the middle of the road, shouting incoherently and excitedly waving his arms and jumping around like a demented demon. The conductor and the other two passengers stared with us in amazement at first then hearing something they all understood, they rushed out to join him. I sat petrified as more and more enthusiastic people appeared from everywhere, forming a crowd on the streets' intersection, some linking arms with obvious strangers as cars and trucks came to a halt around them. Horns began blowing and people erupted out of everywhere and those on bikes skidded to a halt and leaned on them, watching at first, as amazed as I was.

All the ships we could see down in the harbour added to the clamour with continuous blasts of noise, factory sirens joined in and people rang bells or blew horns or whistles, others leaned out or sat on upstairs window sills, some climbing out onto shop veranda roofs, calling to those below – anything to be part of this obviously amazing occasion. Everyone was crying, laughing and yelling all at once and ended up dancing wildly together, some kissing and hugging. Not the restrained Aucklanders I knew!

I sat still, watching silently out the empty tram window. Nothing made sense but apart from feeling really alone, my fear dissipated. Although they may have been behaving in an extraordinary way, people were happy, strangely some tearfully so, and others in the street even began singing loudly. I simply sat and watched these mad entertaining adults with the objectivity of no involvement although I did realise something momentous had happened. Finally the conductor climbed back into the tram and saw me sitting there by myself. He came up and patted me on the head saying 'The war has ended in Europe dear.' (VE Day). That didn't mean much either. Left isolated, it had already felt to me at first as if the world as I had known it had been about to end anyway, which it had of course, for everyone, each in their own way.

Late 1940's

I remember a wedding we went to that included Veronica (who was still quite young so it would have been to the religious ceremony only). We travelled by tram to a church just before the Mt Eden shops on a blustery Auckland day. Mary always loved dress-up occasions, especially weddings, a good excuse to wear large-brimmed decorated hats which she was fond of.

After pulling the overhead cord for the bell, we made our way to the open platform at the front of the tram, where a gusting breeze was concentrated. We had a wait of a minute or two for the tram to slow, getting ready to descend the couple of steps to the tram *zone. Although Mary knew to hold her hat and had it secured with hat-pins as well, it suddenly took off like a wayward kite, skittering, settling and soaring again as the wind dictated – this before the tram had even stopped. Mary in all her finery – jewellery, long full skirt, high heels, gloves and voluminous handbag, leapt off the steps before the wheels stopped turning (usually done smoothly by males – unbecoming for a lady), leaving me to cope with an instantly crying Veronica, and chased down the road in Olympic style to retrieve her gorgeous black hat, its pink rose coming looser with each bounce. She was forced to put her foot on the brim in the end to stop its capricious cavorting and also avoid a couple of cars whose owners had luckily stopped in astonishment. It was usually the men who had a hat problem, not a desperate looking pretty woman dressed like Mary.*

Male passengers were hanging off either side of the tram's platform at the back to watch the performance, yelling encouragement and raised a cheer when a flustered Mary suddenly reverted to being a demure lady again, walking sedately back to Veronica and me waiting on the street platform, slowing so that she didn't have to come and get us until the tram and its boisterous passengers left. We could hear the driver chuckling away with the ticket collector as he took his time to move off. I would think it would have made their day.

It didn't make ours though as Mary scolded us for something and didn't really recover herself enough to enjoy the wedding, although the obligatory tears would have been a welcome relief of built-up tension. It was the only wedding Veronica and I attended that I can remember as most people were still recovering from the effects of war and rationing, so a time of little choice for frock material or an abundance of food for guests.

By the end of the war, the life of trams was all but over although we didn't know that and enjoyed them in Auckland anyway for a few more years. Trams closed down from 1949 and the last one left Queen St. in 1956 and by the end of its journey anything removable had been taken. Horse troughs were also removed where they still existed after horse-drawn street cleaning carts disappeared and like the trams, made way for cars and diesel or electric trolley buses.

The last time I was on a tram was in the early 1950's and for some reason they are one of the things I feel most nostalgic about from that era. It was lovely to be back on a similar one in Melbourne years afterward on holiday.

Chapter 10 Housing

Auckland homes are built on, around and between 50 (or 55 depending on what information is correct), volcanic cones, some of which have now been flattened, scoria often removed, but many are appreciated for their views. Lead paint and asbestos were unrecognised problems and 'leaky houses' a future one.

Renting was usually flats, though not as common as they are now because children stayed at home much longer or boarded with other families from choice, especially if they were male. The flats had varying prices dependent on if they were fully or partly furnished (often tatty), quality and location. Older large homes were the ones lone women could decently make a living from as landladies and often house-keeping and cooking were all they knew, ideal if they chose their boarders wisely. One male friend told me that each night's meal was predictable and wholesome but no-one stayed in on a Sunday as they knew they would be eating left-overs from the rest of the week, however it was the only grumble he had really, grateful he didn't have to cook, clean or do washing. Shared facilities hadn't seemed to bother him.

After the simple original houses in Auckland became slums, private housing varied dependent as always on finances, people's backgrounds and imagination, but in the early 1900's, Victorian English, Californian bungalow or colonial villas, like ours in Levonia St., were popular with their large timber component and the important eaves. Locally made roof tiles were more prevalent when the availability of corrugated iron was unfavourably dictated by import regulations. This was lucky for us because heat and cold were more extreme in uninsulated homes using iron roofing.

Outbuildings housing toilets and a separate wash-house were still around, some attached ones looking stuck-on, and in earlier times kitchens were separate too, until these facilities were eventually incorporated inside the main building. I remember a visit to a villa on a quarter acre section in the eighties which still had an outdoor washhouse and toilet building in the back yard, although the old toilet hole itself had been filled in. The toilet building had become a storage area for garden tools, but the closer washhouse was in use, albeit with a locked door. The 44 gallon drum commonly used for burning paper rubbish (not collected by councils and some of it used for toilet paper) sat next to it.

I know that night soil collections lasted a long time in Otahuhu and it wasn't until 1969 that they all ended. A flush toilet was often installed in an existing washhouse if there was room, like in our Levonia St. bungalow. Though often inconveniently placed for access from sleeping quarters, it was better than outside on a winter night. Toilets were built into new homes but the date that happened would probably have been dictated by whether there was a sewerage system available, which was more likely in the city. City water pressure (from around the 1950's) was necessary for plumbing before indoor toilets could be used. However, the toilet in our Grey Lynn bungalow was inside and had a long chain pull from a water box near the ceiling, as did those in many homes we visited in the 1940's, so there may have been similar alternatives. Being able to afford a toilet also a consideration although council regulations may not have offered an option like a septic tank.

Many of the country places we lived in didn't even have that. A farm where I stayed as late as 1967 had an outside toilet still, although it was attached to the house and the waste was piped downhill to a newly dug septic tank while I was there. Though chamber pots, small and large, plain and elaborate, usually made from china, were still often discreetly hidden under the wire-wove beds with their comfy kapok mattresses (choices were single or double only) for middle of the night needs, and continued for many years although by then mainly for young children and the elderly and incapacitated.

Uncle Ross' old villa in Mt. Eden had power for lights and gas for the stove, with an old Califont heater in the bathroom with a tank for water above and bath underneath. It was lit for weekly ablutions and always tricky to get going as the pilot light was often a problem and the water never heated to any comfortable degree. A toilet had been belatedly stuck in the corner of the outside wall of the added-on bathroom. No hot running water.

By the 1920's we had the highest rate of home ownership in the world. Prime Minister Walter Nash brought back state housing. The State Advances Corporation would only lend finance if a plan was similar to conservative State Housing designs. Without another reasonable source of funding there were few choices for a more innovative design, although a friend said ASB offered a reasonable mortgage rate that could also be paid off in a shorter time. Insulating and heating as we know it today were not options and all homes were oriented toward the street-front not to the sun – so depending on the site orientation that could be great or a disaster.

Our Old Bungalow

The Levonia St. bungalow, our home with our grandparents from 1938 to 1943, sat partway down the side of a hill, the front porch facing north. The 4-metre-square porch was closed in at about adult chest height except for the side with wide steps which led to a sloping asphalt path. That continued on, curving into a corner around a cabbage tree and onward down to the front gate and a few more steps which were set inside retaining walls on both our neighbour's boundary and ours. Our wall continued along the road frontage supporting the front lawn on the public path's edge. Shrubs grew on that raised area and in particular a large fragrant lavender bush, which was regularly cut back, and flourished afterward. That smell is still redolent to me of the old house's upper white weatherboards and black creosoted base.

From our perspective, on the high side of the street, we had a 180-degree view north and west, ideal for watching neighbourhood activity and sunsets when the flocks of hundreds of birds headed to Western Springs and the west coast to roost for the night. The noisy, pulsing black V's used to stream across the layers of back-lit clouds in the distance, till the last sun's rays left just a tinge of delicate apricot and the stragglers dissolved into the formless dusk, their last cries sounding lonely to me. I would be glad it was bedtime by then.

My swing hung from the old fig tree, amongst the other fruit trees, and was my favourite place out the back. I remember the dreamy hours I spent on its soothing sway and no doubt my Nana remembered the peace in the house from my chattering. Before I was five, in the afternoons after the lunch dishes were done, with Nana's quick, efficient hands slotting the knives, forks and spoons with fast 'tings' into their appropriate holes, she would persuade me to have a sleep in her room, lying down on one of the twin beds with her on the other and saying, "Just forty winks and I'll sing a song to you." Waltzing Matilda was the most popular for me of the many Australian outback ones Nana knew although I never seemed able to perfect my first wink, never mind 40, before falling asleep from her singing. She'd always be gone when I woke.

This is the only home I can remember the layout of from a young child's view and can confidently walk through in my dreams. Treasured really. The front rooms were a lounge (perhaps used for visitors as it was not a room we children went in much) on the left off the large square entry hall, probably the same size as the front porch, and a roomy main bedroom off the other side. Straight ahead was a wall with a picture on it with passages off to the left and right. The latter went to two more bedrooms, the first being Granddad's, the end one Nana's. The left passage led to one door straight ahead opening into the bathroom, and another on the right to the back of the house where there was a large kitchen/dining area, a country type one with coal range, plenty of bench space and an eight-seater wooden table and chairs. The table had the marks of where the metal mincer was attached on the end when in use, so was fairly utilitarian. We always seemed to have vases of flowers on it too as the cooking smells mingled with their scent as well as a fruit one. Lemons were picked all year round and other fruit in season, and sometimes there were stringent scents too when the medicine cabinet was opened.

There was a door off the kitchen to the utility room where the toilet was and washing was done, the most interesting place in the house and good for 'hide and seek'. The cupboards and shelves big enough to squeeze under and an alcove with bulky outdoor clothes on pegs to creep behind as well. The back door led out into the quarter acre section with the long cord clothes line, support pole, garden and fruit trees.

Most houses had three bedrooms of various designs and there were grander two storeyed homes for the more affluent but these were not as common. Railway houses were part of the landscape when travelling by train and small by comparison to other homes. To keep costs low they were built from wood that was easily accessible to the railway lines. They came in several standard plans and were added to if it was necessary for larger families, often not in a particularly pleasingly aesthetic way. There were also the small Pegler homes (about the size of some of today's small flats except detached and set on a large section) which were particular to Otahuhu I think and sufficient for an older couple we knew who lived reasonably well in one. The Pegler brothers built about 180 such houses during the Depression era to rent out to families who could not afford to buy.

State Housing

The Labour Government went ahead with state housing in NZ from 1935. First home 1937. Building was a boon for unemployment and there had been much thought given to the designs. The vision was of garden suburbs with trees and flowers and no fences, with modest rentals for the hard working 'middle class' (quoted from the English origins) and to 'stand for security, comfort, and decency'. Most people were pretty grateful to have their own homes. We were. The state houses had several variations of simple and functional basic plans that usually opened up to take advantage of the sun and they were varied by position on the land as well as distance and set on a generous quarter acre. They were often built by local companies and local materials were used when possible. Components were standardised for economy. (I can pick a state house even on its own anywhere in NZ, and by today's standards, their durability, if not the design, is commendable and their simplicity lends them to being adaptable to renovation and addition, which I have done). Rotary clothes lines were installed, saving the back yard for kids instead of the usual one long clothes line, and basic concrete paths were laid. There was a gardening shed as well, which the hand mower (no motor mowers till the mid-fifties) could be stored in along with shovels, spades, hoes, rakes, hand trowels and other needs as in Mary's case hanging onions, and Veronica's bike. It was not quite big enough to be useful as a 'man cave' but probably the closest thing he would get to one and his tools for minor maintenance and other little treasures would have been reasonably safe there.

There were only occasionally under the house headroom areas with a normal door height entry for a bit of storage, the earth slope not dug out and taken advantage of. Useful later though when cars became the norm. No such thing as a garage for coddling cars, although in free-standing houses provision for a carport in the future was made, possibly accidentally, and was usually fitted down one side of the house. In the case of state house tenants, if they were affluent enough to have a car, they probably wouldn't be allocated a state house. People who scored state houses usually felt pretty grateful to have a decent roof over their heads, given the slums they may have had to live in during the Depression.

However there were many struggling families surviving in isolation in pockets around Auckland when community facilities and services did not necessarily flow into new areas immediately, putting stress on women alone with young children all day (few working mothers at first), and buses and shops only reachable by long tiring walks with children in tow. Very lonely for some if depending on the affability of neighbours and whether relations and friends had a vehicle.

By 1950 over 33,000 families had their own state homes (building had been inconsistent over the years and there had been a lull during the war) and up until then middle and low income families could apply. Nevertheless there was still an acute housing shortage of about 50,000 on the waiting list which had increased partly because Maori came to the towns and cities from rural areas. Seventy five percent lived in the country in 1945 but by 1956 they were often living in the city slums.

By the time we wanted a state house, we eventually found you had to be really poor and very lucky, and in Mary's case a bit cheeky to be granted one. She wrote to the then prime minister, to my brother's mortification, explaining she had made an application 10 years earlier and that at present she had no husband, both Ralph and I were boarded out and she and Veronica had to live on the rest of her pitiful women's wage to survive. A solo mum was unusual then (except for perhaps during the war and widowhood) which may have gone in her favour.

To Ralph's amazed shock, Mary got a result. After moving again, but this time all of us together, into our temporary housing in Pasadena we were allocated a permanent 3-bedroomed home in Panmure twelve months later. We were told there was no choice of areas but one couple and their children we eventually knew, lived in the same street as his parents in a private home, which could not have been an accident given the spread of Auckland.

Panmure wasn't even a name we had ever heard before and we were initially appalled at how far out of the city it was and the distance from the shops and transport. However we were very lucky to have private housing in most of our street, including neighbours across the road and next door, and only went past a few state houses at the bottom of the road when we went down to the wharf to swim or fish in the Tamaki estuary. We were grateful we did not live in the middle of the huge housing estate of Pt. England and Glen Innes.

Veronica had some bad experiences at a primary school in that large state housing area. She was bullied quite often as she was very tall for her age at 10, taking after dad, and had lived in the country the first few years of her life so probably wasn't as streetwise as other city kids, nor as educated. Country school teachers could have more than one level to teach. Her new bike was stolen after only a few days at school. She saw it again but the girl was with a group which included Maori. She said it was not an option to take it back in those circumstances and her name wasn't on it as proof. That didn't happen twice.

Standard state houses were very basic. Ours a 3-bedroom, 1 bathroom, 1 toilet, a kitchen/dining and a nearby back entry through the wash house. The lounge was at the other end of the passageway that began at the kitchen, splitting the house and ending at the short passage to the front door entry, the lounge door opposite. Practical for visitors however as we couldn't really afford to light the open fire for the couple of hours it would have been used in the evenings or the odd weekend we were all home, we ended up with a one-bar heater in the kitchen, the warmest place in the house. There was no other heating except the open fire in the lounge.

Second Stepfather

Later my second stepfather, Joe, was to commandeer the lounge for his evenings with a fire going, his favourite piano music playing, reading, smoking and checking his tropical fish in the tank occasionally. I would say he made a happy life for himself. Mary was probably pretty disappointed however as he was no company, did nothing for himself and insisted on paying her board, not actually functioning as a husband as such, and she still had to work after finding out she had a heart condition at 54. No car, just a bus service to the city and long walks each end before and after work where she had been on her feet all day as well. I don't think she had really minded before she started feeling unwell.

My brother and I were paying board initially, although Ralph was working part-time and going to Varsity, and I had just left school, so we were able to afford some of the electric gadgets like a toaster, a jug, a steam iron and an egg beater – all on tick.

After Mary married our second stepfather, both Ralph and I left home, me really upset after finally finding some security and only having it for such a short time. Mary was left with just Veronica and herself to keep which she could have done with the help of a sickness benefit but not with a husband, she was told by the Social Security Dept. I wondered later (as did a neighbour who knew what was going on) if they even discussed a basic financial plan. Probably Mary assumed a husband would support her, not unusual for the times, and he too had assumed things. After Mary's first heart attack though, her husband's days as a partner were numbered. Mary did have a plan for that! This involved me, although it was a shock to me when it began to unfold.

Mary went on holiday with Veronica and only Veronica came home.

I had been roped in to fill a 2-week gap which began to stretch till I gave up. By then I was nagged regularly by my step-father to know when services would resume and who was going to pay the bills? As usual I had no idea where Mary was, although he simply didn't believe me. Par for the course when it involved Mary. Veronica knew, I deduced from odd comments, but wouldn't spill to me or her stepfather whom she had good reasons to dislike. In the end the plan did work and he left – Mary was back in a flash.

Joe had bought a couple of things for the house where his comforts were concerned or he benefitted, a hall runner and a fridge, as we only had the standard indoor safe, and a copper for boiling clothes set in concrete with the double concrete tubs beside it – and this was as late as the fifties. Mary couldn't have been getting his clothes clean enough in it or something because he had eventually relented and bought a new 'Beatty' washing machine. It was the most popular one and it was set on wheels for easy mobility to place near the tubs. The bowl part was about the size of the copper, with an agitator inside and an electric wringer attached to it. (The copper was removed and used decoratively outside later for flowers.)

A washing machine was a boon when working, and although 'Whiteway' auto driers were around, they were bulky and would have been too expensive for most people, even if they could have found room for them. We did not have a matching washing machine that spun, a drier, and sometimes a matching tub too, as we know them today, until in the 1970's although they were around before that. The stove was electric (Shacklock and Atlas are the names that come to mind) as the coal ranges had gone out of favour when electric hot water cylinders could be installed so the need for heating water on the wetback of the coal range was gone.

Also gone though was being able to dry nappies quickly as hot water cupboards were not that much use with more than one baby to keep clean, and many were sealed with screwed up fronts anyway. Drying was a nightmare for most mothers on wet winter days. The standard open fireplace in the separate lounge of most people's homes sometimes had a wooden drier above it that was used drying.

We did have Mary's parents' Axminster squares for the bedrooms and lounge for house warmth. (A few years later, when we first shifted into our own new home we had different coloured cheap squares of Feltex in the bedrooms for warmth instead of carpet or a mat and a runner in the hallway. There was linoleum in the kitchen, which I laid myself matching the pattern with some difficulty. Most people used a mat for warmth on lino in the kitchen by the sink.)

There was little storage space in state houses but perhaps it was not necessary at first anyway as I doubt as a nation we were as materialistic then. The refrigerator was a Frigidaire with rounded corners. Only half of NZ homes had fridges even in 1955 when they were tracked for statistics, the fridge/freezer came much later. Finally Ralph helped Mary with a handsome new radiogram with the record turntable built into it with the radio. There was as a smaller valve radio in the kitchen on the server. (Small portable radios were around but were not really popular till later in the decade.) The huge new power stations in both islands were by then supplying regular electricity, and power cuts became just a memory.

Mary was so pleased to have her own bit of land again and she promptly planted as many varieties of fruit trees that would fit on the back of the section and had prize roses, like 'Peace,' in her front garden. The quarter acre front of the section was not fenced off but there were back fences on each property and a high trellis fence dividing the back from the front on each side of the house, a gate on one side. The trellis Mary planted with sweet peas in season and there was still room left for a vege garden along the back fence which her third husband took charge of while he was there. The volcanic soil, courtesy of Mt. Wellington, and probably help from Yates' Gardening Guide, grew everything quickly and lusciously.

> State House rentals; 'Originally rents were fixed at "fair rent" based on the property value, rates, and insurance. Set in the 1970's as one-sixth of the household income and rose to one quarter in 1984....' *Quote*

When policies changed and State Rental tenants were offered the opportunity to buy the property with a very small deposit and little change in the weekly payments, Mary took advantage of that with a bit of manipulated help from me for the deposit. It did seem to me though it would have been a better policy to encourage people to save while they had the cheap rent and buy or build a home of their own design and where they wanted it, so moving on and letting others run the same cycle. If they couldn't afford to do that and just stayed that was fine too (quote; state house a house for life), but Mary had friends with two cars, a boat and a beach bach in the end, who had not even bothered to buy their state house which they lived in all their lives. They were not struggling and when the wife went back to work they had overseas holidays as well. That did not sit right with me when I knew young people, some of whom lived in really awful circumstances, who had to wait years for a home. Wasn't it them the whole scheme had been meant to support? Perhaps a ceiling on incomes, taking into account children's numbers would have been helpful. If income tested renting was around we didn't personally know of anyone who had been turfed out.

A bizarre remark from a young visiting Australian relation of ours made me think again about our own home when she visited as she asked Mary, "Is the Queen coming to New Zealand?" When Mary said no and asked why she thought that, she replied, "All the houses look as if they have been painted pretty colours especially." I hadn't thought about house colours much till then and realised when I was younger they had been much more limited. By 1958, the year of the Black Budget, I was married with two children and my husband was paid wages in cash on a Thursday for a Friday shop, like most people, because of closed shops at the weekend. Prices were raised on beer, petrol, tobacco, and cigarettes and it was also the year our tax (10 pounds for us on a 100 pound income) was waived because of the incoming PAYE, which seemed a gift. Except that I later worked out they picked it up on PAYE – it's just that it didn't seem to hurt so much as paying out tax at the end of the year. The bonus for us also along with thousands of others was as an alternative to State Housing. The Government offered to help young families starting out by capitalisation of family benefits. It was to be used as a deposit for a family first home along with a State Advances 3%

first mortgage. Ours was eventually approved at 3½ % as our income with overtime that particular year, and only that year, took us just above the cut-off figure. It didn't seem much but made a huge difference to us. However it would have taken us several more years to make it any other way with two young children, so swings and roundabouts.

The total in our case for house and section was 5½ thousand pounds, a pathetic amount by today's standards but it seemed an enormous burden on the day. Being in our early twenties, it meant we would be in our sixties before it was paid off. As life changed that became only for those who stayed in their homes until retirement. In 2010, to my astonishment, I met a couple in their eighties who had not long just paid theirs off. Their property was large and in a valuable position and could easily have been sold and a building more suitable to their needs and size been bought and paid for with an excess as well. They were stoic and stable. Not interested in updating, moving or finances.

Sometimes a smaller second mortgage was needed to cover all costs which were at a higher interest rate, although that had to be approved and the total mortgages, I understood, should be no more than a third of the husband's income. However I knew a family on 8 pound a week that paid 3 pound of that on their rehab mortgage. Some people even privately borrowed a third mortgage as well, from family usually, not a choice we had, but I wouldn't have wanted that anyway. A woman's income, if she had one, was not considered in any equation I was told. I would say that was on the premise that she may become pregnant at any time.

Our privately built home was practical and basic but personalised from a plan I had drawn. Fittings and the choice of colours and location were ours. By the time we shifted in we had allowed for the extras (that had automatically been installed by the state for Mary, like a clothes line and paths). We had also managed to buy a china cabinet, standard lamp and lounge suite in the latest light Scandinavian style and wood. A simpler modern less ostentatious style than Mary's heavy old fashioned dark Kauri timber furniture which would not have fitted anyway, and we already had our bedroom suite in a lightly stained timber.

Modern furniture suited it. Our dining room table was of the ubiquitous Formica, like the bench and server tops, and the table and chair legs of chrome matched, with plastic seats so that all surfaces were easier to clean and table cloths were unnecessary. A most welcome washing/ironing saving. Placemats so much easier to deal with. I was just grateful to have our own home and not be beholden to anyone.

Auckland began opening up, with private companies offering a 'Group Housing' package in a subdivision deal of house and section combined in the price. The standard, simple designs and setup were similar to state housing except that there were more choices of design and finish and you were paying off your own mortgage from the start. Paths and a shed and clothes line may not always have been part of the deal, but it was a step up. I would still always buy a state house if there was a choice between the two. They were standard and relied upon to last and could be altered very simply to be made more appealing.

We also used to visit streets of new houses where individual builders put on 'Showhomes' together. The diversity and imagination in some of their designs were a welcome change and a forerunner of options to come. It was a favourite weekend pastime to view them and queues formed on the paths of the best ones. Dressed to the nines, high-heels, hats and gloves for some, it was dream time for a possible innovative future.

The accompanying building boom in Auckland happened at an acceptable pace at first, but as the economy improved so did the area being covered with quarter-acre sections and eventually there was a scarcity of land until new areas became available further and further out. It felt like the ongoing expansion was a sort of rampaging land rape. Hills would disappear into valleys often including every piece of bush and greenery. There was constant appalling noise for months from huge earthmoving machines, and dust everywhere. The whole topography was changing. Porirua near Wellington was one of the places where this happened and was seen as an engineering and social experiment.

The ultimate dismaying and sometimes unplanned consequences of the state housing effort to form an English based philosophic dream of a 'working man's suburban garden paradise, with variety and diversity and integrated communities with easy access to transport, work and the usual facilities', was lost to the reality of the scale of the enterprise. Initially there were no amenities and the tardiness of commercial enterprises, government or local council support systems to be provided, left people in a kind of limbo-land.

Design standards deteriorated eventually into the uniformity that Savage would probably have abhorred if his government's aim had not all been about altruism but also to satisfy and subdue the mass of the voting population. How ironic that state housing areas have become what they are today. No-one could have envisaged that being the outcome of the dream. Especially not starving families on the scale they are now. That would have seemed more like a 3rd world country.

Auckland's boundaries evolved into their present rambling tentacle shape and our quarter-acre sections were downsized to accommodate the ever-expanding population, which reached half a million by 1964. It was especially disheartening by the time it got to the Bombay Hills, watching the gradual disappearance of the versatile and prolific soil of Pukekohe under concrete, roads, and housing. It seemed more frustrating there than in other districts with their less useful clay. Also, there were parts not so healthy, as in Pakuranga, where swamp land was built on.

Spreading out was no doubt inevitable because we tend to think out not up, but at times it was overwhelmingly sad to me. Nothing for the kids to get excited about any more on a family Sunday drive to the edge of the city to see what had recently been lovely green rolling farms with trees and ponds, and benign cows or passive sheep grazing. It had instead become neatly squared off sections with straight white footpaths and stark sealed roads to define them, the colourful beckoning property signs as decoration. It didn't quite cut it the same. Every generation everywhere will recognise that experience of unwelcome change.

Chapter 11 Neighbours

We experienced relationships with more neighbours than most people; however many of them were fleeting and casual in a time when neighbours were really precious – which they still are for some, perhaps more though in the country than the city and possibly partly to do with age and mobility. Recipes were swapped over the fence, gossip discussing the general goings on and sometimes personal problems confided. Not to be decried according to some health professionals currently. Apparently gossiping often allayed fears and the 'letting off of steam' may have helped save relationships amongst other things. It could also be for something as simple as having access to passed-on mail order catalogues, especially in the country, and magazines like the National Geographic. Those yellow-covered, much-thumbed publications fascinated me the most with pictures of often weird looking animals, different coloured and dressed people, native ones with few clothes and strange and beckoning landscapes. A library may have been around however it was not somewhere easily reachable for us and not at all once we left for the country.

Old Neighbours

We sometimes went back and visited friends and neighbours in Parnell, mostly on a short return to Auckland up from the country between house shifts. I was around 7 to 9 years old. Parnell was where I was christened in the old wooden St. Mary's church which was shifted across the road to where it is now, beside the new one. The first neighbours I remember though were at Levonia St. in Grey Lynn. Mrs. Gibson lived right next door. She was a good-hearted woman and had been a school teacher, although Nana said she couldn't spell for the life of her and also that the large irregular purple birth-mark on the side of her face, had "scarred that woman's mind too". Mrs. Gibson is said to have told Mary, it had come about by her mother trying to abort her. It pulled down the side of her mouth slightly so she always looked a bit crabby to us kids, so we were careful around her although Mrs Gibson was always kind and there when we needed her. When her pretty daughters were born I think she was relieved to find them normal. Fate can be mean though and the story as we heard it was that when one of them in her early teens was biking home from work with her head down in heavy rain, she crashed into the back of a parked furniture van on the side of the road, leaving her with a scar on her face too.

Mrs. Brown and her family across the road had children around our age, as did many families in the street and they became our playmates. Mrs. Brown had lost a baby daughter at about two years old from diphtheria after she went into hospital with an abscess on her lung. At the time the ward was crowded, so the little girl had been put in a corridor where she later died. The whole family was affected for a long time. Grief and guilt are terrible when your child dies before you. Most parents never really recover from it. The Brown family religiously visited her grave every Sunday. Beverly, her other daughter, was my friend, and later did that duty on her own, with instructions from her mum. She was one year older than me so got to experience many things first, like school. I remember Bev always being comfortingly around up till then.

A couple of things hung between our mothers although I doubt it was openly discussed. The one concerning me was the hairdressing session, although it didn't bother me. One day at Bev's place we decided to play hairdressers and I was the customer. Her mother was out, although I think her grandmother was around. Bev had sat me up high on a chair balanced on a low table and draped a sheet around me, and got out the scissors. At the time I had long dark ringlets which Mary habitually wound around her finger every day and I think she was very proud of them as that was the children's fashion then. Anyway, Bev carefully cut them off one by one. There was such a fuss and even Mrs. Gibson cried and wanted to take some drastic action but my ever pragmatic Nana said, "It's no use, what's done is done and we'll just have to make the best of it." So, my hair was cut short all over and it only ever waved a bit again, mostly in the front like Granddad's, so I then had to wear a great big bow on top of my head every day. Luckily, that was fashionable too.

Ralph, older than me by 3½ years, was once playing with his group of boyfriends when things developed into a slanging match between them and the girls, and someone threw a stone and the *others joined in. One caught Bev on the head and there was blood and I think it knocked her down, so things were not too comfortable for a while after that because it had been Ralph who threw it.*

There was no such thing as 'gangs' as we know them today – or at least we didn't come across them. Poorer people were not necessarily grouped together so densely until the government introduced state housing although there were certain city areas which were known as a last choice places to buy or rent in, like Freeman's Bay which had very old housing in it.

There was often local spare land around too where children would gather and further along our street there was a flat area (now part of the North Western motorway) where boys would go off and play their games which of course included rugby. Wilson Whineray was one of the boys in the group and we all later avidly followed his rugby career over the years with the All Blacks. His biography by Sir Anthony O'Reilly in the NZ Herald (26/10/12) after his death was so how we perceived him even at that young age. Perhaps not the granitic quality or the mildly sceptical then but certainly the amused and slightly apart self-reliance was obvious and he was the group leader. His calm fairness and measured tones may only have been developing but the man to come could be seen in the boy. I think he impressed many New Zealanders as iconic and he would have been on my list of most trusted people.

Trolleys were popular. The street intersecting ours was a downhill one, and the boys' favourite weekend sport for a while was taking turns flying down it (no traffic to speak of). After much begging and crying Ralph finally let me have a turn. He didn't mention how to stop the trolley that I remember, and perhaps there weren't brakes anyway. The ride was the most terrifying thing in my life to then – about five years old. With no instructions and not enough strength over bumps to control the steering rope attached to the wooden axle on the front wheels, I came off into the stones when I hit the curb part way down and had cuts and grazes everywhere. I never asked to have a go again. It had been like trying to control a wild animal let loose. I went back to my scooter.

When I was 10 and back living at Arnold's, my real father's place, the neighbour in the state flat joined to ours, a widow I think with two grown sons at home, was really good to me. Once in particular. On my bike riding down a sloping path I had hit something which tipped me against a long uneven stone wall beside it, so that I couldn't brake, and the momentum of the bike dragged me against it for some way until I fell and knocked my head. There was skin and blood everywhere which created a problem, Mary not liking blood, so I had to clean it up before she got back from work. It was pretty painful and I limped home leaning on my bike and sat bleeding and feeling sorry for myself on the back steps, trying not to cry. The elderly neighbour, whose name eludes me, came out and talked to me across the fence. I kept telling her I was fine but she was persistent and in the end I went over and she cleaned and bandaged my ankle and leg for me, offering tea and a biscuit as well. Lovely lady.

I only remember seeing the son of the neighbouring family on the other side and I think he would have just started work. He used his bike to get around too. If I was stuck with a puncture repair or a pump problem which I had to fix, and was doing it down near their footpath, the only convenient place, he would offer to help, although perhaps in a strained sort of way.

I think we were so used to being on the outside, for many reasons, it was just part of our normal life to experience these reactions and I don't think it particularly worried us children anyway. It was normal.

We never became close to neighbours again like those in Levonia St., although Mary must have formed friendships as she would talk about having written to or seen someone from the various places we stayed, mainly towns though, as she wouldn't have had much in common with women from the mill settlements. When we finally settled at Panmure in our state house we did make friends again, mainly with the people each side of us and across the road in the privately owned homes, but it was never on the same friendly terms that we'd had in Levonia St. Also I was 16 by then and had a boyfriend, and girlfriend work mates had become more the norm and it was the same with Ralph at nearly 20.

When Mary was in her 60's and 70's though, she used to receive up to 150 cards at Christmas which she was very proud of. Many of them would be from our old neighbours.

Chapter 12 Health

We seldom went to a doctor and neither did the people we knew. There were few female ones until the fifties. Doctors were often considered 'quacks' by some too and doubtless there were those who deserved it. Easy access to medical help by car was years away and an ambulance only considered in dire circumstances like an accident and/or something being broken or if someone was actually bleeding to death or dying, or appeared to be. Doctors did make house calls but finding a phone to call one was a problem and no-one could afford a doctor unnecessarily until the change of government with Labour's Social Security Act of 1938. No appointment was needed to visit a doctor's surgery which was often at their home and was off-putting from the strong smell of disinfectant. You queued and waited your turn, strict adherence to sequence of arrival jealously monitored by the patients as well as more professionally by the nurse receptionist.

Any doctor 'worth his salt' was well known and long journeys with equally long waits at the end would be made to see them when necessary. There was also an element of secrecy about a visit to the doctor's. Perhaps people only ever went out of desperation, which could mean it was a serious illness, or thought to be, or perhaps a sexual disease or a pregnancy, illegitimate or otherwise. GP's as a rule handled pregnancies but I do know of country areas where it was a local midwife, usually with a good reputation, that was called out to do a home delivery – more common in the earlier part of the century. They were often held in high esteem in the community as in the grandmother of a friend in the New Plymouth area around the turn of the century.

Chemists were consulted about 'over the counter products' and there was a general acceptance of 'home/natural/old wives remedies' for minor ailments along with a level of superstition. Poultices were for several things including sprains and for our family they were hot bread ones on boils to draw them, something best forgotten. Remedies for illnesses were passed around by word of mouth and used by the whole community. Cobwebs to bind a cut, which Mary used on Veronica once when desperate in an isolated mill town (it worked), a dark room for a hit head, butter for burns and for constipation things like liquorice powder, Nyalls Figsen, prunes and if desperate, a laxative. Califig Syrup of Figs or Cascara – not a happy memory.

Carol, Uncle Ross' daughter, was fed some awful concoction for worms which I can't remember the name of, but by her facial expression was enough to put me off when Uncle offered me some. I think he had a slight obsession with worms. It wasn't part of Mary's bag thank goodness. She was into the custom of getting our tonsils out at five years old however so both Ralph and I had ours done at Greenlane Hospital. Lemon juice (there were always lemon trees in back yards) and honey the first choice for a sore throat, Condy's Crystals if you had some. Our option was either Buckley's Canadiol Mixture or more usually Bonnington's Irish Moss because I remember where the bottle was in the kitchen cupboard in Levonia St. and I would ask my Nana if Irish people had to collect moss to make it. I think she gave me vague answers because I would ask her every time someone had to have it.

A cough meant trying to go to sleep with the invasive smell of Vicks Vaporub coming from up from my chest and the itch of Wonder Wool from my pyjamas. This may have been preceded by having a towel or pillow case over my head and awkwardly having to lean over a bowl of boiling water. Usually eucalyptus or Friars Balsam had been added and I would be encouraged to breathe the vapours in to loosen the phlegm in my chest to help me breathe better. The revolting taste of baking soda in hot water was for indigestion, which I seldom admitted to, or Hardy's Indigestion Powder. Dinnefords Magnesia was for winding babies and Reckitts Blue Bags (normally for whitening washing like sheets) for bee stings. Ears were not to be poked, it could lead to deafness and a hot water bottle was laid under the pillow for warmth for earache or peroxide poured messily in ears. At least its fizz was distracting. There was Qtol for sunburn which I would know the scent of again anytime I smelt it, and Rexona soap was for eczema, something our family had. There were still many useless patent medicines around from the earlier part of the century. They were big business but most proved ineffectual at best and some had even been dangerous, but the generation from then still would swear by their effectiveness. It could have been a liking for the alcohol content.

The only remedy for aches, and mainly headaches, was Aspro. Vaseline was used for many things and Rawleigh's ointment was good for cuts and grazes. The Rawleigh's representative used to call regularly in the neighbourhood with a variety of products like cosmetics, flavouring essences, spices, soaps, household cleaners, patent medicines, fly killers like sticky brown strips to be hung from the ceiling, 'Flies Flit' in a pump action spray or (horrifyingly now) DDT. (Cleanliness was competitive and Mary always, always had supplies of Pennant Kerosene, Dettol and Jeyes Fluid.)

There were a variety of other salesmen, the health ones called 'Snake oil salesmen', or 'charlatans' and 'fraudsters' with their 'medical cure claims' and whose products may have worked on some from the 'Placebo effect'. They all lugged around suitcases and some had bikes with a special out-rigger fitted for encyclopaedias, Bon Brushes and makeup, (Electrolux's later with a car) along with visits from a man in a van to sharpen knives and scissors. They were usually welcome, if not for their goods then a chat to break the housewives' monotony although maybe not so much hawkers and pedlars. When I was older, several times I heard more was on offer, in a charming sensual way, giggled at by some and no doubt taken up by others, but not admitted to. I was myself gently propositioned more than once when I had small babies but being so exhausted, the subtleties went right over my head until a neighbour mentioned they had been attracted by some particular travelling salesman.

Young children had to survive all sorts of illnesses that can now be overcome with medical treatment, and there was a much stronger sense of the acceptance of loss of life in general, a flow on no doubt from the deprivations that our parents and grandparents had had to survive. Things like immigrating, wars, depressions and health afflictions like the 1918-19 'flu pandemic, TB (consumption), Infantile Paralysis (polio) with the dread of possibly ending up in an 'Iron Lung', Diphtheria, Rheumatic or Scarlet fever and other children's ailments (mainly the respiratory and infectious ones which now seem minor but were sometimes fatal), had been around for a long time.

A long convalescence period was always encouraged even for minor ailments like mumps, measles, and chickenpox. We did well by world standards though, having the lowest mortality rate until the 1930's. Much of the medicine then used was preventative. Lane's Emulsion was the one I quite enjoyed, unlike the spoonful of castor or cod liver oil and most of the other revolting ones that were accepted remedies, the latter especially for rickets. I hadn't known we were fed Rose Hip Syrup because it was a source of Vitamin C when there was a shortage of imported oranges. When I realised that, I wondered why they hadn't used the Bay of Plenty oranges that seemed abundant when we lived there a few years on. Apparently children of today could do with doses of the latter as rickets are making a return with many preferring indoor games and entertainment to time outside and sun on their skin.

There were no antibiotics as we know them today until the late 1940's. Infant vaccinations had not begun. When they did, many fears for children abated although the horrible concoctions were often nasty to swallow. The discovery of penicillin by Fleming was amazing. Mary talked about the Sulpha drug saving her life in mid-1944 when Veronica was born. She had the common fever associated with childbirth which became puerperal sepsis (septicaemia), and we associated her recovery with the Americans and the Sulpha drug being used. (Unconfirmed)

Health Department Public Nurses visited Maori communities and possibly other people but also schools to check out children's hearing, sight, height, weight, cleanliness, and especially in the country schools with a local Maori population, any signs of impetigo, ringworm and particularly hair lice which people associated with dirty children. I had a mild case of the latter which Mary freaked out about. She was mortified, being so bug conscious she couldn't abide a flea in the house, and we were always being checked for some passing horror. I dreaded taking home a note from a teacher more than whatever was wrong. At Ngongotaha Primary School, with or without nits, everyone was lined up outside an old shed where I knew there was a series of tubs. When I walked through the opening into the windowless dim space, I found out what they were for. They each had a foul smelling solution in them which our heads were unceremoniously dipped into without any warning and we were then shoved out the other side opening, dripping wet with no towel or explanation. The other kids were mostly Maori and had obviously been through this process before and found it very funny when I didn't like it.

Around 1940, school dental nurses were introduced, and one dental clinic was shared with several neighbouring schools, although country ones might not, even if there was a building, distance making it unviable. I think nurses did do a country school round though, as I can remember somewhere a child racing around the playground yelling in terrified, singsong glee, "The nurse is back at the 'Murder House', the nurse is back at the 'Murder House'". At first local dentists followed up with treatment for children requiring attention but later fillings were done by the school nurse using the dreaded pedal-powered drill which sounded like a tractor in the mouth and might miss the tooth and hit the gum or even worse a nerve.

The strong smell of bug-destroying products would be the first indication of the nurse's re-appearance in the city schools and then a pupil from a higher level coming into our classroom and whispering to the teacher. Holding my breath in horror happened every time. Treatment was so painful children would often take off for home when their name was called, especially if they had not been for some time. I was one of them.

There were sure to be cavities or a tooth that needed removing. Not a good outcome when teeth received no attention of course. The treatment was free, not that the children cared. Although it was recommended that the school nurses, with their limited training, should still send children to private properly trained dentists when there were real problems, I can vouch that was not necessarily done. At one school it was however. I fought the nurse, the head prefect and the headmaster all at the same time when they tried to hold me down in the 'Murder House' chair and they couldn't even get my mouth open, no matter how many times the frustrated nurse pleaded, 'Now come along dear'. An appointment was made for me and I was sent off to the Auckland Hospital Board dentist and given 'laughing gas' and they did everything in one go, the few teeth they left me with all filled and a classy gold filling in a front tooth. Some compensation.

My Dutch girlfriend told me her parents did not like their children going to the dentist as they felt the school nurses only added to the bad state of NZ children's teeth, drilling and filling unnecessarily. She and her brothers and sisters had all been born in Holland and didn't come out to NZ until they were all school age or older, perhaps accounting for their healthier teeth.

Cleaning teeth was usually done with equal amounts of baking soda and salt, or separately (and also used for ulcers – common with false teeth) which in the case of one girl from school I knew, who assiduously cleaned hers three times every day, gave her the whitest teeth I had ever seen for the time. My Nana used the pink caked Gibbs Dentrifice for her false teeth. We were told never to take the lid off the aluminium tin or there would be repercussions so maybe it was difficult to come by, perhaps during the war.

The state of our teeth could have depended where in the country we were living. Our family were often in chalky North Island areas which were regarded by locals as having a deficiency in the water leading to more problems than perhaps in other places. The outcome, wherever you lived, was that many people had to have dentures quite young and it was accepted as the best thing to do. People were considered better off without their natural teeth – economically to avoid the continuing source of debt and physically to avoid discomfort and pain. That widespread popular belief was such an accepted part of life, it was recommended for the men in the armed forces to have their teeth removed before they went overseas to alleviate the worry of them. Many took advantage of having dentures fitted without cost. Not much changed that outlook until after the 1950's when water fluoridation was introduced beginning in Hastings then most of the rest of NZ by councils after the 'Commission of Inquiry' was held in 1957.

At 21 I had a phobia about anything to do with dentistry because of continuing really bad teeth, mainly doubles and the eroding enamel along my gums in the front ones, so the removal of them was the reluctant but less painful option in the end after a really bad abscess in my gold filling. Walking around for 3 months with no teeth, as was the custom, prevented smiling and difficulties with food and talking and by the time new dentures were fitted it was like having a mini elephant stuck in my mouth. There were some regrets then for the irrevocable loss of teeth with the realisation of the false ones' limitations. The inability to bite as previously and really enjoy an apple or other fruit, the lower dentures often floating and catching food, especially seeds, underneath them and the sense of control gone. The trade-off was worth it though whenever I watched others with earache and in toothache agony – so many tortured memories!

The relentless, inevitable summer/autumn Infantile Paralysis (Poliomyelitis) epidemic came along in 1947-8, as major ones did about every ten years and to a lesser degree every five years. Schools closed down which meant correspondence school (I don't think we did much work) which that time was for about four months and there were restrictions on going to public places like theatres, swimming pools, churches, holiday camps, parties and picnics. It also altered travel arrangements around the affected areas all over the country. When we resumed normal schooling we had to take our own towels and terrified mothers watched their children like hawks for any signs of the illness appearing. Lucky for me I got the lighter flu version, which kept me inside for weeks, bored and fretting. Many children died though or were left cripples for life and had to wear braces on their legs. Sometimes they were confined in a huge cumbersome, clanking lung machine to keep them breathing – all the time. I wonder if they eventually recovered? Children were not encouraged to ask questions.

These controls were used for the last time from early December 1947 until April 1948 when parents complained, as it was eventually determined the precautions had not worked and also the relentlessly predictable pattern of a specific season had changed. Polio was around more often after the 1948–1949 years; 1952–53 and again in 1955–56. USA made their newly discovered Salk vaccine available free for children in 1956 and NZ was one of the first countries to take up their offer unlike the British who did not accept Salk's findings. In 1959 it was provided to all New Zealanders between 6 months and 21 years and later in 1961 the safer and more effective Sabin was given orally. 95% of pre-school children were then protected, my children amongst them. Such a relief.

Immunisations had become available as well for diphtheria in 1941 and routinely administered, which I missed. In 1947 vaccinations were introduced to schools for TB and I had my little scary scabby result assessed afterwards in the 1950's when I was at Auckland Girls Grammar. Rumour said there could be second shots – to be avoided when possible. Antibiotics like penicillin were eventually developed in 1940, to protect us from blood poisoning.

The insecticide DDT a 'persistent organic pollutant' was introduced in 1948 for various purposes like controlling grass grub and Porina moth and also used on home lawns and in market gardening. We had no idea of the implication of its use, although Rachael Carson's *Silent Spring'* was published earlier, but Mary as always with chemicals, made foreboding sounds long before anyone else acknowledged the possibility and it was eventually restricted in 1970 and banned in 1989.

We heard from my father-in-law that there was a short street of new houses built on the boundary of a farm he knew in New Plymouth where excessive chemicals were used and there were eventually 10 babies lost to miscarriage or stillbirth in that street. No-one in authority seemed interested and when I met a Dow Chemical representative and discussed it with him, he adamantly insisted worries about chemicals were all 'old wives 'tales'. As he would. (I have since found a website which has much more information.)

Driving home one Friday night from work in the 1970's I was impatient to get by a slow-moving tractor on a semi-rural road near our property when I realised what I was reading on the tin that was balancing on the back. It said 245T. The next day we watched as the drifting wind brought waves of fine mist over our house. We didn't know for sure what it was but that night thoroughly hosed off our roof after temporarily blocking the spouting leading to our water tank. However I was ill for several months afterward with a debilitating illness which did not seem to have any apparent explanation. The cancer my spouse suffered and died from was considered caused by chemicals and his dad's farm, where he had lived from about 14 to 28, was two farms over from the Dow Chemical production plant in New Plymouth.

In her eighties, Mary lived her last few years in a council flat. The maintenance of weeds was by using a spray and as her front ranch-sliders were only about a metre and a half from the path where the weeds were controlled, she'd often tell me she felt sick after the spraying was done even though she had shut everything up and gone out as quickly as she could. The same council sprayed on paths children used going to school in the morning until parents complained. Children closer to the ground than adults were more prone to a reaction.

Mary developed huge sores on her back that no-one could decide the cause of, which never went away, and she also eventually died of cancer. I think she had got too old by then to connect the dots about the sprays, thinking she had avoided breathing the fumes, but the residue would still be there at least until the next rain. She did feel she was being poisoned but as I didn't find any of this information out until I talked to another resident after Mary died, I didn't know either. One of the other ladies in the council flats said her husband had died of cancer too and many of the residents regularly became sick and associated it with the spraying. Eventually it was stopped.

Chapter 13 Education/Childhood Experiences

Primary Schools

My first day at school was at Grey Lynn. Our neighbour's daughter, Beryl, who was older and possibly in her early teens, my friend Beverly Brown (a year older than me and from across the road,) along with the other children in the street, walked me the mile or so from home up Chinaman's Hill to Grey Lynn Primary school at the top. Mary didn't come but I think that's how it was done then.

My teacher was an older woman and pretty crabby and when she found I was left-handed, she said, 'A spawn of the devil! Not in my class!' A common belief apparently that I luckily didn't take on board, or the derogatory 'south paw' or 'cack-handed'. She vowed she would change me to using my right hand and she did. It didn't take long. Every time I went to pick up anything with my left hand, she was right there with the ruler cutting me across my tender five-year-old knuckles. Something many other left-hand children of that time experienced, and probably worse.

Forcing my brain to adjust has in fact, often been quite beneficial as in a test I once did, the results were that both sides of my brain were fairly evenly developed and it was also handy for switching hands in tennis to calls of 'Cheat!' It has caused confusion though too, having consciously to reverse natural inclinations perhaps similar to having to adjust to thinking in a second language. More difficult with aging I've found, the brain strongly wanting to ignore learnt ways.

After our stay in the back blocks at Mokai, near Taupo, where we didn't go to school, my education continued in my first country school at Ngongotaha, near Rotorua, where we had shifted to. It was exciting having new children to play with and a novelty to have nearly all Maori classmates – we didn't see Maori in the city much. Although they played with me, most lived in the local 'Pa' and could hardly speak English, consequently picking up little education. They, however, considered it was me that was found wanting when it was discovered that my mother had been divorced. A Scandal! It didn't occur to me that status was important. I accepted them for who they were and couldn't understand why they didn't accept me.

Being ostracised also happened when I went to a school in Rotorua later, which had a bigger mixture of Pakeha and Maori. The kids would sometimes taunt me but as I was used to entertaining myself and didn't really understand why they did it, it was only about Mary after all, and as I don't suppose I behaved as they expected – not responding – they gave up.

The headmaster there was an Australian and our morning assemblies were a culture mix as we sang 'God save the Queen' then 'Waltzing Matilda' and often also Maori songs like 'Pokarekare Ana' and I must have learned the Maori Battalion song there too as I know all the words. (The only time at any school that I can remember where Maori songs were sung.) We also played Maori stick games and some children used poi. No haka though.

Continually changing schools, 23 in the end, 18 in the first 3 years, I had learned to rely on myself and adapt to whatever came along. At some it was easy to fit in, others not. In Katikati there was a clique as the headmaster's daughter was in my class and after a while she must have found something about me that appealed to her and invited me to join her gang of four. I was taken aback by this, it was so unexpected, and politely declined as I was a loner not a follower. She was not impressed and became catty and smart until our male teacher patted me on the head one day in front of her and said, "Our conscientious pupil", no doubt playing his own game, but for some reason she left me alone then. The next time I saw him I asked Ralph what 'conscientious' meant.

Although I went to others, most of the schools were similar in the small mill settlement ones and even in these back block places we received the obligatory free half pint bottles (I have read it was a quarter pint but I doubt that) of full cream milk delivered to the school (initiated in 1937). The school monitor's job was to pick the milk up from the gate, a perk not open to girls, usually a reward for good behaviour, or a pet. We drank it straight from the glass bottles through the cardboard top which had a pre-cut hole we pushed through with our straws. Milk was cheap for years (as was bread) at 3 pence and later 4 pence a pint. A healthy drink for our family when there wasn't much food available, and I drank it in preference to tea or coffee for many years. (No wonder in 1957 New Zealanders were the biggest milk drinkers in the world.) We were also supplied with apples in season during the war. Tart Granny Smiths for some but I remember red apples, probably Cox's Orange. Each came wrapped in tissue paper in neat rows in wooden white pine boxes.

The Teacher

Country schools often had one room in which a very competent teacher had to be in charge, requiring work to be set up for children of all ages, which would have been a horrendous job. Reading, writing and arithmetic were tediously but effectively learned by rote and stayed with the generations that learned that way all their lives. Some places had two rooms, often a 'temporary' prefab, where a novice teacher taught the primers. Some of us used to stay behind after school and help a lone teacher clean up and prepare for the next day. I was often one of these children and used to enjoy it, probably because I wouldn't have bothered making friends and I liked school. It was the nearest to a safe place I knew. Once we had a male teacher who was a red-head and quite charismatic. He seemed to understand that I'd missed things in our rambling life and would question me on various subjects and then give me some extra catch-up work to do. Not much but enough to make sense of things. In return I'd do extra things to help although he never asked me to.

A girl from the after school help group, who I actually quite liked, caught up with me on the way home from the local store one day (which was an unusual addition to the settlement) when my arms were full of shopping and to my surprise she proceeded to attack me. Without a word, she pushed and scratched at me and smacked me in the face until I dropped the flour, which went all over us and the dusty road. At the time I felt horrified, trying to think what I had done to her, not wanting to fight back until she pushed the flour out of my hands. Then I did, as I knew I would cop it from Mary for wasting good money. Thinking back, it could have been jealousy, but as she never spoke to me then or afterwards, I am not sure.

That week for some reason Mary also told me to come straight home from school. Whether she didn't trust the teacher or had heard some gossip I don't know, she didn't tell me why either, but we had a big argument which was unusual. I loved learning and even though one of the kids at that school called me "Teacher's pet", I wanted to keep having the extra tuition. I missed that teacher. In the end I ran home every day.

We moved again a few weeks later and in one sense I was pleased to go for a change although I was also upset. I had found a really nice boyfriend called Desmond, who had given me a kiss on our last night there, when he met me at the gate. I had climbed out the bedroom window. He said, "This is love for us." I don't remember shifting or anything else after that. For a while it felt so wonderful living in this sweet little dreamy bubble where someone loved me, even though I never saw him again. I was all of nine.

> Quote; 'From 1938, primary teachers could not advance beyond a certain salary level until they had served three years at a country school. This drew more experienced teachers to country schools. Also, more emphasis was placed on years of service rather than the size of the school in teachers' salary increases.'

One outcome of this experience by a family friend in the forties was, though both he and his wife trained together at Ardmore Teachers Training College (the only one of its kind in NZ where the trainees lived on site) when he later went to work in the country, his wife was unable to be employed at the same time for some reason. It was when there was a shortage of teachers because of the baby boomers, so it seemed ridiculous. It may have been about them having a family but she did teach anyway although was not paid. The post-war baby boom meant more schools and in 1954 rural service for two years became a required part of teacher training as country positions were often hard to fill. Auckland Teachers Training College was in Epsom.

Many girls still left after primary school if they were of a leaving age and in predominantly farming areas boys often left early too. Girls were considered less intelligent and anyway were going to end up as someone's domestic drudge/wife/mother, so teaching them was considered a waste of resources I would think, although attitudes were changing, in the city anyway.

Girls were expected to do their share and help in the house and look after their siblings, the training that they would need to know about anyway as that would be their own lives within a short time. Fathers would have had different expectations for their sons and I know many families where boys were often the substitute labourers from very young, and certainly on farms. Unless they were still at school, and even then some were expected to stay home at times like haymaking when many hands were needed. School and all the chores often took up a full normal day, Sundays the possible exception. That would be the accepted day of rest and worship as stated in the Bible. A friend, who was one of several boys, had a father who definitely saw them all as workers rather than sons. My friend was often beaten along with his brothers when they didn't do their jobs as perfectly as their father considered they should. They did not get Sundays off. At 14 when they were legally able to leave school, the eldest left home and was followed by most of his brothers. The ones that stayed never got paid and had to work at other jobs as well. In the end, even after promises of being remembered in his will for their loyalty, everything was left to the two girls of the family. There was, as there will always be, often bitterness about the unfairness of how property is split, especially farms here in NZ.

Land is so important no matter how tiny a section or how large a country.

Children would travel to country schools in various ways other than walking, often for many miles. Some came by dinghy like at Ostend, Waiheke Island, rowing across the estuary before the new road reconstruction. Others came in ramshackle buses on unsealed roads – sometimes taking an hour or more – on the back of a farm motorbike or hack which could be a really old flatbed truck or horse & cart, and at one place a tractor regularly blocked the road to drop off a couple of kids. Those ones didn't come far and I think it was when they were running late although they could probably have made it faster by running.

Kids rode to schools on bikes sometimes but that was usually nearer the city. At one of those schools our bus picked up all age groups for primary, intermediate and secondary schools which were set in close proximity. There were mostly girls at our stop and while we waited we would take turns to play a game of trying to identify movie stars by their initials. Not a game I was that good at after coming up from the country where we hardly ever saw movies.

Rural area schools and even ones as close to Auckland as Helensville had a paddock set aside for pupils' horses, somewhere to graze during the day. Shetland ponies were a choice for some but in one particular King Country school, a girl in standard five (form 1) always came on her own full grown horse. He was left in the school grounds in a fenced field with a hitching post and a handy stile to use for mounting. Probably the last of the facilities provided especially for horses. She could watch her mate out of the school window. She loved him so much she would spend time in her lunch hour with him. She was a brilliant artist – exclusively of horses.

At morning break in some of these cold places there would be a big urn on the pot belly stove in each room, (our heating system then) and when it was fine I can remember lining up outside, adjacent to the table and big kettles, waiting to be served and watching our breaths in the air and the steam coming off our mugs of Ovaltine, Milo, Cocoa or Horlicks made from our free bottled milk. We'd have gloves or mittens and coats and hats on, wandering around holding the mugs for warmth on the outside as well as the inside. Frost would be crackling under our feet and any puddles with ice left on were quickly shattered by the boys. The inevitable thick Macrocarpa hedges on the school boundary would still be white with frost around their bases even at midday, so we couldn't play hide and seek in them or the other games we used them for in warmer weather.

There were nearly always mature trees on country school boundaries which we used in lieu of playground equipment and our imagination for games was much more developed than today's children. Older kids did most of the organising if it suited them or we dropped into our own sex and age groups and played games like hop-scotch. I used an old round tobacco tin of John's with a lady and a tobacco leaf picture (Riverhead Gold) filled with dirt for weight which was perfect instead of an uneven stone. There were rope games like skipping that had rhymes and songs to go with them. I especially liked the challenge of the double ropes in the chanted 'Salt, mustard, vinegar, pepper' which went faster and faster until feet tripped or arms got tired turning the rope accurately and the rhythm was lost. When there was enough flat area we competed doing cartwheel flipping, walking on our hands, climbing trees, hide and seek, blind man's buff or just chasing each other playing 'tag' or taking turns at being 'He'. Hula-hoops became really popular after I'd left school but eventually faded out.

Boys could join in and play with us too but they had their own boisterous, rougher games like 'stacks on the mill', 'no man standing', 'king of the castle,' 'cowboys and Indians', 'cops and robbers', any form of football (often soccer with a line to cross instead of a proper net) and ones when they just seemed to tear around everywhere madly for the hell of it. Their marbles all had different values and names (playing either out or inside for these) and there were some very prized spectacular ones in a huge variety of colours. Swapping was part of the game especially if anyone had a destructive steely one (ball bearings). Business acumen started here. Marbles were a mystery to the girls as we were expected to settle for knuckle bones.

Playing with neighbourhood children meant mostly being outside with the usual school games but children often made up their own games for entertainment. Toys would have been a luxury although children weren't usually affected as much as adults were by the lack of money. The ones we knew had few expectations of getting bought toys, including ourselves. As we grew older, cricket and rounders (a simple game like baseball) were more popular with any bats and balls available and could include the girls. At one settlement fathers played with us in the summer. More screams than usual. On wet days, boys played indoor games of soldiers with wooden guns or the more sedate Meccano sets (we had a new one as Ralph was once shouted a set for his birthday although there were no replacement pieces during the war) and wind-up fragile toys like cars and trucks, made from tin plate with bendable/breakable tabs holding them together – not for long if there was rough play or a budding investigative engineer around.

There were playing cards and board games like drafts, Ludo, dominoes, snakes and ladders and I think an English version of Mah-jong plus comics and old books etc. which were usually inherited and well used. 'Colouring in books' to use with crayons and paints, also ones for painting and drawing, were considered a treat for the girls. Books were read if we were near a library or the school had one. Sometimes, as with John, a handyman dad, friend or relation would make wooden toys. They were popular for birthdays or Christmas presents. There were toy trucks and cars or wickets, stilts, trollies and sledges and sometimes girls had dolls' bassinets or beds. They lasted longer and were certainly respected and appreciated more by children then. Lucky were the children who had fathers or uncles who worked in government jobs like the Railways or Post Office with their workshops. I was told that the last few months before Christmas the workshops produced more toys than anything else (workwise) which appeared to be condoned by management as well as the unions.

Chess, Monopoly or Lego may have been around but not for us anyway and seldom were there any children's programmes on the radio even if anyone had one and the area would need to have been reached by a radio station. I always had my swing when we lived in Levonia St. which was till I was nearly six. When it was just girls, baking was an option if an adult female was in the mood but girls usually played house with dolls and their accessories like prams, little beds, and soft toys, often humming or singing happily to their charges. Many rhymes and chants didn't make sense but had familiar catchy phrases, some still around today. Lucky girls like Uncle Ross' daughter Carol had a doll's house – so useful on a wet day as well. If there were rebels like me, we would try and play more interesting games with the boys who could usually outrun and outsmart us, teasing from a distance and with Ralph's gang, no contest.

If boys were at girls' parties, they were coerced into games like 'Musical chairs or cushions', 'Truth and Dare', 'Statues' and 'I spy' or embarrassing kissing and mortifying ones like 'Spin the bottle' and 'Postman's knock', depending on their ages. Parents might organise ball games or hide a present outside when the weather was appropriate but I mostly remember all the noise and the way food was demolished so quickly. Everything home-made with delicious baking, coloured jellies in pretty shapes served with bottled fruit and hand whipped cream (no ice-cream) and lollies like butterscotch and brittle toffee for sweets.

At school, single wooden desks were the norm with attached seats sometimes placed together in pairs. They had lifting lids hinged to a wooden piece across the top with a groove for pens and pencils and a hole to take the inkwell. Pencils only until we changed to ink in standard 4 (year 6) and after that we used long nibs of various sizes that fitted into a pen holder, dipping them in the round ink-wells, and writing about four to five words to the dip. Ink wells were messy things to fill, usually done by an appointed school monitor or the teacher in rural schools. (They were also used for the dunking of girls' pigtails or adding carbide from bike lamps to fizz and create a really obnoxious smell.) If desks didn't have large blotters on them, held by a leather grip, some other way would be needed to blot ink to keep book pages free from smudges and ink blobs. An acquaintance I met recently assured me that she was still using an inkwell in the 1970's in a country school so perhaps there was only a general fading out of the ink pen's use.

There were no ballpoints at Auckland Girls Grammar School (AGGS), in the early fifties anyway, and they were actively discouraged apparently although allowed in school from about 1947 (first British patent 1938 – sold in New York 1945). They were also prohibitively expensive then anyway, about 14 shillings, but did drop down to half a crown (2 shillings and 6 pence) later. At Grammar I used a small fountain pen that was quite precious to me as it fitted my small hand well and it had been expensive.

Mary said they used slates with a slate pencil in her era (1917) with damp rags to wipe their boards clean. She didn't mention if the teacher had chalk and a blackboard. Mary also talked about gaining her 'Proficiency' at Standard 6, (abolished in 1938) although she hadn't even started school till she was seven, so I gathered she did quite well to achieve that. (Five-year-olds were allowed back in school in 1936) It would have allowed her to have gone on to secondary school if she had wanted to and it also functioned as a testimonial for jobs. However, Mary left school at the legal age of 14 which many children did, boys and girls, until that changed to 15 in 1944. In 1945 School Certificate was introduced for 5th formers.

More Impressive Toys

The more affluent families could have a bigger range of outdoor toys similar perhaps to a public park like slides and swings etc. although we had a rope swing when I was young and many back yards did, usually home-made like ours so all different but hung from a tree. A bigger variety of indoor games perhaps like a Meccano set, which Ralph did have along with the materials to make aeroplanes, but especially envied by both adults and children was a Hornby train set, the rails of which in one house went into other rooms through especially made small openings in the large skirting board. A source of great delight to Ralph when we ended up in a home with one after an accident.

We were all staying at Uncle Ross' place and one Sunday Ralph and I had been sent off on our own to visit our Nana at the private nursing home not far away, between Mt. Eden and Manukau Rds. (The trams didn't go that way, across town.) Nana had been admitted there when we had left Auckland for the country. Ralph was on his bike and I had my scooter, which I loved. After the visit, Ralph challenged me with my scooter to beat him on his bike down the long sloping sealed right-of-way drive. Fool me. Sucked in again. The speed was exhilarating until I realised the drive didn't level out enough at the bottom soon enough to stop ending up on the road so it was me that came off my scooter. Ralph had brakes. He must have got a fright when I landed sprawling at his feet though and had gone looking for help as by the time I vaguely came to no-one seemed to be around.

I couldn't hear anything anyway or really remember where I was at first, only aware that my head hurt. I lay there inert for what seemed ages with my eyes still shut trying to figure out what sort of bed I was lying on that stuck things into me. I also remember thinking how mad Mary would be and wondering about our reception back at Uncle's, as we were due to have our photos taken the next day and for sure I would have lost some skin from my face – not to mention the blood. Normal thoughts, like getting myself up weren't happening although my eyes had begun squinting at the light.

I didn't know where he came from but a man appeared on the scene. I couldn't focus on him properly but Ralph wasn't with him and he wasn't someone I knew so I started a bit when he began touching me. But he seemed kind, murmuring away as he carefully felt my limbs and looked at my head, saying something to me quite clearly, which still didn't make much sense. When he bent and picked me up I cried out. That woke me up a bit more as the bits poking me were gravelly and they hurt as I was moved, although most of it dropped off my grazed arms and face. The man carried me out of the nursing home drive and along to the house next door which I presumed was his place although there was still no sign of Ralph.

He carried me through his front door to a lounge and laid me carefully on a couch, which had a clean sheet on it, and was also where Ralph was sitting on the floor by a train set. The man's wife hovered in the background till he moved away and then she fussed over me, covering me up with a rug and dabbing at my bleeding face with a warm flannel. The children of the family began asking questions and were genuinely concerned. Ralph didn't say much, his attention elsewhere on more important things. I was really embarrassed by all this attention and began to cry. They thought it was from pain, but I hardly felt the grazes or my head, I just wanted to go back to Uncle's.

The couple and their children were very kind to us. We stayed a while and were well entertained. The father tried to distract us, probably waiting to see if I got any worse, by getting their train set running properly. They showed us all the lovely engines, carriages and rolling stock cars, intricately built stations, switches, people, buildings, water towers, bridges and tunnels and surrounding rugged countryside with trees, fences, farm houses, tractors, implements and animals, the train set tracks eventually running off into another room.

But much as I wanted to, even knowing Ralph was really fascinated and loving it, I couldn't concentrate for long and my head dropped as the train whizzed around again and seemed to match the feeling in my head. I felt sick too from the slight oily smell and ringing in my ears. I'm sure Ralph would have stayed longer but I think the father was satisfied I wasn't too much worse. He eventually took me out to his car, scooter and all, carrying me against his woollen coat which reminded me disorientingly of my stepfather's tobacco smell. Ralph I think may have biked back to Uncle's after trying to put the moment off for as long as he could. I only remember me in the back seat of the big limousine, wrapped in a lovely soft rug. A comforting memory.

Mary was predictably annoyed when we arrived back although covered it well; profusely thanking the man who was helpfully suggesting doctors or hospital and getting me treated me for concussion, with Mary emphatically agreeing. But as soon as he was gone I remember being harangued although it more or less washed over me as I was so sleepy, spending the next three boring days in bed in the dark where I remember feeling pretty sick and horrible. The cure, as usual was to stay in bed, not a doctor, which must have worked as I obviously recovered. I don't think I saw the scooter again. Punishment enough.

The Orphanage 1946

The silence began for us when the stiff policeman with the sad face ushered us up the curved steps to the very big double doors of a really large building which I could see little else of in the dark. After the policeman had knocked and stepped down a few steps we were totally ignored by him and apparently those who lived there. Veronica, my little sister, had already been crying for our mother Mary when we had been waiting hopefully for her to come back for us at the police station. The policemen had left

Veronica for me to deal with when no amount of their trying to soothe her had made any difference.

Here waiting was no different. One door was finally opened and a uniformed woman indicated we were to come in and the policeman stepped up and leaned in to pass some papers over, grunting something briefly I didn't catch and quickly retreated to his obviously marked car. He was gone before the door was shut.

At nine years old I had no idea what was happening but probably it was another drama I was not privy to although Mary and I appeared to have what was common in those days and now identified as a co-dependent relationship. She may have just left her current husband John, Veronica's father, my stepfather, after one of his violent outbursts. It made sense that the police were involved and also us having a bath that morning although it took me a while to work that out. Mary always had a plan and for this one we needed to be clean. I had been thinking she had fallen apart at the Police Station and we had been taken off her temporarily so she could be given help. It had happened before. Both Veronica and I had been left behind, at different times, mostly me before Veronica was born and normally that meant Mary would eventually swing by and pick us up.

This first night at our South Auckland Presbyterian Orphanage was humiliating for me. I walked into a somehow ominous shadowy and draughty high-ceilinged entry hall which appeared to be the main hub of the building, carrying Veronica on my hip, and nearly slipped over it was so brightly polished. (I would get to understand why.) There was also a faint odour I couldn't quite identify but would ever after recognise anywhere as a particular polish. There were four uniformed women clustered tensely standing by and a fifth more imposing one who had taken the police papers and beckoned us in. She then disappeared into what looked like a nearby office, nodding to her staff as she went.

Veronica and I were separated almost immediately. The stern women came toward where we were standing and separated us quite quickly. It was so unexpected! Not without me trying to keep my grasp on Veronica though and she desperately clinging to me, screaming "Little Mummy, Little Mummy," her name for me. All

I could think of was to say loudly as I panicked, "Stop, stop. Please stop. I'll look after her!" but these women were well practised and immediately the two assigned to me steered me away toward the wide wooden staircase rising up from the entry. Although Veronica was very upset, still screaming out my name as they dragged her reluctantly away down a long high-ceilinged corridor, I assumed it to only be temporary and that she wasn't going far. As it must have been around 10 o'clock by then her tired little legs were not dealing well with walking. Surely she'd be in bed quite soon?

I didn't worry too much at first although the haunting echo of Veronica's high pitched frantic voice reverberated in our ears, taking what seemed ages to die away, which probably meant they had turned into another long corridor. We faced our own seemingly endless walk after climbing the wide daunting stairs lit by the biggest but not brightest lights I had ever seen. I only got a glimpse of them as my head soon drooped from not only physical exhaustion but also mentally trying to absorb what was happening to us. I knew the word 'orphanage' from somewhere but not its real meaning – only a place to be wary of. And where was Mary?

We ended up in a big white tiled and white painted bathroom with high opaque windows and five white baths in it, everything old fashioned and spotless, revealed by high but harsher bright lights here. One bath was filled nearly to the brim with very hot water by the amount of steam coming off it, and there was a smell of some dreadful disinfectant soap. There was no need for speech as it seemed to be a common procedure that everyone else was familiar with except me. My clothes, including my favourite cardy, were thrown in a woven hamper. I never saw them again. One of the two uniformed women, who had watched me as I reluctantly removed my clothes, on a nod from the other one, suddenly grabbed my arm and pushed me into the bath with the water in. That woke me up. I thought, 'She could have at least asked'. She promptly used a brush to scrub me.

I protested sharply, "This water is far too hot. Can I have some cold please? I am quite capable of washing myself thank you and a bit more gently too and anyway I have had my weekly bath already this morning."

Her face froze and I presumed she didn't like that I resisted but I was used to looking after myself – all of 9 years old. She nodded to the other woman who pulled a cord which must have had its other end attached to a bell or similar as within a few seconds a third uniformed woman appeared with a more aggressive demeanour. She also produced a short leather strap out of the side pocket of her darker blue uniform. Tipping her head with her firmly clipped hat stuck on her hair she said, "There will be no more speaking until you are spoken to. Do you understand?" Meanwhile her right hand let the dark brown strap dangle over the curve of the bath, just touching the bit of my shoulder showing above the oh so hot water. I immediately shrank down until it was covered too. I knew all about wet skin and straps.

When I was pushed to get out of the bath then roughly dried, I was given a coarse, cotton, full-length nightgown to put on that had prickly places in it. When I muttered, the stiff woman in charge standing by just watching with her arms folded, the strap back in her pocket, snapped, "Be thankful you have clothes at all and are clean and are also getting a bed to sleep in." As an aside to the other women, "How ungrateful could any child be?" I thought the remarks strange, as although our location often changed we had always had a bed and clothes. Not always a mother of course, like now.

Our little group, reduced to three again, eventually marched along another corridor, me dragging tiredly until I was eventually guided to a long room reminiscent of a hospital ward like Granddad's. (The cleaning process had only taken a few minutes – an indulgence though compared to future weekly bathing ablutions.) There were regular large windows down the outside wall with a neat row of white iron beds placed under them, and from the dim lighting here too I could see they were filled with girls who were covered to the chin by white cotton bedspreads. All were quiet but I felt their eyes on me watching intensely. The other side of the room had small partitioned cubicles with coloured curtains across, which also housed girls, but older ones, from the glimpse of the head that appeared for a quick peep as we passed by. The only empty bed was near the end of the room.

Before getting into it I politely and quietly spoke to the new staff member I had been handed over to, despite the previous warning, because I was so hungry. "I've had nothing to eat since lunch time. Could I have some food please?"

I was told, "Quiet. Get into bed. You can wait for breakfast" and louder, "Quiet!" again as we caught the sound of a stifled giggle. "It's lights out time. No more talking or someone won't get breakfast."

This must have been a threat that worked because no-one spoke and I lay there wondering what had happened to Veronica and when Mary was going to come and claim us. The next day I hoped. There was someone sitting out at a desk in the darkened corridor but after my first taste of real discipline and my food query I wasn't game enough to go and ask about anything else like where Veronica was and could I please go and say goodnight to her?

I thought about this place where no names were used and the woman's threatening attitude in the bathroom. She'd been so forbidding and cold I wondered if she was made of flesh. Nowhere in all our travels had I experienced anyone quite like her, even when I was tricked into staying in hospital on my own to get my tonsils out. She seemed to have no feelings at all, giving sharp orders when necessary which brooked no argument. I came to find out later that she was the all-powerful 'Matron'. I hoped wherever Veronica was the staff were a bit kinder and surely they would be with the smaller girls. Veronica was two and a half – a baby.

Still wondering how we had ended up in this dreadful place and worried about Veronica, I also felt really exhausted so kept dropping into micro-sleeps even with my wet hair, waking momentarily when an unidentifiable noise disturbed me. The last time it was the feeling of a soft hand slithering under the starched sheet instead and a caressing female voice asking to get into bed with me. Everyone else seemed asleep by the amount of snuffling and light snoring that had gradually replaced the silence, so the *intrusion was surprising but not unwelcome. I couldn't see anything of her but this new friendly voice was appreciated after the day's experiences.*

We whispered under the blankets for a while and she said her name was Heather but I kept drifting away from the sound of her voice and falling asleep. I eventually came up out of a deep dense dream-world to consciousness, a seemingly familiar warm body up against mine, and couldn't think why I was awake this time as I was used to Veronica and Mary in our big double bed together. As I was dropping down into the darkness again, a soft little hand crept between my inner thighs and began to rub. I was so shocked; I leapt out of bed immediately and stood looking down in horror at the shadow of my sweet-seeming intruder then pushed her unceremoniously onto the polished wooden floor and hissed at her.

There came the same suppressed giggle behind me and other tittering from girls down both the line of beds. Curtains were pulled back and girls leaned on their elbows to quietly watch. I could see their heads faintly from the dim corridor light. The night watcher there had left her post. Perhaps she was in on it too? This was obviously a common occurrence for a new target and they were waiting to see what the outcome would be and perhaps sometimes it all stayed quiet. The girl scuttled away to her own bed and I jumped back into mine. I tucked the bedclothes around me tightly, lying there for ages waiting, shivering slightly; ready for what might be next.

That seemed to be it though, with everyone gradually settling down again, and eventually sleep shut my eyes and brain down until the morning.

Waking, I got my bearings eventually, relating them to where we were and where the big front entry was. There was a good view out the windows and the girls' dormitory was on the second floor above the entry and to one side.

I only vaguely remembered climbing a wide staircase that had seemed endless the night before. Everything was so large I wondered, in shock still I think, if old fairy tales about giants were really true. The place reminded me of a picture we had at *home when we lived with our grandparents of where Grandad was born and was called 'a grand old English manor'. It had the same sort of front lawn that cricket or football could have been played on and a circular driveway, although this place seemed more oppressive somehow. Perhaps because there were no flower gardens or trees. The place felt undressed in my mind. I eventually found that Veronica's dormitory was in a one storey block at right angles to the main building which I could just see also.*

When the day's routine started everything was done in sequence and timed. Beds made, dressing – I was handed some large knickers, a blouse and an old school gym dress – middling ones were for school, best ones for any ceremonial occasion and old ones for work, I found later. The toilet queue came first then the next to wash, teeth cleaned and hair combed. The line must keep moving, especially with the hand mirror. With someone who had problems getting thick wavy hair to go where it should, there were set punishments which I also found out that first time. It wasn't a missed breakfast luckily, or so I thought. It was dusting. A lot of it and I'd be shown where once only. The fore-runner to every job, like scrubbing or polishing the long corridors, which seemed endless because everything was scaled up compared to a normal home. We children were the skivvies.

All I could think about though was breakfast and Veronica and I couldn't wait to see her. She had been crying when we were separated and she still was when I saw her again. She threw herself on me before anyone could stop her, pitifully asking where Mummy was. I could only hug her and make soothing sounds as I didn't know either. We were pulled apart but allowed to sit at the same table so that when breakfast came I could help her with it. Watching her was more upsetting than anything that had ever happened to me, even the violence. Veronica was inconsolable and I really, really couldn't think about Mary right then. I couldn't bear it for Veronica. I turned my face so she couldn't see me cry, something I seldom did, and wouldn't allow myself to sob.

Breakfast was porridge that she hated anyway and this was more like gruel with lumps and no sugar to help it down, plus a plate of stale bread with dripping instead of butter (like the school lunches later). You had to be quick for it too although there was supposed to be a piece each. I ate Veronica's gruel for her. I was so hungry that day I wanted it but vomited it up later on some subsequent mornings.

This was the forerunner to all meals I was to have with Veronica. Each was a torment listening to her sobs, probably driving everyone crazy although she was ignored. Veronica refused to eat at all quite often and no wonder as the food was overcooked and bland or there were things like tripe and onions which we had never had and tasted absolutely repellent to us. She would choke and vomit if someone came past and forced her so on the whole they left me to deal with Veronica which meant I often had nearly two portions of the same stuff to eat and regurgitate and a swift lesson on bread snatching. Veronica did eventually adjust to certain food and because meals were repetitive, hung out for them. I think drinks of milk might have saved her. It was very cheap then as we already knew as a family so it was probably more available with the little ones.

Like the dozens of other tables set in a huge hall we had all different aged girls at ours, probably families like us, and everything had to be eaten, we were reminded. Aside from a grace being read out, there did not seem to be any other form of worship in this religious establishment.

Several more wooden women sat at a table at the head of the room having their own breakfast and watching and listening. No-one spoke except for a few more staff in uniform who moved around the room monitoring anyone not behaving.

Veronica was sobbing still when it was time to go back to our own buildings again so one of the staff had to carry her away after tearing her off me. I could always hear her calling me anyway even when she was out of range. 'Little Mummy' seemed to go on and on in my head.

A few days after our arrival Veronica and I were unexpectedly taken to join a queue. It was for a haircut and the regular inspection of nits. Veronica had beautiful soft thick hair that dropped down into long dark ringlets. They of course had to go *and we were both given what was called a 'buster' cut (shaved high up the back of the head) because that's the only style the helper knew how to do apparently. Veronica looked at her hair as it fell down and mixed in with all the other girls' colours. Hers stood out as it was longer and she wailed louder than ever. I could imagine Mary's face if she ever came back for us which I had begun to doubt she would do.*

In the line on the day of the new haircut, one of the more vicious girls made it clear what everyone thought. "You better tell your sister to cut out that wailing and get used to this place because parents never come back for their kids."

I turned on her angrily. "You liar. Our mother will!" She laughed in my face as did everyone else lined up watching.

Our first full day there must have been a Sunday as the next morning I was given my school gym dress and white blouse and sent off to the local primary with other girls and a note for the head mistress. We all walked together and were accompanied by a staff member. School was better and not much different to other new schools. I had been to five one year already (ultimately 23), but I kept thinking about Veronica and what was happening to us, so had trouble concentrating. Doubt I learnt much that day or many others for a while.

The next Sunday I found we had a few free hours to ourselves and I was allowed to go down to Veronica's building. There was a small playground where sometimes a swing would cheer her up for a few minutes but her sad little face was the only thing that I really remember, strange though without her curls.

Another Sunday, such a precious day for Veronica and me, we missed seeing each other as it seemed everyone in our age group had to pick fruit in the Orphanage orchard. This felt like being let out of jail and we also mixed with the boys who I hadn't even known were there. A few girls found their brothers and could actually talk to them. We were mainly unsupervised in the open air and it was a sunny day though windy. I found it caused one of my teeth to ache and the ear on the same side so painfully, I eventually, in desperation began eating an apple (on the good side of my mouth) where I could be seen. I was considered ungrateful indulging myself after being given this once a year opportunity to be outside. Apparently not everyone had. This was punishable by scrubbing a hall floor. I remember looking at its length in despair but at least my tooth and ear weren't aching so intensely.

Aside from my terrifying 6ft 5in step-father in a rage, the most upsetting person to me was the visiting school dental nurse wherever we went, usually a white uniformed young woman with her special perky little hat that gave her stature and control in her own little horror-house set on the edge of the playground. She and her odd looking terrifying instruments really put the fear of God into me although I can't actually remember why – except to think 'pain' – so I seldom complained. If I was ever summoned to the horror-house from the class-room I was gone in seconds once outside in the grounds.

When the days and weeks then months went by, eventually almost a year, and Veronica was no better really, what that girl in the hair queue said about parents not coming back was all I could think about, especially when Veronica was around. I only ever saw her crying, possibly as when I was there she thought in her tiny mind I'd finally come to get her and take her away. Because she called me 'Little Mummy' she probably thought I had the power of a real mother and wouldn't have understood I did not.

Apparently one of the staff had told Veronica which window was above my bed in our second storey building and she would gaze up at it at night crying out for me or Mary. Unfortunately Mary had always indulged Veronica, trying to make up for her lonely start to life which had only exacerbated our situation. The Orphanage experience has stayed with me all my life and I know it had an absolutely devastating effect on Veronica.

I don't know how anyone ever really recovers from that sort of heartbreak. It's hard to even write about. The later repercussions around Veronica's mental health suggested she didn't.

We heard nothing from Mary, although the staff may just have had a policy not to tell the children about anyone contacting them. Mary finally turned up just before my tenth birthday on December 10[th,] nearly a year later. I was so angry about what was happening to Veronica, I took Mary for a walk around another of the huge empty grounds never played on by the children they were meant for, to a secluded area behind the building I slept in. I doubt she had ever seen me so angry and upset but I was desperate to help Veronica. What happened to her when I wasn't there was the worry. What punishment was handed out to young children? It wasn't her fault she couldn't adjust and it was just tormenting for her to see me only sometimes. I described our lives and especially Veronica's and told Mary that if she did not at least get Veronica out of there as soon as possible, there were going to be repercussions she would suffer from for the rest of her life that Mary would eventually have to handle. Never mind from me. I think now it was shock I saw on Mary's face. Perhaps she had assumed Veronica had been with me and I had been protecting her as usual.

Mary came for us just days before Christmas.

Revelations, Repercussions and Relaxing.

It was the Christmas School holidays so we went straight down to Onetangi on Waiheke Island, probably one of the most healing places we were familiar with and camped on land Mary and Uncle Ross owned there as we did each year. I had Veronica with me every day. Mary had to go up to work in the city during the week. We went down to the beach, swam, had walks every day and played games. After tea with foods that were familiar to her I would read to Veronica sitting on her bed until she fell asleep. There were nightmares sometimes for a while.

Veronica loved the beach and would sit for hours in the warm puddles the tide had left. She had her precious dolls again. And her hair grew back!

I later learned at an Orphanage reunion that there was another orphanage nearby in Papatoetoe run by the Anglicans where families were allowed to live together in separate chalets. The envy of the Presbyterian kids. It must have just seemed like a dream for them and perhaps it was.

I didn't know where Mary had been or what was happening while we were in the Orphanage. She never said. 60 years later when

Mark (Uncle Ross' son) was in contact again he told me by email that Mary had lived with them for a couple of years without Veronica and me. It could only have been one year though as I know where we were all the other years, but it did fill that gap.

Ralph had also boarded in their big old villa at the same time. He had been boarded out for years with someone once Mary married John. It was for his own safety. I think John was jealous of him. At this time he slept in Mark's big double bedroom with him, the closest thing to a brother he had. Mary had rented one of the other warmer front rooms facing north that had the usual push-up windows onto the villa's front veranda. She had found herself a job and also cooked for what was left of Uncle's family. The mother, who had been her friend, had long gone.

Ralph and I both called our mother Mary as she didn't actually feel very much like a mother. Mary was pretty casual about everything, especially Veronica. She indulged her as this was the second time she had been separated from Mary since she was born. The first was from birth to 6 months old in a home for unmarried mothers with their babies, the only place available. Mary was being treated and recovering from a near fatal illness after her birth. Veronica was always sickly and crying. When we were all together again for a while after Mary was first out of hospital my brother Ralph used to say about Veronica, "Throw her in the lake". We lived on the Rotorua lakefront. She drove us all nuts at times.

Mary eventually gave Veronica 'Condensed Milk' as the only food she could keep down. I have since thought she was probably allergic to full cow's milk as my own children were later.

Once divorced from John, for the rest of her life Mary just winged it as best she could depending on jobs, accommodation and money. I was the main babysitter.

I never experienced any violence at the Orphanage, although I had had the strap at school for sneezing, (a teacher's bad day) but then I never did anything seriously wrong aside from avoiding the Dental Nurse. Harsh punishment was normal though not really suitable or useful for everyone. Boys at the Orphanage would have been considered appropriate. The girls perhaps were only threatened with it. I don't actually know what the smaller children suffered, beside lack of love which we all did. Talking between the 'inmates' was not encouraged so only the long stayers knew what went on. Staff may have been thoughtless, incompetent, over-controlling and sometimes cruel but reading about the sexual molestation in these sorts of places still happening in the 1950's makes me grateful for things not being worse for us.

A few months after we had been there, Veronica's photo was on the front page of the NZ Herald that I was years later proudly shown by Aunt May and her daughter Colleen. The write-up for this Orphanage sounded so good I would have believed it to be true too, as they did. The best way to distract Veronica was with dolls – she always got involved in her imagination and her made up world. They were little people to her and they all had names, and were as precious to her as teddy bears seem to be to many children and adults. The huge lawn the photo was taken on out the front of the main building seemed an idyllic playground. There was a lovely shot of Veronica, who was a pretty little girl, with a worn cane dolls pram and accompanying dolls that set off an idyllic dream.

I never saw anyone on that field ever when I was there nor Veronica not crying. I was amazed and also glad for her that she had some happiness at times. Her appealing photo certainly would have tugged at the heart strings and raised money for the charity if that was the aim. It impressed Aunt May and Colleen.

Ironically it was them turning us away one night that created the situation for us to end up in the Orphanage I found out years later. They never knew. I didn't have the heart to ever tell them and didn't know their side of the story. Colleen anyway would never have wished the Orphanage experience on us.

It was as a consequence of my stepfather's behaviour and his aunty's rejection of us. The stilted memory of going to Aunt May's one evening with our bags and her not allowing us in when we knocked and all the fuss around that was the day before our going to the Orphanage. This memory was indistinct I think because I didn't want to remember. It was the first time I had ever seen Mary cry in front of anyone. It wasn't what she normally did except when John was hitting her but that was behind closed doors. Colleen who stood looking so upset behind her mother was also crying. I remember being really puzzled as we walked back up the hill to get the tram. It was getting dark and we were back in the city not near our last house in the country. We never had much money I knew and now nowhere else to go either.

This had been the plan that normally worked. Aunt May was Veronica's direct bloodline, her great aunt, and she knew how violent her nephew was. It was puzzling although the last time we had stayed Veronica was old enough to want to play with things that Aunt May would possibly not want her to. She had no other young children around. It could have been something else but those sort of questions were never asked.

Colleen would regularly come down to Onetangi for the weekend when we started living there after the Orphanage, bringing food and laughter and always remained my friend until her own Alzheimer's many years later. Then she didn't recognise me although I was the only family she had left, never marrying. I was happy to organise her care and visit. She was the one constant person of only a couple who had known me all my life. Friends were precious.

Also my own behaviour and strong sense of responsibility toward Veronica was answered 80 years later. My enlightenment was revealed on a TV programme in 2021 about young family members spending many hours of their childhood helping look after one of their siblings who had some form of a mental or physical problem, in fact acting as a loving de-facto parent. I recognised that was part of my life so finally something of my bewildering childhood made sense. Many others would have been enlightened too I would think. The programme was about these caring children being recognised and supported as 'Youth Carers' to be paid separately from 'Adult Carers' by the Government. The person supporting that was brilliant.

The words 'abandoned' or 'bewildered' had no meaning to me as a child. It was only much later in life I understood what had *happened to me and why I felt as I did. I realised Mary had often abandoned me. On occasions in Queen St. when I was small, as well as other times, with maybe friends or anyone useful. When Mary was heading up to Auckland, she left me with the grocery store owner who I would guess was charmed by her. His wife was certainly not best pleased when he turned up with me after work. He had been told by Mary I was a good worker so his wife made sure I helped with everything. They had three children under four. I was six and a half. She looked totally exhausted and worn down.*

I think kind Aunt Alice was the one who filled the most gaps, especially long term, but I seemed too often to be somewhere unexpected or trying to find my way back to Mary – sometimes in an unknown area on a long distance bus I'd never been on before or in the city on a tram. Someone would have started me on the journey and I would have had instructions – though not written ones or I'd have probably felt safer. The trams didn't worry me so much as the conductor could be asked questions. I am talking from around 7 years old. It was a different world then and so was Mary.

Intermediate

My first year at an intermediate school was when we were living again with Arnold, my real father. (Std. 5 & 6 or Form 1 & 2 are now called years 7 & 8). Most days I rode my bike to Normal Intermediate in Mt Eden, which was a bit of a shock after the primary years in small mixed classes in country schools. The core curriculum subjects were English, social studies, general science, mathematics, music, physical education and art or crafts. There was also woodwork for the boys and sewing for the girls which, because Mary was quite a skilled seamstress, I seemed to know more about than the teacher. Most of the city children were well ahead of me academically, the result of my going to too many schools, getting subjects repeated and missing others, so I was put in the bottom class.

I don't think it worried me particularly, as I was more interested in what was going on in such a big school. There was more teasing from boys than I had experienced, calls of 'four eyes' for those unfortunate enough to have to wear glasses but especially when breasts began to appear on the girls (me being one) and when the teacher used the word 'period' referring to class times. There was a set of twins, a novelty for everyone as they were identical or seemed so to us and when we saw them in the playground we were fascinated, trying to decide which was which – they were so pretty too. There was a very talented girl called Desiree, whose name sounded exotic which is why I remember it, who could walk the length of the football field on her hands. They had new games, especially skipping ones I had not come across before. It felt a very sophisticated place.

After a while I was moved up a class, this time to a male teacher called Mr. Robinson who everyone seemed quite wary of. I got on fine with him and he even gave me a second chance in an exam once, asking me to go up to his desk and to answer a question on fractions. He asked me several different ways to no avail. I didn't have a clue as I had never come across them before and didn't know what he was getting at. (Later some kind person used a sectioned orange to show me – a revelation and such a simple example!)

It must have put Mr. Robinson off me as not long after he came in one morning, grumpier than usual, and said that the next person that moved would get the strap and unfortunately, I tried to suppress a sneeze. 'The cuts' were given for pretty much anything then. I was marched out of the room into the corridor and told to find a lady teacher to strap me. When I did find one, she was horrified when she found out why, but got her strap and gave me a couple of slaps anyway. I was more puzzled (sneezing wasn't an action I could control) than mortified, especially when I found the upside was I had gained respect from the other children. (Corporal punishment was abolished in the 1980's.) I think Mr. Robinson may have felt bad because later in the year he patted me on the head one day and said; "You'll do". He also gave me a good part in our school play which I enjoyed.

High School

Auckland Girls Grammar School (AGGS)

The first year of Auckland Girls Grammar School was a very different experience. Uniforms were not always worn by children before secondary school, though some intermediates did and also private school pupils from the primers. The heavy, yoked, triple box pleated, navy woollen serge gymslip was a practical solution to the different shapes and sizes of growing girls and was interchangeable between schools with a change of monogram. The length was precise, 4 inches above the knee and was worn with a stiff collared (a pain to starch) long sleeved winter blouse and tie of navy & gold, monogrammed with our school letters entwined, matching our blazer pocket one. Underneath we wore navy bloomers and suspender belts for our stockings, usually rayon or lisle. Hats (felt in winter, panama in summer) had the school hatband and were worn with gloves and polished shoes – all to regulation. This heavy outfit was worn all year round for years and in the Auckland summer heat must have been shocking for pupils. Luckily the new summer lighter weight uniform for the hotter months was introduced in 1951, during the years I was there, the short sleeved white blouse with Peter Pan collar not requiring a tie.

Prefects monitored us as we left the school grounds and if they saw us outside of them not in full regalia, we were punished. I was often pulled up with holes in my stockings (darned holes were acceptable) and crooked seams, but with little money and no Mary around with the darning box, if I saw a prefect I scarpered. It was shoes that worried me the most. Not having worn them much ever and especially not on Waiheke the previous year at school, heavy shoes were painful. They were the bane of my life.

Fitting in

Where I was used to maybe 50 children in a little friendly country style school, not knowing anyone of the thousand girls at Grammar, except Bev Brown my long ago friend from Levonia St., was daunting even for me. I had started late (because of having my appendectomy) in the first term at 12 and was put in the only class that by that time had any spare room, Home (Science) Economics. It all seemed such a waste of time as cooking was nothing new to me, just the full white apron and hat. Other related occupations were familiar too. The girls there were obviously seen by their parents and perhaps others, as getting married fairly quickly so were being taught the housewifely basics, although it could have been the basic course for nurses too. The sewing part of the curriculum was enjoyable though as it appealed to my creative side. (Boys had woodwork and crafts at their schools. I missed their irreverent toilet humour and less intense attitudes.)

The numbers, noise and sheer size of everything was difficult to adjust to and it took a while before I was absorbed into this stream of females in a totally alien environment combined with having to adjust to the formality and snobbish and tiered social structure of each year's level. Getting lost was the worst learning curve, never mind the new subjects. I felt like the proverbial fish out of water, wanting to but also resisting becoming part of the swarm of a thousand girls in repetitious black and white clothes. It was not the colourful, carefree, country style I was used to.

Some girls had come as a group from the same intermediate schools and knew and would help each other, forming their own little cliques. Being late I'd missed the introduction and instructions they'd probably had, so with every girl a stranger in class, it was all very confusing.

We did have our own form room and teacher but we were seldom there and the challenge each day was to keep up with the others and find my way around the huge grounds, old-fashioned buildings, and scattered new prefabs set down below the main building level, never mind the lessons. I daren't go to the toilet other than lunch or play as I'd never find anyone again and get nabbed and punished by a prefect or teacher for not being in class. No-one pointed out a map in the hall to me for months, which had classrooms marked and numbered to match the class timetable. I don't know what else I missed.

If I was ever lucky enough to have a penny or two, there was a 'tuck' shop with a few things on offer but I seldom had the dosh to buy anything so I can't remember, not sweets or soft drinks though I don't think. As the queue for it was never very long I didn't think there was much to miss. Free milk was delivered to Grammar too, although not many of us were interested, especially in the summer unless it was consumed at morning break. Crates were left exposed at a small top gate and the heat from the sun would turn it.

Bev would rescue me some lunch-times. She had always been in contact with us when we were back intermittently in Auckland, and she had visited me in hospital when I'd had my appendix out. I'd been so pleased to see her. She was in a year ahead of me though, so her friends were not impressed and rightly resented her concerned interest but Bev knew some of our family history and looked out for me. Part way through the first year one of the girls in my class, Rita, who I liked and was herself only on the periphery of a popular group, asked if she could be my friend. It was such an unusual experience for me that I turned her down, not even explaining about Bev, and have always regretted it. Also, it was habit to be alone and though I was grateful to Bev, it was strange to have someone take care of me – I sometimes resented it, used to my freedom.

Bullies were the curse of school buses in the country, especially for new kids that weren't onto the local protocols, so I'd had some bad times on them. I must have had enough of that and was very aware of a girl in our class who had her own little gang that would stand behind her, sneering and nodding when she picked on someone. It was awful to watch and most of us couldn't understand why she bothered. She only did it to girls outside a group or when she caught others on their own.

One Friday, after I had felt her eyes on me all week, I thought, 'My turn's coming.' I couldn't bear to think of it all weekend and worry about school on the Monday, so just on home time I caught up with her as she was leaving. She had made some smart remark to her friends and they were laughing as they walked out the door ahead of her, so she was on a high when I confronted her briefly and very carefully and tightly, looking her straight in the eye said, "Don't even think about picking on me or you will be very sorry," and walked away – so I didn't see her reaction. I still worried all weekend as it had taken a lot of my courage to do that after earlier experiences and, as I didn't want to be nasty to anyone, had no idea what I would do if she and her cohorts ganged up on me, but knew I wouldn't just cower.

Monday came but she didn't. She never came back to Grammar and we didn't find out what happened. Whatever the reason I was very careful after that not to even appear to hex anyone again, ever, even when pushed to extremes – and I was. Mind you bullies are usually cowards.

Bev left in my second year and I found my own friends eventually. One was very bright, often coming top in tests and exams. It was good competing with her although I don't think she saw it as a competition, even if I occasionally did better, as she was too self-confident in the knowledge of her ability. Not in a vain way, just that it was who she was. It amazed us all that she could even get her homework done as she was from a large noisy family but had apparently learned to shut herself off and focus. Barbara was also in a Highland Band which intrigued us. She eventually became a hospital matron I think, at least well up in the hospital staff hierarchy – which she would have thoroughly deserved. A capable, competent, and caring person.

My other friend Barbara was a chatterer. She also had a 'thing' about our lovely music teacher, like many other girls, and would rave on about her if I would listen. It wasn't something I understood and it drove me mad, distracting me in class until in the end I had to break up with her, which was really upsetting for everyone. I doubt that either of the Barbaras forgave me but the headmistress had managed to get me a scholarship when Mary had wanted me to leave and go to work at 15. I felt a strong obligation to do well, my way of learning was to picture the day, and I lost concentration with Barbara's constant chatter.

Once I was alone, my mind was clearer and different things caught my attention. Sometimes it was a girl, an incredible artist, who would sit drawing the class accurately with insight and throw the paper in the rubbish at the end of the lesson. I would often rescue it for later to remember when studying. We had some classes part of the year in a prefab, where young guys were *outside painting – that was pretty distracting and memorable. Other times it was the teacher, the colour and style of her frock, what the weather was like, perhaps the interruptions or what was on the board; the lesson would come back to me from those pictures in my mind when I needed them.*

None of this had been achievable with Barbara chatting. She left at the end of the second year at 15, as did many other girls, and although I had already missed her as a friend, it was a relief.

We were all moving forward together each year, but dynamics changed with a smaller class and also when new people came in from other schools. Another Bev, a very gregarious person, became my friend and was one of the best. She was there at a time for me later when no-one else was. Friendships formed in youth are precious and irreplaceable. There sometimes seems to be a finite time to be close with someone too, but the pleasure and comfort of the memories never leave us.

The fifth year was the most challenging intellectually with the School Certificate exam but for the first time I gradually realised I at last had a sense of belonging. Three years was an amazing amount of time to be at the same school, even if I shifted accommodation each year. There was reassurance in knowing I wouldn't be forced to move on to another school as well. It was different too in that it was my final one (the 23rd) and Mary had actually bought me a watch and a signature ring as I did so well. I had blended in with the rest as much as I ever would.

Our teachers became more inter-active as we matured and we had one lovely teacher who, unusually, was married and left in my second year to have a baby and was greatly missed. Our single maths mistress was a strong character, a tiny, older woman who was always interesting and brought up subjects sometimes like the height and shoe sizes of girls of the day. (Probably out of boredom.) She said the average size shoe/boot was an English 3 and a girl's height about five feet, when she was young, which would probably have been at the turn of the century. Mostly we were over five feet with shoe sizes to match and we seemed giants to her, as the girls of today are to our generation, including my own granddaughters.

Joan Hastings, a former swimmer who had won a silver medal as part of the women's 440 yard freestyle relay at the 1950 British Empire Games, was one of our teachers and I came across my last form teacher Miss Hogan, whom we all liked. Years later I became a neighbour of her sister Ngaire. I went to Miss Hogan's funeral with Ngaire to support her, as did other neighbours including my best friend, Ethel, her sister-in-law. I was glad to be there as were representatives from her time as Head Mistress of Rotorua Girls High, which she had been promoted to. Another previous form mistress, Miss Ryburn, also became a head mistress at Westlake Girls High, so we had good teachers.

Although Latin was taught as was chemistry in the senior school the subjects I knew about were elocution, physical education, English, French, typing, core and other maths, science split later to biology and human biology, geography, music, cooking, arts and crafts, sewing and history – mainly British. My own choice of a course, had I been given an option, would have been maths and commercial – typing & office work or professional or even just general. (Offices are where I spent my working life often looking after the money.)

With my spotty education I can't tell whether we were taught about our own country's history, although I would have thought at Grammar we would have been, and maybe we were but I only took History in my last year as a fill-in subject for School Certificate. I knew little about NZ history till well into my forties and that was because I became interested myself when my children came home talking about Maori migration and our wars with them and especially Parihaka.

Our sports mistress was very fit and held herself extremely well so it was difficult to determine her age. Our clothing for her phys-ed classes was full, black pleated cotton rompers, white socks, and white sandshoes with our white open necked blouses. Sports were encouraged and we played in our lunch hour as well sometimes. I enjoyed cricket, basketball (more like today's netball) and swimming, and there was tennis and possibly hockey. Marching (a NZ innovation for girls from the early 1900's, often held in derision) may have been a choice but not mine. We also competed in races at regular sports days, sometimes in the nearby Western Park. When I wanted some peace and quiet, I would go and eat my lunch there too, embracing the harbour view and green grass and trees, yearning for a bit of country around me.

Along with a song, possibly a hymn and maybe a prayer (that obviously made no impression on me), all notices and housekeeping type rules were given each morning at assembly by the headmistress, Rua Gardner, who I doubt ever missed a day at school. She was a strict, fair school head who was very aware of her charges and their problems, and seemed to know everyone's name. She certainly knew mine. I sat outside her office quite often waiting to be seen. Mainly in my first year, especially for being late. Where I had been boarding at that time, the mother used to pop over to neighbours to chat quite early and forget to come back. I couldn't leave the new baby on his own so had to wait. Rua put a stop to that once I finally told her but I never found out how.

One year Rua announced that a senior girl had died, which left us all sad and aware of our own mortality for a while. It wasn't as common as it had once been to hear of the death of a child, although the news may have been kept from us.

The seniors had their own orchestra and produced plays for the school and parents at the end of each year. We combined with Auckland Boys Grammar and the results were inspiring. The one I remember most was just so well produced and performed, the actors could have all been much older if you didn't know. The hero and heroine love scene at the end would have challenged any professional they performed so well.

We had singing lessons in the assembly hall too. It was the centre of the main building with a mezzanine floor above and both floors had classrooms opening off them. If you haven't heard a collection of young female choir voices in an appropriate setting, especially a thousand girls, there is just no way to appreciate the beauty and emotion of that sound. "And did those feet in ancient times, walk upon England's mountains green…" would sound as lovely there as anywhere in the world, especially in this replica of an English building. Miss Gardner would stand looking very proud, in her black gown, on the raised platform, her diamond earrings catching the high ceiling lights whenever she moved her head to look at us all, 'Her girls'.

Ralph

Meantime, Ralph went back and stayed with Aunt Alice and Uncle Henry again, Mary's old friends, and I think he relished his time at Rotorua High School and although he was the youngest boy there, he had good social skills and we did have a happy looking photo of him with a couple of mates who called themselves 'The Three Musketeers'. He had two of his front teeth chipped playing rugby, much to Mary's dismay, which meant like the rest of our family except Veronica, he eventually had all his teeth removed.

In 1947, Ralph spent some time at Mt Albert Grammar, when we lived that year in Three Kings with our own father, and I remember he wore his Air Force cadet's uniform on the days required. I think he felt quite dashing as did several others – just the age for most to be at their best although not perhaps the shorter boys. Many still had growth to come. The following year we went to live down on Waiheke Island so Ralph had to board again. I know he went to Seddon Tech in Wellesley St. but I don't know where he finished up before going to Auckland University although it may have been Auckland Grammar – an all boys' school then. Like other males at 18, Ralph did his territorial service (ACT) and compulsory military training (voted for overwhelmingly by New Zealanders in 1949) in the Royal NZ Air Force.

Chapter 14 Different Cultures

(Some of this information about Maori is from a handed-down memory so I may not have all the details right but there is no offence intended and I apologise in advance if anyone is upset by anything I have written. That goes for other cultures as well. It was simply how I remembered, was told or interpreted situations. Corrections are welcomed.)

Maori were mainly in the North Island and were usually full-blooded in Mary's day and a familiar part of her and our grandparents' lives. They were her dad's work force, living in pas at the turn of the 20th century when he was managing the building and installation of Rotorua town's first Power Station. It was built at the convenient Okere Falls, so Mary spoke a little Maori and could follow a conversation.

They had all known Guide Rangi from Whaka quite well and local Maori still lived there then too in fairly primitive conditions. I can remember some there still in the early 1940's. There were small whares set above the hot pools and some of their cooking was done in them with a string of flax holding the woven baskets that were dropped over the edge. Flaxes, various kinds for their many different purposes, were very precious to Maori.

Near-naked children of all ages were everywhere (no-one seemed worried about the dangers of boiling pools) and from quite young they would ask tourists to throw money off a local bridge into the river and with their practised brown bodies, the kids would dive in after the coins – often big half-pennies and pennies. The human entertainment of the day when they appeared above water quite quickly to the tourist claps – sometimes after a brief fight among themselves as that would be part of their family income. (The water must have been pretty clear then) Although Rotorua and the Whaka geysers were the main attractions, unique in their way, the constant smell of sulphur put many people off visiting but it was the original New Zealand tourist town.

Granddad had a lot of respect for Maori leaders as they seemed to have been born with a Mana that cannot be fabricated. He helped them with our language and like Mary, he too knew a smattering of theirs. I don't think it particularly occurred to him that he might have been judged because of that, although Pakeha society had little to do with Maori socially, that was not most people's way then. There were of course some mixed marriages, a Pakeha man with a Maori woman mainly. (My daughters have a Maori woman ancestor, purported to be a princess, back four generations so it was not uncommon). After Granddad and Nana left Rotorua to live in Auckland in the thirties, they would talk with sadness of all those Maori families they had known dying out. They and the general population genuinely thought it was the end of the Maori race as a people. At the turn of the century in the 1901 Census Maori were only 5.3% of the population. *NZ Herald* 05/03/16. 1920 – 5,300 1930 – 6700.

There was an original Maori Pa still at Okahu Bay close to Auckland City, where the church is now, when I was young. The Maori were forcibly evicted from there in 1952. I understood the excuse used was because there had been a fire. Mary was quite horrified although understood the thinking behind it – but not the awful way it was accomplished. Coincidentally the Queen visited NZ in 1953.

Maori Interaction

Until we shifted next to the Waititi stream in Ngongotaha, near Rotorua, toward the end of the war, we children had not come across Maori so we had no idea how to deal with them. Being familiar ground to Mary she felt comfortable there though and once when Veronica was about two years old, we were sitting in facing seats near the rear of a bus with two Maori women opposite us who were chatting in their language. When our stop came and we rose to go, Mary sweetly thanked them for their kind remarks about how pretty Veronica was. They seemed to be totally stunned that anyone as well spoken and dressed like Mary would have understood Maori. They didn't have time to recover and respond before we were gone.

Ralph however, must have said or done something to upset someone though, perhaps at school, as when he was 11 he was attacked by three big Maori girls on his way home. They wanted his bike. I was abused by girls on the school bus too when I was new and sat in the wrong seat, which may have been from the same three. I think they were just the local bullies and not many would stand up to them.

After the war there was a drift of young Maori to the towns but also the two cities, Wellington and Auckland, where they would be looking for jobs and could initially rely on relations for succour. When it continued too long, I understand it was not always appreciated. Probably dazzled by the city options and appreciating especially the music and entertainment scene, they became part of the city culture. In Auckland in 1948 they had the Maori Community Centre near Freemans Bay to meet with others in similar circumstances and create their own way of life which must have helped with feelings of dislocation.

This period changed Maori and our society forever. Maori didn't die out. According to local gossip, when the Government brought in the Family Benefit, it encouraged families to have more children, which may have been their way to survival. Nana, chatting to their older women when she ran the Post Office at Okere, had assumed from conversations it was common to use native plants to control pregnancies, as from her observation they did not have the large numbers of children they did later. This may have only been the locals though and the different tribes will all have their own stories.

At Grammar in the early 1950's we had two Maori girls in the upper classes, they may have been sisters, but they were the only ones that I remember seeing there – a bit different today. The 6th & 7th formers had their own little eyrie at the top of the main building where they mostly hung out (which I peeped into once), so we only knew about the two girls because there was a fuss over discrimination of some kind and we all were told to be aware of not offending. None of us could imagine we would do it deliberately and I personally felt uncomfortable that the Maori girls had felt bad enough to have it drawn to attention at an assembly.

When working in the BNZ in Queen St. in 1954, there was a well-educated, very well-mannered, bright and aware Maori girl in our intake, maybe the first employed. She was conscious of her behaviour and her unique position and what may affect her employment, probably conscious of others following. She also agreed with our boss when I mentioned to her I had been told off by him for walking down Queen Street holding hands with my boyfriend. I was surprised. (Once intermarriage became more common friendships were easier.)

Other Cultures

I don't know what the fear was about Indians. I only associate them with green-grocery shops in the fifties, vegetable delivery vans, and pretty dark-haired girls at school. A work colleague of mixed Dutch/Indian parentage I met years after, who became my friend, was one of the most beautiful girls I had ever seen. We were more aware of Dutch settlers in the 60s, although 1500 came in during the late forties and early fifties, and Dallies (Dalmatians) were familiar, especially up north.

Pacific Islanders or any other nationalities were off the radar for us. When they did arrive they seemed to congregate in areas like Freeman's Bay which was not a choice piece of real estate. A friend's father had his grocery shop in Ponsonby and used to act as an unpaid social worker for them with general information and helping out with government papers etc.

When my nana first lived in Grey Lynn there may have been a Chinese man with a horse and cart of fruit and vegetables as I remember her talking about one, but not seeing him. When we went to live in Panmure, there were still Chinese market gardens at the top of Kings Rd. in the early 1950's. We passed them on the way to the bus stop.

The families would be out early, weeding and watering the vegetables, I think mostly women (it was hard to tell with their clothing and hats) squatting along the rows, where Mary said the women often also had their babies. This to us was an amazing, unhealthy and an alienating practice. The Chinese restaurants of today were well into the future, rice seen as being a meal for Orientals only, a sweet pudding to us. There also seemed to be a hangover of fear from the past with adults about being invaded by Orientals in general. I don't remember other cultures much at school or anywhere else really and perhaps the people were around but kept to themselves.

Chapter 15 Religion

This was paid homage to. Everyone said they went to church, or at least belonged to a particular faith, even if they didn't, because of a perceived intolerance in society in general for atheists. Going to Sunday services was more about social expectations and face, and one hypocritical boss I had, told me outright that he got many of his business customers from this ritual. I don't think many really cared that much, no-one we knew anyway, except perhaps dedicated Christians. Methodists, Brethren and Catholics come to mind. Some of whom would have gone to church for help and received support and succour, but many felt that the dictatorial, distant, and unrealistic expectations of the clergy did not relate much to ordinary lives. But even those that didn't attend or had different beliefs must have felt reasonably comfortable in accepting the moral and philosophical codes that the churches upheld in general, given society's attitude. During the Depression and the Second World War, praying and Sunday attendances would have been thought about more seriously.

Aside from Mary in later years, our family had always felt sorry for the conforming, dictated to, and particularly constricted lifestyle and lack of choice for many religions, especially the strict Brethren, Methodists, and Catholics. The number of times they went to church on Sundays and the Catholics for having to go to 'Confession', which most saw as amusing, an excuse to repeat offences. I had to laugh years later, when I had a close Catholic (RC) friend, who confided in me that their authoritarian Catholic family, who went many times a day to church on Sunday on the way over to NZ on a boat, felt sorry for anyone that wasn't one. It seemed ironic looking back.

Catholic women in particular, especially when they went shopping, struggled along with all the mandatory children clustered around a worn cane pram, usually with a new baby in it, another not much older balanced on the end and the rest holding hands. One loud outspoken gossip indignantly harangued Mary one day, after seeing her speak to an acquaintance in this situation.

"Fancy a senile old man in Rome telling young people how to live! What would he know about marital relations (these words in a more hushed voice) and coping with all these children and trying to feed them? And for whose benefit? We'll be overrun by Catholics before you know it! They're all so clanny too, giving each other jobs, especially in the government, and thinking they're better than us. Well, poof to them. And as for confession, well, I tell you, it's just an excuse to be able to go off and do it all again! And that Father O'Riley, have you seen the way he ogles the girls!" Etc. etc.

My non-religious neighbour in Otahuhu who had married a Catholic, went to church regularly as she had conscientiously promised to, taking their four children. After about seven years attendance when she was seldom acknowledged and sometimes criticized, and had made no friends, she gave it away. Those people do not know what they missed.

Girls were warned off marrying Catholics, as Catholics were of us. I can remember Mary saying to me, "Don't think you are going to marry a Maori or a Catholic!" Comical really to think about with her record of choices which put me off marrying at all. (My second husband was the one with a Maori princess ancestor. Mary didn't believe it when she found out. He and the girls had very blue eyes.)

To the Catholics we were 'the Heathen doomed to Hell', so intermarriage was unacceptable from either side, and to have the courage to unite in a civil ceremony was considered very brave and foolhardy as well, especially for the girl as she was often cut off from her family for the rest of her life. A few of both sexes acquiesced to the rigours of a faith change, but not anyone we came in contact with except my friend. One couple we did know waited until the girl was 21 and then married. I don't know her parents' side of it, and they were the Catholic ones, but these two were so suited to each other and had waited so long to be together, everyone we knew wished them well. They had a baby after a year or so but the new mother didn't make it home as a previous tennis injury had caused a clot that moved to her heart just after her baby's birth. A tragedy for everyone.

I also had a Jewish friend briefly and she was really paranoid about me not telling anyone else about her faith. I had found out by accident and didn't quite understand her problem as those sorts of religious issues never came up in our family. However I kept her secret and was intrigued by many aspects of her life. Mary said Granddad had the look of a Jew and we probably had been practising Jews in the past. I doubt Granddad would ever have been – he was far too irreverent.

Sunday school was a form of bored torture or sometimes just plain terrifying, depending on the denomination, for us children. Mary sent us off to whatever was available as people were expected to keep up with conformity. She had already transgressed by divorcing.

Peter Lineman, Christian and Religious Historian, I understand has the view that Christianity and religion gives a sense of identity and belonging. I hope it does for some at least and I wish it had been true for me, but it didn't work and I have had many people try to convert me, including my mother and sister as an adult.

I think I was conscious of the feeling of change in the 1960s to people having even less faith in religion, although perhaps not the ultimate outcome, if times were desperate. I personally felt freer and that helped me legitimately to act on my decisions, even though the price later became so high I doubted myself. That was the time when our 'swinging sixties massive social change came to what had been a very conservative and Christian unchanging society.'

Chapter 16 Country Living 1940's to 1950's.

Power

There was no electric power for a long time in the country and even into the 1950's in the city there were power cuts. I also remember more than one farmer having their own generator for back-up for their milking machines, with much abuse about 'the powers that be'. (Farmers were often powerful people themselves in regard to government decisions.) Back-country bush settlements seldom had a power option. Reefton had the first public supply of electricity in NZ including the first street lights in the Southern Hemisphere, first for gold then coal production. Several places had power because it was needed to produce gold or like Rotorua as it was a tourist town. My maternal granddad was involved in that.

A Bushman's Life

My stepfather John was the ideal build for his trade and it served him well. I couldn't imagine him doing anything else although at times he did, sometimes farm work. His huge broad-shouldered physique of 6ft 5in (1.95m) and immense strength was useful both in the bush for wielding an axe or a cross-cut saw and at any time for heavy lifting or shifting in the big steam-run saw-mills. He was a bench-man or a tailer-out in the mill – beware fingers on the big band saws – where he was also later exposed to cyanide and pesticides used to treat pine timber. Not something I understood at the time but which may have accounted for some of his behaviour.

The trees were transported by various means after they were cut. Originally they used bullocks for haulage or wooden lines (unlike trains) for trams and wagons, though sometimes just the steep terrain sufficed. Control was always risky. Where the cutting location was near a river, they could be stored in the water, depending on the timber type. A dam would be erected and then eventually cleared of logs when the water was high enough after removing part of the dam. By the 1940's, normal although closer-set rail lines had been laid and steam engines were used dragging lines of flat-decked wagons of logs. These were the times we may have had use of a ubiquitous trigger to travel to the local town after work hours. Other memories are of the huge and dangerous articulated logging trucks driving on basic roads, not always even metalled. Heavy chains kept the logs in place until they didn't.

Although John's temperament would not have been as suited as his physique to his job and males would only refer to him as 'Lofty' once, there must have been a reasonable level of trust between himself and other bush-men as it was such a dangerous job and men regularly worked in partnerships. In its way a unique job, given the isolation, primitive surroundings and often living conditions. Certainly I was told by an old acquaintance of his at his funeral that John really knew his job and was admired and respected for that and also his incredible power, which most of his work-mates were also wary of, he said.

John probably enjoyed being in the bush the most as it was the sort of life he would be familiar with, the surroundings of his childhood with the trees, birds and streams in often virgin, steep country and although tough and uncomfortable on the job, it was where he would have been happiest.

The men-only accommodation in the bush in his day, around the thirties, was usually a cleared area for buildings, larger in some places for shared quarters, although it may not have been on especially flat ground. Some had a separate cookhouse with a cook employed by the timber company; however, knowing John he would have had a hut on his own – a bit separate. A handy stream would be necessary for water, to be hauled to buildings for ablutions and cooking. If they weren't sure of it for drinking, buckets or any handy containers were placed strategically by the huts for catching roof water as we did at Mokai. There may have been general baths also provided by the company however they were never mentioned.

The simple one room bush-men's huts were common dwellings onsite. Usually built as close as was convenient to work, with materials to hand including shingles made from the timber of the surrounding trees and set over a framework of saplings. The exterior roof and wall cladding were made from corrugated iron along with a distinctively large-bottomed chimney. The heat and the cold would have been very uncomfortable. Most of these huts, whatever they were built from, did not run to glass for windows and if there were any holes cut out, they were usually covered in sacks. The dirt hardened floor was packed down by boots. Open fires would have served up warmth with food cooked in either black pots or camp ovens and cast-iron kettles hung from an internally suspended iron bar. If the fireplace had been made from wood, it would probably have been lined with a plaster of clay and grass. Nikau palm cast-offs were often used in chimneys.

Most of the time in logging situations, depending on the weather, terrain, location and the denseness of overhanging trees, mist and low cloud were common. Everything would be damp and clothing would always need hanging up, which was casually done on a nail straight into the unlined wall supports near the fire to keep dry. (John would often do that in a normal rented house later on too, much to my refined mother's horror.)

Any amount of wood would have been available but tea-tree (Manuka) was the most versatile kind for a handmade washstand-come-bench, a bedside locker, a primitive chair or stool as well as for fire-wood. For his methodical careful shave each morning, while looking into his deteriorating mirror (he always brought it home with him along with the rest of his gear), John used the bench bowl with his old mug, a handy towel and his cut throat razor. He sharpened this on his hanging leather razor strop that had several uses, and the lathered soap for shaving may have been common laundry Sunlight. (No perfumed spray cans of foam or safety razors.)

The bunk bed was usually of rough sacking stretched onto an extra-long frame, probably tea-tree too, and nailed in place. John's height was always a problem so bedding needed to be longer like his substitute mattress, normally made of sacks stuffed with anything available including bracken fern or mingimingi. A top covering of a quilt was common and John used one of Nana's old faded patterned feather ones, with possibly newspaper added for more warmth in winter. However I always associate John with the universally used and distinctive smell of slightly damp, *grey woollen blankets, so he may have been better off than most with one of those.*

Food that would attract rats, like meat, was usually delivered by horse pack with a few other things once a week (unless there was a rail to the mill and a store) and hung high on sheltering trees in a safe along with butter for coolness. Inside the hut rough shelves held things like a set of knife, fork and spoon, plates, tobacco (in its own tin) and any patent medicines – popular in that era. Protective tins, some with scenes on, the only real colour to lighten the often drab and dark dwellings, which stored tea, sugar, biscuits, flour, powdered milk, oats, dried peas and lentils etc., the latter for soups from leftover meat bones.

John's precious crosscut saws (not motorised then) would have hung from the wall, nearly filling one right across with its length. Maintaining them the most religious work he did during his one day off on Sunday. Each tooth carefully sharpened and set, his axes done on a grindstone and jacks cleaned and oiled.

The crosscut saws would be used after a scarf (notch) 8 to 10 feet long was chopped out of a tree near its base. This gave the direction for that side to fall, the area in front of it previously cleared of any growth that would divert it. That could be dangerous. Two men would each begin to saw on the other side of the tree to the scarf and opposite each other. It was very heavy, hard and tiring work and when eventually the tree did drop, knowing first from the sound, they would, 'Quickly scarper!' as the old bushmen told me.

Other men may have played cards to fill their evenings however John I know would have whittled wood carvings from native timber in his spare time, taking infinite care and precision with his sharp knives. His long body and broad shoulders hunched over in concentration in the light from a kerosene lamp or candle, with a roll-your-own cigarette hanging from his clamping lips, their odd colour not so noticeable and the smoke drifting up to his squinting deep, dark set eyes. His huge hands delicately created cradles, trains or anything that took his fancy, like a miniature stump with an axe set in it. A tool I always associated with him, its lines beautifully replicated.

In the times that we lived in the houses in mill settlements with him, a company boat or small train took the men to the work site, and he sometimes had a shed where he would do more woodwork in his time off. He'd fix or make things like a small piece of furniture, sanding the wood carefully to perfection, or something for me to play with if I asked, like stilts or a toboggan. A kindness to me and a pleasure for him.

John was a bush-man at a time when our native trees were being decimated but as far as I know, he was never in the north, where the Kauri grew. They were valuable because they self-pruned, not branching out until at least 10 or 12 metres above ground, their straight trunks especially useful for sailing ships' straight spars on early visitors' and settlers' boats. (NZ timber helped rebuild San Francisco houses destroyed by their earthquake.)

They usually wasted the useful tops, burning them for firewood. There was such an abundance of native trees then like Rimu, Miro, Rata, Kahikatea, Matai, Totara and Tawa although not all were cut. I don't however remember any sense of sadness in their destruction. The idea of conservation or that there would one day be an end to what the bush offered, was not at the top of many people's consciousness. There were square miles and miles of it to be lost in around us. We were more in awe at what had been achieved and the men would have been proud of themselves – it was not a job for weaklings.

It wasn't until I attended several funerals at a much older age I began to realise the regrets the bush-men did have. They used words like 'vandalism' and 'destruction' to describe their jobs and were by then appalled at what we had done to ourselves as a country – and they were the men who had achieved it. It was our own irreplaceably beautiful living, breathing bush we had destroyed – where we could experience so much pleasure and peace just looking at it and being in it. Always the sounds of the birds present and everything was vibrantly alive and flourishing. How could we have done this – as a nation? Like every generation who has watched changes, the full picture came with many regrets. This however was a whole country and after millions of years.

Our first taste of Country

On what I'd originally thought of as Mary and John's honeymoon and had imagined was only a few weeks, my brother Ralph says we lived at Mokai for a while. Mary and John would not have been recently married but I'm not sure how much they actually saw of each other for the first months because of John's war work and living in the company of Granddad and Nana anyway. There would not have been much privacy. Perhaps their calmness was because of the sense of freedom our new home gave us all. It was a small bach or whare in the Taupo area, built along the same lines as John's bush huts, except a bit bigger. Set in a then isolated part of the middle of the North Island, (Mokai now has a Geothermal Power Station not far away from John's property) it was our first shift from Auckland – the precursor to our itinerant lifestyle.

The four of us travelled by car down from Auckland mostly on metal roads that were dusty or muddy depending on the showers, with potholes big enough to break an axle, and during rationing, when to buy benzene (petrol) from a bowser (petrol pump) would have meant having coupons. So that we could make it to our destination, Ralph (about 9½) had to be sent into a Hamilton hardware shop, a source of all sorts of goods, to purchase a tin of turpentine to mix in with the benzene for John's big squarish Essex. Ralph was probably chosen to try and deceive the shop keeper for its purpose. The Essex was a sedan with a useful step up and plenty of room – a luxury for us.

It was a social achievement to be the owner of a car then although not always practical or possible for travelling long distances because of the war. John and his dad had one each as I can remember later that both of them parked together at the Mokai building. There were problems starting either of them at different times and much sweating and swearing when they had to be cranked over by hand from the front near the radiator. I don't know what happened to them eventually and they may have just rusted away from lack of use because of the war shortages or perhaps sold, because we were without a car in all the mill settlements we lived in afterward. (Only 4,000 of the 24,000 cars which had been owned pre-war went back on the road again after the war.)

Near the end of the trip Mary woke us up. We had come to a stop on the isolated, rough country road which ran through a deep clay cutting and with John gathering me up, we stepped out into a magical place of stillness and intense quiet. The rural smells were different to the city's and the night was a much denser black than in Auckland. We could not see past the steep banks to our surroundings so the sky was our focus. There seemed to be hardly any spaces between the stars, there were so many, and it felt as if they had come right down on top of us.

I remember reaching out to touch one and Mary saying, "That's a glow-worm dear, not a star". I didn't really understand the difference although Mary pointed out the Milky Way, the Three Sisters and the Southern Cross and I went back to sleep still mesmerised by the twinkling universe, thinking we were going to live in a glorious place where we could reach the stars and Heaven!

I vaguely remember Ralph and me sleeping in the living area on bunks not far from the wood stove which must have been lit by John for hot water each day. (Most stoves had wet-backs for water heating.) A lovely bonus for sleeping in the winter too. Mary had opened the door to the sun to wake us in the morning as we had slept in. We just saw wonderful sunny space outside that seemed infinite. No roads or fences or people so no boundaries, surrounded by acres of long dry grass contrasting with the green bush-covered hills in the far distance. The revelling freedom to have miles to run and play on the safe flatness was enticing. We may become hungry or thirsty but we'd probably find a stream and some blackberries. With Ralph threatening to leave without me I took toast on the fly and ran. We did find a stream for future fishing expeditions and the next day we also came across an old car wreck by the entry to the road, a great place to imagine journeys on or pretend it was a vehicle with wings for wider exploring.

Reality was different for modern Mary. The contrast between the apparent affluence of having a car and living in what to Mary was such a primitive shelter with its attached lean-to that acted as a carport, couldn't have been more pronounced. No paint was discernible on the old beaten grey weatherboards and rusting iron roof, with only one bedroom and a kitchen/living area with unlined and un-papered walls, except for fading pictures from catalogues and old calendars. No cupboards nor carpet, just a few shelves and an old handmade rag-rug, nails for hanging clothes and no curtains on the windows (but we were lucky to have windows) and no-one for miles around to peep in.

For Mary, who had grown up with electricity, a phone and all mod cons, the lack of power and the basic toilet and washing facilities, which were both outside, would have been a trial. I can't remember if there was an indoor tap and possibly there was as the slightly off-balance water tank was directly outside the kitchen wall on its stand. Items were stored underneath it. Much of the food we subsequently lived on until the garden produced must have been tinned, (no fridge or freezers and we would not have eaten puha) although some meat was probably from John shooting in the bush. Pig perhaps and fish or eels from the handy bush stream. Not rabbit though as John harboured the same maybe unfounded fears Mary and others did about the health of rabbits, possibly retaining poison in their flesh, after attempts at controlling them.

We would all have used potties in the night, which Mary would have had to empty. The toilet was outdoors and I noticed later the door did not have a lock on the inside for some reason but mind you it usually caught on the floor and was difficult to open anyway. Like most exterior toilets, there was a crude piece of wood on the outside of the door that turned on a nail for a handle, keeping it closed. There were holes and warped timber that let in cool air and the wind. Not kind to exposed parts on a cold, wet, miserable day. (I recall staying on a farm as late as 1967 without an indoor toilet still, although it was attached to the outside of the house and a pipe led to a recently-dug septic tank.)

Mary would have hand-washed our clothing and linen in the ever present chipped white enamel bowl placed on a rough-sawn shelf under the attached lean-to. Not sure about the sheets. They may have been soaked in the portable bath. The used precious tank *water was never wasted wherever we were, as the front steps and the vegetable or flowers garden (especially roses for thrips) would benefit from a quick swish of soapy swill. Even when we had normal kitchen sinks later with plumbing and piped water, the use of bowls was so ingrained that Mary went on using them balanced over the sink, as I noticed many women of those earlier generations did. Even a younger friend does now. She is on tank water though.*

If it was too cold to go outside in the mornings, John would use the bowl on the kitchen bench to shave in with his cut throat razor after a quick sharpen on his hanging leather razor strop. He had his systematic routine and no-one was allowed to speak to him until he had completed it – Ralph and I had to remain in our beds until then too.

As summer waned, the drying wind would swirl more often across the wide flat valley. I remember looking back one day after running as far as I could before collapsing and lying on my side panting then spying the tiny, isolated dwelling, no shrubs or trees around, with its wispy curl of smoke like a homing signal. Mary's white sheets were lifting and flapping on the long cord clothesline, sending a faint cracking on the breeze like a message, and I'd think of the tantalising scent of sun and Sunlight soap that would send me to sleep that night. Cuddling under blankets of wool and pillows and quilts stuffed with Eider down (Eider duck feathers) the latter always folded on the end of the bed and pulled up in the night if temperatures dropped. Thankfully I had been allowed to bring my own soft down pillow.

Mary did the ironing in the evening sometimes, especially during the summer when it was cooler, as I remember also listening to the regular rhythmic thump of the cumbersome and heavy irons instead of the usual night sounds. Unlike some dedicated women I doubt she ironed the sheets and underwear. Most clothing needed pressing without our modern types of materials. The Mother-of-Pots irons (or 'Mrs. Potts Sad Irons' according to Google) were heated on the range top, and usually came in sets of 3, so that there was always a hot one ready to pick up using the detachable wooden oak handle.

The readily available wood succumbed to John's routine chopping, starting kindling (thinner dry pieces of wood) set aside for handy access although it was not always needed as the range would be banked for the night with the controlling dampers turned down. In the morning John would have it roaring again very quickly ready for his shave and early morning cup of tea, porridge, toast and depending on what was available (money the decider) the options could be bacon or sausages or chops with eggs. It was common to have a hot cooked breakfast and meat was the biggest food cost (if bought in towns anyway) often routinely eaten three times a day. Mary always fed John well even if we missed out. A hungry John was not good.

Luckily, for toiletry purposes, we must have been at Mokai in the summer. Baths were given weekly in a short portable aluminium bath (about a third of the size of today's baths) which dipped down on the sides and had handles each end. It was brought in from its position hanging on an outside wall in the evening and placed by the stove for convenience and warmth. Used by several people in turn and re-heated regularly from the water-filled black kettles that always sat at the back of the coal (wood) range. When the hot water was being renewed we had to draw up our feet and we'd cook one end and be cool the other, until we moved around and all the water mixed.

Later after Veronica was born she would often be in it with me and would squeal and crawl up me to be sure she was not scalded, Mary trying to soothe her while struggling with the heavy kettle to keep the contents as far away as possible from us as she poured. The last and coolest kettle was kept for rinsing our hair. (The weekly bathing ritual may have stayed around even after power was available because of the cost of the power bill for hot water and an extra bath was deemed an unnecessary luxury. We did sponge sweaty areas often. It was after showers became part of the plumbing fittings in new homes that, we anyway, became used to daily washing, in our case the 1960's.)

Electricity would have taken years to reach some rural areas so in most country places at night we had soft shadowy light from flickering candles and kerosene lamps, but in the bigger rooms like the kitchen, we usually had the stronger white brilliance from a humming incandescent Coleman lamp, which was a bit trickier to light (possibly a Tilley as well). Kerosene and melting candles became a familiar and comforting smell combined with the warmth and scent of burning wood and cooking food. We always really appreciated the range fire at nights in the country after warmer Auckland. Ralph and I had been thrown into each other's company which made me happy but I would not have been his normal choice of a mate with the 3½ year gap in our ages and a girl to boot, but the surroundings were so different to our old home in Levonia St. that the novelty lasted quite a while.

In contrast to many other memories with John, I know we all seemed quite happy at Mokai for ages. Lack of petrol for transport, no buses, no neighbours or friends and perhaps the challenge to survive waned in the end. It later became obvious that Mary was a restless soul and I think perhaps John was too. At least on some level they suited each other. Anyway, we eventually left as there must have been a concern as well about Ralph's education if not mine, and probably money. I don't think John worked while we were there. Mary had become pregnant too with Veronica so we shifted to Masons, a rented property at Ngongotaha, set by the Waititi Stream that flowed into Lake Rotorua.

We all went back up to Auckland for Veronica's birth. It was at a private nursing home in Herne Bay, which was quite a common arrangement, however Mary ended up in Auckland Hospital very ill with septicaemia for six months and nearly died. John went back to Ngongotaha and his job, though Ralph was with Aunt Alice and Uncle Henry in Rotorua. Meantime I was farmed out to whichever friend/acquaintance would take me and later sometimes just anyone, not always kind people, although I did live with Aunty for a while too in the end. I once visited Auckland to see Mary in hospital as she wasn't expected to live. Colleen, John's cousin, took me up to see her from where I was staying with her family in Ponsonby. I don't know if John or Ralph visited or how I even got to Auckland and back. Mary did live after convincing the doctors to stop giving her blood transfusions. Others' blood was not as identifiable as it is today so there were repercussions. Mary said she'd rather die.

John continued working away at his bush-camp job until Mary did return and I came back too, Ralph staying on with Aunty, but John usually only saw us at weekends even then. Ultimately a blessing because of his disposition. Mary was unwell for a long time and self-medicated, mostly with specialised food, like liver, the smell of which made me retch. (That was not unusual for me anyway especially around the time of a full moon.)

Still not recovered and coping with a constantly crying Veronica, who had been looked after in a small orphanage for the six months Mary was hospitalised, Mary's mother, my Nana, died. Although it may have been expected by Mary it must have been a terrible blow for her after what she had just been through. People didn't show their feelings though so I doubt I saw her cry. Perhaps not so much of a blow for Ralph, but our Nana was the only person I had ever felt secure with, so really upsetting for me. Cuddles and comfort were not on offer. Everything was too much for Mary. I think she just took Veronica up for Nana's funeral. Now I know more about life, I feel I was lucky to have had my Nana look after me for as long as I did given what many other children from broken families experience. She was my foundation, my rock from 18 months to 6 years old.

We lived at the Masons for the longest time I can remember being anywhere with John, Ralph still with Aunty. Then our lives changed again and we virtually became itinerants for a few years, John unable to hold down a job because of his temper. That was also the reason Ralph lived with Aunty Alice more permanently and later with other friends in Auckland. We were all separated from John in the end because of his violence. First Ralph, then Veronica and I and Mary, then Veronica and I from Mary as well.

A typical mill settlement

The country settlements we lived in during the John years were owned by the milling companies and had similar settings and often long Maori names. They were usually in a valley at a loose metalled road's dead end, although sometimes it was more basic, the surrounding steep terrain covered in bush, often in the isolated and primitive King Country. We did live in other North

Island areas sometimes. Travelling to most of them, we would wind around constant corners that could open up briefly from the continuous overpowering feeling of being hemmed in by the high dense tree growth, the lower branches grey from dust and torn by passing vehicles. An obscured gleam of water sometimes opened up to a valley view that had a small regrowth space of lovely pongas and ferns clustered together in magic secluded dells where small animals and birds could be spied moving from the road above. Other times we would find ourselves facing an extra high point of the rolling ranges where the unsubstantial low, damp cloud hung hauntingly, obscuring the tallest tip of the terrain, the rugged skyline indistinct and fleeting.

The journeys always seemed endless, drowsiness disturbed by bumping over endemic potholes, until we would finally come down from the steep surroundings into a valley settlement, often in the early evening to what seemed spectral, surreal places, with the sight of smoke rising nearly straight up into the still air from a dozen or so identical chimneys. A pre-evening haze smudging outlines, everyone hushed inside having their tea. There was a sense that everything could disappear overnight, like Brigadoon, and it often surprised me when the vehicle we were in would pull up outside another new to us place and everything was real, although most of these settlements in fact did disappear later, not now on NZ maps. Noises from the houses like a faint baby cry or a man's deep voice or a barking dog, made it a living community, often though it wasn't until the mill started up again early the next day that the place seemed really alive.

Dense bush closed in on many of these small remote settlements too, giving the sense of isolation and being segregated from the world. It was so different from the city. The only form of communication a hitch in a kind neighbour's car or on a logging truck to a far town. Eventually the familiar smells of freshly cut wood and the faint taste of it burning and the escaping wafting smoke, became the norm again. If waking early along with boisterous birds, most kinds of native bird calls could be heard. Tuis were common, with their unique tunes and white baubled throats, flying in groups sometimes. Pukekos with their bright strutty legs and Kereru (wood pigeons) with their white squared off chests, and always the sassy, flitty fantails, and tiny pretty white-eyes. When we were awake in time, the mornings were a continuous crescendo of high pitched competitive bird song – each out-trilling the other – in discordant delight.

The grey warbler's tremulous trill was regularly heard in quiet periods, especially if listened for attentively in spring. They were not that easy to spot unless particularly looking, but a clearing approached in stealth would catch any number of interesting things. Any time I hear the lonely call of a morepork in the night it takes me straight back to the setting but it wasn't for years until I heard it on TV that I really recognised the call of a kiwi which had been another night sound. No-one ever expected to see them in the daytime although hunters would say sometimes a flushed kiwi had taken off suddenly in front of them when a dog had sniffed near it.

Ugly wild pigs mostly stayed away from humans although they could at times be heard snorting and rooting around. Good to avoid them if you didn't have a gun and dogs as they had vicious natures if disturbed. Wetas were the only kind of insect we used to worry about, mainly because they were so big, but finding huhu bugs in rotten logs was absorbing although just to look at, not to eat like the Maori. We thought that a strange practice.

Once we holidayed for a week in someone's ramshackle bach, built in a large flat area near the sea, and it didn't seem to us kids to have anything going for it, except for the water when the tide came in over the mud and the colourful king-fishers. We watched as they regularly caught wriggling fish, diving from nearby cabbage trees into the blue coastal waters with what seemed like casual and sleek skill, their bright feathers giving warning to their prey too late. Aside from the waves, the quiet got to us too.

At the settlements, we were not conscious of noises much other than the background din of the mill. The sawmill buildings dominated the cleared area filled with their massive and dangerous moving structures and saws – especially the huge circular one – waiting for the immense native trunks to arrive, often hundreds of years old, to begin their decimation. The trees had exposed patches of raw wood, mixing the new and old sap which oozed like gold blood, their branches shorn and bark scarred by manhandled tools and yet they still somehow seemed stately as they lay in a supine line for the mill to start up.

Except for lunch and smoko breaks during the day, the reverberating noise of the mill's whining saws formed their own kind of music which rose and fell continuously along with the echo of fracturing timber when cutting the mighty giants. The sound overlay every other until the evenings or weekends. It was only when the mill's machines stopped after the rising and then trailing pitch of the knock-off siren, that we became aware of other noises – somehow leaving us slightly forlorn. It was part of our everyday lives and, in its background way, comforting – so each morning when work began again it gave us a purposeful rhythm to life.

Seeing the controllable, uniform slabs of the finished product emerging from the other end of the mill which were then stacked high in countless rows, with gaps wide enough apart for machinery to drive through (and kids bikes at the weekend) seemed a bit like abandonment, which the mill workers would have laughed at. They were left there for pick up and removal by rail or articulated truck transport and seemed somehow slightly melancholy – in a fanciful way it was like having watched as a mighty king was toppled from his throne and was no more. Majesty certainly comes to mind when touching a full-grown 500–1,000-year-old Kauri tree though. I suppose the achievement was actually really amazing – it just didn't feel that way to me.

At some places whole logs were moved by the trucks too, which most boys aspired to drive. We were not allowed near those roads. We watched their distant tricky manoeuvres sometimes, amazed at the drivers' delicate skills while half hanging out a partly open door to sight the signals from a man on the ground, the truck length making turning difficult. The guys on the ground were not always helpful either. A near miss or occasional crash brought an eruption of uncontrolled swearing and abuse which was clearly heard from where we watched. Their anger never seemed to last though as the men's camaraderie was perhaps akin to wartime relationships with good humour needed around the many dangerous hazards they dealt with, and ultimately *necessary to each other to do their job properly and survive. (As a friend commented once to Mary when referring to John – apparently he was dependable but did not always get jokes which didn't help and was sometimes the cause of his hasty temper.)*

Kids Playing

The inevitable huge piles of sawdust were always part of those unique landscapes. Mostly they too were inaccessible to us children, lying away from the settlement near the mill itself where we were not allowed to play, but in one place when we lived near a town, they were adjacent to the short road the workers' identical houses were built on. During the day the high wooden scaffolding-like conveyer, reminiscent of a semi-permanently placed praying mantis, continually delivered an arcing load of sawdust over its top edge onto the subtly shifting peaked pyramid pile below. On cold winter days of good weather, we would take our toy cars and trucks (usually home made from wood scraps – John made mine) to the bottom of an old unused pile, where we would play in the warm and muggy sliding sawdust with its stronger than usual smell of cut timber.

Boys especially loved it and would play for hours, often creating miniature villages out of wood chips and other handy materials, joining them up with tiny highways over saddle-backed hills, through carefully constructed tunnels and across bridges with water settling underneath. The deeper they dug the warmer and wetter holes would become. Kids never seemed to mind when the rain came and destroyed it all, not unlike the tide on the sand at a beach – except less safe as everything to do with logging was physical and dangerous and like the trees themselves, the sawdust piles had been known to take lives.

In these scattered places in the thirties and forties, even if there was a shop there, with no fridges it meant safes instead, built like a swinging cupboard with fine mesh instead of wood to catch moving air, usually set on an outside south wall away from the sun, or sometimes a portable one hung on a tree (as for camping), but nothing lasted for very long in the summer. Meat was often only delivered once or twice a week so corned silverside was a popular choice as the rest went off quickly if not preserved with vinegar (a common smell and taste) or was cooked up quickly into stews and pies. The remaining meat & bacon bones made soup and were often left on the top of the stove in a big black pot till eaten, which went faster in winter than summer. Meals like tinned corned beef (maybe Spam) or sometimes fish were occasionally used as fill-ins till the next delivery. For us those were mainly oily sardines with their roll-open lid and herrings in tomato sauce.

Bread was delivered at the same time as the meat. It was eaten as toast most of the time and if not carefully tended, ended up with bars of burnt bits from the unpredictable flare of the fire from the open front door of the stove or when laid over the hole on top of the coal range after a cover was removed. We sometimes had a long handled wire toaster, like today's plastic fly swats, giving a more evenly browned (or black) finish depending on how attentive we were. Mary would bake frequently although not bread but scones, sweet or savoury, which were more often used to replace bread. She would fill the cake tins at the same time.

Bagged milk powder was a basic but tinned condensed milk the most popular to have with tea. Aside from the staples like potatoes, onions and perhaps carrots, vegetables were mostly from tins too unless we stayed long enough for the garden to produce, (a rarity) so fresh fruit and veges were a luxury and when a travelling fruit vendor happened to turn up, usually in an open, dust-covered small truck, he would be mobbed.

All the company settlements we lived in were remote, cut off from everywhere except for the company road by the dense bush which seemed to go on forever. In one place however we were lucky enough to be given permission by the company to use their jigger for an evening out. It was unusual I think for the narrow gauge mill rail track to end in a town with shops so they must have used a special engine and flat cars to take the timber out that way perhaps instead of the big articulated trucks.

We were given a push-start by some men out on the tracks behind us and other men took turns to work the jigger handles back and forth. It must have been a reasonably flat area as I don't remember an engine noise so the men would have worked them all the way to town. We couldn't actually see them in the night. (I have since seen a reference to 'bush tramways' which would probably cover what I am describing.)

It was the journey, not the destination, I remember. We squished together in the draughty miniature carriage attached to the back of the jigger. It probably took the men off to work during the day and we sat on their hard narrow wooden seats that ran lengthways under the loose canvas top which came down to the built-in half sides, barely protecting our backs as we shivered under the grey woollen blankets wrapped around us. We were buffeted by wind in exposed places, like crossing a large stream. The smells changed then from one of damp vegetation to the fresher cooler air coming up from the water and the jigger's clackety-clack would alter to a more hollow sound. I remember being pleased I couldn't see down in the dark. I didn't like heights.

We sang songs to help the men with their rhythm – although most of the words would have been lost in the noise from the jigger and the rough talking, swearing and grunting, especially on the way back after the local pub had been visited, which would have been many of the men's reason for their evening's effort.

It must have been a Friday night, the only late shopping time then, as the women had taken us children along with them and I remember the wonder of electric lights on at night again, and the enticement of goods, especially food displayed in windows. A group of us children found a shop with pink and white marshmallows in a big glass jar on the counter and one of them inveigled her dad to give her some money. She generously shared them but I have never eaten marshmallows again. Even two were too much on a stomach unused to those sorts of sweets.

By home time it was well past my normal going to bed hour. In my half-awake state it seemed a weird kind of ride in the heavy, impenetrable darkness; unable to see anything, just feel and smell the breath (some intoxicating) from each other's swaying bodies packed together warmly. The dense overhanging growth, we only knew was there from seeing it in daylight, seemed to have us captured in an endless journey to nowhere. The mugginess that *built up and the rhythmic noise had put me to sleep eventually so it was a surprise when everyone began moving again and we finally saw soft light chinks from the houses where candles had been left lit for the travellers. It remains in my mind as a one-off so I would have only gone that time for the novelty of it, probably with a neighbour's family, as I don't remember Mary or Veronica.*

I returned once to one of the saw-mill settlements when I was in my forties to find the mill itself gone, along with the acres of cut timber and the tall sawdust stacks. A disintegrating ghost town with overgrown fallen piles of creosoted timber, the house foundations, and remnants still recognisably set out in the typical U shape I remembered, protecting the kids' play area in the centre. This abandoned and isolated place incongruously had a tiny 8ft. x 8ft. (2.5 x 2.5 metres) one room building left standing where mail could be posted through a slot in the only door, so I sent a letter off to my brother Ralph in Australia for him to see the postmark on the envelope. He had been there once in the school holidays but probably wouldn't have remembered it as I did.

Time out

I'd often wander on my own on the periphery of the bush as it only took a few steps into the dense fern to become enveloped by seeking clinging tendrils, sharp broken branches or a soft giving of ground cover under my bare feet. Occasionally places had streams where a vague path could be followed beside it and I'd take my lunch or just some raisins and any fruit available with me and wander along looking out for eels in the narrow bevelled cutting of clear cruising water, sometimes running shallower where it rippled over stones. There was usually a small open area intermittently near the stream that had been cleared by someone and was dryer. Perhaps they, like me, had been looking for solitude and silence, a place to paddle their feet and cool off and rest to catch their breath. Lying down perhaps on the soft growth to look up at the distant canopy and moving cloud shapes or closely at plant details with the scents completely controlling the senses. The comforting damp pungent smells from the undergrowth especially, so unmistakeably, so uniquely NZ.

Once in a particularly isolated area we had recently shifted to, which had surrounding patches of secondary growth, I came across a rambling path that didn't seem to have a purpose and I wandered along it intrigued about why it was there, aware to listen for wild pigs. After about a kilometre when I was thinking about going back, the track quite suddenly stopped at a small but fast stream. I determinedly pushed forward along its banks, with ferns and branches flicking back when I had passed, and found the path had vaguely started again but my feet were squishing more into spongy moss, tickling between my toes at each step.

I tried unsuccessfully to keep pace with the narrow racing water, playing a game with it, jumping across to the other side sometimes, when the bush grew right to the very edge in front of me, thickening the deeper I went. There were glimpses of waving eels when an odd shifting sunbeam lit their shadowed retreats, the sudden clarity making the water look shallow and inviting. But it was always deceptive and the straight-sided banks with no discernible grip, and strong cold current, were too risky for a dip. I could see new springs adding fresh water too, the deep clearness of the rippling bottom astonishing to watch. I'd sometimes throw a small flat rock in when I could find one, just to see it dance in the strong upsurge of driven water.

Chanting rhymes and singing to myself, happy in my new adventure, I stopped to eat at patches of glistening blackberries when they appeared, sometimes hindering the way too. We must have moved more north than usual to this settlement, perhaps near the Coromandel area, as a mammoth Kauri trunk nearly stopped me as its twin blocked the opposite bank as well. Kauris often grow together and only usually touch at their roots and crowns where the tall trunks finally culminate in branches and a leafy head. There they compete for the light, their tops too high up and indistinct to be seen through the foliage of shorter trees. These two Kauris would have been several hundred years old they were so huge. They must have been missed by the early voracious bush-men who helped decimate the original forests in this accessible area.

Suddenly the stream had become a small waterfall. I lay mesmerised on a warm grassed area listening to the sound as it changed from deep gurgly swirls to the muted mini roar of falling water – then disappearing, the sound at once absorbed and lost in the thick ferny bush below.

I daydreamed for a while in the stippled sunlight and felt as near to safe there as anywhere I had ever been and drifted in a semi stupor but with intent awareness of tiny things around me, time having no meaning, until I began wondering why this place had grass. I rolled over and saw what may have once been a track so I crawled forward along it, pushing fronds aside until it became more obvious, leading to where the growth grew thinner. Standing up and carefully stepping around sharp lancewood, a young rimu and a few fallen old trees which I was careful not to tread on in case of creepy crawlies that might be in the rotting wood, I was amazed to find myself in a circular glade just big enough for what once had been a house and garden.

All that was left in the centre was a chimney, its brick fireplace home to lichen, not heat now. The bricks continued along forming a short wall at head-height for another metre, turning at a right-angle making a corner. Jasmine covered it all, a creeping canopy of scent, screening the man-made intrusion. It would have looked alien in that place without it although jasmine was not native either. I stood looking around wondering why it was there at all as the mill settlement, like others, was already in an isolated and uninhabited area. It was unusual as this had not been a Maori dwelling either looking at its boundaries. The regeneration of the young native plants nearby meant that a wider circle of land had been cleared at some time too.

Near where the kitchen must have been handy there were straggly potato tops still growing amongst the weeds and long grass. Parsley and mint had survived with other mixed herbs but blackberries were taking over. Closer to the bush were gnarled fruit trees, wild branches entwined with each other, some still bearing fruit. There were shrivelled plums and deformed apples but also the remains of a peach tree, one branch healthy looking, which the birds had obviously found enticing. I climbed it to where I could see there were still some whole peaches left but picked at, screened slightly by a creeper. One at its perfection of ripeness dropped into my hand when I touched it. It looked and smelt so delicious I savoured the moment before the first bite. Warm, slightly furry skin and firm yellow flesh dissolved into juices so sweet that the memory has been the lodestar taste and smell of a peach for me ever since. None has ever compared.

Feeling warm and satisfied, tucked carefully between two branches, I licked my fingers and surveyed my find. Flowers of various colours and shapes popped their heads above the grass here and there and a white trail of clematis hung from a kahikatea. Overall the many greens blended, their growth varying, vying for life. A supple-jack hung near the long grass edge – a natural swing near a fallen trunk for a step or a seat. Strong pleasant scents occasionally wafted through the mild air and hidden birds sang in the distance. A restless lone fantail continuously cocked its head and pecked at the ground on the edge of the glade but no other obvious life was about. There seemed to be no more paths, the desertion complete and long ago.

Peacefulness was the overwhelming feeling in the stillness and a sense of someone or something waiting. Whoever had been here before me somehow seemed to offer the glade's serenity to a fellow appreciator. There was a quality in the contained air of patiently knowing the glade would be re-discovered. My introverted nature felt welcomed and at home in this secret sanctuary. This was one settlement I would be really, really, sorry to leave.

Chapter 17 City Living 1940's to 1950's

There were still places in the inner city that produced things like shirts, (the building for those not necessarily looking like a factory) newspapers and a flour mill amongst many others. John Burns Ltd. down in Custom St. opposite where we walked through to Queen St. from the Auckland Central Bus Terminal was a place I always felt familiar with and happy to see when returning to Auckland. It was with horror and regret that I found it had burnt down when we had been away once. Its destruction had left black forlorn remains with oddly angled timbers hanging over piles of others which weren't immediately cleared. This seemed a desecration to me as a child, as did the windmill when it was taken down years afterward. Near the Karangahape Rd. skyline, it could be seen from many parts of the city including Queen St. When His Majesty's Theatre building went, it was like an act of vandalism and a violation of our values somehow.

Shopping

When I was little, for a treat and our important shopping and social outings, we regularly went into Auckland's Queen Street or Karangahape Rd. and Sunday's best clothes were necessary which included all accessories – purse, hats, (hold onto them getting on and off the tram) gloves, stockings, and high heels for the ladies, suits, ties and hats too for the men. Dressing up gave an underlying feeling of excitement and anticipation.

Afternoon teas would be arranged ahead with friends, especially at Adams Bruce in K'Rd. as they had the best ginger-nuts in town – big, fat and hard, lasting for ages, unless dipped in a cup of tea. My Nana used to take me, and we shared the same mild fetish about them. The right size ice-creams for littlies could also be found there. Tiny, dainty round cones about the size of the bottom half of today's, using a plunger type instrument to slot in the mini delight. I may have another faint fetish for any size ice-cream ever since too.

In local dairies ice-cream and ice-blocks were often home-made. The latter came in an ice-cream cone except that it was a deep square one and the ice-block was much more tasty, interesting and healthier than today's. The Mt. Eden dairy near Uncle Ross' had home-made, large, real fruit and milk ones costing one penny. An extra half-penny would get you a small scoop of ice-cream on top with sprinkles. Such luxuries for so little! 'Heards' were around for sweets but there would be more profit in making lollies on the premises and my favourites from this dairy were crunchy butterscotch and brittle toffee squares.

If power wasn't available and the local store/dairy did not have a generator, ice would be delivered every few days, bought from a commercial company. (To houses as well although we didn't know anyone who could afford what would have been an expensive indulgence.) Ice-cream was put in a special bucket that fitted into a container with crushed ice in between. The first commercial ice-blocks I can remember were TipTop's pineapple Fru-Ju's in the middle fifties in Auckland. In the country we had had 'Eskimo Pies' that were wrapped, oblong ice-creams thinly coated with chocolate – still around but with a possible name change on the cards.

There was always a bigger range in the city – it was one of the things we so looked forward to when we came back for visits when I was older – especially choc bombs.

Not many families we knew had cars till more into the fifties so food shopping was delivered. In Levonia St. in the forties, our part of it was defined by a through road at each end, (no-one owned a car so noise was minimal) and Grey Lynn was our closest local shopping centre. People always knew their grocer and often chatted him up for the local gossip. A good place too to find out about housekeeping or cooking hints or the best local tradesman when needed, from either the grocer's patter or a customer's knowledge.

Things like patterned paper towels, coloured toilet rolls, tissues, spray cleaners, plastic gloves, fluoride toothpaste and disposable nappies didn't exist. Tinned food seemed to have always been around although when our own bottled fruit ran out it was considered a minor extravagance to buy cans of peaches and pears. There was not the variety of today's tinned produce and other edibles.

Pre-prepared foods as we know them now were not known. Dried goods, i.e. biscuits, sugar, tea, rice, tapioca, sago, barley, flour, sultanas, currants, raisins, dates, split peas, salt and washing soda would have been weighed and packaged into plain brown paper bags of various sizes by the store owner. Cheese was cut from a round cake with a wire attached to a wooden handle each end with little variety and bacon was sliced from a long roll – everything open and exposed on the long counters. The shelved shop walls displayed everything from a range of patent medicines for adults, children, and babies ('Glaxo Sunshine Formula Builds Bonnie Babies' and Dinnefords for wind) to Creamoata, Marmite/Vegemite, tinned food, cigarettes (ready made after the war), and Christmas cards. Lined up on a special confectionary counter were large matching glass jars of lollies of all varieties, the shapes, and colours inside brightening the shop and the smells automatically drawing children to them. A penny bought a few boiled sweets, sometimes already prepared in small white paper bags. Three pence bought a feast – the most difficult part was deliberating over which lollies to choose.

The grocer or his assistant collected orders off the shelves that were read out from a customer's shopping list and stacked on the counter, weighing and wrapping as appropriate, brown paper and other bags handy, putting a large order in a box for delivery or fitting things into our own bags or string kits.(No plastic.)

The grocer had a small delivery van but sometimes, to our fascination, deliveries were made by a boy on a bike. It had a smaller front wheel that had a frame for a large basket above it in front of the handles, which must have taken a good deal of strength to keep balanced. It also had stands each side which could be lowered to adjust the balance when the bike was stationary. I think the boy may have also picked up our shopping list for the next week when we couldn't go out. Sometimes meat was delivered the same way to the back door, a friend told me. Their family had a regular order with both butcher and grocer, paying them weekly, which would have made sense, especially when there were limited choices available anyway, particularly during war and afterwards for a while.

When meat was expensive and rationed, we wouldn't have bought that much and probably carried it home ourselves, wrapped in brown paper and string. In Grey Lynn the butcher was a big gruff man in a long blue and white apron who expertly wielded a large, very sharp knife and sometimes a saw, or chopper from the belt around his waist. He would nonchalantly slice into red meat on a chopping block as he chatted away to customers. Bent over, he would look up from under bushy eyebrows at me sometimes and once to my amazement he winked! I had thought only Nana could do that. I would leave with a slice of free luncheon sausage in my hand and the sawdust off the floor clinging to my shoes, especially if they were suede, and Nana used to say to me if I complained, 'Do a little skip'.

After the war the 'Self Help' grocery chain introduced the idea of customers taking their own groceries to the counter and most people were happy to do that although some like my Nana who were short would have needed help with the higher shelves.

We used fruit and veggies in season from our own garden and bought a little from the green grocers. Shops were mainly owned by NZ Europeans as far as I remember, certainly bakeries, and there were some French ones with delicious pastries when I began work, although I could still only gaze at first, not buy. Different areas had a variety of vans come to their streets like bakers, green grocers (sometimes Chinese) fish, meat, and perhaps ice. The milkman called early each morning, originally by horse and cart before small trucks were used, possibly after the war when petrol or diesel would be more available with a larger choice of vehicles – the glass bottles still rattled whatever the delivery mode. I remember myself putting the correct change out in the bottles which would have been when Mary came back up to the city from Waiheke and I was in my last year at AGGS 1953.

Tokens replaced change eventually. I met a good-hearted old couple once who told me they went broke during the Depression because he was a softie milkman and wouldn't send the bill to some families who he knew were always hungry. I don't really think they regretted it, just saw it as a part of the burden of the times and bankruptcy was bound to happen. It may not have been a good idea to put money in bottles in those hard days.

Later into the fifties, bread was delivered along with milk too in our area. (This was before sliced bread was introduced, which became a huge time saver for housewives.) Mary had a prized skill of slicing bread thinly which she used to do by holding the loaf in an upright position and sawing it across with her special bread knife, like lifting the top off an egg, disconcerting to anyone new watching. Bread came in white but differently shaped loaves with names like Raised tin, Sandwich, Vienna, Barracoota and French, and was a big part of our diet. Brown bread was just a different colour because it had treacle or molasses added and came in smaller loaves, not a favourite. All were fresh and crusty and crunchy and very tempting to pull soft slivers off from when breaking a whole loaf (like 'Raised tin') into its two halves. The halves were only lightly joined to be sold separately. I miss that.

General stores in the suburbs and little country places would have a wider range of goods if having to cover for lack of other shops like a fruiterer, butcher, bakery, dairy, stationery, tobacconists/ barber, shoes, and drapery. Although they did their best it was a poor substitute usually. Sometimes a Post Office too like at Onetangi, on Waiheke where they also had a range of cooking utensils, probably for campers, and at another place a barber came in for a few hours a day using a small back room for men clients mostly. I knew two farmers' wives who regularly used a barber. It may have been about time constraints away from the farm, especially getting home in time for the milking. No time for primping.

Aside from beer, and that was usually a man's option or perhaps spirits but not wine, tea was the most popular thirst quencher and made in a tea-pot, one teaspoon of tea leaves per person and one for the pot then steeped to the satisfaction of the brewer. Served with milk and sugar and occasionally with lemon if afternoon tea was being taken on an outing in the summer. The pot may have been rinsed first with hot water. The coffee of today was not available that I know of. It was purchased as an essence as in 'coffee and chicory' or from the very sweet 'Nestles' tins of coffee and milk. I can't remember drinking instant or ground coffee until the 1960's. By then too, there was a bigger variety of bread delivered to the door in the early morning. We had choices of rolls and buns, and milk came with cream, chocolate milk, orange juice and probably other options but that's all we bought.

During the war with all sorts of shortages of imported goods and shopping more limited, extra care was used with irreplaceable things and repairs attempted if possible. ('Planned obsolescence' was an unknown concept.) Queues quickly formed when word got around if there were desirable items like stockings, chocolates, and sweet biscuits available.

Most men smoked when they could afford to. It was usually a pipe with loose tobacco in an envelope-shaped folding pack or in flat square tins for roll-your-own cigarettes, much cheaper than ready-mades – those were for the more affluent – American ones coveted. Lighting up was from wax matches (safety matches were not available always) or a twisted spill lit from an open fire or the coal range, the latter usually continually burning in winter anyway. (It would be tamped down when not in use or if the weather was warm, and banked at night for morning embers and an easy breakfast start for the day. In the city we had used coal and in the country wood – although whether that was just us or generally I don't know). I still like the familiar smell of tobacco, John's pipe especially; the sweet aroma always enticed me closer. An old friend in later years looked out of place without his pipe and the smell of his particular brand had always been comforting.

My brother probably wouldn't have given up smoking even knowing the brutal consequences and grief it could cause. He died of cancer. It was a way of life and I think men felt more masculine with a cigarette in their stained fingers. Even for those who hadn't smoked until they went to war, most never gave it up when they got home. I don't remember a male friend or relation who didn't smoke. It was 'unseemly' for women to indulge themselves by smoking, although no doubt they did behind closed doors. I remember watching one of the brave footballers' wives, when I was a 17-year-old bride, who openly rolled-her-own at a game much to the other wives' sententious horror. When women did smoke in public, they could buy various designs of cigarette containers, sometimes a combination with a makeup and mirror compact as well. I was given one as a present once. It didn't help the nausea I felt from a cigarette. Lucky for me.

The tobacco companies, I have since discovered, paid millions to expensively promote smoking in movies where the debonair hero always held a (named) cigarette in his fingers and lady stars used cigarette holders as they sat around looking glamorous – health concerns not even considered. Smoking in theatres themselves was forbidden, mainly from fear of fires.

For many years not much changed and all serious fashion shopping was done in what was considered the sophisticated Auckland CBD. K'Rd. had Rendells, Woolworths, McKenzies and George Courts as well as specialty shops. There were cosmopolitan menswear outfitters (still there many years later) and a good variety of wool and material shops – very important for knitting and home sewing. Up-market jewellery outlets fitted in well and I can guarantee their status.

A Bracelet

After I was married I took my first baby girl into one of them to buy a long-saved-for gold bracelet for her one-year-old birthday present. We were both fashionably dressed – hers the latest expensive dress and bonnet outfit from the specialty baby shop around the corner, both beautifully embroidered. Only to be used on special occasions. Her pushchair was new and so was my own carefully replicated frock of the latest design – the way anyone with skills normally owned clothes. Clean, well-mannered and dressed and coiffed we may have been but we were ushered out again quite quickly with a brisk 'You don't belong here!' pompously spoken in my ear by the large, overbearing suited gentleman guarding the entry. I felt like a schoolgirl again who, along with the others from Grammar, used to drool over their lovely window jewellery on our way home. I have no idea why I was ushered out of the jewellers. It was bizarre.

I went back years later and finished my purchase, just for a different birthday. I was welcomed that time.

St. Kevin's Arcade, with its tearooms and smaller odd shops like a tobacconist/newsagents, had wide steps opening at the back that led down to Myer's Park where kids could have a break and play. In George Courts, we would go up the wide, gracefully curved stairway to the different floors or in an old-fashioned double-door lift that let us see out through the clanging grilles. The polite formally outfitted lift-men wore dark doorman suits, hats and gloves and called out each level's type of clothing or furnishing:

"Going up, going up! Ladies frocks, underwear, and accessories. Next floor ...," all said in a loud, commanding, slightly sing-song cultivated voice so that the timid could only be heard faintly requesting something not mentioned and the response would be, "Certainly madam/sir. We have the very thing two floors up."

Beside our purses and shopping bags, we often had a useful string kit tucked away for excessive spending. It was see-through as the string-like stretchy material was joined at intervals culminating in two handles. It may have been machine crocheted. Mary once used a heavier coloured string for a matching hat and bag, which she was complimented on.

In elegant Queen Street, quote, 'the most famous street in the country, the beacon of international city sophistication and the centre of everything', there were larger enticing department stores like Smith & Caughey and Milne & Choice with their fashionable creatively artistic window displays. Milnes also once had a full size Michelangelo 'David' replica placed in the middle of their ground floor. It totally dominated the shop interior and was tall enough to reach up past the mezzanine floor – good viewing! At 16 in the early fifties, after the Post Office job, I worked at the main branch of the BNZ bank next door so a daily visit was a must. My girlfriend's father had an account that she could use there on special occasions, to my amazement and unusual passing envy. I couldn't believe she had access to all the new lovely summer bathing suits and opulent ladies' wear. It did define the differences in our living standards and was probably the closest thing I came to recognising what would have been a class structure in another country. Not that it really bothered me that much ultimately as at the time I really thought she was just spoiled. In my world when you wanted something you saved up and paid for it yourself or went without. Good training!

John Courts, referred to as 'The Corner', at the intersection of Queen and Victoria Streets (Albert Park handy for lunch just up the hill) was a favourite meeting spot as it was approximately half way up the main shopping part of Queen Street. It was where the 1958 unique innovative 'Barnes Dance' system stopped all traffic allowing pedestrians to cross the road diagonally and straight across. John Courts itself was where Colleen my cousin worked, so I was often there. It had a variety of goods and was a great place to have a read if too early for an appointment or a boring lunch hour.

Further up the rise was the exclusive Smith & Caughey's on the corner of Queen and Wellesley St. It had/has several entry levels with its multiple storeys and large windows. Lifts were in various areas (eventually escalators too) and there were high narrow chairs provided at the counter for the tired and elderly waiting for purchases, with wide spaces between counters. There never seemed to be any rush, customers would drift around and discreet staff would approach them if they felt they were needed, offering quiet suggestions. Sometimes at the glove counter someone would make a request for a certain pair of gloves. They would appear magically from a smoothly efficient bank of drawers like a sleight of hand trick, presented as if they were diamonds.

As a young child it would all have been very entertaining, particularly their fascinatingly efficient way of taking a payment. An overhead mechanised pneumatic vacuum system called 'Lamson Tubes' sorted Mary or Nana's proffered money. Along with the docket from the counter staff, it went into a hand-held shuttle which was then pushed into an opening in a silver tube that was placed handily to the counter, and with a delicious sound, was sucked off through it. We would watch in admiration and listen to the tuneless light clanking and sucking and its faintly rattling express journey up through the glinting silver tube, reflecting the shop lights, contorting its way above us toward a glassed-in extension that appeared attached to the very high ceiling. The cashier's quick movements could be vaguely seen behind the reflections as she accessed, sorted and replaced the docket and change which would speedily return back to us by the same route although perhaps in its own matching tube until the shuttle landed back at our counter again. Excitement. On my first visits in a push-chair, it had been the nearest thing to a not-very-frightening monster, however later it was the only place I ever really wanted to visit in the city – except for the ice-cream and gingernut shop.

I had a temporary job in their restaurant upstairs in the summer school holidays when I was 15 in 1952 (not that they knew my age). I swapped a dark school uniform for a white one, including a hat, not unlike a then nurse's outfit. It was a very lovely setting with one large lavishly set table up at stage level, at the back of the spacious high-ceilinged room where the city's wealthy gathered for lunch and no doubt business meetings too – not a table I would be serving. There would have been large windows to make it impressive and the décor certainly was but I don't remember a view. Note pads were not used – memory was it, no matter how many place settings were filled. The waitresses who had been the longest serving were the only ones allowed to wait literally at 'the top table'. The woman pianist who played soft background music was a very cultured and pleasant lady who produced tunes played by ear. I would hum them to myself when passing and she pulled me aside once in a quiet moment and asked me to sing some of the latest tunes to her. I was amazed as she picked them up in seconds and after that she would wink at me whenever I passed and she was playing one.

A friend of Ralph's from University and his beautifully dressed mother and friends arrived one lunch hour and he was quite taken aback to see me there as a waitress. He shouldn't have been really as he had been to many of Ralph's Uni parties Mary allowed at our state house. However he was embarrassed and held back from the table, making some quiet remark to me which I can't really remember. I just poked my tongue out at him and went on working. It did not go unnoticed. The manageress pulled me aside and I was told off for being disrespectful to their customers. I laughed and said he was a friend. She obviously didn't believe me by the look on her face. It may have been my last day but a new school year wasn't far off anyway.

Later, smaller unique shops often with exquisitely dressed windows were in arcades and sometimes up the steep side streets away from the main bustling flow, but really worth visiting for their chic one-off fashion designs, even if it was only to look. They were also tucked into odd corners or spaces between the larger grander buildings, each of which was interesting compared to the predominance of glass today, and would appear suddenly, enough room for just one gorgeous frock displayed in the glassed front. (I did buy my wedding frock and night trousseau at them and discovered in my thirties my father's sister probably owned one of them and ran it herself until she was in her seventies.) Their exclusive and beautifully designed street-wear could be matched at recommended shoe shops, and Vulcan Lane was one of the better places to find them. When it was eventually closed off to traffic and became more people-friendly, it was a lovely sheltered place to sit in the sun with a cut lunch and soak up the city atmosphere crowd watching. Mary would have frequented it too when she was first married. She was the one who would find the time to spend the whole day in Queen St. – a must for ladies. It was entertainment as well as shopping. Morning, afternoon tea and lunch were part of the whole adventure, the numerous tearooms the place for a rest and recuperation from the bustling, hectic thriving city. By the sixties the lights had come back on.

Farmers shopping was an experience in itself. The building had six storeys, considered high outside of the main street and full of goodies. Innovative for the times anyway. From 1922 buses ran from the Farmers (which changed to a tram in 1936) up Hobson St. and Pitt St and around the corner to Beresford St., K'Rd. a step away. We usually got the free bus up the steep Wyndham St. hill from Queen St., as it was more interesting and a change from the tram. Both became electric trolley buses in 1938 and their starting points had underground toilets in the street which both fascinated and frightened us children and we were warned not to go into them, the Beresford one being male only anyway. When I did eventually really need to use one later in my teens, luckily I had a penny to fit in the door's coin slot, as I don't think anyone had warned me.

Children could tease 'Hector the Parrot' (actually an Oz sulphur crested cockatoo) upstairs at the top level of the multi-storeyed

Farmers. There was a large black rocking horse, pedal cars, bikes, and swings and slides all in a safe uncovered area for children and also it had a spectacular look-out over the city and harbour up an open flight of stairs. The play area was eventually covered although adults could still see out but the scenic stairs were closed.

Santa would be around at Christmas for knee-sitting, hugs and photos. The adults, meanwhile, could play ladies in the nearby tea-rooms. One side was a help-yourself area and the other side served meals in a cavernous room which had a view of the harbour out of the high arched and elegantly draped windows. Small red goldfish darted and hid in the small rocks or plants of a low fountained stone pool, set near the entrance wall in the slightly genteel surroundings of stylish tables and chairs. Children would sit sideways on the half-moon flat pool edge and watch patiently for the fish to appear from under plants as their elders preened at nearby tables and were waited on.

An institution in its own right, the Farmers had nearly everything for a household that you would ever need under the one roof, each floor with different products and they even had a basement food-hall in the fifties. Previously it had been a bargain basement (nothing over 2/6 pence) and anything could be returned and would apparently be accepted. They would replace older ladies' worn-out undergarments for years as a contribution to the aged. Time payment/hire purchase was interest-free which was a Godsend to many newly married couples, especially for washing machines and fridges for a new home. They were the first Auckland department store to have an escalator in 1954, which would have attracted customers even if it was only to sample something so innovative. In 1955 the Farmers built its own multi-storied 500 space car park, which was useful not only for parking but for viewing as well.

Mary worked at the Farmers for a while about 10 years before retiring and would have spent her whole pay there except for our delivered meat, bread, and milk. She loved time payment and the Farmers always had specials and sales – sooo tempting. Special staff used to work all year to have their spectacular annual Christmas Parade ready and there was always the huge red-hatted

Santa Claus on the outside corner of the building, nearly the height of the Farmers itself, an overwhelming figure to littlies, with the exaggerated wide space between his eyes, one of which winked, plus the slightly bizarre big beckoning finger inviting everyone in. (Inherited by Whitcoulls [originally 'Whitcombe & Tombs] and added to the festive display on 'The Corner' of Queen & Victoria Sts., which had also been John Courts in the past.) It was a score to be able to participate in the annual Santa Parade (which Mary did), even if it was often a long hot walk from the Town Hall, down Queen St. around Customs St. and back up Hobson St. to the Farmers. (My memory thinks it was that direction but it could have been the reverse.) It went on for several generations.

The public loved it and in the last years, parking would be at a premium. Children would remember for the rest of their lives the colour and action in the parade of floats of fairy tales from familiar children's stories, the fanfare of music included bands and the bagpipes, uniformed marching girls, stilt people, balloons, clowns and dressed up nursery figures and Santa at the end, sitting high up on his sleigh with his imitation reindeer in front attached to a large unseen truck.

When the Farmers closed, there was a definite sad feeling of a city icon lost to us. (I did once sample the transformed Art Deco Heritage Hotel's Grand Tearoom with its amazing atrium.)

Aside from the Farmers 'Bargain Basement' the nearest equivalent of today's $2 shop and probably T&T and any haberdashery shops or Emporiums (a throwback), were the large and prolific Woolworths and McKenzies variety stores, although with a much wider selection, including things like enamel saucepans which Mary had bought once and regretted. The heated milk in the pot eventually turned our custard green. She did take them back as there was a money back guarantee. They had all sorts of cheap and handy things to browse through. They were displayed in square open wooden containers at counter level around the shop and people seldom left empty handed, goods paid for or otherwise.

It was all so tempting and would no doubt be emptied in a week by shop-lifters today. Security was up to the assistants and I remember walking around in one of their big suburban stores, desperate to find a silk and wool singlet for my asthmatic daughter at a price I could afford, which wasn't much. When I did find it, it was just a couple of pennies too dear and I stood there for ages so tempted to steal it. There wasn't an assistant in sight. Something interesting must have been happening out the back as no-one came out to stop temptation overcoming me. In the end I did walk out without it.

Innovation is always a selling attraction and to get the perfect shoe size fit, when I could finally afford to buy them, some retail shops offered a new machine which x-rayed your foot in a shoe. The dangers of x-rays meant it was a short-lived gimmick, but it drew people in, fascinated to be looking through and inside to their foot. A NZ novel innovation became famous in 1957 when we produced the jandal, the name a compilation of Japanese and sandal, but it is disputed who was the first to invent them although that did not stop the raging success they became.

According to Foodtown records when I checked with them, their first NZ supermarket opened in Otahuhu in 1958. It was actually closer to Papatoetoe, a few hundred metres from the brewery on the main Great South Rd. and in my memory, and as I happened to live in Otahuhu at the time, I recall it being opened from 1960. I cannot reconcile their date with my memory. We hadn't shifted to Otahuhu until after my son was born and that wasn't until 1959. However, that will probably only be of interest to me. I didn't go down the first day as I had no car and there would have been little space for parking anyway as apparently people turned up from everywhere to view this new phenomenon. It became our one-stop shop and made the weekly groceries, vegetables and meat purchases a breeze compared to walking down Otahuhu's main street with two babies and then struggling back up weighed down.

It may not have been as cheap as other local options but it was certainly convenient and it had goods normally only found in specialty stores as well, all goods usefully parcelled up in large brown paper bags. My neighbour, who used to run me down to shop sometimes, regularly bought her son a cheap toy. This to our family seemed really extravagant.

I don't associate the forties and fifties with people rushing around or not having time either. The 40-hour working week was accepted as normal for men with maybe some overtime. Shop hours were Mon-Thurs 9 to 5, weekends off. Late night shopping was when places were open till 9 pm, usually a Friday. On the whole, regular hours for coming and going were probably predictable. (Our neighbours in Panmure used to check their clocks against my stepfather, Joe, leaving for work and arriving home for the day.) During the war it may have been different, with more of a sense of urgency for some things anyway and women working too.

There was no Saturday morning shopping as it was abolished in 1946, weekend trading hours not reinstated until 1981 because of strong union resistance. Sundays were sacrosanct. I wish they were today sometimes for a bit of peace and quiet from hammers, nail guns, electric drills, power saws, motor mowers, water blasters, leaf blowers, weed eaters, wood chippers, lawn trimmers, hedge trimmers, stump removers etc., never mind traffic.

There is no bridging that gap of constant noise pollution between my grandchildren and me. They seem to accept and thrive on it as much as I am repelled by it to their puzzlement.

Chapter 18 Events

Royalty

This was a momentous year for the Commonwealth with the coronation of Queen Elizabeth and for me the highlight of working at the (Chief/Central) General Post Office in the city and being able to see the Queen and the Duke of Edinburgh on their NZ visit. The motorcade came along Quay St., (which still had train lines) from the Royal Yacht *SS Gothic* in the harbour and rounded the corner into lower Queen St., passing the G.P.O. The staff had access to the second floor windows and we had a great view and saw them clearly as we hung out of the lower part that pushed up. The crowd gave deference to them, and we joined in their cheerful cheering.

Royalty was popular and very welcome in NZ for a long time and most people showed enthusiasm. The older people may have still had fond memories of their own parents' stories of the pomp and pageantry of English Royalty and how great the British Empire had been, especially in India where everything seemed so brilliantly coloured and exotic and often excessive. Their buildings so imaginative, their jewellery and clothes magnificent, perhaps outrageous by western standards and riding around on decorated elephants, though all may have had a sense of unreality. An era which was coming to an end as British power slowly waned, begun around WWI. The proud feeling of being part of the Empire was discernible, Mary said when paying homage to King George V (Emperor as well) on his 25th Silver Jubilee in 1935. The first time the whole Empire heard his voice was in 1933 which began the royal tradition of broadcasting important speeches.

Mary may have achieved some of her unwanted notoriety as her name was 'Simpson' as in Wallis Simpson the divorcee who married Edward VIII. Mary had divorced a few years after his abdication. King George VI was reigning when I first became aware of royalty which was during WWII. The King and Queen and their two daughters were the ones that I related to after hearing people talking about the support they offered to everyone during the war. An immigrant friend told us about the sad circumstances surrounding Princess Elizabeth when she found out about her father dying. This friend was a teen when her English parents owned 'Tree Tops' in Kenya where Elizabeth stayed. The rooms were built high on poles with a view from a flat roof and balcony surrounded by a group of trees, smaller in front. The pool below was where the wild animals drank, often at dusk. A spectacularly colourful and vibrant setting. The antithesis of London and her new responsibilities.

Our family always listened to the Queen's annual Christmas radio speech (maybe in a supine position) when she came to power as we had her father's before her and many New Zealanders related to her like my friend Bev, her mother being English. (On the whole I don't think Granddad himself was a royalist. Although he probably enjoyed festooning the Rotorua Gardens with lights in 1920 for Edward the Prince of Wales. He often took the mickey out of anyone who had too much of a sense of self-importance.)

The most impression anything made on me as a child was my world atlas. So many countries were coloured red.

Achievements

We felt Ed Hillary and Tenzing Norgay conquering Everest was a great contribution of loyalty to the Crown and a huge boost to our general morale. Dashing and daring Sir Edmund Hillary, who grew up in that era, became the iconic epitome and quintessential hero of what was expected from those generations. It was as if Ed had given us personal permission to be able to achieve anything we wanted to.

Yvette Williams had earned her gold medal the year before at the Helsinki Olympics and in 1954 set a new world long jump record so even we women felt part of the nation.

The later victory over the Springboks in 1956 by the All Blacks seemed the pinnacle of NZ achievements. Quote – 'Rugby is the measure of a man', certainly expressed by a male.

Tangiwai

Unfortunately 1953 was also the Christmas of the Tangiwai rail disaster on the main trunk line in the Central North Island when the Auckland-bound midnight express from Wellington crashed. Amongst the passengers were those en route to Auckland to see the Queen and others to join friends and family for Christmas celebrations. So a very poignant, sad and shocking Christmas Eve for everyone. With a population of only two million we all knew someone that was affected by the tragedy. I think the country went into shock.

A lahar from the Crater Lake on Mt Ruapehu flooded the area around and including the Whangaehu River. A pier from the railway bridge over the river at Tangiwai had given way only minutes before the train reached it, and the train caused the bridge to collapse. The steam engine and the five front second-class carriages sped straight on into the river nearly reaching the other side. Some passengers in the first class carriages at the back of the train, which had miraculously stayed on the rails initially, probably because of the train driver sanding them to slow the speed, watched with unbelieving eyes when a still-lit carriage floated away below them. One first class carriage which had been teetering on the edge of the bridge eventually dropped down into the water and mud but except for a young girl who drowned, all the other passengers were saved.

Of the 255 train passengers on board 151 people were killed. Many bodies went on being found later in the river near various settlements including by local farmers in the Mangamahu area. They went even as far as the river mouth. 20 passengers were never found and may have been washed out to sea.

William Inglis and Arthur Bell were later awarded the British Empire Medal, Cyril Ellis and John Holeman the George Medal. I think there were probably other heroes that night too. Certainly the train driver Charles Parker and fireman Lance Redman did their best. Tangiwai was the worst rail disaster in NZ history. (There is much more information, some of which is contradictory, on Google. A book titled '*The Tangiwai Disaster. A Christmas Eve Tragedy*' by Stewart Graham sounds interesting.

Post Office Job

Working in the telegraph department of the General Post Office meant the next day we fielded the hundreds of telegrams that resulted from the non-stop, clattering, rhythmic telex machines. Fingers flew over keys and constantly moving personnel sorted and directed incoming and outgoing telegrams till late in the evening. The huge high-ceilinged room was a busy sultry hive of movement with the dedicated staff intent in passing on all information as quickly as possible. Forwarded telegrams were received by local Post Offices and usually delivered by boys on bikes as quickly as they could be. They were the main means of fast communication used then and made heart-breaking reading. (Land-line telephones were not universally in homes.)

The earlier ones would question if the person/people (some families with multiple members) had boarded the train in Wellington and the follow-ups were either reassuring or stilted and brief with grief. Terrible news to receive in black telex typing stuck onto a yellow form. It would have taken many back to the dreaded days of the war, less than 10 years previously, when being notified about the death of a loved one.

At our short smoko breaks there were groups of people huddled around others trying to console them. We were not really aware of many details although the bosses may have been – except that there had been a disastrous rail accident on the main trunk line in the middle of the North Island – but some of the staff had recognised the names of passengers enquired about and were apprehensive too. I had only been working there a couple of weeks so didn't really know anyone well enough to empathise. I was probably one of the few though that had actually lived near that isolated area so perhaps had a better picture of it but it was all too bewildering and sad to really think about at 16.

Most people knew someone, or of someone in the crash, (as they did later with the Erebus disaster) so it affected the whole of the NZ population, it being so small then. My brother lost a childhood neighbour from when we lived in Ngongotaha. He was only 19, so it was quite hard to deal with, as kids of today know when they lose mates in car accidents. He didn't know straight away either so it was an added shock later.

A story we heard from a family friend who lived in Mangamahu was about his neighbour who had gone to help. That was a shocking drive – over one of the worst roads in the area – and the father said his teenage son had asked him what the white sheets were doing floating in the water. They were the white shirts on the backs of men's bodies.

One of the incongruous cruelties of the night was that the raging, tumultuous river reverted to its normal strength again around 45 minutes later albeit flowing through very differently shaped terrain as well as the remains of the wrecked bridge, engine and carriages.

Mary said a legend from the Rotorua Maori was there would always be a disaster when Royalty visited at Christmas.

Bus Crash

NZ's worst ever bus crash on the Brynderwyns in February 1963 haunted me every time I drove north for many years. I had always thought it had happened on the corner at the very bottom of the road where the terrain had levelled out and I wondered why there had been so many killed. Why hadn't the driver just gone straight ahead onto relatively flat grassland instead of trying to take a bend? It wasn't until a recent TV programme that I fully understood how horrifying the accident must have been. They hadn't got that far. I hadn't known either that the victims were mostly of Maori heritage although I do remember they were coming back from the Waitangi celebrations. It had obviously meant so much to them to be there – all the more reason for the accident to be stuck in our psyche. (No TV news pictures then.)

The Wahine

That disaster seemed unbelievable – it could not be happening in NZ. It all seemed to unfold in slow motion to those of us listening to the upset radio commentator, his voice stopping and starting as he described the indistinct glimpses of the upturning boat through the formidable storm. It sounded as if he couldn't take in what he was seeing. In some way the shock has never really left those of us I know who were listening (or watching) when it was actually happening and then later the stories of heroism and the many personal experiences, sometimes the helplessness felt as others died. All part of the interwoven degrees of grief that touched our nation.

Weeks later I received a letter from the Post Office asking me to call in at the Christchurch main branch. I didn't go straight away as it wasn't a particularly convenient time and there was no reason given so no indication of urgency. When I did go and gave a staff member the P.O. letter, she whispered something to her colleague and I was ushered with some underlying feeling of tension into a small backroom and told to look on a certain shelf amongst many others. They all seemed to contain rubbishy and grubby paper and unrecognisable debris with a faint but distinct smell. I was told I could look all around as well in case there were other items that might belong to me. She disappeared quite quickly shutting the door behind her.

It wasn't until I recognised my own distinctive backhand hand writing on a 6 page letter, the first page missing, that I realised it was from an Easter gift parcel I had posted north weeks earlier, that I really understood. The embarrassed P.O. employee had assumed someone had told me that the room contents I would be looking at were from some damaged mailbags rescued from the Wahine.

There was nowhere to sit down and it was very claustrophobic. The smell became stronger the longer I stood there so I only quickly glanced at the other shelves and just grabbed what I could see in front of me and went out. Slightly gasping, I shut the door after me and leaned on it. There was no-one around in this back area so I slowly slid down onto my haunches and stared at what that terrible storm had left me. The folded water-stained paper with the legible writing seemed very unreal. There were even shiny gold wrappings from chocolate Easter eggs amongst the other unrecognisable bits of what may have been dirtied dismembered bits of soft toys along with my letter. It was almost obscene in a way that it and parts of the toys should survive and people hadn't. Silent grief overwhelmed me for a while as I *thought of all those drowned souls and it wasn't until I stood up again and looked around for a back exit and found my car that I felt free to sob.*

I didn't want the flotsam so I wrote to my girlfriend again, airmail, explaining what had happened. She was thrilled to be able to own part of our history and was happy for me to re-post her my letter at least. I was glad she wanted it. I probably couldn't have thrown it away so have no idea what I would have done with it.

There had always been shipwrecks given that shipping was the major distributor of goods and people, and the size of our sometimes rugged coastline and often huge surrounding seas. It was a major part of our economy then. Other disasters like mine accidents, the 1943 Huntly mine disaster the closest, seemed mainly in the south so not so much in our Auckland consciousness. That may seem unfeeling, but unless someone had a relative with a miner's or seaman's background, which we didn't, it was a passing drama. Not that we weren't horrified but it all seemed so remote then and there wasn't the media coverage like today with the Pike River Mine explosion and their up-to-date information. People were interviewed and photos were on TV, which we can visually relate to. (The *Wahine* brought shipping disasters home to me.)

Chapter 19 Teenagers

The strong vision by parents for their children was to enjoy the current era's lifestyle which would have seemed very precious to them after the Depression and the war. It was felt that the younger generation should not have to suffer their parents' financial disadvantages and boys, the main bread winners to be, were encouraged to go for a safe job (Govt.) and train for a career. Apprenticeships were especially valued and a Uni education pursued if possible. In these circumstances of dependence and the low minimum wage for most 'teens' (not a word in our language then) giving fewer options of living choices, children often stayed at home till they were married, their behaviour consequently controlled or at least modified for much longer, even 10 years. If like me you were a girl, your job would barely be able to pay for board and bus fares, and clothes if you were lucky, never mind having the money for a flat and its needs, or cigarettes and booze – or drugs had they been around. Girls, always on lower wages than a male to start with anyway, were not usually promoted ahead of the boys. (Advertising to entice workers was not like it is today either.)

The parents' dream was that by the time their children moved on, they were expected to marry and have children (for the grandparents to enjoy them too) with a permanent job and promotional options, preferably a secure government one, which would last them for 40 years. The end payoff being a private superannuation and perhaps a gold watch, with possibly the mortgage paid and enough money saved to cover the cost of a trip overseas. (Mortgages could be for 30 years or more)

Only a few parents seemed to question what their children's quality of life would be when they retired at age 60. Realistically they may have physical or mental disabilities or may not even be alive. Those of us born in the 1930's knew only the circumstances we were brought up in, and although we were influenced by our parents' and grandparents' thinking, unlike them, the Depression deprivation and the war restrictions meant we had had little to miss. We were not necessarily affected in the same way as them either by painful war memories, depending on our ages and by whether anyone we knew or remembered had been killed, wounded, or lost. Grief had not impacted as strongly and was not as familiar to most of us.

After the war, the economy and the country progressed and with all the new electrical gadgets to be had it was too fast for some industries. It led to the huge new developments of hydroelectric power stations. (Granddad's job as 'Engineer in Charge' on the small Okere Falls site in the early 1900's minuscule compared with what was opening up on NZ's largest rivers.) The government continually struggled to keep up with the power supply so we often had unexpected shut downs at inconvenient times. For Mary it was that her sponge cakes used to go flat and she would rue the waste of eggs but we were also used to not having the convenience of electricity and reverted to candles and the open fire for warmth when necessary without really noticing. It was serious for hospitals though and in the large industrial working sites that were developing along with all kinds of businesses.

There were jobs for all, many of us were confident and hopeful of the future and had a more positive attitude, and it also led us to expect progress in other ways. The lifestyle that was achieved with the focus on homes and families, emphasising women's clear maternal role in our society, eventually meant though that the underlying sense of women needing to rely on men to implement their decisions was beginning to erode for them. Along with a more obvious rebelliousness from young males towards their parents' careful conserving survival scenario, becoming fed up with their continuing fear about the future, so warnings from our elders were not heeded.

Their ways seemed too tame to us. We needed more to look forward to and wanted to live life and get on with it, as youth does. For someone who no doubt should have been striving for just that stable situation Mary was concerned about, I too wanted more options and rewards sooner, not the instant gratification expected by many of today, but a sense of achieving a better life style not too far in the future. Working for it was a given, for most males anyway, and in the 1950's it was possible.

By then more people of both sexes were educated for longer and males anyway, considered taking the risk of going into business for themselves or opted for private firms, not the advocated safe jobs. With the larger influx of English immigrants and a few other nationalities from 1947 (the English peaked in 1954) we had become more aware of other places in the world too and we were becoming more impatient to make our own way in our own manner.

Our generation was the beginning of the unsettled feeling I think which lured us into the major OEs (Overseas Experiences) – even if it was by back-packing – to go and find out about these countries (like the previous youth of the wars that volunteered) even if it was only a few of us and as close as Australia. The guys could afford to go further and for longer of course. I had a girlfriend we all envied, whose parents shouted her extended trip to Oz.

Eventually the NZ Post Office and Engineering (Telecom) built into their employment conditions that people could go on overseas trips for up to 2 years (although not in one trip) and come back to their jobs at the same level of pay and conditions. We had no perception of how lucky we were to be offered that and also of living in a country like ours, even with its limitations.

The extreme of the change in youth was epitomised by 'the appalling 1954 sensational murderers, Pauline Parker and Juliet Hulme, who were portrayed in Peter Jackson's film *"Heavenly Creatures"*. They wanted more, but more desperately or perhaps arrogantly than most. The term 'juvenile delinquents' was an 'indicator of teenagers getting out of hand' according to the 1954 'Mazengarb Report Commission of Inquiry into the moral delinquency of NZ Youth'. It was released and delivered free to families receiving the Family Benefit, not that I remember it arriving at our family home. If Mary even read it she would have probably binned it. She was one of the working mothers it blamed.

The report didn't stop anything. The technical revolution gave media the opportunity to show us the current behaviour of other cultures and countries, adding to our frustration, along with the global social upheaval of youth. With phones becoming more acceptable in homes, even if they were huge, dial-up, heavy black ones that discouraged long conversations because of an aching arm; they were the key to rebellion as communication always is.

Bright fashion colours and longer hair began emerging, reflecting attitudes. Bodgies and Widgies particularly with their own brand of haircuts slicked down with Brylcreem, as well as outlandish clothes based on English Edwardian era but adapted to NZ styles with their tight pants, pullovers, windcheaters and neckerchiefs. Girls were considered to be an employment risk from several points of view including having 'time-wasting, inappropriately dressed, badly behaved disruptive mates visit', who were variously described as yahoos, larrikins, hooligans, and yobs. Their female Widgies, in a fashion reversal, favoured a scraped back pony-tail look and were dressed down in colourless dark clothes, sometimes jeans (worn by both), leaving their boyfriends to be 'Cocks of the walk'.

Beware the 'Milk-bar Cowboys' in their leather bomber jackets, peaked caps, drainpipe trousers and flying boots (when they could afford them) and their insolent cheeky ways, their slang appalling to many. They sometimes had what were considered 'rough girls', called 'Pillion Pets', sitting behind them on their motor-bike seats. (A pillion pet I met in her middle years was as traditional as any other mother her age and very fastidious.) They in contrast to the boys, like the Widgies, dressed down too. Their favourite hangouts during the day were the notorious Curries Milk Bar, which I had not been in, and Somerville's Milk Bar halfway down Queen St. They parked their motorbikes directly out front on the road with several in one car space.

> The 1954 Petone Milk Bar gang youths were 'revealed as having a shocking degree of immoral conduct which spread into sexual orgies in several private homes etc.' and 'Perhaps the most startling feature is the changed mental attitude of many young people toward this evil.' 'It was reported that some of the girls were either unconcerned or unashamed and even proud, of what they had done... The situation is a serious one, and something must be done.' (Quotes from *NZ Herald* August 24th 2014.)

The Auckland literati and artistic types fraternised at Somerville's so it was a popular if not always an appropriate place to frequent. It was one of the few milk bars that still served real American style coffee, as they had for the Yanks when they were here. There was a soda fountain and they made milk shakes and served ice-cream sundaes in long glass dishes with 3 ice-cream scoops, supplying the requested toppings with real strawberries in season. Most milk bars had slippery plastic bench seating, red a favourite colour, finished in shiny chrome, with the centre table tops in Formica – as in at least one Burger King I've seen recently.

Literature, art, movies, and music often pre-date change as they did for our rebellious young in the middle fifties. Juke boxes played the latest overseas tunes, banned on radio, and were the best places to go to hear Rock'n'roll, Chuck Berry, Fats Domino, King Creole, Elvis and Bill Haley and the Comets records, the actual movie *'Rock Around the Clock'* not being shown here until 1956. Another movie that caught the censor's attention several times before being released was *'The Wild One'* with hero Marlon Brando as a motor bike gang leader. This was seen as 'glamorising gang lifestyles and encouraging antisocial and undesirable behaviour and eroding traditional values.' *'The Man with the Golden Arm'* (controversially about drugs) the *'Blackboard Jungle'* as well as James Dean's *'Rebel without a Cause'*, didn't help to calm anyone down. All having 'the pernicious effect of American culture' and 'adding to teenagers' unpredictability'.

The sensual innuendo in songs (which went right over the heads of some of us), the dancing antics of Elvis and other pop singers and groups, the new provocative ones particularly aimed at youth, along with often having access to more money with less stringent rules, meant that sex became openly talked about even if practised secretly, so it was inevitable singers and movies were all blamed for having 'undue influence on youth'. People were shocked and irritated and felt very strongly about the emergence of these unpredictable and upstart youths.

For girls who worked in the city, there was always a feeling of excitement when avoiding the Milk-bar Cowboys' overt stares and ignoring the catcalls and whistles when passing by the group, and we daren't look back or we could be followed, a few yards (metres) at least, and that was better not risked at night – especially when they hung out at the Queen St. Majestic movie theatre.

The so-called 'Milk Bar Murder' that frightened people had happened at Somerville's, and had been during the day. A young girl had rejected her suitor when she found out he was already married. He had been reading newspaper articles etc. about young lovers, it was said at his trial, which had encouraged him to try and get her sympathy and love back by threatening her with a gun. The thwarted suitor had been waiting in the milk bar where he knew she would come down for a milkshake in her lunch break and hadn't intended to kill her. Whatever the plan, he shot her and she died later in hospital. This unusual happening in a major commercial thoroughfare was horrifying to most but I would think part of the Milk-bar Cowboys' cultivated aura, especially as the lover was subsequently hung. Luckily I hadn't been aware of the murder at the time or at least not associated it with that milk bar. The 'Mazengarb Report' instigators would have felt completely justified as there was another murder the same year at the 'Hole in the Wall', again in Auckland.

Teenagers were forerunners to me of the simmering social change which began to happen more quickly in the early sixties, especially after drug use became prolific, although I was a bemused and non-participating observer of the hippy, bra burning, sex, drugs and rock & roll revolution when, as a male friend has since commented, 'romance went out the door'. Maybe, but young women along with male youths had begun to come into their own, for good or bad, and we were not surprised or particularly unhappy when the 1960's turned out as they did. The world changed for us forever. The 1950's and early 60's is seen by some as, on the whole, a 'Golden Era' in many ways.

Chapter 20 Marriage and Social Expectations in the 40's and 50's

Marriage

Women were brought up to marry. What else would we do? Not something I had understood at the time. I was busy just surviving, not welcome to live in our own home that we had waited so long for at 16, once Mary remarried. Flatting was for guys on bigger wages which became obvious fairly quickly. Wanting to work and being independent my achievement, not particularly ambitious although responsibility didn't worry me, certainly not seeing males as the answer for me but they were then, without parents for support. I would say men thought 'I didn't know my place'. I didn't have much respect for them on the whole after some of my experiences in life and without a decent father of my own.

Although happiness for life with a soul-mate partner was a pretty unreasonable expectation for everyone and an objective look at marriages around us would have made that obvious, nevertheless personal happiness and fulfilment was the goal for most and young girls anyway wanted to believe in fairy-tale romantic relationships that promised and were to encompass love, loyalty, fairness, honour, sacrifice, integrity and truth. It was the sentimentality promoted by books and though I don't remember 'Mills and Boons', women's magazines had love stories, and there were always the movies hype of 'happy ever after' endings in a marriage – love hijacked by Hollywood.

Girls were encouraged to live their dream of 'The Big Wedding Day' and it was lovely to have a day when the centre of attention was us and hope and good wishes for a rewarding and happy future were made (if not envisaged) from all, but that sometimes became the focus, not how the actual marriage would survive, and how they would get along with their partner afterwards. A man saying he loved you and wanting to marry you was enough for most. I doubt either asked 'What does love actually mean to you? What are your expectations of me?' Experiencing legal sex and all the accompanying emotions would have been predominant and discussions about the delicate art of power sharing and compromise, compatibility, cooperation, and caring communication I would think be a given, by the wife to be anyway. Certainly responsibility when she had experienced it from her own father.

One of the AGGS teachers did encourage us to learn about a variety of subjects so we could have intelligent conversations with our spouses – suggesting he might otherwise have his head stuck in the paper over breakfast. As she hadn't married herself we thought her quaint. It is surprising to many how different life is when people actually live together even if they had known each other for a long time. And there are always those fortunate ones who married caring people and did love each other and their families. I have known their children and they have no idea how blessed they have been. To tell them would not change anything.

Young women were admonished if they didn't behave 'properly' and caused a scandal, which meant they had to be acquiescent, not swearing, not putting on airs and graces or attracting attention to themselves to be talked about i.e. not have someone say; "No wonder she hooked him! She set her cap at him right from the start". Having fun was to be controlled – hard for the gigglier young girls. It was important not to lose our reputation which could cut our chances of a 'good' marriage back to nothing; so many parents were overprotective and controlling. (Luckily I didn't have that problem.) Several friends told me their husbands had asked their fathers for 'their daughter's hand in marriage' although whether this was general I don't know. We were also warned not to break off engagements with a betrothed when we found the 'love of our life' was not what he seemed to be after a while – 'you might be sued.' It may have been a possibility although no-one I ever met had been and it could have been said to stabilise nerves even though the girls were probably right in their conclusions. Loyalty was often misplaced too, before and after a marriage.

Girls married young, usually by 22, and did so up to the nineteen sixties. In 1960 there were 1,213 males and 1,196 females in NZ. (*The NZ Official Year Book*.) Even young unmarried women were called spinsters and the word 'chastity' was often used in relation to them. Men were referred to as bachelors.

Women usually defined themselves by their husband's position in society and were used to being controlled, often just going from a father to a husband, who would usually enforce the same patterns of entitlement. Given that we all tend to marry what we know, that could be good or bad. They may have had a male boss for a short time in between and sometimes employment lasted for a while after marriage, if the husband agreed and becoming pregnant hadn't happened straight away. Sometimes it had already. No-one I knew had talked about protection from pregnancy to me and I don't think it was discussed generally, especially if you were married. Babies were expected forthwith. Women stayed home. The sex subject was avoided, by women anyway.

Trousseau preparations were often begun in a 'glory box' (or bottom drawer) long before a suitable suitor appeared. Useful items were hoarded, mainly good linen, towels, and perhaps Tupperware later. Inherited family items would hopefully be added to as wedding presents. If not all the necessary items were given as presents, people would sometimes offer things they no longer had use for to 'get the couple started'. This could mean ending up with sheets of various sizes (all white then although usually good linen), various coloured towels, and tea towels, square and round tablecloths, and perhaps plastic ones, a hodgepodge of saucepans and containers that were often useful especially as most newlyweds lived in furnished rental accommodation.

Honeymoons

Honeymoons were not always affordable. A week away was possible, a fortnight thought vaguely extravagant, but many like my own was for a one or two night stay at a local hotel or possibly one a short drive away. My only relatively lavish spending, other than my wedding frock which I also bought myself, was a beautiful, drifting, full-length, white diaphanous nightie with accompanying long sleeved over-gown. (A bit different to the usual long, all-covering, winceyette nighties or pyjamas.)

Abortion

Being all locked into a constricting community of stifled and suppressed sexual passion often led to confusion and lack of understanding about our natural emotions, for some creating smouldering resentment, frustration, and rebellion. The dangers though of falling for a boy and letting him 'have his way with you' and the 'evils of sex' were warnings we girls were all given. Sweet innocent virgins were apparently the only ones decent men would marry – of course they were the ones that were often caught out too because of their very naivety. Girls that had experimented could be canny enough not to get pregnant. Shameful examples of 'used fallen girls' were whispered about, "You'll end up on the street like so-and-so!" or "The poor thing. They sent her off to ...," a town or city as far away as possible where there might be a useful relative or a home for 'bad girls' where she had the illegitimate baby (or little bastard) adopted out. "Getting into trouble (pregnant)" was hugely scandalous. The biggest gossips were often the ones who had themselves been in that situation or their daughters had. Possibly suffering from the loss of their potential child/grandchild and their grief came out as spite.

Maybe girls were sent off to Australia if the baby was known about early enough and there was the money and connections for an abortion. There was occasional loss of life when girls, who were brave or desperate enough to go to a back-street abortionist, encountered a particularly cheap, butchering one. Going to any abortionist was usually hushed up and seen as disgraceful and those girls who kept their children were viewed in the same way for having "the temerity to keep them". Either way you were damned. Safe medical abortion for girls without money was not an option until 1977, so unless they tried the gin, hot bath and jumping up and down on a wire-wove bed routine (this sometimes worked apparently as I understand some women can vouch for – or possibly not – as miscarriage is common) they lived with the consequences. Others were perhaps relieved when they had a stillbirth or miscarried naturally.

Some women never really recovered from losing a baby they had conceived in love, or sometimes just plain ignorance or rape, and had had them aborted or adopted out – often forcefully. Stories were handed down in many families about a female relative (like my second husband's – it would have been his unwed aunty, the youngest in the family) in baby loss circumstances who had died of a broken heart which is now medically accepted as a legitimate cause, others committing suicide. Or a baby was abandoned on the steps of a church or anywhere really. If they were lucky and survived, an adoption could be arranged but their parenthood would probably never be known, especially earlier in the century, for those who craved the knowledge. It may seem unbelievable in today's world but there were serious social and economic consequences then if women didn't marry. It was called a shotgun wedding if they were pregnant and did.

Miscarriage

Married women or unmarried women, who had simply miscarried and were grieving, often did so silently for various reasons including shame, privacy, grief, and fear of being condemned as having procured an abortion or self-aborting. An attitude that adds terrible guilt for them sometimes still. Many in the community believed it was somehow the mother's own fault that she had lost her baby. (1 in 4 women miscarry and the largest percentage of those had pregnancies that were never viable for many reasons, the most common one being chromosomal abnormality – like a zip that doesn't come together perfectly.)

The grief from a miscarriage can haunt women all their lives, some more than others. It can be assuaged partly sometimes by having another baby but not necessarily. The dates they died, like stillbirths, are often recognised in some way even if it is only the mother that remembers and it is good if she names them – a name that could be for either sex if she didn't know. It also depends on the personal circumstances and experience. The first of mine was not good, as it was after a kicking so I was in shock about that anyway as well as being blamed for the loss. The second time with a different husband I was more distraught for him, he was so upset. He was also left on his own in a waiting area for hours not knowing what was going on and I was in a dark room on my own in pain. The doctor had been called away quite quickly without any discussion and didn't come back for several hours by which time I felt like screaming. He arranged for an operating theatre immediately and when I asked my husband be told, he agreed. A pity he hadn't let him stay with me for both our sakes – but no-one was allowed in the delivery room then, theatre or not.

In the 20 years I ran our miscarriage group I came across all sorts of circumstances including an 80-year-old who had been too ashamed, frightened and in such grief, she told no-one about hers including her husband, who had recently died, until she told me. Even then she apologised for taking up my time. So sad. Men surprised me too. They often suppressed their own grief to support their wives. www.miscarriagesupport.org.nz

Adoptions

Adoptions were often as painful for both mother and child in their own way. Frequently guilt for the mother and maybe the father too if he knew. After her lovely adoptive parents had died, one friend in 2000 tracked her 70-year-old birth mother down. She was rejected again by her. The shame the mother had always felt perhaps so deep or she would not, even then, go against her husband's wishes and acknowledge her or tell those in the family who didn't know. Perhaps both. My friend is such a lovely person I couldn't help thinking how much her real mother missed. Other women can't wait to find and acknowledge their children once their situation is reasonably viable and the law allows. One way or another it will always be painful for someone.

Couples sometimes couldn't afford to get married in the Depression; they could wait up to 8 years or more, so there were long engagements, and nature took its course, although the marriage may not have. For some reason, the condemnation of unmarried mothers was less common once 'The Pill' became available in the sixties.

The most horrifying of moralistic attitudes toward women in the early part of the century was what files revealed about aging women who were still found in state-run mental hospitals in the middle of the century. They had been incarcerated by their parents as young women and left there for 'moral degradation', code for having a baby outside of marriage. What happened to their babies? Was adoption also a part of that scenario?

A Wife's Duties

Without the helpful household accessories we have currently, the practicalities of married life took over fairly quickly. Quote – 'A drudgery oppressively imposed'. The responsibility of a household may have been a shock to some and perhaps others enjoyed it, but either way there was always something to do – especially as children arrived. Cooking, dishes, washing, ironing, vacuuming, sweeping, scrubbing and polishing floors, sewing, knitting, mending, gardening, shopping and the rest, often tamed the eagerness and idealism of youth.

The strong commitments of tradition would usually cut in with the wedding ceremony, for the husband anyway, and the expectation that it would be for life, like their own parents, with whatever that entailed. Unfortunate if a bad choice had been made. Other patterns emerged too once children were born, often with unexpected or unacceptable behaviour, but it was the wife who usually acceded to the husband's wishes. Coming down to reality from the high expectations of youth could create feelings of failure and the unfairness of life, disappointment, resentment and depression.

Once the improbability of the dream of easy success was obvious, except for those lucky or well matched couples, most people got on with life as best they could. It was up to everyone to face the hardships and stresses, either individually or together, along with whatever pleasure and satisfaction they may experience of having children, and to form their own unit of strength. If they were from larger families themselves they may have found that brothers and sisters were closer and more loyal, reliable and supportive than others, which was often the way. I found that especially in the country where the whole family may have been expected to work if they were on a farm, the husband and wife doing the milking until children were old enough to help out. There were also women's groups like the 'Country Women's Institute', which I experienced as Mary once joined in Kauri Point, Katikati where they had access for meetings in a local hall. (Looking back that group seemed an unlikely choice for her but it was an area we lived in longer than most, albeit with my stepfather changing jobs but not necessarily the house that time.)

Families

Life became about the family, although children did not seem as precious in the early part of the century as they generally are today with fewer children, although not necessarily in all households of course. Perhaps infertility was not common so children were easily conceived as there were few couples without children. Depending on the woman and perhaps her husband's or older children's help, or lack of it, stress would have been a problem, especially with large families when there may have been too much for mothers to do and too many mouths to feed. It may also have been because children died much more frequently from diseases, so parents protected their feelings by not becoming too attached to their offspring. They would grieve no doubt but were probably expected to move on fairly quickly and would have needed to with the constant call on their time. Another baby would have been considered the answer, by males at least. Post-WWII, the government encouraged women to reproduce in abundance to replace population lost to the war, and they too promoted idealistic family values (encouraged by the Family Benefit), hence the 'baby boomers' (1946–1964).

Without the modern scan Mary was often consulted about what sex a baby might be and the favoured trick was to hang the woman's wedding ring on a longer piece of her hair or a cotton thread and hold it over her pregnant tummy. The ring was supposed to have a life of its own and begin moving in a circle for girl and backwards and forwards if it was a boy. As I didn't put much store in this mode of divining I don't know for sure if that is correct. Other people said they could tell the sex by how high or low the baby was being carried and there were plenty of other old wives' tales about other methods.

The prevailing public position, which remained through to the sixties, about allowing a pregnancy bulge to show or referring to what was obvious, was considered ill-mannered and women were expected to wear clothing to disguise it. A euphemism for how your wife was progressing might be, '…and how's the Missus?' or if a pregnancy was only suspected, it could be a straightforward ignorant, 'Is she up the duff?' or 'A bun in the oven then?' The later 'Has it popped it out yet?' which was pretty offensive considering what many women suffered through.

When relations were visiting toward the end of my first retained pregnancy, my four-year-old-nephew asked me why my tummy had got so fat so I told him about the baby inside. I was roundly reproved by his mother, my sister-in-law. Sometimes women withdrew entirely from socialising, staying home before they were showing much but certainly more so toward the end of the pregnancy. That denial often left women feeling ashamed of their condition, as if pregnancy was something unnatural. A public announcement in the newspaper was common at births, announcing that 'so and so' had given birth to a 'bouncing baby boy or girl' which could come as a shock to those 'not in the know' and also if it was soon after a marriage.

Parenting

The huge adjustment to being a parent was all-consuming and my previous life was hardly even a memory it was so far from the reality of each hour of the day being so dictated to by routines. With a sick and constantly crying new baby who was also mentally retarded, and the beginning of another pregnancy of vomiting and nausea starting again six months later, life was exhausting. I also felt consumed, absorbed and diluted into the eternal elemental stream of maternal consciousness, my identity disintegrating and dissolving as if I didn't really exist as a separate entity. In the tired, mindless, ritualistic and soul-alienating isolation of existence then, I fought hard to hold onto the 'me' I knew. Trying to survive and be normal while still living up to the expectation of others, supporting a sister with big problems and a mother with an unsupportive husband (like my own), especially after she discovered she had a heart condition. I'd occasionally simply just sit, hardly able to function but forced to in the end by the needs of the children playing around me.

As well as the 'Missus' I was also referred to by my spouse and other men as the 'little wife' or 'wifie' and sometimes called 'mother' too, (which I didn't respond to at 21) but seldom my name, furthering the sense of being lost in this world of servicing other's needs which was also expected to be achieved with a cheerful attitude. People assumed that women would cope so it was not unusual for them to be treated this way, each in their own circumstances.

Adult company, especially other women's for comparing coping strategies, would have been valuable, but that would have taken so much effort even if it had been available, it would have been beyond my capabilities anyway for many months. Just walking up to the shops a kilometre away was a big deal with no car. The need for something more to look forward to though gradually did surface in me again and although everyday connections were not an option, I did eventually manage to get to see my sister-in-law when I could. She'd had babies young too.

My experience with all our near neighbours out working and their children being older may not be typical of the times either, but certainly lack of easy communication was. Cars were a luxury item for many, particularly a young average family and anyway the husband usually had it to get to work if they could afford one. Other people made it hard for themselves because they simply mistrusted things they did not understand, for instance they wouldn't have a phone in the house whether they could afford it or not (never mind such a thing as a cell – not even envisaged then). It was hard for me to grasp that sort of attitude as well, as all that kept me from having anything modern was a lack of money.

Adjusting to one wage was a big problem after marriage, with women not being expected to work, so along with the extra outgoings for a new arrival, attention to budgeting was really serious. Even if a woman had been employed on a low pay-rate they would have missed it.

If husbands conscientiously sorted out the family finances, as many did, life would be reasonable unless they were particularly low paid or he was mean. However if the family outgoings were dictated to by the husband's needs, like not wishing to cut back on pub spending with his mates or give up gambling, women's needs were often the last consideration and most men of that time were traditionalists. Unlike me I found later, women did not usually handle the money – that is what was left in the opened wage packet I received – better than none by comparison to some. Every penny was treasured and carefully put aside each week for necessities like food, perhaps material for sewing clothes or wool for knitting, the mortgage, power, annual outgoings like tax and rates and any time-payments which would have been for things like a clothes-line, a rug, a heater and fridge (one at a time in our first house) all worked out to the last shilling.

Eventually 'keeping up with the Jones', easier communication and the convenience of home entertainment with TV, which finally arrived in the sixties, won out for most people to more pay-as-you-go type options. Although not to be done without today, they were considered an extravagance then by many. Women could end up forced back into employment to cover the spending once that happened, babies or not. 'From small acorns... ' to today's (to me) horrifying debts for the 'now' generation.

A child was ultimately a woman's responsibility and a wife was expected to deal with their children's behaviour. Rules were very clear and there were extra manners to be observed if eating out but the general ones taught were: please and thank you, to be quiet when told and especially for grace to be said before food was eaten, no talking with a full mouth, never to use fingers or knife to eat off or push food onto fork, never put elbows on the table, not reach over the table but ask for something to be passed and say thank you, make sure your mouth was empty before drinking, put knives and forks together tidily on the plate when finished, covering mouth when coughing, sneezing or yawning, apologise for burping and flatulence and move away from others, not remark on elders' noises and embarrass them, not pick noses, no spitting, apologise when knocking into someone and for being late, saying 'excuse me' when wishing to pass, not gawking or laughing at others – especially those who may have a physical deformity or mental problem (nervous giggles hard to control), men to open doors for ladies, offer to carry parcels or bags, give up seats for elders on buses/trams, not to fiddle when answering questions and to speak clearly, not to point (I noticed royalty doesn't have a problem with that these days) and to defer to adults' wisdom, experience and authority, no matter how stuffy and stolid they seemed, with respect for God, religious leaders, police, elders and 'betters' and refer to adults as Mr. or Mrs. or as pseudo Aunt and Uncle etc. Not to say we achieved all these things but they were the expectations for us and our children.

Discipline, sometimes physical, and control of children was expected and they did more clearly understand their boundaries and learned not to back-chat adults. There was stricter religion taught at schools some of which was frightening. Open classrooms were a later development so supervision was easier and loud noises, running in the corridors or on stairs was forbidden. Good posture was encouraged – shoulders back, head up, stomach in – and attention to the teacher and especially the headmaster – a terrifying figure to many. It would be the 'Dunce's Corner' or the strap for infringements, even for girls as I found out on a bad day. There was often seething repression though, especially with boys.

The father might have the total responsibility of 'bringing home the bacon etc.' and DIY and outside jobs like the lawns and gardening and dealing to minor maintenance problems, but the mother did everything else. Although much of the early part of the century Victorian and Edwardian-type formality of relationships with their children had dissipated, men we knew took no particular interest in or bothered to show a baby or young child any real affection. That was the woman's domain. Although some men may have felt really proud of their children and loved them, they probably wouldn't have displayed it. I remember my husband making fun of that and shaking hands with our son when he was about three, who responded seriously to the formality. As was shown in the interviews with Arthur Lydiard's group in '*The Golden Hour*' (2012 TV production), fathers were very important and could dictate a child's aspirations – for good or bad – especially if the children only experienced criticism. Arthur filled the nurturing gap for several. Boys were expected to live up to their father's ambitions and honour them whatever they were, suitable or not for their sons, and were seen by their fathers as an extension of themselves. A big responsibility if the son was not up to it, dictating their lives, and the cause of much heartache, frustration, and sadness. Suicide was not a subject I remember being reported on and I personally only heard about one. I'm sure there were many more.

Men usually took a back seat to everything domestic. Even if a man did offer to help, as an older friend commented once, "I think I made a mistake in not letting my husband help when he offered to early in our marriage. I took it as a slur on my competence rather than the helpful offer that it was. He never did again, so five quick children later, life was hard."

This attitude continued after the war with fathers of baby boomers, and many wives aware of the war's effect on their husbands, would caution the children to behave and 'mind their father' (meaning 'do as you are told'), which they usually did. The consequences of not 'toeing the line', if the transgression was serious enough, would be 'wait till your father gets home!' When he did it was usually the strap or a whack or two from the hand and this would have disturbed his routine of wanting peace and quiet, to relax in his slippers and perhaps have a smoke and read the paper, after an 8-hour day and 40-hour working week. Babies and the younger children would perhaps be kept up long enough to see their father and then be fed and put to bed early so that only the older children would be at the 'sit down at the table' home-cooked meal of possibly soup first in the winter, meat, three fresh vegetables and a sweet – standard for an average home.

For some families this was a pleasant time of being together and discussing the day or a subject particular to their interests and for others it was a 'no talking' time. Late for dinner meant finding your plate of food on a simmering saucepan, with a lid covering the plate to keep it heated or alternatively, dried to a crisp in the oven – depending on how forgiving the cook was.

As children grew and especially if it was a boy, there was more attention given and a father might find time to play with his son and sometimes daughter. Along with the parents' controlling influence, especially the father, this sense of estrangement often lasted until adulthood and for some all their lives, or at least to when the father began to show his age and loss of physical strength, then positions could reverse if grudges weren't held.

There would always have been a variety of exceptions to the general mould of course, including other cultures' ideas, and lucky the children who had a different kind of father. My own son's father baulked when I suggested one day he could do with a cuddle after some trauma had occurred, however his idea of comfort was another tentative shake of the hand. Anyone who indulged their children or showed them what was thought of as an inappropriate amount of love was considered foolish.

There was in many relationships a certain amount of resentment at the time taken up by children and especially a new arrival. The lack of attention given to the breadwinner especially, particularly his sexual needs, which may have remained the same when his wife's probably had not, the thought of another baby not at the top of her agenda. It was a distinct possibility with the limited precaution options available.

Some couples could rely on breastfeeding as a pregnancy deterrent, and for those where that worked, there was often a distinct pattern of 2 year intervals between babies. When it didn't work, it was not unusual to hear of another baby being born even as early as 9 months after the first. It wasn't till well into my own 1950's marriage I can remember preventative measures being referred to discreetly and finally got some control over my life, like others, instead of relying on the abstinence or withdrawal and sometimes the condom option, which the male may not be interested in using.

It was no doubt objectionable for a husband having to forgo his natural/pleasurable/rightful procreation act. If you were lucky you could reluctantly be fitted for 'the cap' (made from rubber) by a doctor, which usually came with a moral lecture, mainly about men's rights along with religious overtones, and often whether the husband had given his agreement. Having your tubes tied was a procedure seldom offered to anyone under thirty and usually reluctantly even if they had several children, unless there was a life-threatening situation, and even then your husband's signed permission was needed. A friend told me recently her doctor was very kind and because her husband was a known philanderer and her mother had standing in the community, they arranged for her to have an operation privately. Ultimately though her husband had to sign it off. Apparently he was persuaded to, I would say by his very stern mother-in-law.

There was the 'rhythm' method too accepted by the Catholic Church which involved taking your temperature and guessing the time of ovulation and refraining from sexual relations around that time (I understand). They all came with their flaws, but given the number of children in most Catholic families, their option wasn't of much help. I knew a few girls desperate not to have more babies that it didn't work for although perhaps it did for others. Some enjoyed big families. Marriages, especially those interrupted by the war, often produced late babies (religious parents or otherwise) that were seen as 'after-thoughts'. Unfortunately a higher percentage of those were born with a physical or mental disability possibly from deteriorating women's eggs and men's sperm.

By the early 1960's, when more reliable contraception as in 'The Pill' became available, population statistics had already peaked, the women I chatted to anyway did not want large families, no matter what the government encouraged. The birth rate had dropped during the Depression even without good contraception which meant New Zealanders were only replacing themselves and with the war as well, it was understandable where the government was coming from. Families of four children were common, which was generally accepted as a compromise. Not getting pregnant was women's foremost worry, aside from the everyday family hassles. I lived in apprehension of becoming pregnant for many reasons. It stayed with me until I was well past 'the change of life' (menopause).

I did have one Dutch Catholic friend who was from a family of 12, which was not unusual for them apparently, and when she couldn't conceive, she worried that there would be no-one to look after her in her old age. This was not a reason I had heard spoken about by New Zealanders, living in a welfare state, but may have been part of the thoughts that led to large families.

The sense of idealism about marriage and having a family meant there were few people who didn't follow that pattern and I only knew one couple who took a long time to have children, and theirs may have been a fertility problem. Either way, they had bought a house and a car before having their first. Unfortunately, on his way home from visiting his wife and baby in hospital, the husband was knocked off his bike and killed. It was so shocking we couldn't get our heads around it. It made no sense. Especially to those of us who thought their decision had been sensible and they had done everything the right way around. It was the timing that upset us most I think. Poor man. Poor wife and child. His family had been provided for but that was no compensation for not having a loving husband and father.

There would have been others who were reluctant to admit not being able to conceive and would say to anyone nosy or insensitive enough to ask that, 'it was their business and their choice'. Whether you didn't have a family from choice or otherwise it could be awkward socially. Invites to occasions may not be forthcoming unless perhaps couples were part of a club and because it was unusual not to have children, there seemed to me to always be a sense of those couples 'not being good enough' around them but also some jealousy or envy.

My Baby Experiences

Women did not really talk about their birth experiences to each other much, including my own mother, although she did about its aftermath. A friend that I asked would not tell me. It had been such a distressing and difficult time, she said later, so she did not want to be the one to put me off when it may not be the same for me. It was. My sister-in-law Kay, on the other hand, was always lucky to even make it to a hospital and only just did with their fifth (and last) boy child.

He literally dropped out past her briefs onto the hospital entry hall floor, to my brother Ralph's absolute horror. He had a thing about blood like the rest of our family. The nurses came back about 10 minutes later to assure him both mother and baby were fine and found him standing in the same place in shock. He was still holding his wife's suitcase and staring at the blood spattered white dishes on the nearby large hospital kitchen trolley.

I thought it would have been much better to be prepared for the shock of birthing – it was such a painful, life-changing event – than live in fear and ignorance at just 20. I had already lost a baby to miscarriage which had been reasonably painful so the only small comfort I hung onto through hours of tormenting labour was remembering Mary saying that it couldn't last forever, although after three days it seemed like it. Obviously no-one suggested a caesarean operation and the nurses had already made it clear that noise was disapproved of, screaming not an option, so all this fear and misery was suppressed, although what was thought of as 'foreign' women, like Greeks, had no such inhibitions.

The outcome was, from my one brief glimpse, a dark-blue, limp baby girl with thick black hair, who did not cry, and was hurriedly rushed away. No medical person remarked on why I couldn't hold her although I hadn't known whether that was the normal procedure, or that I had to still pass a placenta. I had thought it was all over and when the strong pains came back again, was horrified it wasn't. The pacing doctor said, 'About time' with not even the usual patronising 'There, there dear' on offer. The just-as-impatient nurses showed no emotion, although they may have been upset and covering for the hospital at the way the birth had turned out. All a negative experience anyway. The only plus that stays in my mind was that I no longer felt nauseous. I was sooo hungry. They just wheeled me out of the theatre and said I could see my daughter later. That took half a day and, by then, she was the right colour although she seemed unable to breast feed.

A brusque nurse forced her onto my painful breasts muttering about 'useless new mothers'. No medical person actually told me what had happened at my baby's birth or that there would be consequences to be dealt with, like brain damage and her possible early death. The inability for her to suck was just the beginning. At home a bottle sorted that.

I hadn't even understood that she had been dead and was resuscitated until years later when some-one told me about their birth experience. We just accepted things then. When I asked for Shanla's birth records years after, I was told the Hospital did not have them any longer. I often had the thought how fitting it would have been to just drop my baby off to the incompetent doctor for 24 hours (which would have been more than enough I would think for anyone). He could experience the practical result of his decisions and see how well he coped with a constantly crying baby, who could not keep milk down so needed to be fed continuously and only slept the odd few hours in 24. He may have been as appalled as I feel writing about this now.

There were several possibilities for the cause of Shanla's retardation although her birth probably did the most damage. One was I had been given radiation treatment at 15 to help with acne. That Pacific Island women had experienced jelly-like babies being born after being close to the French Bomb testing was not publicised that I know of. (I was 30 before I found out about those effects of radiation from the Auckland Public Library and have wondered about Shanla since.) Secondly, I was so ill with 'hyperemesis gravida sum' (like Kate with her royal babies) that I hardly kept anything down for months, even vomiting up water 24/7 losing serious weight (as I did with all my pregnancies only not quite as extreme). What would that have done to any baby? I tried to get help from a medical professional but he had no answers. Thirdly, a chemist recommended me taking 'travel sickness pills', which I did. As they made little or no difference I stopped after about 10 days. (It wasn't until the Thalidomide babies became news I even thought about the possibility of those affecting her.) My husband had possibly cost me one loss, but there had been no violence near the baby this time.

I also have no memory of anyone checking for my baby's heart beat during labour and I don't know if they even did in those days. I remember thinking more than once as the pregnancy had progressed, 'My baby doesn't move much.'

I thought women who talked about the 'joy of having a baby' could not be mothers.

How could anyone use the word 'joy' in relation to the huge new responsibility of a constantly crying and vomiting baby? The strong need of awareness for the life of a delicate, tiny human being was overwhelming. Shanla dominated every moment of life, awake or asleep. Nights were torture. The longest sleep for years was two and a half hours at a time. If I'd had it, I would have given a million dollars for even one night's peaceful, irresponsible, unbroken, and dreamless sleep. I craved sleep like people craved cigarettes or alcohol.

A local doctor I consulted only offered his opinion that his wife had to get up to their baby too, insinuating I was just a new moaning mother, so I struggled on with a sick child who had Galactocaemia, which may or may not have been recognised back then by a competent physician.

As a result of constant antibiotics for her infections all the teeth in Shanla's head rotted and had to be removed at about three years old. The city dentist who removed them under an anaesthetic roundly chastised me in front of a waiting room full of people afterwards. I couldn't even think about defending myself with a screaming, terrified child desperately clinging to me with blood still leaking out of her mouth. They had taken her off me with ear splitting howls and brought her back the same way. I would have said that we had no money for the luxury of sweets and had had to save for weeks even for the taxi fare home. Unable to chew until her second teeth came in, Shanla from then could only eat mashed food. She'd even ask Bevan, her younger brother, to bite her nails for her. She wouldn't let me cut them.

I had a boy baby 15 months after my daughter. Not from choice. Arriving at National Women's Hospital after beginning labour I was put in with a small group of women who were also. The room we were in was separated into cubicles which just fitted a bed and a small dresser at one end with a cupboard underneath for clothes etc. and medical needs and water on top. There was a curtain over the open entry and a chair outside for the support person, not necessarily a husband. We could not see each other so when what turned out to be a quiet Maori lady in the next cubicle called out that her baby had come, I was shocked. There was no response from a nurse (no buzzer) so I went to try and comfort her, but yelled loudly instead to get real help. So much blood!

Although it was as painful as Shanla's birth, Bevan's didn't take as long. He blew me away as he came out yelling and wriggling, his strong little body very much alive – a shock really compared to Shanla. I couldn't believe the life in him!

I just watched him, amazed. He fed well from a bottle (to the nurses' disgust for not breast feeding) always aware and moving, his bright blue eyes seemed focused looking up at me as much as to say, "So you're my mother!" On the second day after I had developed breast fever I leaned over from the bed to pick him up out of his plastic bassinet for a cuddle but I simply didn't seem strong enough to manage it. I thought, 'Wow, I got weak really quickly with this infection,' and made more effort. Bevan suddenly came over onto the bed with me – plus the bassinet. He was still gripping its curved edge with one tiny fist, the supporting frame and wheels skittering away. I couldn't believe it. I had to fight him to peel his fist open to make him let go.

Physically strong, independent, capable, observant and quick, Bevan didn't really change much all his life. The antithesis of his sister. He also reacted to milk, however. He preferred real food anyway and was on home grown vegies by two months. He used to eye our plates at dinner from his highchair as if a bit of meat would be appreciated. Without him I sometimes wondered later how we would have survived so well.

What seemed to me to be a barbaric but accepted traditional ritual of circumcision was one I did not want to put my little son through, but the custom was so ingrained and believed to be the most hygienic, I gave in to my husband's persistence. On the appointed day at the local surgery, the doctor's staff just took him off me and told me to leave for 15 minutes. I cried my way around the local shops wheeling Shanla, which meant she cried too. We returned to find him so distressed; it took a long time to calm him down. I don't know how it was done or if any form of anaesthetic was used as it wasn't a time when doctors' decisions were questioned. I just gave my son lots of extra cuddles.

Shanla spent the first few years on my hip most of the time along with Bevan on the other for a short time. If one cried the other would too. Holding them both, the exhaustion was so extreme I would even fall asleep, if I was sitting down, and not drop them.

Shanla needed constant monitoring. Thankfully she thought I had eyes in the back of my head when I once sharply told her to stop poking a small tea-spoon handle into a power point without turning around. I could see her in the kitchen windows' reflection. A good ploy in her case. She'd feel under my hair at the back sometimes after that but I'd tell her my other eyes were asleep. Bevan wouldn't be held for long. He'd usually wriggle down after a while and squirm his way to a toy or something that caught his eye. At 5 months he clawed his way up onto their rocking horse and would climb up anything he could including, when he was a little bit older, pushing a chair to the kitchen sink to get himself a drink of water when I was busy with Shanla.

I had no idea what normal stages of development were so Bevan was a revelation. I accepted that when he needed something he would get it himself if he could. He was a doer not a talker. When Bevan walked at 7 months, then ran not long after, Shanla was so jealous she started trying to walk too. She had crawled once he did. It took a while as at 2 she did not have a strong body or coordination like him but eventually she succeeded. That memory stays in my mind as we were all so focused, me encouraging her to reach out and take my hands and Bevan hovering in case she fell. I suddenly realised what joy was. For me it wasn't ecstatic like I had watched in others, it was a quiet flood of thankfulness for Bevan's patience with Shanla and gratitude that she could now lead at least a partially normal life. Bevan had watched and waited and was pleased when they could walk together, him leading of course, holding her hand.

We had eventually built our own home near shops and life had become less stressful. (Post-natal depression not a diagnosis then.) Trips up to the shops were still slow and a worry with Shanla's asthma and her unpredictable reactions to things. I eventually managed to save enough money to buy Bevan a tricycle and had a seat attached to the back of it so she could ride too. They both loved that.

Shanla surprisingly talked clearly from very young. She and Bevan also developed their own way of communicating as well and by 2, like my other two children later, they were both easily understood. Unfortunately however it also meant Shanla understood enough to know she was not normal and resented it. Thank goodness for our lovely neighbour Ethel and her 4 children who accepted Shanla for who she was. Shanla slowly learned. Bevan was her best teacher as she could not abide him doing something she couldn't, which I had always known but not necessarily implemented. She went to school after the primer mistress had a chat with me when I was up there one day with her.

Shanla stayed slim and small all her life. She was bullied and teased at school when Bevan wasn't around and really had no idea about friendship. She would talk only to the teachers and smaller kids. She did become a competent reader, although not always comprehending the 'Herald' information. Real paper money was just to play with, pennies meant more to her.

Like autistic children she had her own rules and ideas. She would put herself to bed at seven if I hadn't and was asleep in seconds. Not for all night of course. I think she was unable to identify the difference between reality and dreaming – she would sometimes growl at me for something she said I had done after she had woken up. She would cry from pain but not identify where or how bad it was unless I guessed or found the place. She was often frightened, unable to identify her fears. She still hadn't properly developed cognitively at 10. The social niceties totally eluded her. Her fine motor skills remained a problem all her life. Shanla never fitted in anywhere. Not even at IHC when I left her there for a day once. They told me she was far too disruptive to stay. Shanla wasn't bothered. She said to me, "Never take me back to where those stupid kids live." Right! She was very strong willed but often bewildered. Later she did find solace with her own aviary.

I think she and the birds connected on their own special level.

The Education Specialist, who evaluated her around 3, told me what he thought her life would be like, but did not offer any help.

I ignored the information he gave partly because I didn't think I could cope if I believed it but also she had already done some of the things he said she wouldn't. And Shanla did so much more. He also said she would die around 28 and he was only a year short about that. I had ignored his comment with the rest. Maybe he knew that from statistics.

Whatever the reason for Shanla's brain damage, it was so severe the pathologist who did her autopsy when she died at 27, was also doubtful about what I said she had achieved in life – he had envisaged her wheel-chair bound, dribbling and incontinent. Trying to make sense of it I spoke about Shanla's life once to the now Sir Richard Faull, Professor & Director of The Centre for Brain Research of Auckland University and his comment was,

"We still know so little about the brain."

He had no idea how much it meant to me when he rang me one Saturday morning and said what a great job I must have done for Shanla to achieve as much as she had. I couldn't speak. He was the only person I had ever met who had really appreciated and understood what our lives had been like. It meant so much to me him acknowledging that after all the criticism. Moments like those are just so precious. Never forgotten. I eventually found my voice and thanked him.

Now in my eighties grief has become familiar. Each experience was unique, painful and sad in its own way, and they were all subtly compounded with those previous experiences. Covid has created a grief resurgence for me, as it will have for many.

The death of James K Baxter, the poet, the only stranger but in another way the most memorable because of his public fame and the police presence in our home and their questionable behaviour. However, none it seemed to me were more devastating than the loss of children from my own body. Of the 7 babies I had, the first pregnancy of twins was from a stillbirth after physical abuse, however knowing what I know now about baby loss, it may only have been a trigger for what would have happened anyway.

The second borderline miscarriage/stillbirth conceived with my second husband Bruce, was more devastating for him than me at the time. I hadn't wanted another damaged child though, which the loss suggested, to have to struggle with life like Shanla. Bevan died too but much later at 54 from prostate cancer whilst I and my 2 last daughters, Kerry and Jenny and his best friend's wife watched over him as the hospital staff helped him out of his pain and misery. He died from the same cause as the girls' father Bruce, not long before.

The one thing I am sure of is – loss never leaves us. Accumulative grief can involve all sorts of levels of trauma and also over different periods of time. A date, and event, or even the smallest loss can trigger a reaction. Each person has to find their own way to grieve. Acceptance, forgiving our 'what ifs', being kind to ourselves, exercising, and especially learning resilience does help. There is no magic bullet to recovery.

https://www.joincake.com/blog/cumulative-grief/

The Flower

My sister had the strangest dream
of a naked-lady near a stream.
It grew alone on leafless stem,
its lovely head a great burden.

There was a sadness in its stance
as if it knew 'twas not by chance,
it was without its likeness near,
also a sense of unknown fear.

My sister woke with foreboding
in her desperation hoping,
the fear inside her would soon pass
and that the dream had been a farce.

A phone call brought the news she knew
would break my heart, her sadness grew.
They'd found my daughter in the shower,
Dead and as lonely as the flower.

Baby Life in General.

We had proper roomy prams for babies then. Large old English styles were available (Pedigree) and cane ones were popular. They all faced the mother so babies could be checked on and they were comforted by seeing their mothers' faces. We bought a modern pram. It had a separate wheels and frame that supported the actual carrycot part that held the baby. That carrycot was made from coloured canvas with its own lighter frame and attached handles. After shopping, just lifting the whole thing out and not disturbing the baby was so useful instead of struggling with the whole pram up steps and banging the baby awake. For a toddler it also had an attachable seat that fitted across the end of the carrycot part. It was common to have an outside sheltered spot for the baby to get some fresh air when the weather was fine, using a muslin net to go right over the top of the pram hood, preventing flies from waking them.

Pushchairs were a separate item with different sizes and portable as now, but used only for toddlers and facing away from the mother usually, although cane ones didn't. Those did lie back for a tired toddler to sleep comfortably though.

The standard layette of baby clothes was not always enough for the amount of soiling that happened with some babies. The 3 sets of clothes were oversized to begin with, to extend their life for the fast-growing baby. This was especially so for the long Viyella nighties, made from a Karitane pattern, with pleats in the shoulders designed so they would last up to at least 6 months. They were worn day and night for girl or boy babies, sometimes pinned or domed along the bottom to keep in the warmth and to stop them riding up. There were (new or second hand) sets of 3 matinee jackets, bonnets and/or helmets and singlets, cotton for summer and a mixture of silk and wool for winter or hand knitted 2-ply wool ones. Several bibs, bootie sets, small soft muslin flannels and small towels were needed. 3 thick wool flannel domed or buttoned over-pants (to absorb moisture & keep warmth in – plastic pants available but not always used) a pack of large locking safety pins, (I still have a pink one) small cuddly blankets, and decorated bassinet and pram covers. These latter could also be crocheted or knitted.

Sometimes for summer they were made of Viyella too and crocheted around the edge. Large shawls of expensive materials like fine wool or silk and lace bought (or made) for a christening were often more extravagant with delicate larger areas of embroidery, crocheting and fringed edges. The more beautiful ones could be handed down for generations and those were nearly always hand-sewn.

Lastly, usually 3 dozen square cotton nappies – carefully folded into the standard triangle for girls and a T shape for boys, straight off the clothes line when dry. They were also used for new babies who were firmly cocooned in them for sleeping, looking like an Indian papoose.

The whole layette could be hand-sewn too and I once saw a treasured heirloom of a baby's white/cream set, mostly made from very fine cotton. It had the tiniest, daintiest of even stitching and everything was embroidered with delicate smocking and crochet-edged hems. The beautifully decorated long Christening gown and bonnet were of pure silk. The patience, skill and time required are not of today's world, that I know of anyway.

Hand-knitted basic woollen garments were especially popular and winter baby clothes were given as presents in sizes for up to 12 months. Once the baby was born colours were introduced – blue for boys and pink for girls. Unless you believed the results of a wedding ring experiment, no coloured clothing presents were encouraged before the birth.

Babies and young children often had long hair up to 3 years old, especially if it was curly or wavy, although clothes by that stage would usually differentiate the sex.

Bevan had lovely light golden hair I was reluctant to cut till he was nearly 3. He came first at the local baby show, across the road from us, at 18 months after we had shifted into our new home.

As it was for most of us in the social setup of the day then, looking after a baby was a totally encompassing life. There were daily rituals of necessity which seemed more arduous when exhausted. Like, baby bathing, preparing glass baby bottles (plastic ones not available in 1958 or much of anything plastic although acrylic plastics were invented in 1936) or if breast feeding was a problem. The continuous changing of dirty cloth nappies, wet bedding and maybe vomited-on clothing, could be a burden with a winter baby. Weather watching was compulsory for drying. Thank goodness for the new Hill's Hoist rotary clotheslines if you had one. It was also a time when there was not always an electric washing machine nor clothes dryers nor even an old-fashioned coal/wood range to help with drying especially in new homes. One nappy, singlet, and nightie at a time could be dried off in a hot water cupboard if the screws were removed from the permanently closed opening where a door should have been (some State regulation against it at the time).

Youth was helpful from the point of view of the ability to adjust quickly to being a mother but the vacuum of knowledge about dealing with the basics, created unnecessary problems with first babies. Normal household chores and cooking meals as well would often seem just too much at first. Time did help.

It never felt right to me that a young mother was sent home from hospital after the compulsory fortnight stay confined to a bed, treated as if she had an illness and her baby usually looked after in the nursery part time. She was then expected to cope alone without any further support or information – unless she was lucky enough to have a helpful husband – although men were not expected to help with babies. Some new mothers would have had relations and perhaps help from others.

Women with other children would not have cuddled them for that fortnight either, hospital staff trying to keep the super-bugs out. Children were thought to be carriers and parents were told to keep them away. I remember little longing faces being lifted up to windows from the grassed area around each ward of the old one-storeyed National Women's Hospital. However, I did hear one farmer's wife say she looked forward to her break from milking and the children.

Being protected from the super-bugs didn't work for Shanla. She came home with a huge ugly boil that looked like a third eye in the middle of her forehead and it took months of sugary antibiotics to heal. Her crossed eyes didn't help her odd appearance. (Her eyes were corrected at the recommended time of 2 years old.)

Although their efforts have since been labelled inadequate, at least if a Plunket nurse visited, it helped reassure new young mothers especially about breast feeding. These vulnerable mothers were often very grateful for them. (Mine had no answers although she offered help from the live-in Karitane Home which my husband vetoed.) The nurses did their best, calling at regular weekly intervals for the first 6 weeks. They were there to track the baby's weight and length progress, recording it on charts for comparison to normal growth lines. So perhaps more for the babies than the mothers? Doctors, mostly male, handled pregnancies. It wouldn't have felt so overwhelming for first-time mothers if some female carers, like today's LMC's (Lead Maternity Carers) had been available, State or otherwise.

After 6 weeks babies could be taken to the Plunket Rooms, if there were any nearby and you had transport or could walk. The Plunket's little blue and white record books were precious and treated seriously at times in a court case for child custody, used to prove a mother 'fit' to look after her child. The 1950's to 1960's were the middle of the 'Baby-Boomer years' – although we didn't know it at the time.

There were few family cars, which the husband would have used for work anyway, only fish and chips for take-aways, seldom any land-line phones, and no TVs or computers. Communication was particularly difficult for those living in newly-formed housing communities, so isolation and loneliness were often a problem. Most women would have spent the last few months of pregnancy indoors. There was a sense of shame rather than celebration for many. Neighbours could also all be workers as the mother probably had been herself. Men making comments like, 'So, the wife's got a bun in the oven.' or 'I hear she's up the duff' wasn't helpful. Breast-feeding in public was not done. In these large new estates, shops were seldom handy and bus times infrequent. There were no gathering places unless you were a church-goer, and even then getting there could have still been a struggle. I think many mothers felt isolated anyway wherever they lived, from conversations I've had. Not so bad once the children grew and made friends

Reading years after in '*Superwoman*', it seems native customs were still observed in parts of the world. This meant women experienced in baby matters gathered around in support of each other, sharing responsibility for all the children, not just when the mother was recovering after birth or in the early weeks, but as a way of life. It seemed to be an ideal survival scenario for the critical and busy years of early childhood, for parents and child.

Chapter 21 Working Women's Histories

This section is about giving women today an idea of how our options have improved in the past 100 years from my Nana's generation, albeit slowly, but it does put our modern day life in perspective. For my generation, by the 1960's, it was about the realisation of our choices and the inability in the climate we lived in then to be able to achieve them. We had our dreams but no encouragement. It was the men's financial support and permission we needed, whether it was a father, husband, brother or other male relation or bank manager if we had no inheritance.

Some men felt threatened by women generally and also thought that education especially was wasted on them. They were genuinely appalled when it became known that 'girls were Dux in 19 out of 22 unspecified schools' earlier in the century. That was men's reaction to many aspects of women's lives, especially women who were forward thinkers. The use of things like ignoring women, sarcasm, patronising paternalism, to verbally belittling (with terms like 'silly young thing', 'the little woman', 'brainless blonde' and especially 'neurotic' from doctors as well) along with other more modern derogatory expressions was probably true of a certain type of man and in some cases still is. Bullying, teasing, sexual innuendoes and touching were often covered by humour.

Luckily for us education-wise, early on the Scots continued their tradition of offering learning to both sexes so at least there were opportunities, especially if money was available. One of the reasons Scottish settlers voyaged to the other side of the world was their belief and commitment to education and they created their Otago University in 1869, where women were admitted from the outset and it was also the first in Australasia to do so. (The University also prevented having to send their children back home for an education.)

The first woman graduated in the Arts in 1885. Elizabeth Macomb's sisters went to University in Christchurch and she became politically active, beginning a long association with the Christchurch City Council, eventually becoming the first woman

MP in 1933. 14 years later in 1947 Mabel Howard became the first woman Cabinet Minister. I remember her being talked about, especially by the men, muttering about her flamboyancy at times. This was more than half a century after women had won the right to vote.

Even when a woman was compassionate, capable and intelligent enough and felt drawn to a medical career and was supported, she could be ostracised at university by the men, so running the gauntlet to become a doctor would have taken much courage. Part of the prejudice was generated by the University staff themselves with their problem of how to combine decorum and teaching. It would have been embarrassing and 'unseemly' in anatomy classes, seen as a really important issue then. Their attitude toward women was more about tolerance than enthusiasm.

Emily Seidenberg entered the medical school in 1891, and was the first woman graduate in 1896 as well as studying overseas. She was followed the next year by her friend Margaret Cruickshank, who became New Zealand's first registered general practitioner in 1897 at Waimate. (She died later in 1918 after contracting the pandemic flu while administering to her patients.) In 1907 there were 20 women and the situation had slowly improved so that by 1938 there were 100 women doctors and in the forties the female entrance figures rose to above 20%. (There were 799 in 1980.) They still had to prove themselves in practice as non-acceptance of women as doctors was general from men and women, patients or professionals – seeing them as women first and doctors second.

In the past anyway, co-dependence has always been a huge issue, women needing to depend on men for their own and their children's survival, so it was the pragmatic and normal way to live with the few other socially acceptable options, including jobs being available to women that paid enough for them and their families to survive. Marriage was looked upon as the stabilising foundation of our society and each partner's role was set up by law and custom. (In earlier centuries 'Love' was once seen as 'a silly reason for a match'.)

Some women have always been behind men, playing an active role in a family business or on farms or running the family finances very capably, but there was very little acknowledgement or appreciation shown. It was an expectation. I'd known nothing about any of our New Zealand women forebears trying to do better for us, and perhaps they were not included in our school history lessons because it was felt their stories just weren't deemed worthy of telling when all the important changes were usually made by men. (It may also have been because I missed so much schooling.) I had only ever vaguely heard of Kate Sheppard until it became a street name and also a maternity group was named after her in 2000. Later in 2012 I watched her story, *'What Really Happened – The Women's Vote'* on TV.

It was interesting that Kate was English and educated in Scotland and that she had a forbearing husband and only the one child at a time of large families. With her socially clever and passionate but quiet persuasive approach, the tenacious Kate Sheppard achieved an amazing feat for women, supported by other determined and strong females and a few empathetic males. New Zealand was the first country to implement the women's vote in 1893, although women could and often would follow a father or husband's dictate.

Kate Sheppard's example encouraged others to join her in the 'Suffragettes' movement, raising awareness of alcohol abuse as well with the 'Women's Christian Temperance Union'. She wanted women accepted and appreciated, for them to have equal education and rights and a better deal for their daughters. There have been women MP's as well as other brave role models since then like the incredible Jean Batten and, although they weren't the norm, they were examples of what women could achieve. The courage it must have taken for all of them to make their stand is probably not appreciated in our times.

Until WWII most women had not experienced real independence. They would have needed to have had money in their own right. It could have been from widowhood or a family estate, or they had been to University and got a degree, which would usually have required an indulgent father or tolerant husband as well. I don't know how a single woman without family support survived before the war except for the most obvious answer. Once all the fighting men went away though, men's jobs were often done by women. It brought a revelation that would never be forgotten by them. It must have also surprised many of the men who had grown up assuming women were naturally inferior and they would probably not have expected the capable reliability and responsibility they showed.

The impact on society generally would have been enormous at the time and it certainly made a difference to females, and even if it didn't change the thinking of older generations, it did many of the young ones. Just being shown what was possible, by even a few, was enough to encourage others and hope for a less constricted and limiting lifestyle. No matter what the government legislated against, when women had to stand down again afterwards for the returned soldiers, like many things after the war, the repercussions would not go away so simply. I don't remember anyone personally who said the men didn't deserve their jobs back, which they did after what they had been through.

There were always some women happy to give up and even saw that as their right, but others wanted to work on and have their independence and resented the government's stand encouraging reproduction and being the 'good little woman' again, not workers. The unthinking and paternalistic sexist male attitudes were stifling to them.

The Government's betrayal, in a way, of forcing women out of their often well-paid, rewarding jobs, was not really referred to much. That underlying knowledge and acceptance though that we women actually could do all these things that had been so locked into men's territory, wasn't forgotten.

By the time I realised women didn't have to become just wives and mothers and that there were choices, although we may have to be ready to fight for them, I was already well married.

Married women still could not sign things like time payment contracts. They needed their husbands to do it for them and even the 'NZ Committee of Women' endorsed that in 1952. Women can be their own worst enemies. When one married girlfriend told me around that time that her husband insisted she be wearing makeup, high heels and stockings and be neat and tidy with a clean pinafore on in the kitchen when he arrived home from work, (like the adverts) and serve his meal at exactly 5:30pm, I understood that this was the males' dream not ours. (The divorce rate in NZ had increased by the 1940's and given that attitude no wonder.)

Sometimes as a way of handling situations they don't feel comfortable in, like inappropriate behaviour of overbearing bullying and put-downs from partners in public, I notice elderly women often still react with a nervous laugh as well as with other men who are behaving rudely, including bosses. These are the women who put up with and even now 'stay with their man through thick and thin'. I do know of one brave one who left in her seventies when she could receive her own separate pension and claim half their worldly goods.

Careers were mainly for men and the only ones for women that were seen as acceptable, (an earlier generation hangover) were perhaps a librarian or hospitality employee, school teaching and usually nursing although the attitude to the latter was often polarising; either an angel or a whore – 'all that dirty stuff they had to do'. Many became spinsters. Midwives were in a class of their own and often revered for the quality of work they did and the large areas of the country they had to cover. On both sides of our family there are past relatives who were midwives and were remembered years later fondly and gratefully by the locals for their dedication and caring of their families, often saving babies and their lives. Pregnant women who did not from choice or were unable to reach a hospital or nursing home were glad of them. In the city particularly, even the gutter for a birth was preferrable knowing that at a hospital where there were doctors, the chances of infection and death were high. The need for sanitation was not understood and doctors went from patient to patient without washing. (Puerperal fever was what Mary nearly died of even in 1943 when my half-sister was born.)

For years there were menial jobs like domestic helpers or a housekeeper (a euphemism in some cases for a live-in sex partner as well, an expectation which Mary often experienced and accounted for our being without a place to sleep at times, which happened even in large country estates) washer women, cleaners, cooks, waitresses, factory workers, care workers (although the expectation was that family would look after family but they were required in orphanages and other institutions at least). During WWII the necessary land girls were often complained about by farmers' wives as being promiscuous or 'fast'. I'm not sure what their attraction was with their dress-down uniforms. They wore large shapeless, sexless overalls covering their legs and breasts, a work shirt and their feet were in clumsy gumboots, all of which, it would have been thought, made them unappealing and awkwardly dressed for any 'quickie' or 'roll in the hay'. (Slacks were not a particularly fashionable type of clothing for women till a few years later.) Perhaps it was simply opportunity.

Not many women were in positions of power, like managers, or ran their own businesses and if they did, their worst critics would often be other women as they were in many areas of life. Certainly not many women were professionals.

With fewer children and less effort required for housework, modern floor coverings easier to clean (less scrubbing and polishing of floors), the improved economy and electrical appliances like irons, vacuum cleaners, washing machines, dryers, and fridges etc. becoming readily available, more women began drifting back to jobs, perhaps starting part time at first during school hours like I did. Women in the work-force doubled after WWII from 169,000 to 380,000 by 1971. That number was measured again later between 1966 and 1976 and was the biggest jump. The middle sixties also offered a choice of careers that had become generally acceptable too but tolerated more by one level of society than another. Men and women could both be quite critical of working women and voiced it, but the economic benefits were so alluring it must have been hard not to 'go with the flow' in the end. Work was more of a necessity in some households than others and some women were happier at home. They and their husbands often became 'Derby and Joan' couples in their retirement.

Legal Advice

The only career woman I met and consulted with around that time was Dame Augusta Wallace DBE, one of the few women lawyers in our area in the early 1960's. She eventually became the first woman in New Zealand to be appointed as a judge to the District Court in 1976. In 1993 she was made a Dame Commander of the Order of the British Empire. In my opinion, given her advice which I did not take, she didn't seem to me to really understand the circumstances I was trying to survive in and I think I was given the usual opinion of any lawyer of the day. I thought, as a woman, she would have understood more but later realised no-one, unless they have experienced or witnessed a violent relationship close up, ever really does.

Some women with serious careers and a reasonable income may have chosen not to marry as they would probably have felt they would have been suborned by children and their husband's needs and choices.

The acceptable and usual employment was as a receptionist or manager (not necessarily acknowledged by that title) in hotels and other hospitality venues, shop or office worker and maybe a florist and those attracting apprenticeships, like dressmakers, pattern drafters and milliners. The hairdressing and the chemistry trades were recognised from 1926 although in any situation where work was seen as part of a man's world, like the Bakers and Pastry Cook Award, modifications and conditions were redesigned to restrict women to the less skilled area than their male counterparts. Men could have feared for their jobs as women were cheaper to employ. My Nana ran the local Post Office at Okere Falls, near Rotorua, at the turn of the century, the biggest part of her job being on the switchboard although it would not have been that busy. (They lived in a government house as part of my Granddad's job anyway so she worked from home.) Switchboards were acceptable as a woman's job and boarding house owners were often women, sometimes widows, or spinsters using family money left to them.

Even in the fifties inexperienced girls straight from school could be taken advantage of (sometimes including sexually) by being given quite responsible jobs without the remuneration or title that a male youth would have expected. At the BNZ though, the line was very clear; girls were not acceptable as tellers and seldom handled money. Although there may have eventually been equal pay in some government jobs, it would be a different story with promotions which in most instances was about being a male and length of service, not ability or education or experience level, certainly in Telecom. The males often became inept managers at a time when inadequate training was given and sometimes even when it was good.

In the old Post Office for instance, I knew several male managers who had started off as telegraph boys at 15, which was not unusual, and made their way up the system to a fairly high level management position and were often clueless. A woman friend who had seniority as well as being competent was held back from promotion for years. When it eventually came through I was so thrilled for her, but a girlfriend remarked, "She'd better keep her back to the wall". Some women did happily break into men's employment and one we knew in the early sixties, who really did consider herself 'a cut above', was a cutter in the clothing trade and well paid. She was from overseas somewhere, her long black hair was always freshly coiffed in the latest fashion (at the time of beehive hairdos), and she wore the most imaginative and sophisticated outfits, even to Carlaw Park to watch the senior Rugby League games. A few generations ahead, there were probably more job opportunities in that area than others, like clothing designers and drafters. I wonder now how her wages compared to a male counterpart.

The first in NZ to acknowledge and see the need to support equal pay for women was the National Council of Women in 1896 when they passed their first resolution. Like many areas needing attention that lost traction after that time, not much appeared to change. An example of the wage difference between men and women from the Insurance Industry in the mid-1950's is 727 pounds per annum for men and 450 pounds for women. The gap has since closed up more but women still generally only earn 86% of a man's wage. (*TV1 News 29/10/14*)

Mary was lucky as a milliner in the late thirties. Her boss was a woman who owned her own company, and gave Mary carte blanche to design and make what she wanted and paid her extra. Of course Nana had had her own hat shops in Rotorua so Mary already had an eye for fashion. Building drafting was an acceptable compromise for women, although probably not extended to being an architect, and there were some trained girls but they may have had trouble finding a willing company to employ them.

A very small percentage of lucky girls, with good looks and figures to match, became models. They were much more dignified and respected than some of today's, not in the headlines or seen as icons of fashion particularly, to us at least, although may have in the more sophisticated and wealthier circles they were usually from. We Grammar girls once went to see a fashion parade in the Auckland Town Hall. Those ladies were in their twenties, gave the impression of being quite classy, and were absolutely drop dead gorgeous and unlike current models, had slim but full womanly figures, their long legs striding down the catwalk while holding themselves in perfect control. They were happy to flash their lovely smiles. I don't think they would have had enough ongoing work though to make a living full time but they may not have had to depend on their earnings. They were probably not the models that posed for those so unrealistic adverts showing housewives sprucely dressed in high-heels, makeup and with every hair in place but incongruously aproned, as they presented washing machines, fridges and the other latest electrical household items. Draped female figures over or around a car were very popular too, perhaps not quite as blatantly sexily as is done now.

I had a petite girlfriend when I worked at the BNZ, who was like a pocket Venus, she was just so exquisitely and beautifully proportioned, and she did part-time modelling of underwear at night. The bank guys hung around her like bees at a honey-pot. Beauty queens were crowned in popular annual competitions, like at beach resorts, and one I knew went on to eventually become an air hostess, a much envied group.

That was a fairly elite occupation of the few and it wasn't until flying became more popular and affordable later on after the war, that it was a more viable option.

But all these jobs were seen as fillers until marriage, by men anyway, and unless you were very lucky, you would need to marry to survive. Ultimately my marriage at 17 was as much about pragmatism, as anything else after Mary had remarried and it was 'the thing to do.' If you weren't married by 22 you were considered 'left on the shelf' and no-one wanted to be a 'spinster'. The word itself was horrifying enough with the visions of past relations and their dull, captive and sexless (we presumed) lives, usually looking after aged relatives.

I can't imagine that many people made a good living from the theatre or any of the arts. The exceptional writers, artists, comedians, singers (opera or pop), poets, photographers (mainly black & white photos then which could be hand painted), sculptors, potters, musicians, producers, directors, comedians, actors, ballet or other dancers may have done, but for most, unless they went overseas, NZ was and is usually too small a country for them to be able to make a continuous good living. Some may have been content to stay in NZ anyway but it would have probably meant 'don't give up your day job', the double meaning also that maybe you were not good enough. However, the likelihood of a New Zealander, particularly a woman, achieving what has since been done in politics and several of the arts or of anyone becoming equal to or surpassing what a Hollywood movie star or film producer did or receiving the 'Booker' or similar prize, were so far off the planet, it would have been thought ludicrous.

The other more lucrative, independent, but risky option was to derive an income from the sex industry. Although I do not recall any staff member ever referring to the fact when I was at Auckland Girls Grammar, the school is set below what was then the sleazier end of Karangahape Rd. The old buildings housed sex shops and the appropriate clubs, in what was a known night area for street workers. Large, colourful and suggestively dressed figures on bill-board cut-outs sat ostentatiously above on the shop overhangs, lit by pale neon during the day, garish by night. Shop models were posed in sexy attire and posture in the shop front window in a version of underwear and suspender belt unlikely to be found in most homes then. The young school girls who accessed Grammar from the 'K' road direction were exposed to this display five days a week. And no doubt some of them would have been drawn to that lifestyle too.

Crafts

At times handcrafts were done from necessity, but were more usually accepted as relaxation, helping to pass the time for the pleasure of creating something through individuality of expression, and also therapeutic to my mind. Sheep farmers' wives in particular often spun their own wool on small spinning wheels and like most women did hand knitting (perhaps machine knitting as well), along with tatting, embroidery, crocheting, smocking, hand sewing, and mending. It was usually done at night with the family in the living room and the radio going, around the fire in cooler evenings. We had a family work basket which contained things like thimbles, a wooden mushroom for mending (mainly woollen socks), cotton on wooden reels and balls and skeins of wool of various colours and all kinds and sizes of needles for knitting and sewing. Most people had Singer treadle sewing machines which were used for all sorts of jobs; men's collars turned, adults clothing re-designed and re-sewn for children, (no T&T or The Warehouse) adjusting children's clothes to fit other sizes by shortening or lengthening hems (although that often showed the last hemline unless ribbon or lace were creatively sewn over). White linen sheets were cut through the centre, where they had worn, and were re-sewn with the outside edges together in the middle or used as pillow cases with ties instead of envelope openings as now. Elbows of jumpers were sometimes patched with soft leather scraps and became popular for a while.

Clothing tissue-weight paper patterns of the latest trends were borrowed when starting from scratch with a piece of new material, which was usually carefully saved up for. After the pattern had been cut out and the material pinned together and then tacked, there would be a first fitting for adjustments (seldom would any shop-bought pattern fit perfectly and not many women had a dress model to fit it on, only themselves, always awkward). The tacking running thread would be adjusted for alterations then the pieces sewn by machine or at times by hand, although hems and finishing areas were always done that way after being carefully ironed into place. I never quite matched the expertise of my Nana's invisible stitching. I think she used a slip basting one that was for matching pattern edges and she always wore a real silver thimble on her finger. As well as the hemming stitch there was back stitch, blanket stitch, top stitch, flat-fell & French stitch, button-holing, gathering and fancy stitches like cross, feather and saddle stitches for decoration which older women often used, all starting and finishing with three inconspicuous tiny stitches. Some used small knots but each person had their own preferences. No stretch materials as we now know them.

Specialty wool shops were also common and, other than the farmer's wives who pursued their craft and could buy from the locals or home farm, wool was normally bought by the skein (a large coiled loop) and had to be wound into balls before use.

Nana would sit in a chair opposite me and I would hold the wool hank taut between my wrists in front of me while she expertly and quickly wound the balls, usually singing her Oz songs to entertain me and distract me from my tiring arms. Sometimes she would unravel a hand knitted jumper or cardy that still had good wool in it and that would be re-knitted into something smaller or combined with other wool to perhaps make a Fair Isle pattern for a man to fill in for the yarn that was lost to wear and tear.

Mary liked crocheting the most I think, although she had earlier sewed and knitted most of our baby clothes with appropriate coloured pink (or for me apricot) or blue smocking and crocheted rosettes. Mary kept some of Ralph's clothes for over 30 years and I used them once for my son when we were visiting, after he had managed to wet or dirty all his. They did not look out of place in the bus going home.

Embroidered tablecloths and tea showers, the latter a see-through light square of material thrown over a table perhaps set with food for morning or afternoon teas to deter flies, used mainly when visitors were expected. Aunt Alice had a framed verse in cross-stitch on the wall of the living room which started off 'If you have a job to do, do it now, if it's one you wish was through, do it now..." the rest of which eludes me, but I got the message.

Chapter 22 Hypocrisy / Divorce / Violence / Murder

Quotes: "Some people just have 'chronic dissatisfaction' – not something time changes." "Resilience and self-control were needed for a reasonable survival. Some people simply deal with stress easier than others."

The 1930's was a parochial, ingenuous, trusting time of relative innocence is the thought uppermost in my memory. However, anyone showing an individualist streak in belief systems, other than the accepted norm of the basic political or religious ideologies, was considered 'odd' and those people could expect to be ignored or worse and sometimes took their stance in peril.

Living-in-sin was 'an absolute no-no' and never admitted to. Though in the early 60's I remember a pensioner couple living together as they weren't willing to sacrifice their separate pensions for face. As it would have for many at that time, it made me feel really uncomfortable when they admitted to it one night over dinner. (A joke now. For me too later.) The trend of not always bothering to marry has increased although couples might after having a family, which to older people is the antithesis of their own youth. I know of several friendships that broke up because of the different influences in the generational thinking, although historically in earlier centuries it was thought a good idea to wait till women proved their fertility. My grand-daughter, at around seven years old, asked me innocently once if her mother was a flower-girl at my wedding to her granddad. Aside from the obvious 'no', I couldn't immediately think of an answer as to why that would have been unacceptable at the time that would make sense to her. I changed the subject.

Conscientious objectors were openly ridiculed and abused, even when their strict religious beliefs forbad them to go to war or they were genuine pacifists as the poet James K. Baxter's family experienced. They were treated more harshly in the camps they were confined to than in other commonwealth countries too. It took more courage to be different, not less.

Our judgemental society was fine if you stayed within the boundaries, but there were many brave, intelligent, and creative people, as well as unfortunate ones, who were culturally stifled and stepped over. Sometimes their talents, money, or sense of humour could save them in certain sectors, where their idiosyncrasies would be more acceptable. Be careful though you did not become a 'tall poppy'. 'Self-aggrandisement is no recommendation' and 'he's a blowhard' are two comments that stick in my mind.

You could be turned on if your behaviour was not seemly and it was a long way to fall. Living up to being humble and gracious with integrity, someone to be trusted and having an independent spirit helped, with fairness and compassion as a given. (Arrogant, entitled, misogynistic men were always about and to be avoided.)

There were, no doubt, suffering or elderly people who were secretly put to sleep, perhaps sometimes in agreement, and we had the usual embezzlers, con-men, thieves, rapists and sexual perverts – but aside from the talk of postcards from earlier in the century pornography was not a word many of us were familiar with. I know of several cases where the people, who are now dead, committed crimes (especially sexual ones, including incest) that were covered up by family or professional loyalty and thieving or misappropriation of funds was often 'swept under the carpet' by club or company embarrassment, as happens today still.

Murder was unusual enough for most people to be shocked and ones that made newspaper headlines like the notorious Basset Rd, Auckland, double murders with the 'Chicago comes to Auckland' headline and comments on an 'Al Capone style gangland killing' were rare. Everyone was horrified and appalled, especially with it happening in the elite suburb of Remuera. The use of a machine gun and being related to the illegal manufacture and sale of liquor were horrifying. The murders were talked about and referred back to for years with the infamous 'Jorgenson' name always associated with that time. An indication that 'this sort of thing' only occurred occasionally.

The passive, compliant, and dutiful housewife of the 1950's existed but there weren't that many among the women I knew who were not harbouring some level of resentment at having to fall into line with the role-play they'd been cast in. As always, what went on between a married man and his wife behind closed doors of course was their business, unfortunately for some. As it is today, ultimate outright violence, sexual or otherwise, was usually only done where no-one could bear witness. Women's mistreatment and what is now marital rape, were not addressed until they grew older and more able to think for themselves, although they still may not have done anything about it.

Domestic Abuse

In the thirties when Mary was first married, the trauma of being beaten up regularly was common and probably always had been. She had a friend whose daughter was born without a fully formed arm. From the elbow down there was just a string of flesh and skin. The daughter was about my age and I was in the room when the girl's mother and Mary were discussing it and the woman was so sad. Her husband was a quiet brutish type despite the fact that they were both well-educated and lived in an upmarket home. The wife blamed his treatment of her as the reason for the deformity, which had obviously never been seriously dealt with by medical professionals, and I think the mother felt terrible guilt about the whole situation. Denial was common in many areas of life and domestic violence was rarely referred to that I can ever remember, except for that occasion, other than an odd knowing nod.

The law would only grant a divorce after seven years separation or desertion, and adultery a bit sooner if proved, as Mary understood it anyway when she wanted to divorce my father, her first husband, in the early 1940's. Luckily for her, Arnold's adultery wasn't hard to prove. His sexual habits were fairly well known. He was acknowledged as a 'womaniser'. She said her main reason for leaving him at the time was always wondering what venereal disease she was letting herself in for by staying and I think all her life she waited for that ultimate disaster to arise – it never did happen. She wouldn't have asked anyone what the timeline was for 'it' eventuating. (No Google.)

Mary's marriages and divorces were fascinating to some people and abhorrent to others in a time when even risking the shame and disgrace of a separation was considered a drastic action. She was no doubt seen in some quarters as being a racy gay divorcée or there were worse connotations but if they were ever expressed in her presence I'd be surprised. I think most people forgave Mary on the whole, initially anyway after the first divorce. Others in normal relationships probably re-thought that when she divorced a second time from my stepfather, John. I came across some of those sanctimonious people myself later. Mary did have good reasons for leaving John as she was beaten too, although the divorce went through on the grounds of desertion, but knowing her, she possibly didn't tell people the real circumstances or much else. It would have been I that spilled the beans if I'd been asked. Mary was right onto it when it came to survival, not like her eldest daughter, a much less self-focused and more trusting person, as my life showed.

Mary's divorced situation affected us children, although I can only speak for myself but I know Veronica was teased. Adults occasionally maybe would say something to me – usually too politely. Any subtle remarks would have by-passed me anyway, but at times there were definite obvious snubs and looks, a 'drawing aside of skirts' as it were. Other than the usual kids hectoring, with not much response from me, I was only really hurt once I can remember.

This episode was unexpected. It was when we were back living with Arnold when I was 10. There was a girl a bit younger than me who lived nearby, with the same name as me. We had played together after school off and on for months but when I called out to her house from the street as usual one afternoon, after picking up Veronica, her mother came out instead and abused me. "You get home to your own place and don't come around here calling out my daughter's name (never mind it was mine too – that must have bitten!). You're not good enough to play with her. Your mother's just a slut living like that!" As it was my own father and mother together this time, the apparent insult didn't make sense to me; I just thought she was stupid. The cruelty of laws was something I'd not knowingly experienced then. My little friend must have felt the same way as her mother, or at least obeyed her, as she didn't play with me again.

She was only one of many lost friends so I moved on as always. Sometimes I wouldn't make any effort to have friends. We moved so much would it even be worth it? I found it difficult relating to other children too, especially if it was around a bad period in our lives. Their conversations often seemed frivolous. It was obvious I couldn't share my thoughts with them so there was no point. It was easier to drift along on a superficial level and join in sometimes when appropriate like a game of skipping or rounders but otherwise keep to myself.

There would have been secret infidelities on either side as today, but for women anyway, the gamble would be huge as they would pay the bigger price if caught out, one way or another. The stigma after a separation and divorce was that the men's behaviour was considered 'a low class activity' (physical violence) from uneducated and labourer types. Women were seen as being besmirched and disreputable. Unlike today, men seldom opted for the role of child carers and stay-at-home husbands and if fathering an illegitimate child, it wasn't and still isn't usually so bad for the man, as he can walk away and more easily make up lost ground with his larger wage when unencumbered. Decent men taking responsibility is more common now which is great for the kids as well.

Consequently loyalty was strong and women often pragmatically hung on to their fantasy programming – well past the point when the union was obviously not working for them anyway. Many women also continued to love their husbands, so giving up on the idealism of love and marriage and dealing with the daunting outcome of relationship breakdown and the effect on their children. Their survival would be a huge struggle. Living with the known fear of the partner against the fear of the unknown plus the hardship of the full responsibility of the family, and there could be several children, as well as having to deal with the distress of the physical separation and handling the money, perhaps for the first time. It could often all feel too overwhelming and be enough to keep women in unsuitable relationships.

They may have no support either as people often do not realise what actually goes on behind closed doors and inevitably take sides. Relations and friends sometimes reluctantly feel forced into it, especially when influenced by their spouses. The public's critical response had to be borne as well either way. If violence was obvious, onlookers may see the answer as simple. Leave. Outsiders, male or female who said that, would have had no experience to be able to appreciate how huge that decision would be and what it involved. If you have a friend who needs help, before doing anything, use the internet to find some answers first about the best way to approach the problem for both your sakes. Being judgemental will not help.

Thoughts, Observations & Conclusions – from my own experiences and others who have confided in me.

Leaving could mean trauma of a different kind. It meant women lost their financial support, their home, and possibly their children. Facing the world with dependents, insecurity, no financial or emotional support such as it may have been, maybe loss of safe sex, homelessness, loss of a job, marriage failure and public criticism.

It was unsettling for all at a time when women's wages were very low and would hardly have been enough to survive on even if a babysitter and a job were available. (In the 1920's a divorced woman could apply to the courts for child maintenance such as it was. Mary also caustically mentioned once there was a pitiful 'Deserted Wives' Pension'. The DPB was yet unheard of.)

Fearing the future which could still include physical violence and trauma, with always a percentage leading to injury and/or death, usually the woman's. A certain kind of focussed, arrogant, obsessive, vindictive, intimidating behaviour of a male means danger. The apparently inherent male belief in some men, especially narcissistic ones, is that they are 'entitled' or 'have a right' to whatever they perceive as an appropriate relationship. Also an addiction to power and control, without considering or showing any empathy for their partner's needs, (or as a boss to their employees) and that seems normal to them. They often cover their greed and the vanity that goes with it when money is involved. None of this behaviour necessarily shows before a live-in relationship unfortunately. They may appear very different in public.

ADHD or similar recently identified mental health problems can be responsible in some cases as well, but I understand that the person is not necessarily aware that their behaviour is not appropriate. Whatever is involved, these relationships are based on a mental health problem which in the past, the women who loved their partners were forced to deal with – and still can be. As they are the ones who are the focus of the problem, how can they? History alone means they are bound to obey their partners and many men expect it. Mental health problems require qualified people to sort them; preferably men in abuse cases as they can better relate to each other and are more likely to be listened to.

When I was first married in 1955, most relationships that I thought I understood about the trauma inherited in historical violence were based on the old acceptance of women being men's personal property. Perhaps not by all men and also probably to different degrees. They had interpreted their rights as entitlement to use whatever means to control their wives they fancied e.g. power, isolation, humiliation, intimidation, manipulation, belittling, subjugation and bullying which included physical and mental abuse. They may have also just been repeating their own family backgrounds (called genetic 'Neanderthal behaviour' by some abused partners). I thought that had begun to change, which it probably had for some of my friends of the same age, and for us as well, I expected, based on our current relationship. More one as an equal partnership.

I was shocked and disillusioned on the first day of our honeymoon and I can remember thinking that there was something fundamentally very wrong with my husband's sudden obsessive behaviour and that I simply did not have any skills to help either of us at 17, but I was basically expected by society to sort the problems myself. The unbelievable depth of cunning and deceit used for control is something I found personally the most insidious, especially coming from someone who constantly told me how much he loved me.

Apparently the 'fear of these love obsessed and troubled men' see focussing on controlling their partner as the only way to create the loving intimate relationship they so fundamentally desire. It seems to them it is the only way they can feel better when their partner is not living up to their expectations in one way or another – perhaps expecting someone to behave more like their mother and being too different from them? Or the opposite.

Unfortunately, when the husband's behaviour toward their partner doesn't work, a good percentage of them end up frustrated and enraged.

> *Quotes from abused woman; 'They can't understand us and need us so much.'*

> *'I accepted the blame for the things that happened. I thought it was my fault.'*

I found it unbelievable at first that one woman's story was much like another's, including my own, when they have lived with a certain type of man. In this often 'toxic love situation' an old Scottish doctor once told me, 'Mental manipulation and/or physical violence and bullying relationships ultimately end up in 1 of 3 ways; one of the partners leaves, one commits suicide, or one kills the other.' (This applies when the woman is the aggressor as well.) Apparently no amount of reassurance from a partner makes a difference to them so the outcome is predictable. It is the timing that is unpredictable.

It seems to me that these men appear to have simply not grown up properly and are often looking for a mother replacement. The reasons are more complex than others in some cases, for instance, their mother may have been lost to them physically, for whatever reason, or it may have been that their mother wasn't 'there for them', even if present, or had abused them in some way. Perhaps like Elliot Gould, as an extreme example of being totally indulged, the spoilt 'Mummy's Little Murderer', whose behaviour was unfortunately condoned by both his rich parents. (Being an only child not helpful either as in this case.)

When women are being physically hurt, the abuse is obvious and undeniable (although it often is by a forgiving and/or frightened partner) and in many cases horrific but it is usually preceded by emotional abuse which is much harder to identify. Although not necessarily obvious to a woman in love, as they probably wouldn't associate it with their partner's behaviour, but however much she does not want to believe the man she trusts to help, provide and protect her and their family from harm, he does want to control her.

What begins to happen is not the expectations that come from being continually told, 'I love you' and then eventually, 'I love you and you are so lucky because no-one else could.' This can be the beginning of a carefully calculated and timed programme of different forms of mental punishment. His behaviour may seem thoughtless or that he is angry (or on drugs or drunk) at the time but on the contrary many men's considered behaviour is like a subtle sex predator. He has been grooming her and already insidiously getting in little derogatory digs in front of other people for instance, which may be denied if commented on and apologies also offered.

That is part of the mind game – and can sound really sincere and believable. And he may be if he can see he has overstepped the boundaries too soon and there could be repercussions that will expose and hurt him and what he feels he needs to achieve. Sorry for himself in reality.

> Louise Doughty in 'Apple Tree Yard' says her friend felt, 'We are taught we can redeem them as soon as we can read. We can turn the beast into a prince, if only we love him enough. We eventually know instinctively how bad it's going to get when we leave, so we keep putting it off. We think that if we are with them we might be able to control them a bit, but we know once we leave, we will be in real danger.' (abridged)

Often paralysed by fear of harm being done to themselves or their children they live in daily tension. Unfortunately there is often an unspoken strong bond not usually acknowledged between partners, which is hard to define, that repeatedly brings the leaver back again and again. I think of that relationship as a 'lethal love bond'.

Perversely, there could be times of relative harmony, weeks and sometimes months but the rules of the power game would not have changed and they would come back into force around the time the woman was feeling more reassured or if jealousy was a trigger – which may have seemed endearing at the beginning of the relationship. Initially, the partner can be left with feelings of guilt and that of 'He loves me and I haven't made him happy – I shall have to try harder'.

This kind of thinking is actually the beginning of the end because 'wanting to help' along with loyalty and pity are three of the strongest motivations women may feel in this situation, to their detriment. These kind, caring, empathetic young girls who would make great mothers are often men's focus. Once a woman has taken that attitude it's just a matter of time, which can be years, before she reaches her limit of tolerance and forgiveness and the destruction of her preconceived expectations. By then her happiness, humour and even hope can have been affected so much that her life is hollow, just a shell of what might have been. (One woman asked, "Why does he want to eat my smile?") Her diminishing self-confidence and assurance affected her belief in herself and her own judgement, doubting her ability and sanity sometimes, making a mockery of the time and care she has invested in their life so far. Her self-esteem can be so low she will feel she doesn't deserve anything better anyway and she can feel nearly destroyed. Shame can be a huge factor – in all sorts of ways – however she is not the one who should be ashamed.

Often women become isolated just by staying with a partner who is seen by some others for what he is, but he has often deliberately set up the split from friends and relations with lies to protect himself and destroy their support for her. For anyone unfamiliar with this type of person, it is often still hard to believe nothing is what it seems and they find it very difficult and confusing to accept someone would actually behave as this person does. It goes against reason especially when the partner/husband tormentor will profess how much he loves and needs his partner (which he probably does in his way) and behaves so charmingly and well in public, especially if they are a respected public or sports figure or are a loved, charismatic person. People do not want their heroes sullied.

No-one would take the woman's side anyway. It's all uphill. The woman is often classed a troublemaker and even humiliatingly seen as ungrateful.

If depression, alcohol, or drugs are involved, a crisis point can be reached faster and unexpectedly. When there are children to complicate thoughts of escape in an increasingly intolerable situation and the wife has finally worked out at least part of what is going on, she will realise they too can be used as another controlling factor and become pawns. Their gullibility could be influenced by his needs and exploited for his ends. (The NZ quins said their stepfather threatened to hurt them if their mother did not co-operate. He killed her and then himself eventually.)

Leaving means ingrained belief systems from where all decisions that arise, have to be addressed. Once the woman has reached this stage, even the most forgiving of them understand that leaving is their most dangerous time, and they have often paid the ultimate price if their plan came apart or they were unable to get enough help and protect themselves. The extremes of these men, the ones more likely to kill, I have read, are apparently inclined to self-righteousness and self-pity, rejection is also common. They blame their wives for their unsuccessful lives, cannot get their act together and are humiliated by their failure. Others, more paranoid, may feel that their family is in danger from the world's decaying moral standards and needs his version of protection.

The terror they and their children live in has to be experienced to be appreciated. Self-disgust can be paralysing when you eventually understand you are a brainwashed victim. There are so many situations to deal with and the underlying fear of retaliation is constant, with good reason, and life is fragile. These women may recover in time, but no-one having lived through such a traumatic situation is ever the same afterwards. PTSD is an apt diagnosis for many abused wives.

Breaking up the relationship is a total life changer. For 12 years, subtly at first, I had felt like a trapped prisoner of war except that I was alone, the only prisoner, no others to commiserate with or share the brunt of the attacks. Also, needing to act in public as if life was normal while living in total fear. (I am sorry if POW's take offence.)

Leaving Home

My terror level increased with each slow minute of new morning light and my home felt like it was seeping away from me. I had been awake most of the night so was already exhausted. Every time I had briefly slept it was to realise again what I was going to do when I woke. Once he had gone to work I still lay in bed for another hour, half expecting him to creep back in again and torment me saying, 'Ha! You thought I didn't know didn't you? Didn't you? I will always know what you are thinking – never doubt it bitch!' It had taken me months to train my face to blankness but he would still sometimes give me a look and say, 'I know, I know!' He seemed able to read my mind uncannily at times and he could do that to other people as well.

Would he come back this morning and gloat and laugh and threaten me – leaving it until the last minute as I was backing down the drive?

Not reacting to anything was the only way I could think of to protect myself, no matter what went on. I had lost 3 stone in the last 3 months, felt like I was losing my mind as well and I could always feel the cold – it felt like it had been trickling its way into my bones – even being burnt from the open fire didn't warm me. The insides of our bedroom windows were icy this October morning, the only heater we had was in the kitchen, a gift from Mary, so I dressed in three layers of clothes then carefully and quietly went down the hall to the kitchen and turned it on. By the time the kids got up for breakfast the edge of the cold would have lifted.

I couldn't eat or drink as residual bile was caught in the back of my throat, burning and bitter, the fear so great anyone near me would have smelt it. I sat there trying to think through my carefully planned moves and their sequence once more. What had I forgotten? How would the kids behave once they knew what was going to happen? Would the woman from the Social Welfare turn up on time? Would the police come as an officer had promised or would he have told my husband instead? He had friends in the force.

The car had had its check-up at a different service station than the usual one and the petrol tank was full. My lawyer, from another district, instructed me to tell no-one I was leaving, not even my best friend next door. Certainly not the only two other friends I had left after my husband had been to see them all, or anyone at work either. My boss would be furious. It felt horrible as it seemed like a betrayal to all of them and everyone else I knew. I may never see any of them again either and that was so painful. How could I do this? What would become of us?

Mary knew – she had to or we would not have had anywhere to go. Certainly not her place. If I couldn't trust her with this one thing when I had supported her for months when she did a flit from her last husband plus many other times, our relationship would be in a bad way. She had arranged for my first few nights to be spent out of town with her church friend who my husband didn't know. This was the beginning of probably many more moves, already around 40 so far in my life for other reasons, if I was to succeed in staying alive. I had had to accept I may not after his threats and the shocking statistics about women not surviving after leaving (and men) I'd been told about. 'If I can't have you no other bastard will!' his most common refrain.

There was no-one in the drive. I had been watching down our long right-of-way since the sun came up. Hope was not an emotion I would allow myself. My shaking had gradually stopped when I heard my son get up. I was trying to control myself so that neither of my children would see my fear, especially my daughter. They both came into the kitchen to dress in front of the heater and then have breakfast. When I saw them I thought, 'I can't do this! Take them away from their father, their home, their school, their friends and their life, especially Bevan with his football.' I went to the toilet so they wouldn't see me crying. I was totally aware this gamble I was taking was for them too as a drunk, nasty and sometimes violent father was no life for them either. Shanla had a knack of saying the wrong thing at the wrong time as she had got older, so he was threatening her too now at 10, Bevan 8½. I couldn't shut her up forever. Bevan had more sense but was rebelling too lately. I knew I would do it. Leave and never come back despite what others may think, especially the police as they had said that was the pattern.

Not mine. It had taken 12 years for me to make really sure that was the only answer. Waiting for my partner to grow up was not a good plan any more. I was also now more frightened of what I may do to him when he was drunk if I stayed. Enough was enough.

The big clock in the kitchen was showing nearly 8am when I went back. There was no-one in the drive when I could bring myself to look. I said to both children that I was sorry but we were leaving home this morning and they needed to be good so that I could remember everything I had to do. I had put large, sturdy, paper bags at the end of their bed and they were to go and pack the toys they wanted to take with them. Shanla immediately said her pram would not fit. Bevan kept looking at me then slowly went into his bedroom and did what I asked. He came and sat down again but in the adjacent lounge and was very quiet. Shanla went and sat beside him on the couch after a while and took his hand.

There was no-one in the drive. The fear and shaking came back anyway. The Social Welfare woman was due shortly so I finally put my plan into action, trying not to think about anything, concentrating on the immediacy of the moment. I brought out the innocent looking brown bags like the ones for the kids which had been carefully hidden, and packed the previously-prepared stacks of clothes in the drawers straight into them with anything else that I could fit the kids might miss. Taking a minute I checked again. There was no-one in the drive. My best new green frock I had deliberately soaked was in the washhouse along with some of the kids clothes. I left them but packed as much as I could in the two adult suitcases which had been in their usual place in the top of the wardrobes, one hiding the .303 rifle. I placed everything just inside the front door as they were filled, including my pillow, checking out the drive each time. There was no-one there.

Then there was someone there. I saw a car dropping off a young woman at our entrance, laughing at the man driving as he peeled away with a flourish. She walked confidently, high heels clicking on the concrete, her smart business suit matching her fawn purse, gold handle catching the sun, smiling as she saw me waiting at the open glass door. She introduced herself, saying, 'And how are you today?' Normality wasn't something I could handle so I just nodded and asked her if she would mind helping me to load the car. She would know my name. It was a large second-hand 4 cylinder Vauxhall Wyvern so quite roomy but 'had no grunt' as guys would say. It was mine though, carefully bought and paid for. I didn't want to think about the cost. It was the reason I was able to do what I needed to.

The Welfare lady didn't offer any other comment except to mention that she was a qualified university graduate with a degree in sociology. (Or its equivalent – I wondered if she had been taught how to deal with a stressed-out wife and children and a possibly violent husband.) She'd obviously picked up on my state of mind. With everything loaded she asked some questions about the police and tried talking to the kids who weren't particularly responsive either. I sat looking down the driveway from the kitchen through the porch window. The car was ready to back out. I'd been too nervous to make any unusual changes, again waiting for the police who hadn't arrived at the time we had agreed on, plus checking that no-one else had either. My nerves started getting the better of me again, my fear really obvious as my shaking came back worse than ever and the kids were restless. Bevan came over and hugged me, trying to comfort me. Shanla especially was getting more upset the longer we waited, crying that she did not want to leave. She didn't want to be cuddled either as she was angry with me. She didn't develop asthma though – a blessing.

I sat looking around at the house I had designed and had had built, sacrificing so much for the deposit from meagre savings from part-time work and anything I could squeeze from the minimal house-keeping I was allowed, all the time having to rely on my husband to sign everything off and hope he was still earning. 12 jobs in 12 years. Everything in our home was carefully paid for. It all meant so much to me after my childhood. My home, my security, my stability, my only real roots. I had lived here longer than anywhere else in my life. I could never casually explain why it was so important to me and was the biggest reason I had stayed so long. It was devastating. I could hardly function by then.

The restless Welfare lady told me to phone the police to check but when I went to call, my fingers were unable to stay on the right numbers to dial. The together lady from the Welfare suddenly started falling apart too and grabbed the phone impatiently off me and dialled the police herself. They simply said they wouldn't be long, she told me. I said, 'What does that mean?' desperate for support. She then yelled down the phone to say that wasn't good enough and who she represented. Apparently that must have got some action as her face smoothed out a bit and her tone became more moderate, although her hands had formed fists.

Bevan was nervous now as well and asked me what his dad would do if he came back and found we were leaving. He looked frightened thinking about it so I tried to reassure him but he wasn't having it. He kept saying, 'You know Mum. You know.' I stood looking down the drive with an arm around him, Shanla avoiding me, when a police car pulled up, parking and blocking off the drive exit, the car facing the wrong way. I thought, 'Okay. So it's all over. I tried.' Ridiculously, a sense of total calm flooded through me for the first time in months as I watched a strapping cop in uniform stride toward me, carefully adjusting his hat at the same time. I had nothing to say, feeling paralysed, I just stood there on the front porch waiting. If the police were stopping us leaving what did they think was going to happen to us? I felt bereft, totally alone and so fragile, forgetting to even breathe at first.

Bevan had watched this big policeman come and tugged at me saying, 'we'll be all right now Mum.' I shut my eyes and slowly opened them taking in a big breath as he arrived, putting his hand out to shake mine which I automatically did as I was standing on the same level as him, the porch a few feet off the ground. I thought, 'Why did I do that?' He was speaking to me but I was still in resigned shock and couldn't really take in what he was saying.

The Welfare lady suddenly spoke to him from behind me so she could make sense of what was happening too I surmised, and reached out, grabbing my arm saying in huge relief, 'He has only blocked off the exit so that no-one else can and he will escort you as far as the motorway when you're ready.' It just wouldn't sink into my brain.

He stepped up and took my other arm telling the kids to get into the car while he talked to me. We went inside and he guided me into a chair saying, 'You are safe now and need to have a minute to think if there is anything else you want to take with you.' The word 'safe' bounced around in my brain. I thought 'I have never been safe. What does that even mean?' I just stared at him. He said, 'I have done this before. If something important isn't remembered till later, no-one wants to go back.'

We were sitting at the kitchen table beside some open shelves I had curtained off for my sewing machine. I had thought at least I could make a living from sewing if all else failed. I'd nearly forgotten it. I couldn't believe it. The policeman grinned slightly at the look on my face and picked it up when I moved the curtain and took it out to the car for me saying he would also back me out. I was really grateful and thanked him. I don't know what happened to the Welfare lady but she locked the house up and brought me the key, saying goodbye, wishing me luck through the car window, looking in a bit of shock herself. I watched my home numbly as it got further away.

The policeman gave me a minute to get my act together once he had shifted his car and I had driven onto the road. He then followed us to the motorway north entry, giving us a toot as he peeled off. It had all happened so fast in the end I couldn't believe it. We were free – for now anyway!

We stayed on the motorway until it ended after crossing the Harbour Bridge and continued north to turn off to Coatesville. Just before the bend at the end of the straight after passing the Coatesville shop, the sun suddenly appeared again from behind a stray cloud and lit up a lone, beautifully shaped fruit tree. It was in full pink blossom in the middle of a lush green paddock. Its loveliness brought me to tears but from possible hope this time. (Years later I lived on the 10 acre block of my dream only a *couple of miles away up the hill as the crow flies and this Coatesville area was the beginning of our long view I had seen.)*

Aftermath

My husband was the sole legal guardian of our children, as all men were, and the court confirmed that as by the time our case came up, he lived in the family home with the children and I had no current job, so I was classed as destitute and homeless. I'd had to leave my employment the day before because of his disrupting behaviour when he had abused me there. I had already been forced to leave where I had been flatting as a chatty neighbour warned me a guy had been asking around. (Thank God for a friend who helped me. She had had known me all my life and did not believe his lies when he approached her too.) The defence of saying I was nuts, an often used ploy by lawyers, had not worked as I had been to a psychiatrist who pronounced me sane in writing. I was told by the judge to go back home. One of the lawyers commented, 'He must have had his hand slapped last night!' On the other hand, the police had already told me outright to leave the country if I could afford to when I was being followed by my husband, and to stay away for as long as possible. They said they couldn't protect me night and day and it was impossible to stop an attack, especially so soon after a separation. One policeman also told me quietly not to trust lawyers as they could be persuaded to pass on information to each other – which made sense to me. There had been just too many coincidences when my husband had kept catching up with me.

I had been taunted by my husband about the courts when I lived with him. Just for the sake of it, he would read out from the Herald headlines of the time about wives coming off worst and abusive men going free, saying, "What do I have to fear?" On the whole men forgave each other far easier than women, for many things, not only male domestic violence. This was later confirmed for me by several men who had been in powerful positions themselves.

I eventually lost everything. My children when the police later removed them from me after I refused to go home. Then any job I found subsequently when being harassed. My car as well when I ran out of money. Then before I left Auckland, nearly my life on more than one occasion – hunted and threatened – and eventually again almost my sanity. The thought of probably never seeing my children again was unbearable. At the time I thought that the intensity of that grief was worse than if they had died. I had known the cost would be high. And it was – but surviving under intimidation, coercion, violence, and fear is still not a life. What the situation did do is change the person I had been forever.

Women I have spoken to about their young lives have had more threating family experiences than public ones so maybe my circumstances and experiences were not necessarily typical of the times. In my early teens I had an older boyfriend for over three years and while I was with him, life felt much more normal – there was a man in it. I realise thinking back about it now, it wasn't until he went overseas with the army and there was no man around again, things went back to how life had been previously, necessitating having to be more on my guard again. Being open and friendly was not an option.

Once Shanla was accepted at school at 7, life became less unpredictable and I was able to find a part time job. Working with adults again made a difference to how I felt about men, especially the helpful ones I met then. Most had a sense of humour and were on the whole kind and caring decent people so it is good to acknowledge them. I have since met many more over the years and to this day have offers of help for jobs I struggle with. Their thoughtfulness, caring, consideration, kindness and physical help has made such a difference to my life. Some of them have even said to me they feel guilty on behalf of those other less caring men. I'd like to thank them all especially for just being themselves. They made such a difference in my life.

N.B.

A possible alternative may have been the following life; a woman with four young children I knew around the same time in the early 1960's, had kept her home because of her mother's testimony of violence by the husband that she had witnessed. The mother said her two-year-old baby still didn't speak for fear of a slap after several years. She herself lived in familiar fear and slept with a knife under her pillow, not only for if her violent ex-husband turned up, but also for the unwanted, blatantly sexual advances from regularly visiting local detectives.

When the children were given to their father by the courts, things were initially reasonable as far as the Social Welfare could tell me. From information that I found out about later, despite my continual weekly requests for them to check, this was not true. When I had left Auckland the previous year on the advice of the police, my lawyer, sister, mother and last remaining friend Bev, I was reassured by everyone they would keep an eye on my children. For the first few months they were apparently fine, looked after by a young house keeper.

However that didn't last. A year went by and during that time, the house deteriorated; household accounts went unpaid, including the power bill, which affected them the most, especially Shanla's asthma. Finally the police had gone to pick Shanla up after a neighbour rang to say there was a child sitting in the gutter in the dark and cold at 10pm, heaving with asthma. Bevan was apparently asleep in a truck parked up at the pub where his father was, which had not been known about. If he had been picked up then too I may have been given custody of him as well. One of the neighbours told me later they had been too nervous to do anything for fear of repercussions.

Bevan was over eight years old (nine and quarter) the usual age for sons to go with their father after a separation. The Social Welfare had given his father a week to find appropriate alternate accommodation which he did. Bevan did eventually come to stay with me for some school holidays. By the time I was told about a Government mortgagee sale pending for our home there were only 3 days left to save it. I couldn't believe it. It had meant so much to me – I'd gone without many things. A low offer for it had been made through lawyers on the condition the buyer was not revealed. I agreed as I had a good idea who it was anyway. We had a 'family home' so both signatures were required (only a man's was usually) which was achieved in time. My eventual half from the sale was about a third of our home's value.

The repercussions for that year were many: No fish and chips were ever eaten again for tea by Shanla she was so over them, Weetbix for breakfast and a 'proper' school lunch were appreciated but there were some bad habits to undo. Shanla was ten and a half and was not wanted by her father then or later. The Social Welfare, who the police had given her to, had temporarily placed her with a minister and his wife. The wife was very short with me, when I picked her up. The whole situation was a very different to what I had allowed myself to hope for, but, for once, I could see maybe things would improve. Although the scarring from Bevan's loss stayed with me, other people would always tell me quite openly how much he loved me. 'Count our blessings and always be grateful for what we have' is a good lesson for life.

Educating our Children

Recently a 17-year-old daughter of a friend, who is still at college and is bright, intelligent, top of her class, strong and perceptive, experienced emotional abuse but neither she nor her mother recognised it. If information relating to her experience had been available for this gullible and caring young woman she could have avoided the abuse she received, including blackmail with threats of suicide – very familiar. Without more knowledge a pattern could easily form for her, attracting the same type of person in the next relationship. Listening to other girls' and women's stories was like hearing my own all over again albeit in different time-frames, life-styles and with a wider range of abuse.

If brought up in a loving home or at least a reasonable one, when 'falling in love', what these women never expected to have to deal with in a relationship and may not have known of or recognised in their partner's behaviour, was their entrenched deceitfulness and insidious intimidation, domination and callousness, and for her the resulting disillusion, humiliation, isolation, guilt, loneliness, unhappiness, fear and a sense of betrayal and loss of power. She would be confused and have no answers or tools to deal with this kind of behaviour. All in the name of love which he was probably saying he felt for her. Their sexual relations always such a critical part of the relationship especially if they had a good one. This could leave her desperate for answers to understand what was going on.

This emotional and physically abusive behaviour needs to be defined and guidelines taught in schools' sexual education so that young girls can relate to and recognise what is happening to them. Also information for boys about how not to behave in a relationship so neither end up in a situation they could never have envisaged. (Apparently boundaries are being taught at school now so that will be a great help to all and perhaps curb our tendency to having co-dependent relationships.)

Repressed Feelings

Some women would have been very frustrated being mothers and stay-at-home wives doing all the housework, often finding no acceptance in a predominantly man's world when they had a good education and a useful brain. Perhaps better than their husband's sometimes. The reaction to that varied depending partly on the woman's upbringing. In my grandmother's case she had been needed on the farm until the younger son grew, so had come into her own as her life bore that out. She was a capable, trustworthy person, handling physical work and the farm's books and working after marriage. Out of step however in the late 1800's with the way society accepted women, Nana still passed on her independence to Mary and Mary to me and I in turn to my daughters.

One of the outcomes for intelligent/independent/capable women who were generally patronised, was to feel angry and frustrated when they couldn't achieve anything because of legal constrictions (i.e. fathers or husbands had to sign documents for them and men were the sole legal guardians of the household including their children) or lack of control of the money, which may be gambled, used for boys-toys, spent on other women, invested unwisely, or simply squandered away or drunk, with the outcome affecting the whole family.

The feelings that repression and dictatorship set up caused a reaction in some women that could be overt anger and show itself in a violent confrontation or in many cases, the women would become what Ralph described as 'wind-up merchants' with a simmering but covert anger (passive-aggressive). Once you knew what to look for it wasn't difficult to identify them, even though they were often quiet, restrained, and genteel as in Mary's case.

Mary only had to walk into a room where my brother or my current husband were and the seething underneath would appear in smooth off-hand usually subtly snide remarks that needled men and pushed their buttons. (In between husbands Mary's most common saying was, "I hate men".) My husbands and I had the worst rows we ever had as did Ralph and his wife Kay, after a seemingly innocent visit from Mary, and she had swanned off. She was not invited back that often. Ralph's quote, 'Manipulative Mary had a predilection for drama'.

Summing Up

For the man, I understand it is the ultimate rejection when their partner leaves a relationship of ill-treatment; a double 'not good enough' is engendered into their thoughts. A husband/partner will flout a restraining order, ignoring the law (often seen as a joke), determined to seek revenge. They seem to justify it to themselves as them being the one who is wronged. When a really obsessive/fixated/vindictive person means harm, they are the hardest to escape from and survivors often live with a residual fear of an attack. I don't think 'revenge' is too strong a word for these guys. The most repeated terrifying words that are said to their partners are, as I can verify, 'If I can't have you no-one else will'. (I heard recently from a man that women say that as well.) In other words you are their property.

Divorces had increased by the sixties as it became a more socially acceptable option and the change of legislation made it easier. Now that domestic violence is openly acknowledged women do fight back and are not so cowed, but often to their detriment as there are more deaths around domestic violence than there were. Abused women need to go for help. It is not a situation they can handle alone, no matter what their partner promises. Their abusive partner's first blow should be their last. Being persuaded to return home by a temporarily regretful abuser is often what goes against them the next time. And there will be a next time.

He is regretful for what he is missing when you're not there, not for what he has done.

As the Women's Refuges say today, 'Physical abuse destroys the body, psychological abuse destroys the soul'. They once quoted that a female partner was murdered every 10 days in NZ and the 12/04/09 report from New York's prestigious 'Leitner Centre for International Law and Justice' say family violence affects a third of all women during their lifetime and that 45% of murders in New Zealand are family violence-related. Around 14 per annum in 2018. 27 murders in 2019. I read that the NZ Police have call-outs approximately every four minutes for Domestic Abuse. It has not gone away. Those Police statistics for family violence are truly shocking.

(For more information and the latest stats see
http://www.amazon.com/Verbally-Abusive-Relationship-Expanded-Edition/dp/1440504636)

Chapter 23 Sexual Preferences and Experiences, Homosexuality

Males seldom admitted to being homosexual or sexually differently oriented unless they wanted to be shunned and the butt of every joke and often violence. (I never met a girl or woman who was openly gay or even vaguely had the thought except the one experience in the orphanage at 9 when I was horrified, not that I had a word for it at the time.) There were anyway many wandering single men in the era between the wars which would have been made up partly of some 'queers' no doubt along with genuinely homeless guys and wanderers.

Some were simply not able to fit back into society for whatever reason including being wounded in the First World War and still suffered from shell shock or the then unrecognised PTSD (Post Traumatic Stress Disorder) or depression. Others perhaps had too much pride to ask someone to marry them without adequate income to support a family. There was little official mental health support like counselling in the form we know today apart from religious help, which was seen as being offered with strings, especially with men being encouraged to change their sexual habits. People were considered either normal or not and often we were teased as children about the 'men in white coats coming for us' if we didn't behave or were thought to be crazy. No idle threat. Everyone knew about 'Asylums'.

Cross-dressers and other unusual forms of sexual differences were not obvious nor had a name known to us. They were just 'queers' or 'people of doubtful sex'. After living on Waiheke, when I was back in the city it surprised me when people were critical of someone, as one of the first people I met at Onetangi worked in the local store and was a woman (I think) dressed similarly to a man and spoke in a deep voice – and no-one ever commented.

The ever hopeful gold-panners made their own lifestyle choice but from reading and my conversations with older men, they were often forced to live away from their families and in single status through necessity, especially during the Depression. They worked in council/government frontier-style jobs in isolated places like mines or on road-works in all-male groups.

Accommodation was often scarce, people slept together in a way we would never do now, so it was the accepted norm, and perhaps situations then were not so much homosexual as bi-sexual from lack of options. People too, who have had little affection as a child or adult can be desperate to be loved by anyone and can look for a substitute through inappropriate behaviour with others sometimes, as has been told to me, with their own siblings, either sex.

It would have been easier to cover homosexuality then too as society was not so openly conscious of sexual behaviour other than the conventional norm – although what people actually thought may have been very different. Talking to males of that generation I had the sense that there was a level of indulgence about men being together and it was quite common in an underbelly way and accepted by some without stigma. (This may not be true and is only my impression.) As long as nothing was admitted to or discovered, most people would have believed the myth that single men were all just reluctant or even happy bachelors although parents would make comments we didn't understand, like veiled warnings to their sons. (See the *'Mates & Lovers'* book by Dr Chris Brickall, senior lecturer in gender studies at the University of Otago, which goes back to colonial times).

The law around homosexual relationships was adopted when we became part of the British Empire in 1840 and later punishment was changed from death to life imprisonment, hard labour and flogging and in 1893 was called 'sexual assault' even if consensual. Reflecting changes in attitudes in 1961 the penalties were reduced again.

> 'In 1968 a petition signed by 75 prominent citizens and calling for legislative change was presented to (and rejected by) parliament.[3]' 'The New Zealand Homosexual Law Reform Act 1986 is a law that legalised consensual sex between men aged 16 and older. It removed the provisions of the Crimes Act 1961 that criminalised this behaviour'.

However acceptance of homosexuality by the public varies and our sports teams were under scrutiny re the 'consequences of Gays coming out'. A *NZ Herald* 17/05/15 online contributor commented that 'This country is extremely homophobic.'

Children of Rape

22/02/20, 84% of Sexual Assaults are not reported.

The betrayal when the true reality of the girl's situation becomes clear to her as seen in the eyes of the community and often other family members, who may reject her, is usually totally overwhelming, appalling and shocking. If it was her father, and the mother knew, it would be unimaginable how the family would survive. Although all the spoken and unspoken things in the family would ultimately destroy it anyway, the child would be the one who would have to survive the most repercussions.

Who has her back? Who could she ever trust again? Who should she be loyal to? Who would normally survive in those circumstances? Besides remembering the physical pain and violence and the results of that, ongoing rape may have awakened sexual feelings that would unfortunately forever be associated with those times. Rape can be so repulsive and terrifying to a normal person I think it prevents us from actually really thinking about the consequences for the survivor, which can influence our reaction to it, say on a jury. If religious teachings are part of ours or the girl's life that will also bring another layer of influence to everyone's thinking. Positive or negative judgement, depending on the person.

There are just so many words to describe what changes rape can create in an innocent, vulnerable person.

Some that come to mind are them being seen as: gullible, disgraced, stigmatised, ostracised, devalued, dysfunctional, undeserving, damaged goods, judged a slut. They may feel: betrayed, unworthy, fearful, anxious, depressed, guilty, embarrassed, stressed, ashamed, dirty, worthless, isolated, used, different, rejected, lost, bullied, intimidated, grief, devastated, devalued, alone, lonely, undeserving, deprived, worthless, rubbish, suicidal, angry, frustrated, defiant, powerless, invalidated, disillusioned, disrespected, belittled, misunderstood, humiliated, unsupported, insecure, looked down on and not belonging.

Their understanding of who they really are, so: the loss of self, innocence, security, safety, the unbelievable lost family love and also of many others around them, and the possible self-loathing, self-blame, regretted gullibility, the guilt and the pain and their ability to survive.

The questions of: Do I deserve to be loved? Could anyone love me anyway? Can I now love anyone? Can I trust anyone? How will I handle normal? Especially sex? How do I deal with my perpetrator? Will he still have power over me? How do I control the anger/fear/terror/disgust that sometimes overwhelms me? Do I deserve to live? Is my life over?

The devastating and appalling repercussions for anyone are life-changing and life-long. Rape affects them physically, mentally, emotionally, psychically and spiritually. I think also in some undefinable core part of themselves. If they are still children the hope would be they receive the appropriate treatment and are placed in someone's loving and understanding care for the best outcome.

A police woman I once chatted to felt children do often recognise and play on their ability and sexuality to tease the opposite sex, especially girls, with adult men. Responsible adult men were not mentioned. I was shocked at her attitude in the late 1960's and wondered how generally accepted that was. If that was a normal police attitude, no wonder guilt by the survivor was so prevalent.

For adults, feelings may never happen on a level that means they can function normally again. Unless someone they really care about sticks by them, many probably feel they will just have to do their best to survive by themselves however and wherever they can. This was especially applicable to women in the past. They may never confide their experience if they have escaped from their situation or even when they don't. Shame is a very powerful, controlling emotion, hindering healing with its secretive consequences and often preventing someone seeking help professionally, when they do have a choice, or even from an empathetic, non-judgemental person when offered. This was my experience sometimes but who could they trust? Telling a friend may or may not have been useful.

I also eventually realised there were other people I knew too who had probably had to deal with sexual trauma, although only in retrospect after writing about rape. If you know for sure about one person the patterns are often there to see. Perhaps not exactly about what happened and only similar behaviours, but that something had.

Children Born After Rape

When the baby is kept the fall-out for the child of rape, legal or illegal, has its own repercussions. The generation that was aware of the circumstances of the child's conception are often unable to disassociate the perpetrator from the baby to respond normally to the growing child – including the mother. How could she? Rape within a marriage is the most difficult trap. Separating from the father does not necessarily mean having the choice of giving up the child even when wanting to. Whatever the decision made, it will always have complications. An unmarried mother for instance.

Consciously or subconsciously, people's lingering feeling in response to rape, especially women's, appear to me to be projected onto the child. They may only be as mild as dismay or pity, but the child will feel them even if unaware of the cause. The fact that the child's father will at the very least be judged and at worst vilified and perhaps feared and hated, the child still unfortunately has his genes. Even when hoping for the best outcome of a loving upbringing, the question will always remain in people's minds instinctively, especially if the child is a male, whether they will take after their father. It doesn't help when the child has a strong likeness to the father, which is what happened in our family.

Rape repercussions can seem endless, especially when the secret is kept, and the innocent sense things and may feel rejected. This I can vouch for. Luckily for me my grandmother was my main caregiver for my first few years (probably a frequent answer to a difficult situation) and covered her feelings better than most. Her own natural defiance, adaptability, resilience and common sense, which she had needed when she was required to take a male's role on her own family farm growing up, some of it rubbed off on me, thank goodness.

It wasn't until our mother Mary was actually dying when I was 50 that my half-sister chose to let me know I had never been wanted, unlike her and my brother. Life then finally made real sense. It wasn't that I hadn't known somewhere in my mind on some level, it was more confirmation after gradually putting together conversations and overheard remarks during the years and also our cousin Colleen saying to me once that Mary had unexpectedly one day said to her about me, 'I don't like looking at her face'.

Forgiving helps, especially from a distance, and once I understood what had happened, what else could I do? I also know that I was the one my mother relied on and trusted all her life, even with her reservations. Mary once said to me that even when I wasn't with her, I was with her.

In some ways I consider myself relatively lucky. Life could have been worse. I may not have been loved in the normal way like my half-sister and brother, but I did stay within the family, such as our life was which was not traditional in any sense anyway. Our family was often split after our Nana became ill when I was 6 and died a year later.

Institutional Rape

There are just no words to express what my feelings are about institutional rape, especially religious perpetrators' horrendous use of their innocent naïve victims for their own sexual satisfaction and the depths that the church hierarchy will go to deny their responsibilities. Their insidious deceit of using God as their cover, the extra deceit of also destroying the person's faith, is unbelievable. I understand boys suffered the most for various reasons, often their parents forgiving the clergy because of their own beliefs. I wonder how their sons felt about that? The scale of the little sexual abuse I knew about was appalling enough for me.

Since these revelations this century I realised luck had also held for Veronica and myself as we had escaped the situation that many hadn't when we were incarcerated (it seems the most appropriate word to me considering our previous freedom under Mary's often lax parenting). We were ruled in an orphanage by fear not bars for a year in 1945. It was run by the Presbyterian Church and the girls were separated from the boys and luckily staff by gender.

Others' Experiences

The consequences from any rape experience, single or ongoing, seems to me to mean the chances of a normal life of happiness and fulfilment are limited. With rape by incest, there are family repercussions even years afterwards if a sibling exposes their childhood sexual harassment as an adult, even in their retirement, splitting families into a 'for and against' situation, so that the unhealed psyche wound is exposed again with little assuaging and more stress. The male offender will often repudiate the accusations and compound it by invalidating his victim, belittling her as a person, and damning her as a trouble maker. He would have been in denial all his life and unlikely to ever change. And this is what happened in three cases I know of in large families. To protect them they are anonymous – that doesn't mean it didn't happen nor lessen rape's effect.

I watched three women and one man struggle with the aftermath of rape all their lives, although not understanding the cause of their dysfunctional behaviour until the very end. The following are my recollections. Except for one, they were all introverts, with very few friends – never close ones. One eventually told me she understood how lepers felt. Joy was not an emotion I saw them ever experience, although they may have. There was a sense of containment and reserve in their manner. Light hearted or carefree would never be a description I would imagine them having either and only a strained sense of humour, their laughter often unexpected and I think a relief to themselves. Life was serious and there was a sense of them being on guard. In retrospect, after being told their life secret, their inability to live life as others did was just so sad. I would have trusted them with my life though.

They had all held their natural caring and empathetic natures for others contained in case they totally fell apart themselves. Especially the male with anger. Their whole lives were blighted, not by the single act of a stranger, but by the atrocious and repeated predatory behaviour of a male family member. Not the father in their cases.

Another two friends in their eighties recently confided in me about their brothers abusing them. One for about four years from when she was 10 until he left home. She was not explicit and it was a secret she had not told anyone else about either until she became ill with Alzheimer's, when the torment came out with all the other repressed feelings, but even then she would not say which brother. She died without revealing him – for good or bad, although thinking about it, I would say some in her immediate family knew because of how she behaved around them, and how I have seen them treat her. Her own children didn't know which I understand is not unusual. When speaking to me earlier she had philosophically accepted that it was the lot of many in her generation. It had a definite effect on her life as many odd attitudes made sense about her once I knew.

As others have now, this second molested friend has also died and may not have told others. She was terrified of one of her brothers too, having to pass his bedroom door to get to the toilet, and was so intimidated and frightened when he was at home that she'd wet her pants and have hidings instead of running the gauntlet. Many in this age group lived in villas and had toilet facilities tacked onto the back of the house when indoor plumbing arrived or were still outside. That would be even more terrifying knowing he could be waiting to attack in the dark. Something to be said for toilet chambers of the time.

The only extrovert I knew who had been raped was a brilliant actress (not a stage one), good looking, well-dressed, socially presentable, friendly, pleasant and caring. She was liked and even loved, and many friends and people trusted and confided in her. They were often protective of her too, although probably in response to an instinct, rather than an obvious reason. Very few who knew her would have believed her background – as with many people who have serious secrets in life.

She could not handle stress though, so in her dark times she would disengage from everyone and simply disappear. Sometimes for good from where she had been living and people would go looking for her, imagining the worst, until word filtered back she was okay. Sometimes it took a while when she went overseas. Reassuring letters would eventually arrive with a plausible excuse. Friends would be puzzled at her behaviour, but would forgive her and continued to like her and men to pursue her in some cases. An intuitive friend may have eventually realised there was a serious underlying problem but I doubt they would have found out what. Established denial is difficult to break, especially when it is covering anger and resentment. (Extraction) In a way her whole life was a fabrication.

If the perpetrator doing the molesting is a trusted person in a girl's life, rape can be the most devastating thing especially if he used threats to silence her. A family friend, a close companion of her father's, did to one girl I know who became pregnant at 14. She was abused while babysitting his children. She let the family think the father was a boy she had been friendly with. The real father eventually shifted away. That baby was adopted out and she then had the double grief of losing her child in disgrace and having to live with that loss for the rest of her life, while not being supported by the people she loved the most. There would have been confusion should the adopted child ever try tracking their heritage unless the truth came out from someone.

When rape occurs at a young more vulnerable and innocent age, persuasive lies are more easily believed or the threats more insidious. It was the reason one girl I heard about committed suicide and similar situations also probably created most of the women who made/make a living as professional prostitutes.

I once rented a room for a few weeks in a large lovely old villa in a good area with a variety of other people, including professionals, who each had a large room too. One of them was a street girl who had a front porch bedroom with a convenient large push-up window. On a night when just the two of us were in the kitchen, she told me her story which included a detailed description of her father's behaviour, admitting she liked sex –

'resolute' and 'brave' are words I find appropriate for survivors like her.

Many older women (and probably younger ones too) will relate to these insidious situations and we all probably thought that we were the only ones having to cope with the sly sexual harassment and sometimes rape as well – especially from a family member. The subsequent consequences could keep girls quiet and more often than not, if anyone told, the situation was handled by blaming the victim rather than disrupt others' lives.

A girl-friend recently confided to me about how her maternal grandfather always liked her to sit on his knee and rock in his rocking-chair, the excuse to hold her firmly against him, after managing to make it sound natural for her to take her knickers off first. This was from very young and it was years before she understood what was going on and when she complained to her grandmother and then her parents, they dismissed what she said and growled at her for making up stories. When she later had her own daughters and wouldn't keep up the pretence of normality and make the trip to visit the old family home any more, especially as her granddad was still in his rocking chair, she was berated for it. This disbelief and rejection was critical to who she developed into. Luckily because she was an open person with a good sense of humour and married to a lovely guy, she dealt with it better than most, although her relationship with her mother is still often rocky.

Stranger rape is the headline that gets the publicity and sympathy and sometimes retribution and justice, and so it should, although the stats are against it whoever the rapist is. Often a court case can make the person feel like she/he is being re-raped by their treatment in a courtroom and the unwelcome memories being relived. Hopefully that situation is improving. However I think the ongoing covert family scenarios are just as damaging, with huge control given to the older predator by them using the fear of the threat of future insecurity with a family break-up and the possible punishment for the perpetrator. It would be beyond a young person to deal with. Her/his silence the goal. The cruel undeserved guilt would be shocking.

For the victim/survivor of rape, after forgiving their perpetrator, perhaps the most difficult aspect of coming to terms with life and some sort of normality in the end, they then needed to forgive themselves. Although not their fault, the abused I knew as an adult at least partly blamed themselves, even though they probably had very little idea of what the word 'sex' actually entailed before their forced childhood encounters. There was a woeful lack of even basic information for children and young adults in the post Victorian/Edwardian era. Abuse in any form, including rape, is certainly a terrible start to a young life and as horrifying to an adult.

'Both the child and adult of rape or abuse and the child born from rape have the right to live'. That is so important for them to know.

Earlier, without counsellors around, the main options for help were a religious person or perhaps a psychiatrist and they were usually men, which would have been off-putting for girls, and could have had unwished-for repercussions as well.

Even when abortions became a choice, the girl's own conscience could have prevented her from taking that option, especially if it was a sister or brother. Adoption was a whole other scenario, perhaps the best for everyone when there was a choice.

Many women have survived and coped with ordinary living but often at a very high cost emotionally and mentally and sometimes physically. Perhaps they were lucky enough to find good husbands that they could tell who understood and supported them. For others it might be a lifetime secret and/or lead to using sex to make a living.

Trying to survive and live a normal life takes the kind of courage many people who haven't been there could never appreciate or envisage. A different kind of courage, tenacity and resilience to what is expected of men unless they too were in the same situation, but just as resolutely necessary for woman. Soul-destroying without it. Good for those whichever way it is they've managed. Whatever success anyone makes in life, especially when a pregnancy is the result of rape, they deserve any happiness and support that comes their way.

Sexual Harassment

Quote from Helen Mirren, "One did not speak about sex when I was growing up. It was thought to be unbelievably sluttish to even have a bra strap showing". That was my era. No-one openly referred to sex and the term 'sex education' had not been 'coined'. Parents were still far too inhibited. The only people to find anything out from were girlfriends and we were usually as ignorant as each other.

On Waiheke 'we just joined the rest of the misfits' as I think of us. We went to live there year round when I was about 11 instead of just the holidays. Its variety of people, according to gossip, had more misfits per head of population than anywhere else in NZ. Some out of step with society one way and another like new immigrants speaking little English, alternate and possibly some unhealthy lifestyles, free-spirits and dreamers, odd religious types – no cults that we heard about anyway.

One old man taught a group of us Onetangi girls the Esperanto language for a while until one of our parents discovered he had built a centre room only accessible from underneath his house with a window in the roof. He said it was for sunbathing nude. He should never have used the word 'nude'. I only remember he offered us bottles of free Coke hanging from a homemade holder in the kitchen which we were too polite to take and that Esperanto meant 'One who has hope'. Pity about that.

No-one was that much into judgement either. For instance, there was some level of acceptance for a woman who had apparently had a baby to an American soldier during the war – there were many illegitimate children born then. Usually 'those' sort of babies were just adopted out and never mentioned, a family secret – especially if you were married. Not hers however.

Some people had physical and emotional problems, others mental ones. There was one brave woman who lived in isolation in an undeveloped area a bit inland from Onetangi Beach, who only brought out her handicapped children late in the day, just after sunset. We would see her hurrying along behind them. They were nearly as big as she was but not as co-ordinated, as their ungainly gait was obvious as they ran along near the cliff edge calling to each other, the mother with apprehension in her voice. I don't know if anyone ever actually met them.

Many however were just glad to be away from the city environment for some peace and quiet and healthier living conditions and were mostly good natured and harmless except for the few. Still, a secretive place in its way then, Waiheke, and parts of it probably still are.

As a child, although I lived in fear, I did not fear men other than my step-father. It was more about fear for Mary's and Ralph's safety. My step-father was the tallest, most well-built and violent man I had ever met, however his anger was not directed at me or Veronica, and Mary did our disciplining, such as it was. Ralph first, then Mary was the next in line, except with a closed fist, at least once a month around a full moon. I wished we could all leave! The women's unwritten code of 'Safety in Silence' had always really been 'Suffering in silence', but it avoided the disbelief, belittling and bullying disparaging of many men's attitudes towards women.

Being believed is a huge issue. Sometimes also compounded by other women saying, "She's a liar". Girls learnt that quite young. Hence not complaining when the boys harassed me and later as well when men did too. Perhaps not so for others if supportive fathers took their daughter's side. Attracting boys was flattering but mysterious and distasteful at the same time and they did sort of refer to sex, but in a smutty, sly way, so what was going on was still an enigma to me.

I knew about the meaningless of the word 'safe'. No-one had ever offered to help Mary when she was attacked and I couldn't help though I always tried and my screaming had alerted neighbours. A neighbour Mary met years later on a bus trip said she still had nightmares of my screams. Having survived living with John, other men didn't seem worth worrying about. I had so much more to learn.

More pain that may never completely heal can come from a manipulating, deceitful, sly and devious person. Once, when it was me who was the focus of that treatment, to save my sanity and survive constant threats meant I needed to use similar tactics myself – to my horror!

Also the fallibility of this theory about not fearing males was that I discounted boys. They seemed pathetic around girls when it came to sexuality. I did not understand the power that would control them as they grew.

In the following bush boys' case, Mary would have brushed the incident aside, not the only one to by any means. I'd got away with it she would have said and it was my own silly fault anyway. My step-father could have gone and found the boys and given them a hiding, which from him would have turned out seriously. Our lives would have been impossible in the small community, mine especially as it was usually the female's fault. There were no police to appeal to in small settlements like that and the outcome wouldn't probably have been too different. It was a lone young female's voice against a group of boys and the men would be judging them. One of the boys was the son of the boss. A 'pragmatic decision' my Nana would say.

Although Mary seemed to understand about boys she never warned either myself or my half-sister how vulnerable we were to predators especially after she left our step-father. We were young and she may not have realised how soon that would be a problem having always had a mother and a father herself. The unspoken, publically perceived protection that a man in the house gave us was now gone. We were fair game. Ralph knew though. Once after he came back to live with us, he confronted an old man at a bus stop who had been sidling up to Veronica and making suggestions to her, while she waited for Ralph who was meeting her there. She was quite lost and embarrassed but Ralph was so angry and kept hassling the man until he went away and missed his bus.

I saved myself many times with my ability to run very fast or if that wasn't possible initially, talk my way out of a situation – then run. Boys often just wanted to feel my breasts or watch them wobble as in a Physical Education class at school which I caught onto fairly quickly and got myself to the back of the group. This at least ceased at high school being all girls and Mary eventually bought me some bras.

1940's Boys

The Bush Boys

In the 1940's, from around the age of 8 to 9 years old, I had begun developing a figure. This resulted in attention being paid to me when I was obviously still very innocent.

Self-defence wasn't something anyone even thought about being necessary for a girl either. No-one openly spoke about what could happen to a girl if she ended up in a situation alone with boys or a man or men, so the first few times the situations arose, they were pretty shocking for me – especially as I got on well with boys. Perhaps I was more adventurous than some girls when taking up a challenge from them like diving into a deep spot off rocks at the beach. Maybe the problem arose partly because of my lack of fear around them too.

Anything more serious physically usually began with a sly suggestion first. In the bush settlements I began to realise I needed to be more careful when I went off on my own. About six boys with an older one of around 15, the predator, thought they had me trapped once about half a mile from the houses where there was a small bush clearing, a favourite dreaming place of mine.

I had only just arrived so they had been waiting. As they began surrounding me, the salacious 15-year-old droolingly described the things they were going to do to me as he exposed himself. Most of it eluded me as I just stood there like a frozen idiot in shock. Some of the boys, who I thought were my friends, looked slyly sheepish and couldn't meet my gaze. Their leader shouldn't have done and said what he did without holding me down first. I got my act together and was gone in a flash through one of the closing gaps. Running was my specialty – trees and undergrowth or not.

I don't know what the boys expected but afterward one or two of them hesitatingly tried to speak to me at school but I would have none of it. I'd gone home and into my bedroom and sat on my bed, repulsed and horrified, shaking in anger – mainly from the frustration of knowing there was nothing I could do about what had happened. We left again not long after. Me more disillusioned and wary than when we had arrived.

Mt Eden Pool.

Once a group of boys cornered me at the Mt. Eden swimming pool. I'd thought I was being watched when I was swimming but could never have imagined what was being dreamt up. They were a few years older than me mostly. I was about 9 I think, just developing. They had followed me out of the pool and into the girls' empty changing rooms, sliding on the wet floor in their haste. They closed in on me before I could even get to my clothes. I was backed tightly into a corner as they cut me off, totally trapping me in seconds. We all stood there. They were scarily quiet and watchful, partly waiting to see what I'd do, I think now. Eager sweating faces, staring eyes, bodies becoming restless.

Shaking and terrified, I couldn't see a way out for the life of me (I never even thought about screaming – inbuilt instructions – 'Don't scream! Don't cry!') The boldest and biggest of the leering boys, who was about 14, grabbed my bathing suit top, trying to rip it off, dragging me to the toilets at the same time. I was too busy struggling to notice when a parent walked in until she called out to see if her daughter was there.

She stood there looking blank when she first saw the boys in the girls' area, not spotting me at the back, and for a few seconds their attention was off me. Quickly smacking off the big boy's hands, his strong grip having already partially relaxed, I fled. Squeezing through a small gap that had opened when the boys had turned, I raced past at least one guilty looking face and shot out of there so fast, grabbing my bag off the seat as I went, and was gone before anyone else moved.

I knew they would follow me as when I was going through the exit turnstile at the end of the pool I heard one yell, "There she is". I flew out the entrance, not the exit way, as it was the nearest, desperately pushing past people and ran to the nearest house without a gate and plenty of shrubs and trees and hid. The main road was too wide and the view too long to be able start walking back to Uncle Ross' place a couple of miles away. I crouched there shivering with cold and fear, carefully not changing position, my bag clutched to me, watching until the boys gave up looking. They never came anywhere near my bolt hole and eventually broke up.

Calling out to each other as they walked off, some looked ashamed while others were jeering and swearing. I eventually felt safe enough to move. I pulled on my frock over the wet cold bathing suit, mostly feeling angry by then, not so frightened, and thought disgustedly, 'Another place not to go alone'.

1940's Men

The Old Men

At Onetangi, one of the oddballs was the old man neighbour who stored our Christmas camping gear under his house. As usual each year, we all had to help lug things up the hill from his place across the wide track (now a road) to the camp site at the top of the hill, which we did in dribs and drabs, until I went back alone for the last of the pots. As I pushed aside the scrub that had grown out over the little used pathway; I saw that the back door of his house was open, which it hadn't been. We had thought Mr. Jones had gone out because we were taking so long, but I could see him inside vaguely and something didn't look right. Even at 8, not wanting to be rude, I avoided looking. Thinking I heard him call out though I focussed again and realised I was seeing his angled reflection in the mirrored wardrobe door of his bedroom. He was standing there starkers, holding his penis in his hand waving it at me.

I was so shocked I turned and ran like a hare back to the camp and the safety of other people around. Uncle Ross, who looked after us until Mary arrived, nagged away at me for ages to go back and get the pots but I wouldn't and he got quite annoyed but he was a man too and whom did you tell? One of the boys went in the end. When Carol, Uncle's daughter, and I walked along the beach after that, we would often catch him waving to us from the lupines, naked and exposed as usual. We made a joke of it in later *years and laughing would run past as quickly as we could dragging little Veronica along with us. There was another Mr. Jones further down the hill who would do similar things but we'd already got used to the one we knew before he started his antics, so he didn't bother us.*

Travel Encounters

Once I began boarding trams in the city from the age of twelve and my breasts had nearly fully developed, I became even more vulnerable. Going to secondary school by tram a different kind of harassment began. There wouldn't be many people on board around 3:45pm but there were often old men. They would obviously look out for someone on their own and who no doubt looked quiet or shy, I was both. Spotting me they would slide into the spare seat beside me even if I had put my bag on it, taking up most of the room. They'd persist and shove until they had squeezed in, then a silent intrusive game of "I will", "No you won't" would begin.

It was all carried out under the nose of the conductor, as an unseen hand would slip under my skirt and try to get under the elastic in my knickers. I would stab at it with a pencil I kept in a pocket, pushing and fending it off while the man would lean against me trying to control my hand movements and preventing me from standing up. All the time he would be looking away across the aisle out the window on the other side of the tram, as if nothing was going on, relying on a scared young female not to make a fuss – God forbid!

I got more adept at dealing with these creeps as time went on pushing one off balance and onto the floor and accidentally stepping on him when I moved to another seat. I'd timed that push to happen when I knew a jolt was coming up where there was a problem with the tram lines. Another one would have got deep scratches across his face as I forced my way out of the seat, dragging my hand behind me, and got off the tram at my stop. The weirdest thing was that I never really saw their faces as they would come from behind, turn their heads away, and never look at me. I would smell them though. They all had a strange musky scent which I recognised years later.

As adults on the whole had not been helpful or protective in my life and usually turned a blind eye to anything unsavoury, I'd been expected to look after myself, which I know many other girls had experienced too. I handled the situations as best I could with the least fuss. Besides I didn't have a lot of faith that anyone would believe me and if I appealed to a man, like the conductor, whose side would he take anyway? And things might get worse.

I dealt to all the old men eventually in our silent struggles and I think they may have got on other trams because a few weeks after my last encounter, at morning assembly at Grammar, we were warned about such carryings on and told to report them. In these types of situations I had always thought it was me who had unknowingly in my ignorance been doing something to create them, so I was astonished that someone else who had obviously been hassled as well, had actually told a parent or teacher and some action was being taken.

Going home late after school detention though there was no help, as the city workers leaving early from Queen St. had already packed the tram by my stop in Symonds St., so I would end up being out on the platform where all the men were. They'd never let me through to the main part of the tram by stubbornness, design or because it was simply too crowded. There would always be at least two hands feeling about. I'd smack them off and shift around as best I could but it was difficult to tell where the hands were coming from as everyone looked ahead in innocence or indifference. I'd often give up, get off, and walk home, sometimes in the rain and dark for several miles, but I felt safer even if I wasn't. At least I could see what was going on around me – besides I had faith in my running and had already found that at night was the best time for swiftness.

First Job

Employed in places like the General Post Office at the bottom of Queen St., the opportunities for abuse were rife. There were so many choices of areas to get waylaid. Some guys would be openly brazen and often did and said things in a jocular way which, although offensive, were certainly not taken as seriously as today. Some women who reacted strongly were left alone (and called bitches out of their hearing) but on the whole it was just part of life and women and girls put up with it. If it was totally over the top, something might be said, but men were the bosses and supported each other, so if an incident was hushed up, no-one complained too loudly. Jobs were jobs.

I know at times I was sort of warned by other women about not getting myself into a vulnerable situation with certain guys at work, like in the lift, dead-end corridors, near cleaners' cupboards or basements, but nothing was really said openly, just hinted at, and as subtlety often eluded me, it was not usually helpful.

Around the Christmas period it was very unwise to go to the toilet alone after dark in the dim lighting, some bulbs having actually been removed, and the back area of the Post Office was a rabbit warren. Working late enough for it to be dark didn't happen often but at that busy time of year and being on a salary, we didn't leave until our boss said we could go. Aside from the men and boys working there, the public could also wander in various back entrances without too much of a problem because there was no security – not even thought of – just a 'staff only' or ' No Entry' sign outside which most people respected.

The proximity of the wharfs could make sailors a problem outside as well and going home after finishing late one night, I used the back entrance to get to the bus terminal more quickly for my ride, after one of the nicer guys had offered to walk me through the corridors. Once outside on my own I slipped on a soggy cream balloon at the bottom of the steps, noticing there were quite a few lying around, and thought they were pretty colourless for that time of the year.

Further out into the dark parking area where the open exit gates to the road were, several sailors had been crossing the footpath and stopped to watch me as I went toward them and the lights. I was so concerned about missing my bus and having to wait nearly an hour for the next one, by the time I began to seriously think about the sailors and that it had perhaps been a mistake to come this way, it was a bit late. They'd moved toward me as a group, giving me cheek in guttural English and making lewd *finger suggestions. I'd already slowed down but stopped all together then and began back-pedalling but thinking 'I'm never going to make it back to the steps in time as well as having to race along the threatening passageways'. I turned to try anyway and nearly walked right into my boss' arms. A lovely man. I was so embarrassed I could feel myself going red but he just nonchalantly took my arm and smoothly turned me around again saying, "I think we are going in the same direction," and guided me past the sailors who were by then standing about as if they had nothing but the purest thoughts in their minds.*

Part time employment

These were probably the jobs where women were the most vulnerable, especially to bosses, but it did help to have numbers of people around to make the harassment less acceptable when tried openly.

At 16 I took a part-time weekend job to fill the hours after my boyfriend went overseas. I'd get a taxi from my regular job in the city on a Friday night down to a popular café in Newmarket where they made good coffee. The other waitress/helper there was a recent Dutch immigrant who had a husband and new baby. We got on okay but she was older and wasn't someone I would want for a friend as I simply did not understand her attitude and some of her beliefs.

I was often there early Saturday mornings on my own as well with the male proprietor, making the day's sandwiches in the tightly set up kitchen and I noticed he would be forever going in and out unnecessarily, pushing himself against me as he went by. If I said anything he would look at me innocently as if I was accusing him unfairly and brush it off. I mentioned this to the Dutch girl, asking if he did this with her. She obviously thought I had a problem, not him. One morning when lack of sleep from working too many hours caught up with me, he hesitated a bit too long pushing past as I was cutting the sandwiches. I moved slightly sideways along the bench, turning and bringing the bread-knife up in front of me as I did and just stood there looking straight at him. I was furious but he moved off quickly and nothing was actually said, which had become the norm. His wife came in to help with counter work about 11am and they were chatting out the front of the shop between serving customers. When I went back out to the kitchen carrying the dishes after I'd just cleared off the tables, she followed me and accused me in a high agitated voice of making a pass at her husband. I couldn't believe it and just laughed and asked, "What, with a knife?" I couldn't get over that she had been sucked in by him. She sacked me on the spot so I grabbed my things and walked out saying, "Ask yourself why I would look at a dirty old man like him," pointing as I passed him. She was furious and said something I didn't catch. I was just so glad to be out of that place.

I realised that the Dutch girl was due to start work as I walked toward the bus stop so that 'spontaneous' angry sacking had been timed. I ran into her after I crossed at the intersection of Remuera Rd. and Broadway and she stopped and asked me why I was leaving at that hour, so I told her, more upset than I thought I was. She looked at me strangely and said in her thick English, "But that is always part of employment." Shocked at what she understood New Zealanders expected I asked what her husband thought about that. She said, "I am to do whatever my boss asks. We need the money." Sexual harassment was probably pretty prolific in those days so perhaps her attitude was not so different from other women's, but it appalled me. I even went up to the local Police Station and the guy interviewing me obviously thought I had a nerve, and waved/laughed me off.

Work Colleague's Mates

Angela and I worked together when I was 17 at a private firm after leaving our BNZ bank job together, mainly for better money. I went to weekend dances with her and her boyfriend, James, when my boyfriend was away. James brought along a group of mates one evening who mostly sat around drinking surreptitiously, politely asking me for a dance sometimes when I didn't net a partner. Toward the end of the night I made movements to leave before the final dance as otherwise I would miss the last bus home. It was only across the road so no problem. Angela said the boys were on their way to the Army Camp at Papakura and had offered to drop me off at Panmure also on the way south, if I wanted to stay till the end. I hadn't really talked to them much as I'd been sitting next to her most of the evening and the guys had been together in a small group including her own boyfriend, so I didn't get their names even. I wasn't worried about going with them though, trusting Angela. We all said our goodbyes and the six of us squeezed into a small car they had parked off the main road. I sat in the back on three guys' knees and moved around a bit when it became uncomfortable.

We followed the main Great South Rd. initially, everyone flirting and chatting, all making jokes and in good spirits so the guys appeared likeable and carefree. After a while one of them, James, with whom I had danced the last waltz, distracted me admiring my outfit and commenting on my hair. I still had my eye on our route however as I wasn't sure they knew the right one, until I saw a building go by that was not where we should have been. It was Greenlane Hospital that I was very familiar with. At the very least it was the long way around.

When I commented that whoever was driving seemed to have lost his way slightly they all laughed and said it was I that didn't know the shortcuts. In fact I knew Auckland pretty well, having lived in so many places. We started arguing and meantime the guy driving continued on, and as I knew the road would eventually take us back to the main one south, I relaxed a bit until he suddenly made an unexpected turn into Cornwall Park.

I protested but James with his arm around my waist tightened it and another laid his hand across my thigh. I realised I was in deep trouble then but in the end just laughed and said, "You guys want to play. Why didn't you say? I thought you had to get back to camp". They smirked and laughed self-consciously, relieved there wasn't going to be a problem. We pulled over and eased off the road onto the grass a fair way into the park grounds next to some large trees set amongst plenty of surrounding ground covering. There was little light and the boys became a bit awkward then, no-one speaking at first and in the short silence we could hear a party going on not far away. I heard Maori being yelled out so knew there was no help there and anyway one of the boys made a smart remark about what happens at Maori parties. In the end I said I'd get out of the car first.

They must still have been slightly suspicious or perhaps eager as several of them made to get out as well, but I stopped them saying, "One at a time please guys. I'm a bit shy. Could I have my coat to lie on please?" It was a coolish night and damp on the grass, so they handed it out fairly quickly. If I had known much about anything I could have got away with asking for my purse as well by saying I had condoms in it, but it wasn't something that came to mind.

I lay my lovely, expensive, warm winter coat down (a time payment job and very precious) for what I saw as the last time and before I'd even got myself comfortable on it, James dropped down, nearly on top of me. He pushed at my shoulders and began kissing me passionately. After a few seconds he rolled off slightly to undo his fly buttons and began pulling off his trousers, so I said, "I'll just take off my skirt too so it doesn't get wrinkled." It was a full circle black taffeta one that came down to just above the ankle so quite a bit of material that would have been hampering us. He half lay there on his back, his hands suspended at his knees after pushing at his trousers and watched like the others, peering through the dark out of the car windows. I stood up and as I was the only one on my feet then – I ran.

An Olympic sprinter wouldn't have caught me in that few seconds. Running in fear was instinctive and I was out of sight in the darkness under the trees heavy shadows before any of them woke up to being duped. I could hear their angry frustrated yells fading as I headed in a direct line for the main road, lights and people, although there probably wouldn't be many at what was then about 12:30 am.

I had just reached the park's road a couple of hundred metres before it joined the main Greenlane Rd. again, when I heard a car coming from behind me. I was out of breath but realised it might be the boys so backed off to see if it was and where they would go. The car stopped and it was them. They would know I would be heading that way. Unless I could climb the waist-high stone wall of the park which ran along parallel to the main road, without being seen or before they could reach me, which I didn't think was possible, back-tracking was my only option.

At first they just sat in the car waiting so I backed away carefully and slowly but kept them in sight After a couple of minutes they worked out I might have seen them, so they came hunting, They kept yelling out, checking with each other, but were also using cajoling words for me, offering to take me home now and that I'd be okay.

I kept ahead of them, dodging between the trees without being spotted until the greenery began curving around the road boundary which was leading back towards where the Maori party noise was, which was louder. I realised I could see ahead more easily now as some of the growth was shorter and denser. That was good and bad. I hesitated and looked back hoping the hunters would be thinking about giving up. But they weren't. My choices were an open grass field with a wire fence boundary on my right, crossing the road to the left or straight ahead to the party.

In the end I did move the party way a bit as I'd caught sight of one of the last big old trees among a few smaller sparser ones. From my angle of view it looked like it had a slight inward curve in its trunk. It was also in a darker shadow from where the boys would be seeing it. Moving cautiously, even more aware of my surroundings and the extra threat, and making sure I wasn't seen from either direction, I slowly bent down and lifting my skirt and petticoat, crawled carefully into the old tree's shadow. My clothes were covered in leaves and sticks (and who knows what else – hopefully not a weta) and the knobbly bark of the trunk jabbed at me when I leaned into it. Keeping my movements slow I bent forward and keeping my black petticoat down my back, pulled my dark full skirt up from my waist and over my head, wrapping it around me, my feet tucked tightly in so no part of me showed. The skirt made a soft rustle if I moved even slightly so I locked myself in position as best I could and sucked up air as I waited.

I had been aware of calling voices getting closer but was too absorbed in what I had been doing to take much notice, except I knew they weren't right on top of me. The hardest thing to do was to control my breathing. Taking in air made a noisy rasping sound and terror kept me from breathing at all as their calls got closer. I eased one hand to loosely cover my mouth and nose and tried to intermittently take tiny quiet breaths instead of holding one in, in case I made a bigger noise when forced to. The smell of gum and dampness arose around me and the pricks of small sharp sticks dug into my bottom. I blotted out everything to remain still and silent. The Maori party sounded like it was getting a bit nasty, it was certainly noisier.

As the boys got nearer they must have been able to hear the Maori too and would also have seen the end of the trees. They had stopped again and were yelling at each other about going back to the car. They decided they'd probably missed me and it would be better to use the car to catch up with me again.

The boys were fairly well spread out but the one closest and most determined, I realised, was not that far from me and had kept walking as he was answering. He must have been thinking about where I would have gone and swore under his breath. I thought, if he comes any further forward or looks down he will see me, and I felt myself beginning to shake. I thought, 'I am not going to get caught now', so I stuck my nails into my cheek for distraction and some control until it really hurt.

My hunter's breathing was quite heavy and his shoes slithered on the leaves as he moved his restless body looking around. He was the most frightening one as he seemed to be the leader from what I had heard of their earlier loud conversations but he suddenly said, "Let's go. I've had enough of this crap. The bitch could be anywhere". They moved off arguing with each other, some for just leaving the whole thing, but one guy further away still reckoned they should go back to check the road again before giving up.

I just stayed there, still huddled hard against my refuge, taking in great heaving breaths when out from under my skirt, eventually really shaking from the release of tension. You can read about being hunted and you can perhaps imagine it, but until you actually are, nothing about the reality of that terrifying pursuit comes close to what must be an inherent fear in all of us. The fact that it was done in a relatively peaceful setting did not stop me from feeling hounded and at bay like any animal and the deep *dread of exposure to a group of determined boys/men, who may have had no pity, was petrifying.*

I was so cold from reaction and the night by then, all I really wanted to do was stay there till the light came in the morning. It took a while and the Maoris' noise had changed to rumbling with the odd yell or drunken laugh, before I could persuade my legs to stand me up, and when they did they wouldn't hold me properly at first. I leaned against my tree for a while working things out and realised that the guys probably did have to be back in camp by a certain time so I decided to move. I wondered what they would do with my things including my wages? My coat alone was a huge loss, never mind getting to work next week.

I walked carefully back to the junction of Greenlane Rd. and the park road entrance, stopping in the tree shadows again to watch when anything came by, and sat still for ages by the stone wall entry when I got there. Timing it to make sure there was no car lights coming along either way, I raced across the road and on down toward the curve where I knew once I was around it, there were houses and plenty of lights to be seen nearby and in the distance at the major Greenlane and Great South Roads intersection.

I made it across and was beginning to relax, slowing down my pace so I wouldn't look so desperate once people could see me, but just after I rounded the path on the big corner where the traffic lights could be seen in the distance, I vaguely heard a car come around behind me so I swung closer to the fenced properties. The path was really wide there and anyone trying to grab me would have to stop at a dangerous place and get out and walk or run toward me, but I would have time to move first. The car passed me and I stopped dead. It was them. They didn't see me at first but they suddenly swerved into the curb about 50 metres ahead and began to back up. I did too so they stopped, no doubt aware of other vehicles possibly coming around the curve and worried about a crash and their own safety.

Any of them trying to grab me would hesitate I thought on a main road like this and a built-up area with street lamps. Nothing happened for a while as I stood quietly but tensely waiting and watching near the fence of a respectable looking house which also had lights on. Thoughts of possible scenarios were running through my head and depended on what they did but I also started shaking again.

In that minute of stand-off and relative safety, I realised this time I was feeling a sudden surge of anger. How dare they behave like this! I think I would have flown at anyone who came for me then and would have screamed and screamed till someone heard, which I had felt like doing for the last few hours anyway.

Finally, one of the guys opened the back door of the car and stood exposed in the light on the curb of the broad pavement and calling to me said; "Don't worry," hesitating on my name, "Come and get in the car and we'll take you home. You'll be okay."

As I didn't move or speak and they already knew how fast I could run, he got back in and after a few seconds leaned out placing my coat and purse on the edge of the footpath. They waited to see what I would do and when I still didn't move they revved up and took off. I watched till they got to the lights and turned right into Gt. South Rd., the route to Papakura, but it was also the beginning of my own way home.

I gradually slid down the fence onto the damp crunchy path, as by then my legs had given out again – in relief. The passionate heat from the fury of my anger had dissipated and I rested for a few minutes, meanwhile keenly studying the traffic coming towards me that had turned into the road I was in from the direction their car had disappeared. After a while, when nothing threatening had happened, I rubbed at the marks on my face where I'd stuck my nails, and slowly stood up, then stumbling at first, went towards the changing colours of the traffic lights, picking up my belongings on the way and pulling on my lovely warm coat – so relieved to have it back on some level, although hardly able to register anything in my brain except the terrifying night. I wasn't in a hurry by then as it was a long way home. Tired and exhausted already from being hunted, I knew the distance only too well having walked it before – farther as it had been from the central city and for a similar reason – only one guy that time.

I warily reached the corner and pushed the crossing button as a couple of late buses from the city pulled up over the road, the signal against them. I waited for the pedestrian sign to go green until my sluggish, still fearful brain eventually registered that one of the buses was going my way. At first I didn't believe it as the last advertised bus was around 11:30pm. Suddenly coming to life again, I raced across the road against the 'no crossing' signal in sheer exhilaration, waving my arms in front of the slowly revving bus to hold it. I leaped on board so gratefully when the doors opened, thanking the driver from the steps, and scrabbling in my purse for any small change I had, offering it to him for my fare. I then leaned against the cool glass of the inside partition for support in amazed relief.

After a few panting breaths of respite I glanced sideways at the other passengers, wondering whatever I looked like and what they were thinking, but all the seats were taken and there was standing room only right to the top of the steps where I was. The air was humid and fuggy and only a few of the drowsy people near the front would have seen anything but none seemed perturbed. I couldn't believe it, but one of them was my brother Ralph. He hadn't said anything as I think he was astonished to see me but also he was too far away to talk over the engine noise and he couldn't reach me without causing a fuss from the standing passengers.

By the time we got to the bus stop at the top of our road in Panmure, about 20 minutes later, we were both too tired to talk sensibly and he never did ask what that had been about. It was so good to be able to walk down our long hill to home with someone though. Ralph had no idea how much. My jumping nerves weren't as fatigued as my brain. I probably wouldn't have told him what had happened anyway if he had asked as I didn't tell Mary or anyone else either.

Back at work on the Monday, Angela made an offhand remark about loose girls and she was obviously pretty disgusted with me so I didn't even bother to explain. If she believed her boyfriend's *mates' version without even asking for mine, and he was the one who had set me up, nothing I said would have made any difference and who needed that sort of friend? Angela left to marry not long afterward when she became pregnant, a relief to both her and me, but I felt sad for Angela about her choice of husband. I should have kept that sorrow for myself as my own choice not long after was little better.*

Chapter 24 Fashion

Women's Fashion

Like the Second World War, change was reflected in fashion following the First World War. There was a period of turbulence, liberalism, and increased cultural exchanges, especially between America and Europe, including African-American jazz music. The 1920's was Mary's decade growing up. She had just left school and had a real awareness of fashion, partly inherited from her mother and her shops, but she was pretty so aware of what looking good could achieve. I don't know how much other families were interested and it may have been no big deal, the subject treated as frivolous. Also women may not always have been able afford to keep up with the latest designs, but inevitably they would have changed their dress styles as others did, even if it was a few years out of date. There had to have been relief from the earlier more military, prudish, and constricted dress fashions of a sheath frock or the voluminous, petticoated skirts and the still encouraged wasp-waisted steel and whale-bone corsets.

In a 1916 crowd photo, frocks had long sleeves and skirts, although not dragging, and were belted and primly high necked. Every woman wore a hat which seemed to depend more on their personal taste than a consistent fashion. The children also, as hats were recommended because it was thought they protected them from the sun and the dreaded Polio. The girls' clothes were similar to those Mary had worn, shapeless, long bodied, knee length 'French frocks'. Hers though had been covered by a full, usually decorated apron which was worn inside and outside of the house, and especially to school. Although the apron may not have been on for special occasions, like the girls in the photo, practically it would have prevented staining and have saved time to be able to wash the apron rather than the frock. Stout boots were worn by boys and girls, the latter over dark wool stockings. Usually leather sandals in the summer.

Modern dress options as we know them began in the twenties. Women were the primary consumers the market aimed at and Mary talked about Coco Chanel, the fashion designer (particularly her chic suits), and Clara Bow, the actress, both exponents of the latest trends, leading to the liberating changes they instigated, simplifying women's lives. The contrast when it came in couldn't have been more striking.

The flippant, boyishly flat-chested, practical flapper dress with the slim dropped waist and shorter hem lines must have seemed amazing. The revolutionary style was often made from soft flowing jersey fabrics and was easier for anyone to sew or knit at home. The *Mirror Magazine* even had free patterns so garments became more individual with fewer fitting problems and less material and shop-bought ready-made clothes came into their own. The straighter shaped corsets would have brought a sense of freedom and encouraged physical mobility.

Fashion was no longer just worn by the more affluent. By 1925 the conservative middle class were slowly adapting to the appealing styles as hemlines dropped to below the knee-line. Dressy outfits were colour co-ordinated, Louis XV high-heeled pointed toe shoes, patterned stockings and Dior costume jewellery were popular. For the more discerning, fabrics used were often luxurious like light chiffons, silk georgette and crepe and for evening lace, satins, velvet and fur. They were artistically enhanced by jewels, beads and sequins set in frills, shoulder straps, ruffles, fringes, flounces, with low hips emphasised by a decorated girdle, belt, or sash. Embroidered satin evening shoes could be matching as well. The Queen Mother Mary also followed the shapeless fashion with her wedding dress in 1926.

Mary's Choices

This innovative time gave Mary a sense of liberation after the previous era of constricting and restricted fashion and she left home at 16 and came up to Auckland for a while. I doubt though that Mary went for the outdoor type clothes that became trendy and certainly not trousers, including tailored pantsuits. It was unusual to see them on anyone anyway.

The flexible clothing (trousers for the daring) were welcomed by the more athletic ladies who played tennis, went swimming, biking or horse riding. For Mary, it had been more about the 'Charleston' and picnicking and parading along the beach with a parasol. No sunbathing was allowed on Auckland beaches until 1933. I doubt she would have worn the baggy, woollen two-piece swimsuit anyway. Surprisingly, as they exposed legs to just above the knee, they were introduced in 1913 and stayed around regardless of other fashion in clothes for years although some preferred the popular Australian suit. It was a fitting, slightly clinging one piece made from wool too. In the 1930's a new range of bathing styles appeared with a more conventional mid-calf hem length. They came in an all-in-one sleeveless garment, with a variety of colours and materials exposing the body shape in a closer fit.

Mary, as part of the Rotorua social scene, had posed photos taken showing her in flapper frocks with material hair bands (Alice bands) on her by then short hair and Mary-Jane T bar shoes with their buckled strap and rounded toes. She obviously enjoyed living through the 'roaring twenties' and the much more acceptable sporty life. Not by all though as a woman once told me. She had been the fastest woman sprinter in NZ at the time, and so proud of her achievement, but her father eventually stopped her from competing. He would not have her '*displaying herself for all to see*'.

Nana's millinery shops in Rotorua stocked bell-shaped cloche hats made out of felt which were her biggest seller. They were worn low on the forehead over by the then radical bobbed or shingled short hairstyle. Long wrap-over coats with fur collars or wraps complemented the hats and Mary, like others then, seemed to have a fascination for real fur and for many years she always had at least one fur coat. (Consciousness of an animal being killed to supply it wasn't an issue.)

1930's & 1940's

The twenties avant-garde styles gave way to a more shapely and a softer natural feminine curve by 1930, corsets all-in-one, and the more conventional mid-calf hem length, the conservative middle class adapting more easily to this fashion. The 'little black dress', initially in velvet, made its first appearance in 1935 too and has never really gone away. Mary made her own clothes and followed the move toward the softer romantic styles. She was fond of the empire waistline and bias cut and full pleated skirts, the latter more expensive with so much material, so she mostly wore slim pencil skirts to work accessorised by the popular strings of pearls, gloves, hat and silk stockings.

Mary still had a beaded handbag from that time many years later. She never went out without a purse or a hat (which women always seemed to have worn then, probably following the fashion rule of trying to look at least 40 and staying there forever) right up into her eighties. Her hair was white, wavy, and long again but caught into a bun, and she always wore the fashionable solid clunky high-heeled shoes of her youth that lasted for many years. Slippers had heels too and women that worked on their feet all day, like shop assistants, needed them as their leg muscles were used to that height and became sore when flat shoes were worn.

There is no particular mention of fashion colour I can find during the early thirties or forties, except that at funerals black was always worn (and Nana said that when she was young – the late 1800's – once women were in their thirties, they often wore it too). In 1939 clothing choices were affected by the war. Women's fashion dresses used minimum material in simple styles, as was seen as decent, in a 6 gore skirt the length just below the knee or around mid-calf unless it was evening wear when they could be longer but slimmer to save material. Colour was encouraged in accessories to lift morale including patterned high heels which were considered smart and perhaps lifted the spirits of those who wore them and others around them. Anything jaunty that contributed would be appreciated in those depressing times.

The severe drab and utilitarian officer-style tailored coats, with their squared padded shoulders and belted jackets, evolved as the war years went on. They would be worn with pants with more acceptability as they were practical, which was partly also to do with the jobs women were expected to do. They did not have flies as in pants today (what for?) but were zipped at the side like skirts. Certain patterns in materials like checks, tartans, houndstooth, and paisley, waxed and waned in popularity as did stripes and florals, large and small for summer wear. Wool was the basis of winter clothing right up until the sixties. Browns, greys, and beige were the war colours in vogue, though by war's end that must have changed as many photos show bright floral cotton, and art silk fabrics were popular for summer dresses although with quite prim necklines.

Hats reflected the times and were less fussy and more formal; sometimes just a beret, or they were replaced by a coloured scarf, commonly worn over shoulder length hair. Shoes were sturdy and sometimes had more than one colour, like navy and white, and wedgies were popular. I had a pair of blue suede wedgies shoes after the war which I just loved. Someone else admired them too and they were stolen one day at the beach. A totally unsuitable place to take them but my minor fetish would have me wear them. Mary was really annoyed saying, 'I told you so' several times amongst other more vehement things.

As kids Veronica and I would trawl through Mary's jewellery box at play, not distinguishing between values, just the attractiveness of the piece. There was a large, real gold bangle Mary had worn on her upper forearm she said, genuine pearls, and other expensive pieces amongst the jumbled cheaper costume imitations, the majority being bracelets and brooches. There were not that many rings and no earrings.

About 1948, I remember Mary making herself some full length 'culottes', the wide legs looking like a skirt until she moved. We must have been staying in Auckland, probably with Uncle Ross, and we saw her coming home after a day out. She had gone shopping, meandering up and down Queen St. and along Karangahape Rd. and found a new wide-brimmed hat and accessories to match. The neighbours were as impressed as Uncle's family and we were. People watching her was something Mary was used to and she handled it well. She'd enjoyed her day.

1950's & 60's

Stilettos came in the later 50' and 60's and were the cause of many painful feet and probably other parts of the body – like today. Slipping over was always embarrassing and they were downright dangerous on carpeted stairs – especially the Civic theatre. The other extreme was jandals becoming popular around the fifties too, only other countries had their own name for them.

Rationing was still around after the war and meant generally fewer clothes were bought, perhaps two items a year, unlike the disposable rate we are used to now, although if you were a seamstress it would have been easier, perhaps combining materials for a new design from another year's outfits. Twenty-six clothing coupons were doled out six-monthly and covered the household linen as well. Each clothing item was allotted a set number of coupons and special coupons were for a pair of possibly lisle, or rayon – artificial silk or fully fashioned silk stockings. A total disaster when ladders ran in the latter. (Silk stockings became impossible to buy with Japan being silk's sole source.) Nylons had come in after the war or earlier from Americans if you were one of the lucky ones. Stockings had a seam sewn up the back then, from the toe to the top, and it was important to have seams sitting straight .They were held up by a suspender-belt with a gap between the top of the stockings at mid-thigh and the briefer scanties/panties (no all-in-one pantyhose as today). Failing that, legs could be painted with the appropriate coloured cream (light brown mostly) and sham seams sketched up the back of the leg, usually with eyebrow pencil. Unglamorous bloomers, with their longer legs to just above the knees where they were held by a band or elastic when available, were still popular and covered the exposed thigh in winter, although usually the older generation's choice.

White weddings were the exception for a while given the scarcities; women often wore a suit with perhaps more decorative accessories than the norm. Mary wore shades of blue most of her life and the one exception I remember was a green frock which she made after finally coming out of hospital alive after having Veronica. The first time she wore it was the day she found out that Nana had died. I never saw her in anything other than blue or teal again after that.

After 1945 dress lengths increased but Mary also embraced and welcomed Dior's 'New look' guilt-free fashion a couple of years later with the lovely billowing, long skirts and petticoats (worn by some just above the ankle) with cinched-in waists, fuller bosoms, wide shoulders and wider brimmed hats back again. A luxury after the war's frugality and the virtuousness of having to 'make do'. The new fashions lifted women's spirits and they looked more rounded and feminine – girls without much to show would stuff their bras or wear padded ones to keep up with fashion.

I once had to dispose of our old cousin Colleen's house contents (which included paperwork that had never escaped right back from the year I was born in 1937) and the variety of the dozens of gloves I came across distinguishing each era. There were also beautifully home-made evening frocks (she was a seamstress), their elaborate embroidered, brocade and taffeta materials looking as good as new. (Someone eventually stole them from where she was being looked after. In a way, she may not have minded if someone could use them.)

By the fifties new synthetic fabrics were more common and the 'wash and wear' nylons, polyesters, and acrylics were time-saving for working women. Girls in office jobs dressed with a sense of demure formality, sometimes suits, particularly if they were secretaries, with a suggestion of femininity with perhaps a softer material for a ruffled blouse. Skirt lengths were to the calf and yellow and 'powder blue' colours came back in too so Mary was in vogue again with her limited colour choices. Hats were small and could be worn with full face or half face veils, allowing women to feel mysterious and seductive.

Dior's influence with rounded womanly type fashions remained in favour right into the sixties, hems a flattering length and paper patterns were kept for years and would be exchanged or modified and sometimes mixed. Wide, flattering to the waist cummerbunds had a period of fashion before more separates were worn and gathered, pleated or straight slim skirts were useful and popular once more, especially for work. One of the frocks I particularly enjoyed making had a long waist and a wide striped material which I pleated carefully for the skirt so that when it moved while walking, the pink of the top showed the grey underneath.

Separate bras (brassieres) and corsets (from the waist down only, as opposed to the all-in-one), replaced what had been the accepted steel and/or whale boned corsets that supported and pushed everything up to the breasts from below – the wearers had actually found that more comfortable according to women of the time. (Victorian women wore them all day, doing their housework in them, including scrubbing floors. Women who didn't wear them were considered 'loose' – the origin of the term.) Corsets were self-supporting, the boning and lacing stopped them collapsing in on themselves. Our NZ climate however must have made them a terrible bore in the summer.

The substituted 'girdles and elasticised pull-on Easies' made when 2-way stretch 'Latex' was discovered, held everything in from the waist down. They had detachable suspenders and were popular as figure controls and stayed around at least till the late fifties as I was castigated by a shop assistant for not wearing one after my first baby. She was also surprised I hadn't been swaddled after the birth. I hadn't even known about that but when I mentioned it to Mary she said it had been common to be bound or wear something firm around the stomach to help slack muscles go back into place. It would have been handy to know.

Brassieres and the Cycles of Taste

Varying accounts exist of who invented the modern bra, but Sigmund Lindauer, who came from a German family of corset makers, patented an elastic version in 1913 and began mass producing the garments. *(http://tvnz.co.nz/world-news/medieval-bras-found-in-austrian-castle-4977754)* The twin cup bras were first designed to flatten the chest and any weight was carried by the shoulders, which could be uncomfortable with bigger bosoms, especially with the lightweight silk material used in 1929. In 1936 a more developed A, B & C cup sizing came in. In the early 1940's a choice of bras with some padding was on offer but materials went from natural to synthetic with the war shortages.

After the Second World War, with the help of fibre technology, a more generous rounded shape was designed, using elasticised materials, with boning and padding when required. (Ralph's Uni mates referred to flat-chested girls as the ones 'that hung their tits on the end of the bed at night'.) The 1947 re-introduction of corsets by Christian Dior appalled Coco Chanel, but not Mary and probably others of her age. She had worn corsets for the 1920's 'little boy look' up until I urged her to buy some bras, when I was quite young. She would have switched to the bra and corset separates reluctantly I think. From 1947 on she continually wore the Christian Dior ones right up to her death at 85 although had trouble by then forcing the bones back in their worn pockets when they popped out or finding a replacement 'foundation garment' (as they had become known) unless she went to an expensive specialist. She said she found them comfortable and needed them for warmth and back support. (Underwire bras eventually took the place of bone and 'long-line brassieres' reached to the waist, making it nipped in again.)

Cycles of fashion.

I had a nearly fully developed figure at 12 years old and I suddenly couldn't fit into children's clothes anymore and as Mary had an account at the Farmers, she let me buy a black 2-piece midriff bathing suit (not skimpy though like the bikini that was introduced in Paris in 1946) but to my embarrassment, she resisted buying my first bra for me until 1950, nearly two years later. These were conical shaped cotton, stitched in a circular pattern for support and strength (spoofed later by Madonna and others). I had needed some body control during cricket, basketball, and running at school and the long line and conical shape fitted me well. The latter worn with a fitting skirt made a sexy silhouette when combined with fitting woollen sweaters.

(Not a good move as like other girls, I embarrassingly received lots of hubba-hubba calls and whistles which was not always appreciated by the current boyfriend. He would know why better than me.)

By 1956 bras were a more natural shape which evolved eventually in the late sixties to Lycra being used in most. Another innovation of an all-in-one, long-line but firm and natural looking bra was made with a suspender belt below for under the long-waisted styles to keep a smooth shape. (They are now accepted as sexy outerwear, without the actual suspenders themselves although I have seen them too)

It wasn't till the era of the Sunday Newspaper publishing (page 3, I think) bare breasted women that most of us even realised that breasts were all different shapes. I at least had thought they were all cone shaped.

Women's 'vital statistics' of 36-24-36 (bust, waist and hip measurements in inches) were the ideal 1950 figure to acquire, padding or otherwise. Bras were a dominating fetish in a way that seemed to represent to some the restriction of women, given the 1968 bra-burning episode (and perhaps not so well-known other clothing also like female underwear and high-heels) protesting against a male oriented society and for the freedom and liberation of women. I and the women I knew did not burn ours. We needed them for comfort and support not unlike older generations, but with more reasons, with the variety of sport available to women by then.

The phenomenon of men who talked to our chest and not our face just had to be tolerated – as it mostly still is – although I was told a story by a well-endowed young lady recently. She said she pushed her breasts together at a staring young man and dropping her head said coquettishly to the totally mortified offending male, "Hello!"

In the swinging sixties, fashion switched from the few exclusive, chic Paris salons to Carnaby Street and King Street in London and morphed even further when it reached NZ. Barbara Bernard commented, 'fashion and design became a matter of concept, more than merely good taste.'

Hair

Before Coco Chanel appeared on the fashion scene the trend for hair was long. Aside from the awkwardness and time spent washing and drying it without the modern facilities (even showers) and the dryers and potions of today, it was easy enough to style at home if no elaboration was required. Arranging hair would depend partly on time and patience but also the straightness, waviness, curliness and also thickness for style possibilities which could be limiting, especially if hair was thin. Money made a difference but if you could afford regular visits to a salon, problems could be overcome. Alternatively, girlfriends were handy. (Young girls wore plaits to school as Mary had earlier, partly to avoid any 'vermin'.)

Mary was one who went for Coco's radical change to shorter hair in the twenties. (Much to Granddad's horror when she did it. He wept, as many other dismayed parents probably did too). Mary had lovely long, dark wavy hair which was seen in those times as 'a woman's crowning glory' to be treasured and brushed 100 times a night before sleep. She had it cut to the bobbed fashion and short hair meant cuts were needed regularly to keep the shape and there were fewer options for styling. 'Cut, shampoo and set' the mainstay of hairdressing, was not something many could have afforded to keep up during the Depression when it came.

Hair pins and especially hair clips, the crimp invented by a New Zealander, seemed to stay around well after other hair accessories waned, like hairnets that were for keeping hair under control and also perhaps for covering unwashed hair. They could be worn during the day or at night and sleeping in them kept a set in place. I associate hairnets with the Depression and especially the war, as the use of them was necessary in factory workers' jobs. Hair could be caught in machinery and an older friend grossed me out once with a detailed description of a bloody scene in the place where she had worked.

Hair fashion during the war was generally around shoulder length which was curled in rollers and could be either flicked back and up or under, the latter was called a 'page boy' style. Even covered wire pipe cleaners could be used by rolling the hair in them and then turning the ends inward (easier to sleep in). Butterfly clips held big waves in place when hair was drying – more easily set by a professional. Long tresses never seemed to really go out of fashion though, partly because of the variety of ways long hair could be worn. The 'bun' at the back, sometimes covered an artificial shop-bought round one, or a roll, for bulk and control and in the fifties and sixties, the back-combed 'beehive' and French roll or high 'pony tails' for teenagers were copied from the Hollywood movie stars as were many things.

Bright coloured plastic hair rollers came in around then too and were used to control hair to achieve a natural looking wave or curl as shorter hairstyles came back or when a perm couldn't be afforded. Damping hair down before rolling it up was often done last thing at night so morning just meant it needed combing or brushing out. Women could be seen out shopping in bright rollers – not even bothering to cover them up with a scarf. English people tended to wear scarves more than us, possibly because of the Queen's affinity to them.

For those who couldn't afford hair salon prices, home perms were introduced and were relatively easy for do-it-yourselfers who could however end up with a frizz if the perm solution was left on too long or the wrong strength used. My girlfriends and I of the time, around 1947, used to perm each other's hair, and discovered after some disasters (especially on me as I had very thick hair) that having a haircut afterwards got rid of the ends frizz anyway and was great for a more natural look.

Ladies' hair styles are an individual choice usually, although sometimes partners (or dads) do have a say apparently, but we are influenced by others around us and it could be a stylish hairdo an actress had or fashion magazines. Sometimes the hairdresser. For me, by the time I went to work about 1953, it was Audrey Hepburn with her gamin look which Auckland men stylists adapted very well. The prices for a really good professional hair cut were just beginning to rise as recognition of an expert at his/her job became acknowledged and names were recommended. Working in the BNZ in the city I was able to access the best before their prices soared out of my budget range. Personal hair dryers appeared on the market a few years later and made a huge difference to how home hair maintenance could be managed.

I would imagine nearly every woman has at least one scary story about hair colouring. Blondes the most obvious users, quite often for ladies that had been fair in their youth and their hair colour had turned mousy later. More flamboyant types also, but covering the white and/or grey was probably the most often reason used for colour. When Mary's hair had turned white overnight after having Veronica in her thirties, she was an avid user of do-it-yourself dyeing that lasted into her fifties. When she stopped, after re-joining her old church, it grew out thick and wavy, and pure white. It became very long but following the church beliefs, was always tightly restricted in a bun at the back.

Miscellaneous

Cardigans deserve a special mention. They were so handy their popularity stayed around for years. Every woman had a short cardy and most had several – always one for best (probably not so much in bad times). Twin-sets (a cardy with a matching coloured short sleeved jumper for under it) worn with gored skirts were a comfortable outfit, the short-sleeved jumper acceptable if the cardy was removed when the temperature changed. It was difficult to imagine life without one, I think partly because of the unpredictability of the NZ weather. Mary would often wear two as she got older and felt the cold more. Even on the hottest day she would have one twin-set on. She reckoned she had Aussie blood that couldn't adjust to NZ temperatures.

My age group was a great fashion decade to grow up in. Mary and I could even interchange each other's clothes, as once past childhood, girls automatically dressed in adults' clothes, appropriate or not. There were no specific young ladies fashions here so a group of young innovative Auckland girls formed a committee and voted on the suitability of clothes for their age group. It was picked up by the market and I also made more age appropriate styled clothes after that.

Creative Section

I would love to have been an architect or draftswoman or home designer/colour consultant and I do succumb to friendly envy of others sometimes, which includes admiration for one of my daughters who now does that job, but I am happy she has the choice. It took the courage and stamina of earlier generations for her to be able to achieve it.

Designing was not considered a job as such, not by mainstream people, although it may have been with moneyed ones. It had always fascinated me and within our budget I would try and match and decorate with a sense of harmony, making whatever I could like bed covers, drapes and cushions and even upholstering an expensive suite base myself after persuading the manufacturer to let me buy the frames of two lounge chairs. A reasonably plain couch with matching legs blended, and the covering material had a self-pattern to break the plainness. That meant when we were able to afford carpet a pattern could be used to help with wear and tear (popular Axminster carpet not on my list). Keeping the flow in the room meant not much furniture beside a coffee table and a custom made bookcase to fit by the chimney with small china and glass display cabinet and another for the combined radio/record player, which was pretty much the norm for most families with new modern houses.

It wasn't until I went back to an old friend's place from the neighbourhood of my first home after about 25 years, that I realised not everyone saw things the way I did, and perhaps colours and their surroundings weren't as important to them as they were to me. My friend had never changed houses or redecorated hers in any way. Everything was worn, the painted areas and furniture the worst. The wallpaper was the original and even the cheapest pictures or none would have looked better than the outdated and faded ones she still had. The patterned wallpaper showed in squares where others had been, the brightest colours in the room now. Money of course would always have been an issue, she was a very kind, and caring person, and she no doubt felt she had better things to do with the little she probably had.

That friend was not the only one over the years. People who had made a huge initial outlay, the house sometimes built by the husband with a long term mortgage, furnishings and fittings bought as they went, could stick with them for 50 years or more, probably comforted and proud of their surroundings – and why not if it made them happy.

Being a designer in the clothing trade would have made me just as happy as I made my own clothes, mixing up patterns, but especially children's, which I drafted up and made for my own kids. Later I drooled over the 'Pumpkin Patch' clothes!

Sewing

For years married on a low income, before the days of cheap children's imports, I was able to keep our whole family well dressed, even if we may have only had one best outfit at a time. It seemed essential then to have that, I guess mainly for some special celebrations for adults anyway, like a wedding. I remember once thinking I should wear my best frock more often as we weren't church goers and didn't get out much so it would go out of date – not that fashions came and went as frequently as today. It was possible then to be fashionable in the same clothes for as many as three years depending on where we lived, what we did, and whether we wore classics.

In Mary's day there wasn't much obvious makeup worn. She used to always put 'Ponds' face cream on at night (she had a good skin always) and lipstick for going out, usually shades of red rather than pink, and a touch of loose powder.

Glasses

These were not a fashion item and may not have been worn by girls (and perhaps men) even with serious sight problems.

Handkerchiefs

Hankies were de rigueur for everyone. Business men were expected to have a clean white one every day, a coloured patterned one acceptable for others and women a lace-edged, daintier or coloured version. Men had useful pockets and women their purses or their sleeves for convenience. For years Mary wrapped her pound notes in a special hanky and inserted them in the front of her bras for safety when out, only keeping her change and 10 shilling notes in her purse. It could be embarrassing to us kids when she had to retrieve them in a hurry although others probably had no idea as she was very discreet.

Men's Fashion

In contrast to the extremes that women's fashion attire were prone to, the changes in men's clothes have mainly revolved around the suit. Coats came and went as we belatedly followed the European fashions until eventually our own casual attire became more acceptable. Unless they were worn every day for work, suits were saved for funerals and weddings and often out-of-date ones were used, even a father's old one for a first job for instance – but usually for a funeral – sometimes his. When my brother was growing up after the war, on cooler days waistcoats of matching material were used but he, like others, also had a series of sleeveless pullovers in a mixture of coloured patterns as a knitted wool waistcoat replacement. The common ones were Argyle and diamonds but some had more elaborate and coloured designs when hand-knitted from balls of wool left over from other knitting and utilised for a Fair Isle pattern.

Most men working outdoors were more likely to wear casual or work clothes; heavy warm material for trousers like wool for the cold and one farmer I knew would not waste an old wool suit and used the trousers. (Incongruous in the cow shed.) Although some men may have made an effort with their clothes for a Friday night visit to town, a special outing or going to an A&P show, (Agricultural and Pastoral Show, i.e. a country exhibition and fair) farmers seldom changed their work hat. The tendency for outdoor workers to wear shorts in all weathers wasn't until later in the century, and it wasn't for everyone.

Men's underwear hardly changed during the early part of the 1900's with long-johns and undershirt worn, no matter the weather, except for the black singlet. It evolved into today's variety from before the turn of the century and was created by an Australian shearer ripping out the restraining sleeves on his undershirt. Made from heavy wool, it came to just above the knee, covering the lower back warmly, especially appreciated by NZ shearers as well at the end of a working day. After the First World War navy blue was added, the colours covering light soiling, making it acceptable for other outdoor workers and athletes as well.

Further changes in the 40's and 50's with looser armholes and a scooped neck meant it was suitable for a wider variety of labour intensive occupations and black became the preferred colour. It is now iconic to NZ, recognised and satirised as good 'Kiwi blokes' gear. The outdoor Swanndri or patterned wool bush shirt is still as popular too. It was made and patented in NZ in the early part of the century although processing has improved since then. There is nostalgia nearly as strong around it as the black singlet.

Men (and some women) would and still do stick to fashion styles of their 'heyday' feeling comfortable in their chosen era. Braces and even winged collars were worn into the Second World War period, some with fob watches in their pocket with the chain across their stomach (we still have Granddad's real gold one). Many men hung onto their braces, possibly not trusting the new-fangled zip to keep their pants up. Collars on shirts were turned to increase their life and cardies darned or patched on the elbows, sometimes with leather.

One summer at the weekend down at Waiheke, I can remember borrowing a short sleeved, soft white knit shirt of my brother's, originally used for tennis, and wishing they made them for women too – a fashion to come. Although jeans were worn they were not a particularly familiar sight, not really coming into popularity till the sixties, however if they had been as raggedy and with as many holes in them as worn today, our first thoughts would not have been about which designer label they were, but how embarrassingly and terribly poor that person must be.

The fifties continued with change in many ways especially with casual street-wear and even shades of socks became more vibrant and individual. Relaxing, coloured, casual button-down shirts caught on right across the world, although they began as beachwear. Some were bright, in-your-face floral patterned Hawaiian ones. Suits had become popular again with some males, the flashier Zoot suits favoured by some youth, resuscitated from the London's Edwardian fashion. Long, black, woollen coats are a picture I remember from a cold bleak winter's day, especially shopping in the city, although Bodgies' coats were longer and fuller. Narrow trousers, although not perhaps 'stove pipes', became acceptable for work in the office and the more casual dress shorts with white knee-high socks and short sleeved shirts. These were worn with no tie and a soft collared shirt, a revolt against the uniform look that went with matching pants and jacket.

Ties that had culminated in the 1920's to the current bias cut that created a tidily hanging accessory, had always been the most individual way men could express themselves, with colour anyway, and began to become louder and more creative, featuring images and graphics. Not all men were impressed with those options and retained their usual conservative, dignified selection which could be years old and have belonged to their fathers as well. The history of the evolved modern tie and its predecessors, the possibilities of what it could actually represent and the status it denoted over the centuries makes fascinating reading.

Men's Hair

Hair was cut on a regular basis at a barber. (Men were at risk of being called a 'poof' for a long time if they went to specialised salons and had their hair washed as well.) Barber shops had a distinctive round red, white, and blue advertising tube turning outside their shop in most towns and city suburbs and were sometimes incorporated with a tobacconist. The favoured short back and sides style was much quicker to do when electric hair clippers appeared in the 1920's and the shorter cuts stayed around till about the 1960's along with the scent of sprayed Bay Rum oil as a finishing off tonic to stimulate hair growth. (Perhaps that was more for the barber's profit than balding men.) That familiar smell was considered manly and was also acceptable as an after-shave lotion in an era when anything that smacked of femininity was avoided. I am not sure when Brylcreem became popular, but it was a familiar smell that seemed to stay around for years. I know Ralph wore it to try and contain his hair which was even thicker and curlier than Granddad's.

Younger men could choose to follow their father's look when they reached adulthood, as they did with clothes, or more controversially, by the early fifties when the economy had lifted and real changes were being made, 'teenagers' wanted to try the popular new movie star styles and some fathers tended to then follow their sons instead. This 'fancy haircut' craze copying overseas trends, including the British Teddy Boys, was not particularly popular with the barbers who had to learn the different cuts, and there were many types all with their own names, and barbers could still only charge two shillings and sixpence. Although barbers no longer did shaves, they trimmed beards which were predominantly worn by older men and changed shape with fashion. Granddad had a short pointed one all his life from about 30. I only remember it being white, matching his thick wavy hair, reminiscent of George Bernard Shaw. Moustaches seemed popular still with some although not as elaborate and different as they had been in the past.

Accessories

Fob watches and walking sticks began to fade out around the Second World War although many senior men hung on to them like their haircuts. Very distinguished looking they were too.

There are few bare heads in any outdoor photos from the early part of the century I have seen and the custom of men wearing hats only faded out gradually and was perhaps noticed more by other people with older men in their lives. The English boyfriend I had when I was 13 in 1950 wore one and Uncle Ross remarked to me he didn't know enough to take it off in the house. Perhaps it was a generation thing as much as a fashion but as it was an individual decision and taking into account styles, head protection at work, the local weather, a predisposition to balding running in a family, and comments from wives, mates and perhaps insecurity issues, it all took a bit of time.

Men were not always recognised without one either, especially if they only had them on at work where people had met them previously. Hats still remained common though and I know they were being made and worn in the early sixties, as I'd seen them removed at a passing funeral cortege in the street while shopping. They were also worn at Saturday afternoon football games. The one time I was at Eden Park trying to watch a rugby game from the standing area, the only thing I saw of the ball over the hats of the crowd, was when Don Clarke kicked his goals.

Chapter 25 Entertainment & Leisure

Few could have afforded what entertainment there was in the Depression years or the war ones. With 'tourism' and the choices and distractions that came along with it, such as restaurants, fast cheap eating places, large scale shopping, night clubs and any hair-raising physical adventures etc. things began to change. In 1968 a friend and I visited Queenstown and noticed a bright light in the sky one night, which was obviously not a star, but it wasn't until the next day when we were leaving that we commented on it and got vague looks from the motel staff. It took a fellow visitor to say it was the new gondola and worth a ride. That ignorance about a tourist highlight is not something that would happen today – especially not there.

Celebrating Guy Fawkes was more about friends and neighbours getting together around a huge bonfire in someone's backyard. People would have been adding burnable rubbish to it for weeks, and there was usually a scarecrow stuck on top closer to the night. There was often a friendly combining of our few fireworks which may have lasted an hour after dark if we were lucky. Just staying up late was exhilarating enough in itself, playing scary games and listening to everyone's laughter, a safe outside releasing and freeing experience in the dark and I would sometimes get into a comical mood on a high and have kids and often adults laughing. (I would experience watching myself from the outside at these times and wonder wherever I was coming from and why I was behaving like that, but others seemed to accept it as a natural part of who I was.)

Late night shopping in my teens in the city on a Friday was interesting and if I was going to the movies, I'd sometimes muck around dreaming and inspecting each store for anything I could afford, especially the many small specialty shops, trying things on and looking out for material bargains. Cheaper pieces might not be as good as they seemed and needed to be checked for possible shrinking, colours running and the amount of ironing needed. It was always fascinating people-watching in Queen St. with the option of popping up to the Farmers in its special bus, however that could be a trap, there was so much to see and I always identified time there like the drifting airport wait when I got older. You knew you had to leave and it was wise to keep checking your watch. Tea in town was the usual crumpet and milkshake. The three hours till the set 8pm movie session went quite fast.

Circuses would regularly come to town and were loved by most, not so much the animals for me, but certainly the clowns and clever trapeze acts, and just watching the way of life of these people was fascinating. They moved all the time as we had, except more often, but they also had each other like a mini town and I wondered what that was like.

Everyone seemed to go the annual Easter Show at the Show Grounds in Greenlane with the scary, fast and high rides, side shows and if you were interested, to see the animals in the big arena. Sticky toffee apples did it for me, they lasted so long. Other smaller shows did the rounds; one quite regularly down in Sandringham was our handy favourite, with its Ferris Wheel ride the right size and price. The heights and fears of the likes of 'Rainbow's End' were never contemplated. Franquin the hypnotist was someone that fascinated me and I even booked to go once but never made it.

Tupperware parties became part of life as we knew it and a pre-wedding one for the bride was practical and useful and was sorted out by the party hostess. 50 years later I still have some originals as do friends.

In 1929 bookmakers were made illegal however that didn't stop them and along with our flouted drinking hours 'became another manifestation of natural hypocrisy'. 'Up your nose' in other words. Eventually, as it could not be prevented, betting was regulated and in 1951 the government opened our TAB's. By 1980 these often scungy-looking hole-in-the-wall premises, with discarded cigarette butts and racing forms for floor decoration, were in nearly every suburb.

By contrast our attractive racecourses with gardens and green spaces were admired by overseas English visitors and also not having to put up with bookmakers on the course. They had faded away. Racing was for adults and Christmas and New Year the optimum times to go. Because of my father's penchant for gambling, whenever I went it was with a set amount of money and a fixation on backing the most popular jockey – and I often won. For many it was more about the fashionistas (not a term used then) and the excitement and general festive feel, than the horses. That was where, if you let your hair down, it was an acceptable place to do it and people were much more real – especially when they lost. The reality of a big one hard to cover with all the emotion being displayed.

Right back to Mary's youth, entertainment was often a picnic, usually at a beach or picnic/park grounds. If it was a large group of people, like extended family or say an organised church get-together, or club or school with all age groups, women would outdo each other with food and titillating gossip. Clothing was less formal as the years passed, shorts or sun-frocks worn on the few times I remember them after the war.

If picnic grounds were near bush it may have meant children making a hut in the trees with anything lying around but we always played the usual school games. Except when smaller children were the first ones out in games and there were tears and disappointment, (seldom tantrums) everyone seemed to have a good time. Tin buckets and wooden spades for the sea and swimming and creeks, rivers and waterholes for diving and generally challenging behaviour, the danger from home-made or small boats not taken very seriously nor the differences between safe beaches and ones with rips – consequently drowning was once known as the 'NZ death'.

When there were open fields for more adult outdoor-oriented entertainment there was 'Catch the (raw) egg' with two opposing rows of partners taking a step back after each successful throw, sprinting, a 'three legged race' when we tied each of the couples' inside ankles together (often with an old stocking) and ran a short distance, 'statues' – freezing in mid cavorting when 'stop' was called out, the longest to hold a pose consistently without twitching being the winner, a 'piggy back race' – usually a male with his partner, 'a sack race' – stepping inside a rough jute sack holding it up under our arms and running/staggering/jumping for the finish line. Children could also participate if they were big enough.

Games with a circle of people and a player in the middle trying to intercept a ball as it was passed over our head and a 'tug-of-war' if someone had a strong enough rope (big muscles displayed to advantage by adult males). Ball games were casual football (similar to 'Touch Rugby' but a bit rougher), rounders (like baseball with whatever bat was available), cricket and soccer all with made-up rules of the day as the games went along, by the (dis)organiser or the person that yelled the loudest – always up for dispute of course to yells of 'cheat'. The main aim was to have a laugh for our simple light-hearted holiday break.

We may have made a fire on a beach for cooking pipis or mussels but I don't remember BBQ's being around and it wasn't until about 1958 they were offered for sale by retailers although there could have been home-made ones before then. The family's favourite foods were prepared well ahead and was always sandwiches or sometimes the ingredients to make our own. On one occasion at a picnic in a vineyard, that meant bright red beetroot spilt across a clean tablecloth on the ground at the beginning of the meal. Not good. Pies, sweet and savoury, and fresh fruit were swished down with made-up orange and raspberry syrup cordial and bottles of Coke or fifty-fifty (orange and lemon). The men brought their own drinks, and if we were by water, found a place they could cool bottles safely. The large ones that beer came in then were awkward and heavy to drink out of, although it never took long to disappear. (Early in the century, the drinking problem in families, rebelled against by women, was indicated by nearly every main city intersection having a pub on each corner. The problem did not go away with their disappearance.) There were bottle drives and those collected were sold back to suppliers, sometimes by the crate if there had been a celebration, and the money often used for donation to schools or worthy charities.

With the advent of the easier cans and eventually smaller beer bottles probably even more was consumed. By the 1960's, generally beer was drunk by men and wine by women. If women did drink beer, especially straight out of a bottle, there were looks.

If Maori were involved that could mean a hangi being set down earlier in the day in the backyard of a private home, usually by a group of men, helped along by a few beers, to be ready for an early evening meal. A joke once played by three mates (by then well in their cups) was one of them yelling out to stop eating the recently served food. He pointed out that the house toilet was being flushed (by a partner) and the accompanying water rising up from the hangi pit. Much retching, spitting and coughing ensured before a wily guest found the house hose tap on full, the buried end obviously in the pit.

Communal picnics died out gradually for various reasons, the war being a predominant one. Unable to go to beaches because of the threat of invasion and the precautions taken, with wires on some, lack of petrol for cars and families split by the fighting, there would have been a natural winding down of trips to anywhere. Our regular trek to Waiheke for the summer meant we were by the sea anyway and for others, when cars became more available and affordable, caravans and camping, and beach baches were the norm for most, with a few hiccups over petrol rationing or weather.

At an adult party there could be a 'rave-up' and someone would play a piano, guitar or a mouth organ accompanying sing-alongs of old favourites or current hits (no Karaoke). Perhaps unsophisticated but usually clean and witty jokes and party tricks and games were all part of the fun, especially kissing ones like those played at kids parties, with variations, although later in the evening when only inebriated adults were about, things could become more entertaining. Some Dutch games were very suggestive I found out from experience and there was much teasing when I was caught up (as in set up) in one. The clincher – the look on my face.

There could also often be a rascal relation everyone would love to hate (a wag, a likeable rogue) who was sometimes the best value. Maybe envied by the more straight-laced and perhaps cherished by a doting old mother. People in general certainly whistled and sang more then than they do now, although that could also be more to do with portable entertainment developments.

Larger, more formal celebrations were about christenings (whether the family was religious or not), an engagement or marriage for the daughter with the father giving her away at a white wedding (with a behind-the-hand whisper often heard – 'How could she wear white when everyone knows she is not a virgin and probably at least 3 months pregnant? Shame on the family!') or a 21st for the son a similar 'Do', except more money was spent if parents were well enough off and the celebration would also be catered for.

It would be a local church or lodge hall with a small band for entertainment and trestle tables set out in a 'U' shape with the top of it being set aside for the honoured guest/s and their families. Kegs of beer were to the side for the serious drinkers, the majority of them men – women usually more discreet – and tables with white cloths had groups of mixed soft drinks bottles for a bit of colour and perhaps if anyone had any creativeness there may have been a flower or two beside the usual plain table setting to go with the unimaginative food.

The young men could just be paying lip service at their formal 21sts as it could seem more like a celebration for their parents than them, especially as older family members would be there and prolonged speeches were such a big part of the evening, similar to a wedding. Respect would need to be shown so the real party would have been before or after with their mates. No-one was considered an adult and by law was not treated as one in various ways till 21.

Men would form separate groups at any gathering anyway, usually smoking, and no doubt the guffaws of laughter indicated coarser wit and higher levels of intoxication, beer the main lubricant, but even so I seldom heard anyone swear in front of women. Bars with the 6 o'clock closing were places to stay well away from though, especially at closing time. Only 'floozies', 'loose' or 'hard' women drank in pubs. The temporary 5–6pm 'swill' lasted from 1917 to 1967. Ironically, as is often the case try and no doubt accounted for our obsessive need to win. though we were small and at the bottom of the world, we make a difference and we wanted the chance on home turf ove it. The early competitive, proud preening of a nation of e but resilient people proving their worth to a patronising h Empire and the world, our solitariness, our uniqueness ur aggressive need for approval, often giving us the edge. background is still apparent.

ing

Zealanders are amongst the greatest readers. My brother began before he went to school with books that took his like the '*Boys Own*' ones: *Swiss Family Robinson, son Crusoe* and like adventure stories or anything to do flying. I started on comics he left around progressing to the cs which fascinated me until I read the originals.

ay have had access to library books in the city but did not libraries in the country towns we were in, but sometimes came across a much handled *Woman's Day* or the like. Order catalogues were fascinating with their pictures of cts (orders by mail – money back guaranteed) which we when isolated in mill towns, drooling over the possibilities. *nal Geographic* magazines were really intriguing with s of other peoples of the world and where they lived. tive races were often photographed and seemed from er planet as did the animals and strange landscapes. They early in my young memory and I think they were passed d the neighbourhood. When we returned to the city I would ravenously, and although *Readers Digest* was one of the available magazines, I was more discriminating by the time t to Grammar, and would stay awake into the early hours of orning reading anything interesting I could get my hands on en I was supposed to be helping around the house or ng. Once at work at the BNZ, I managed to wheedle my onto the young guys' circuit that passed around the den Mickey Spillane books. Including modern style comics were described as 'basically designed for low-mentality '. The '1954 Amendment Act' considered them a bad

with laws, it was introduced by the governmen[t]
consumption.

It wasn't until the late sixties that I went into
afternoon with a friend, thinking it would be [at]
least as it was a local holiday resort, but the at[mosphere]
male clientele could have been cut with a [knife].
Around this time, wine or spirits were more l[ikely]
drunk by women if at all. I once bought a jar o[f]
small vineyard on the North Shore in case i[t]
gathering. It was the most disgusting wine I ha[d]
much like vinegar I used it as such. The flouris[hing]
we now have was just a future dream.

The most popular weekend sports for girls from
age were outdoor basketball (which evolved in[to]
swimming (suitable bathing suits and often f[ull]
were worn), tennis, table tennis, cricket, marc[hing]
for precision and dressing-up) and gymnastic[s]
school we had short distance running and re[lays]
sometimes competing against other schools. Th[ose]
parents had the option of skiing and winter
North or South Island. A pretty petite girlfri[end]
just after leaving school enjoyed being the cox
team which was fairly unusual. Roller skating
top of Khyber Pass was something I did but I
that popular.

The men's perennial rugby, rugby league, and
focus, the international sport competition f[or]
giving us something to look forward to.
Springboks 1956 tour was an eye-opener in m[any]
to the sporting public. Our rather casual attitu[de]
own country was not particularly acknowled[ged]
shock generally to think we had anything in
South Africans.

It felt great to have the British Empire games h[ere]
opportunities to our youth to improve their spo[rt]
them perform. Having home-born heroes who
in world stage sport validated our worth and

influence on the young and they were banned. All the more reason to read them.

Aside from annual plays at secondary school, our orchestra performing and our music class, unlike today, NZ writers, artists, sculptors, composers, musicians, opera singers, ballet dancers, actors or anyone involved in the arts scene were not talked about much at school or anywhere else that is memorable really.

TV

Some law changes, like the liberalisation of Sunday entertainment in 1953, meant more freedom of choice although not everyone was pleased. It wasn't until 1960 the first official TV transmission was made in Auckland though televisions weren't available until June. Politicians were aware of the impact TV could have on elections that had happened in other countries, and the possible negatives, which may have been the reason we were without it for so long. But the advantage by the 60's was that the technology had improved and we had 'by far superior quality compared to USA and British'. Colour didn't come until 1974. The first broadcast was in black and white on TV 'receivers' with limited programmes and time frames. Veronica had a strong singing voice that was good enough for her to belong to Uncle Tom's choir and she had been in his group who sang for Auckland's fledgling TV station, one of the first shows recorded locally.

It took a while before televisions were common in homes. In the meantime people went to friends or hung out around shops that had a working receiver displayed in their front window, which was only at night at first. When we could afford one, with the TV licence as well, dinner for the children was definitely over before 6pm so that they could go into the lounge and watch when the programmes started. There were often comedy shows on but it didn't seem to matter what it was really – they even loved the commercials.

Theatres

Although we now have a high proportion of our own productions in ballet, opera, theatre, music and TV, Mary said that in her day it was the visiting performing arts like the vaudeville acts (the most popular) dance, drama and theatre companies, pop operas, musical comedies and singers that her generation went to see. Wonderful artists from different parts of the world – UK, Australia, America, and Europe – would visit and perform including ballet star Anna Pavlova, Dame Nellie Melba and even Yehudi Menuhin – who was in shorts. Overseas accents were preferred for live theatre and thrilled, ardent theatre goers knew actors' names as we now know movie stars'.

But the Depression and films nearly drove theatre from the stage and there were few live shows for years. Orchestras or organists were retained while there was no sound from the movies, playing the appropriate music to the story, but eventually they went too.

Aside from a few occasions, it wasn't until well after the war that we were back on a more limited overseas circuit again and famous international ballet, opera, and drama companies, classical singers, and eventually the orchestras had a new audience.

Others preferred jazz, pop and rock concerts, singers and musicals. For those who could afford them they were usually performed in the city at His Majesty's Theatre (now demolished, not without regrets), the Town Hall, and sometimes movie theatres like the St James or the Civic. Live entertainment was a personal preference so it didn't attract my attention that much, especially when finances were really tight, but we did go to the odd choir, orchestral and singers' performances and did eventually see Roger Hall's *'Glide Time'* but on the TV screen.

Few were really aware of the struggles that had gone on trying to lift NZ's cultural level aside from Prime Minister Peter Fraser announcing in 1946 'NZ would have a full time symphony city orchestra' as part of NBS. We didn't hear much more after the new government came in.

The Civic theatre

Local groups did perform as I went to a pantomime once at the Civic. I think it was in the school holidays and I would have been about 8, probably up from the country for a few days. We had waited outside the corner of the fantastic Civic building for a little while before the tall doors had opened. Mary bought my ticket at the counter and after instructions of where to go when the show was over, left with baby Veronica. I was impressed by the theatre's peculiarly sumptuous and ancient Indian/Persian style, especially the large high lobby area with the two spectacular graceful curved stairways each side (which people often tripped over going down). I got lost at the top there, distracted by the many large carvings including elephants and a Buddha (although a funny fat man to me then) and trying to find my way to the right steps and right door to the theatre proper through the spooky maze of archways, open rooms and alcoves.

The fantasy atmosphere and oversized exotic décor and gold ornamentation everywhere continued in there as well and there were a pair of lions with flashing red eyes that seemed to hover each side at the front of the embellished stage with the open dark pit below it. When the lights went down the setting sun's rays above the stage faded too and the ceiling became a sky of twinkling stars (800) where vague clouds seemed to drift by. I thought the roof had magically disappeared at first it was such a high stud and the building was so unlike any place I'd ever seen before. I felt anything could happen.

The seating was very steep and made me a bit nervous looking down at the tiny people who seemed a very scary long way away. A kind lady with a large party of children must have noticed me there on my own in the sparsely filled seats around me and sent a boy across to invite me to sit with them. I was so pleased to have somebody a bit closer.

When I went to the Ladies Room at half time I found it was just as oversize and flash as everywhere else with dainty, beautifully covered chairs set before mirrors and all the fittings matched the gold of the rest of the theatre. I have no idea what the pantomime was about, the strange theatre was more memorable in the end.

Movies

People were fascinated by the movies, especially American ones although there were objections to their speech and the level of intelligence of the content, some preferring English movies.

Censorship had been around since early in the century and there was also an appeal board appointed in 1928 so the public were protected.

The American soldiers appreciated the spectacular grand and unique Civic when they came during the war, feeling at home there. It compared to the best Hollywood picture palaces could offer, the dream of one man who had contracted a well-known Australian firm specialising in building individually designed theatres, filling the hole in the ground on the corner of Queen and Wellesley Streets, that had deliberately been left (and abandoned for years) for the benefit of the citizens of Auckland.

Providentially, and probably anticipated, by the time it was finished in 1929 'Talkies' had arrived. Although there were hundreds of theatres around NZ, many originally built for earlier live shows, nothing compared to the size and lavishness of the Civic. It acted as a theatre, cinema and had the late evening 'Winter Garden Cabaret', three thousand tickets being sold out in a few hours especially in the war years. (I never saw the 'Lucky Ladies' floor show but did hear about the infamous gold painted nude lady and I saw her interviewed on TV years afterwards. I think she might have had a good time on the day [night].) A proper orchestra played on a raised golden barge that came up out of the floor. The Wurlitzer Organ also ascended (and I think turned – during intermission for the movies too) with the accomplished player seated and already performing which were all overlooked by the big lions with their sparkling eyes from my pantomime days. It was refurbished in the 1990's.

The acceptable city cinemas were run by Kerridge-Odeon and Amalgamated Theatres and were uptown. Aside from the Civic there were the Majestic, St. James and later the Odeon and Western, Plaza, Century, Embassy, and the Regent which was a popular meeting place for couples. For me while I was still at school it was on a Friday night at 7:30pm. There were other cinemas, some more individual like the Art Deco Century but eventually the two opposite the Chief Post Office, in the sleazy area at the bottom of town, became pretty grungy. One was the Roxy but I can't recall the other one's name – it was inappropriate though. It was partly I think because they were adjacent to the waterfront where overseas sailors hung out, not that anyone actually said that. The local suburbs all had picture theatres as well however they tended to be below standard too and eventually their aging buildings were justifiably referred to as 'flea-pits' or 'flea-houses', especially after 1960 when attendance numbers dropped because of TV.

In all of them though, bizarrely, no matter how disreputable they looked, at the beginning of the movies we had to stand and sing 'God save the Queen'. If you didn't the ushers could reprimand you although there was no law that said we must. Sir Robert Kerridge was a keen supporter of royalty and the 'Motherland' so it was probably more likely to be in a Kerridge theatre than in others toward the end when people revolted (as did I) and wouldn't and the habit faded into the seventies.

Peak time for movie theatres was at the end of the war when there were around 550 throughout NZ. Set times for shows were 11am, 2pm, 5pm and 8pm. Saturday afternoon matinees were institutionalised by then and we went for our weekly 2pm movie fix to the Cameo at the Grey Lynn shops with the other neighbourhood kids, about 15 years down to 5. We would be strung out over the half mile or so up the hill from Levonia St., the boys tearing along in front and the older girls watching out for the younger children.

Sometimes in the summer the hot bitumen on the road would be melting and we would stop and pull at the tar-like bubbles, getting our fingers all black and sticky. Someone said you could chew it like gum. I tried it once but it tasted disgusting. Adverts and shorts, cartoons and regular mini serials featuring 'Cowboys and Indians' or maybe 'Tarzan' came first, travelogues at the 8pm sessions, then the 10 minute half-time interval before the main film, for dashing to the theatre sweet shop to join the pushing queues for ice creams or a chosen lolly, the struggle and delight of the day.

At some sessions, and probably more in the evenings, a boy in uniform and small hat would stand down at the front of the theatre with a wide band slung around his neck that held a curved tray which stuck out in front of him. It contained Nestles chocolate products and at intermission, ice-creams in cones. As he was paid on commission, after the first rush, he would also respond to indications from seated adults to buy, which could be awkward if they didn't make an effort to come to the aisle at the end of the row. However they usually would as they found it more dignified to buy from him than join the sweet shop scramble. As everyone returned to their seats, the boy would wait down at the front of the theatre in full view of the whole audience right up until the lights went down, in the hope of further patronage. I admired the one in our theatre for being able to even just stand there alone and also felt sorry for him hoping an adult would buy something. That would have been more poignant during the Depression.

Mary talked about the silent movie stars that she was familiar with as 'Matinee Idols', and much like her idolising of Micky Savage, she related to the handsomeness of the men and the gorgeous, sophisticated women with the same respect and admiration. (She staunchly defended the dashing Rudolph Valentino, who had appeared in the popular movie 'The Sheik', saying he was not 'queer', as was often derogatorily suggested by men – and she was possibly right. I was sorry I couldn't do the same for Rock Hudson later.) Part of the adoration was, I guess, the hope they apparently held for a better life in the future during the Depression years, with the 'Happy ever after' film endings, fantasy though it may have been by either star or politician. Mary also had the popular figure and features of the times as well, and could relate and feel comfortable with their images perhaps better than most.

The 1940's was the 'Golden Age' of movies and unfortunately I was just that bit too young to appreciate it. We had also moved to the country and then down to Waiheke, where there were no local theatres either, so we missed the early part of that era. The odd school that was near a town took us to see a suitable movie under the guise of education, and in Katikati it was the never forgotten 'Black Beauty' and Elizabeth Taylor, my favourite star for life for many reasons beside her loveliness and acting, which included her multiple relationships that I could relate to courtesy of Mary.

There are just too many stand-out movies and stars in the forties to mention. The American influence did not affect me as much as some others, especially in the city, because of our lack of opportunity and also money to see them. One of them I have subsequently seen, the epic and enjoyable 'Gone with the Wind' which was as much about history as entertainment for someone who had such a mixed schooling. I missed the Walt Disney fantasies and the humour of the comedians which must have been loved by so many children.

Mary occasionally had some money so we could come up on the boat from Waiheke. She would usually have had her own purpose and would not have wanted me around, so I would be able to go to the 'Flicks'. Colourful musicals were in around then which suited me fine and once I went to two in one day, Gene Kelly performing, such amazing dancing as well (Fred Astaire my eventual favourite). So I saw a few of the 1950's 184 musicals (according to Google) and experienced a totally indulgent, luxurious escape from reality that they were, with the hard ice-cream in a cone in between, although with my often aching teeth, having to wait until the ice-cream softened a bit.

It wasn't until 1954 that 'Cinemascope', the 'new miracle curved screen' arrived in Auckland at the Civic and the first movie it showed was 'The Robe', a spectacular biblical epic with a cast of top Hollywood actors. By then Mary, Veronica and I were back in the city at Panmure and I would think my throat cut if I didn't go to a movie once a week, usually Friday night. I was glad I saw Marilyn Monroe and Jane Russell in 'Gentlemen prefer Blondes' and also a couple of Grace Kelly's movies before she upped and married Prince Rainier of Monaco. James Dean in 'Rebel Without a Cause' was finally passed for screening in 1956 although 'The Wild One' with hero Marlon Brando as a motor bike gang leader was censored several times before being released – 'too bad an influence on already impressionable wild youth' – 'Blackboard Jungle' and 'The Man with the Golden Arm', controversially about drugs, which I am not sure registered with me or many others.

Our English teacher at Grammar suggested we not only be dazzled by the latest Hollywood production but give some thought to the film content, the values expounded and who the director was. Good advice, just not really appreciated by girls besotted with their handsome dishy heroes and stars like James Dean, Marlon Brando, William Holden, Paul Newman and the gorgeous ladies like Marilyn Monroe, Audrey Hepburn, Grace Kelly to admire and Natalie Wood who was probably closer to our age. And the fabulous, graceful lady dancers like Cyd Charisse and Lesley Caron to dream about becoming.

Home movies were unheard of except maybe for unsophisticated family ones.

NB 2018; The moth-balled rotting old St James in Queen St. is one of the last two iconic early 20th Century theatres in Auckland. Its demise had seemed unbelievable and shamefully sad to those of us who once used it regularly. Heritage NZ says the 1928 built St James is one of the best preserved vaudeville theatres in the country. It is now scheduled as a Category A heritage building in the Auckland Unitary Plan and can move forward with Government approving the application to the Heritage EQUIP fund.

Music

There are some things I wonder how life would be without their existence. Music especially is such an amazing healer and a joy to listen and dance to, with time encapsulated songs that are forever locked into the memory of that era. I wonder too if the composers, people who play instruments and the singers – anyone in the music genre – ever really get just how much their contribution means to the world. There are so many memories associated with songs and their words giving the right message, the music's rhythm and the perfect sound to enhance special times, especially (to my teenage generation) of the fifties and the sixties along with the usually more moody and intense classics.

From my Nana's Aussie songs, children's tunes, the rousing, consoling, and happy ditties of the war years, our school choir pieces to the sentimental ones in my early teen years and later the appropriate ones for funerals – they all have unforgettable significance. I have a very clear picture of even trivial moments like when boarding at Uncle Ross' while I was at Grammar. One of the pop songs of the day I used to sing along to on the radio was Johnnie Ray's 'The little white cloud that cried'. A lady relation of Uncle's from the country was staying in his spare front room for a few days and she said, "I will never hear that song again without remembering my lovely little holiday," and saying, quite surprisingly, "How happy you all are." There were four of us young ones staying there at the time.

After I changed jobs from the old Post Office and worked in the Queen St. BNZ in 1954, I along with other staff was lucky enough to get complimentary tickets to many of the big acts that came to NZ. The performer who remains the strongest in memory was Nat King Cole. His gentle manner and soft, melodious, romantic songs combined with his tall, slender, swaying frame stay in my mind as a silhouette of sadness. He must have survived so much to reach his popularity, given the attitude to Black people in the USA then and even now.

When Ralph was about 19 and we were living at Panmure, he bought a record player so we could listen first-hand to male tenors like Mario Lanza and his songs 'Funiculi Funicula' and 'Drink, drink, drink' from 'The Student Prince', that he and his mates liked and emulated. Long playing records were available in Auckland by 1951, 33⅓ revolutions per minute playing for 25 minutes. The small 45 records (around the size of a CD) only had a single song each side.

Ralph bought the pop operas Porgy and Bess, Carmen Jones, La Traviata and El Toreador which were favoured along with any current musicals. Mary bought the more inspiring classics, preferring piano and orchestral pieces and the tenors Enrico Caruso or Richard Tauber. We never did get a record of our own Oscar Natzka. (I sat in the desk he had used when he was at school at Ostend on Waiheke Is. Other kids thought I was privileged. He'd carved his name on it.) Taught music by Catholic nuns as a teenager, Mary had sung herself and could have played the new piano she had bought, but never did. She said it was too long ago since she had learned. I think the piano was more a status symbol and perhaps a comfort to her from her youth. It did have a beautiful tone and was a modern elegant design. Ralph's big bear of a mate Ted played it beautifully at parties, and we made sure there was plenty of food for supper for him.

Many of the big artists like the suave-suited crooner Bing Crosby with his restrained smooth voice from the Depression years, Jazz singers and the big bands like Tommy Dorsey and Glen Miller faded with the forties after the war as did the patriotic and nostalgic songs of Vera Lynn and to a lesser degree Gracie Fields. By 1947 change began with the more active perennial Frank Sinatra, the amiable Dean Martin, and the movie musicals with Jane Powell and Debbie Reynolds which brought light-hearted ballads into our lives. That change continued bringing a larger variety of music types and singers. Betty Grable, June Allyson, Kathryn Grayson, Judy Garland, Doris Day, Esther Williams, and Vera-Ellen come to mind.

Country and Western was always around like Hank Williams and Tennessee Ernie Ford, but was seen more as having a back country, cult type following which Elvis embraced along with other genres to make his own special sound. His interpretation opened up an era of a more uninhibited type of performance and raunchy rhetoric. Rock & roll came into its own in NZ with the 1950's movies 'Blackboard Jungle' and the musical 'Rock Around the Clock', the title song sung by Bill Haley and his band the Comets. Many of us went to see these movies several times, just for the singing and dancing – in the theatre aisles. The beginning of a whole new generation of music. The influence music has had on my life made living possible when sometimes little else could have. The distraction of being able to live in the moment, enjoy music and be happy, so consoling and healing. Singing along, not always knowing all the words didn't matter, it was time out.

Dancing

I've always loved dancing. Perhaps nurtured from when Mary took me to tap dancing lessons in Grey Lynn at around 4 years old and later going to ballet lessons around 10, both for short times, which was the one really good memory of staying with Arnold, my father. Several of us from the neighbourhood went to a local hall once a week to learn the basics. Something to look forward to and enjoy.

Mary's third husband-to-be Joe had a shop with a door leading directly off it to a hall at Onetangi, Waiheke Is. It was available for playing bowls and table-tennis during the day, cards and probably other things in the evening like Christmas dances for the holiday visitors. Mary let me stay up for them from about 11 years old. Cousin Colleen and another holiday friend called Shirley, who was between us in age, probably about 15, were there too with Mary not far away behind the shop counter. She would pop into the hall herself when she was not busy and sometimes have a dance with Joe or a local.

We would have been working hard all week on our tans to get them at an even peak and would apply the palest pink polish to finger and toe nails, considering it quite daring. Hours would be spent on hairdos, getting them just right. Curlers were used when we couldn't afford a home perm but removing the sea water first was a major as we spent most of the summer swimming and fresh tank water was always at a premium as there was often not much rain over the holiday period.

Black, wide stretch belts were worn for showing off small waists and calf length, full circle skirts had become fashionable and lovely for swirling in the fast dances, no doubt exposing too much leg and in fact were banned in some places. In earlier years most girls had worn their best fitting white shorts (ours having been put under our mattresses the night before for pressing – no power for irons and too hot for lighting the stove to heat other kinds) with halter line bra tops and sandals (no jandals) on our feet which were usually off by the end of the evening. Sometimes bras could be too and if not done discreetly, seen by anyone who happened to go for a moonlight stroll along the beach afterward.

There was always an initial awkwardness at social occasions like a dance. It was usual to sit with other girls on benches around the hall, and we would just become part of the NZ segregated scene. The guys huddled in self-conscious groups by the double-door exit from where they would regularly disappear outside for a short time. On return they would continue to surreptitiously eye us, more boldly as the booze took effect, jostling and egging each other on to approach a girl and ask for a dance. It would take a few brave couples until about the third dance before things really got under way. Once that happened, it was usually an easy going happy crowd. With a live band of piano, drums, guitar and maybe a saxophone or other instrument and sometimes a singer imitating a popular overseas artist, the evening would liven up. There were no security problems even though the sly grog truck with its beer keg was parked near the exit door (which made using the outside toilet slightly embarrassing). I don't think there were any real pubs as such on the Island and perhaps the one police officer, who would have to have known about the truck, must have turned a blind eye.

We girls did all eventually get asked, although I don't think many of us would have without the men's 'Dutch courage'. There was a short break for supper, usually sandwiches, cakes and tea served on a trestle table and for the band something a bit more fortifying. There were strict dance protocols to stick to, like if someone had already asked for a dance and been refused it was not polite to get up with someone else, which was adhered to by us but perhaps not others. I regret missing the one guy I wanted to dance with, when both girlfriends said I shouldn't, after turning down someone I didn't fancy. He was too shy to ask again. There would be a variety of dances, sometimes a samba, but mostly quicksteps and foxtrots, perhaps the Hokey-Tokey and a supper waltz. Couples who could swing and jitter bug or jive with a bit of flair would end up having the floor to themselves as others were fascinated to watch their skilled moves (the Americans had introduced us to the new dances like boogie-woogie moves during the war). One year a particular couple, the guy a recent arrival from Canada, were as good as any professionals and were a pleasure to see in action.

For the last dance – the important one – the band always played a slow romantic waltz, sometimes to 'Now is the hour', and with the lights lowered trysts were probably whispered. As we were all supposed to be virgins and no-one admitted to having sex, it's hard to say what proportion of guys got their way, although I would think unwanted pregnancies would have been at their highest numbers by late January.

After Mary had helped lock up, Veronica, around 4 years old, would have to be woken up (she slept in Joe's bed for a few hours when Mary worked late) but I don't think she minded as it was a little adventure for her to do things in the dark. Mary always made sure we walked home along the metalled road on a dance night so that we wouldn't trip over couples partially hidden in the undulating sand amongst the dry, stalky growth and swelling succulents. Normally we'd be off down to the water for a quick paddle and a run along the firm sand surface above the edge of the waves, avoiding the often quite deep and wide puddles that were lovely to lie in on a hot day. The flat ocean seemed endless but the green rolling headlands in the distance, on both sides of the long white beach, eventually curved slightly around, giving a sense of sheltering and safety, framing the moon with its wavery silver reflection like a beckoning path to some imagined Nirvana.

Sometimes when we got home, if it was a still night and we were staying in a bach right on the beachfront, I would race down to the sea over the slippery sand dunes, discarding my towel in the last few steps to the water and dive in nude. Swimming out way too far at first, revelling in the coolness and novelty of the sensuous freedom of unconfined body movement. Eventually floating, with the smell of salt water on my face, I would gaze up at the night's sparkling panorama that seemed overwhelmingly and impossibly huge and also nearly touchable in the clear air. I wanted to stay forever in that infinite universe, a part of it and it a part of me. A time for treasuring.

I'd be nearly asleep by the time Colleen came in. A guy would have walked her home separately, the long way around, and she would come in afterwards, giggling and chatting on to Mary about her latest conquest, often referring to his body feeling very hard when he pressed up against her for a goodnight kiss, the real meaning of which eluded me at the time. They would ultimately discuss whether he was a prospective husband. Mary would encourage her and join in the fairy tale way Colleen saw thrilling romance and life, and although Mary should have been well over that, she was a romantic and vicariously enjoyed Colleen's dreaming.

A few years on, when we were back in Auckland, Friday night was movie night and Saturday was dance night referred to as the local hop. There were dances in many Auckland venues. The ones we knew about were often community or Parish halls like St. Septs. at the top of Khyber Pass, and halls at Ellerslie and Remuera, the Orange Dance Hall near the top of Symonds St.

On the North Shore there was the Takapuna Boating Club at Bayswater, right on the wharf itself where I did end up once. It was very romantic to be able to go out on the balcony over the sea and still hear the music. Ye Olde Pirate Shippe at Milford was I think the most popular with an open sea setting on one side and grass on the other. They both required a ferry trip and for city-siders with other connections afterwards staying too late was a problem. There was the extra cost as well and girls anyway would have had a problem without a boyfriend or parents to help out.

There were balls and the BNZ where I worked my first year after school, had theirs on the top floor of the Farmers. It was a lovely setting with its high draped windows and decorated ceiling, the harbour lights seen when taking a breath after a dance. We also had access to every floor and it was so amazing to be able to race around in our ball gowns and high heels, looking at everything without being frustrated by crowds of shoppers, not that we were supposed to. Being employed by the bank, I guess there would have been an assumption we could be trusted, which was probably true, except perhaps for the few that sampled the beds.

For the more sophisticated and perhaps older and those more well-heeled than teenagers, there was the Crystal Palace I think beneath the Mt. Eden movie theatre (a two minute walk from Uncle Ross') Peter Pan at the top of Queen St. (no full skirts for rock & roll) where I did go to a Gay Show once in the sixties for some reason – possibly for the novelty of it in a time when it would have been pretty courageous to perform.

There was one hall, the Masonic I think, in Upper Queen St. where they ran old fashioned dancing exclusively on a Thursday night which my boyfriend of the time and I sometimes went to. Those dances were my favourites as it was more interesting *learning the steps and keeping in line with the synchronised groups, ones like the Valeta, Maxina, the Gay Gordons and the 3 Step Polonaise. In the latter after forming a circle partners were continually changing which could be interesting, especially if the guys had been drinking. But also for my adult boyfriend, as in fact he said in the 3 Step, married women were harder to repulse politely than single women. He was very good looking and used to being treated as 'a piece of meat' although it didn't always bother him. I think it was the numbers that threw him there.*

There were 'Ladies dances' where women got a turn to ask the men (not always well patronised and my boyfriend would disappear) or other dances when a tap on the shoulder meant your male partner had to relinquish you to a new one. These night dances all seemed to have the same romantic breathless air of buoyant expectancy which the music enhanced, creating innocent pleasure for most of the young girls and no doubt more ardent thoughts too. The males displayed their arm muscles after shirt sleeves were rolled up when jackets were discarded early in the evening but restrained politeness on their part covered any obvious lust which however could quite often be felt. Dance halls were usually safe, friendly, and happy environments where romance flourished and led to not only dancing partners but no doubt life-long ones too.

Dancing was such a pleasure and a real expression of creativity for me and I enjoyed every type. Ballroom was a much yearned for kind, but I couldn't afford the frocks or the fees to join the specialised private classes, so made do on the odd occasion when a dance partner had been trained. Once when going to the dance at St. Septs with a girlfriend, I met a male workmate. He had taken ballroom dancing lessons and encouraged me to try some steps with him. He held me quite close and said to just feel his body movement and follow. I thought the equivalent of, 'Yeah right', but in fact he was such a good dancer it was easy and we suddenly had the floor to ourselves with an audience in a circle around us. It was an electrifying and terrifying few minutes until the band's number ended.

New dance crazes came along, the widgies with their jive, rock & roll and 'The Twist' about 1960, and after I was married, even if

I didn't get to go to parties or football 'Do's' much, (mainly because of children and no baby sitter but also the effects booze had on the guys) I could still do those at home because partners weren't needed. My close neighbour and I would practice the steps to them on our front deck, switching from the slightly different beat of each to the sound of 45s singles records.

Making up my own moves to the music's beat was the most rewarding. At a friend's party in another time, a guy I barely knew came up and dancing close to me said, "You really just love to dance don't you?" It impressed me that a guy should notice that.

Chapter 26 Food

When we had choices as I was growing up in the late 1930's our days began with a cup of tea and a biscuit or buttered bread, then a cooked breakfast a little later. After our regular rolled oats there was usually meat like thick bacon strips, sausages, ham or steak with eggs, possibly the night before's leftovers of veges – everything mixed together and lightly fried (bubble & squeak) – cut up or mashed potato on their own and fried bread, perhaps only soaked in milk instead of egg. Full cream milk and butter our only options and always a cup of tea with every food break.

The war changed all that for a while, although we still had porridge of some sort, until by the early 1950's we were back to more reasonably normal times for us when we could eat a cooked breakfast again, mainly at the weekends. I associate that with Ralph usually when he was in his hungry teens. Sometimes Weetbix instead of oats first but the frying pan was always half full of heated fat kept from a roast and with the option of the usual meats again as well as lambs fry (dipped in flour and salt first) that he particularly fancied. Eggs would be fried, scrambled or made into a light omelette with beaten whites, all dripping in fat to be slithered onto fried bread or toast covered with lashings of butter. The grease would set on the plate before the meal was finished and the dishwashing water had to be really hot to dissolve it and leave the plate clean (no dishwashers). It smelt revolting to me as I had a bout of 'Yellow Jaundice' (Hepatitis) at 16 and never ate cream (ice-cream the exception) or really fatty food after that.

10am was morning tea with fresh scones or home-made biscuits, meat again at lunch but usually cold with a salad or a soup in winter, and afternoon tea was more likely to be some kind of cake.

The basic evening meal in the winter, always served with bread and butter, was a 3 course dinner; soup, a main and always a sweet. Soup not so much in the summer. Usually 3 but sometimes 2 vegetables, depending on availability from our own garden and whatever was in season and cheap – cost always a consideration.

Supper was any baking left over and for us children, cocoa made with milk. We did not drink tea although many families did allow their children to have it. (We once watched a chatty male visitor cheerfully scoop 3 teaspoons of sugar into one of our best dainty china cups, without pause in conversation. He didn't even register no-one was listening. We were all horrified – there was barely enough room for the tea. We children were shushed as we started to protest, reminded about our manners. We had always thought 2 sugars extravagant. The visitor was not invited back.)

Meat was hogget, fat lamb/mutton, beef/veal and pork – no venison. Beef was the main meat minced. Corned beef and cabbage a staple. Bacon, ham, sausages, and mince were produced by the local butcher as he cut up his own meat in his shop, the hanging carcase often in full view of the public, sawdust to catch any drips. Don't know what he did about flies. The usual cuts were available, each family with their own favourites, steak like veal or sirloin being a treat for us, eye fillet a rare one. Chops were usually pork and lamb and the less tender meat, the ones mostly used, were for stewing – dumplings for those and Yorkshire pudding for roast beef. Our Sunday lunch roasts were rolled I think as the memory of string being on the serving dish is strong, mutton and hogget the first choice.

Any extra meat from them needed to be eaten in the warmer weather as cold cuts by Monday night, with a salad and new potatoes, the rest minced by hand. The utensil had a handle for turning the contained screw that ground the meat, all enclosed in a heavy metal casing. As the kitchen table was used then as we do a bench now, it was firmly attached to our wooden table top – something to keep children's inquisitive fingers clear of. This cooked meat rolled easily into meat patties or was made into a delicious Shepherds/Cottage Pie with veges and gravy. What remained, including any bones, was used in a soup with onions, barley, lentils, dried peas, and other similar ingredients.

Other bases for soups we used were shin meat, oxtails and bacon bones, although there were other suitable cuts as well, leeks an added favourite and sometimes done in a white sauce instead. As I had never tasted rabbit I looked it up and found a dressed rabbit carcase could have been bought at the butchers, but Mary had a horror of catching a disease from them as they had been poisoned in different parts of NZ and she did not trust that the survivors were not carrying some form of contamination.

Juices from roasts were used for making gravy and some fat, so greasier than most today, the rest was stored in glass preserving jars for cooking and baking and sometimes used as a savoury spread on bread. Fat/dripping was used in other ways too like on squeaky stairs and doors and there were recipes around for soap making although we didn't have it. Uncle Ross stored his in tins and he had heaps of them, the old ones at the back often smelling rancid or off anyway. They were in a cabinet the legs of which were set in lids of something to deter ants but the ants were welcome to all the tins really. (Ants were the bane of many housewives' lives.) Uncle did not like 'vermin' and also hung sticky, curled, treated paper ribbons from the ceiling for flies which were a light brown treacly colour that looked repulsive to our family – and sounded unsettling when waiting for the buzzing flies to die.

There were not many home-cooked fresh fish meals. Cousin Colleen's family boarded a man who worked on a fishing boat so they had fish regularly. Some suburban areas had fish & chip shops with wet fish for sale as well and fish vans called in some streets weekly. But more usually, fish came from a neighbour or friend who were hobby fishermen and maybe had an old dinghy or were near a local wharf. There were no rules about the amount caught so if it had been a good day everyone benefitted. Home-made smoking containers were popular. Pipis and mussels were a Waiheke treat collected by us kids and devoured pretty quickly once they opened in a pot of boiling water or after being thrown straight into an open fire and rescued with a stick. Whitebait fritters were a welcome late addition to our diet. Chicken was a total luxury, an alternative Christmas meat, as in the unfortunate chook (chicken) that lay the least in our run. Duck or turkey may have been served up by some families or on farms as a special dish for a celebration. Curries, pasta, and rice were considered 'foreign' dishes, rice only ever served occasionally as a sweet. Food in our house was served up on plates by Mary not placed in serving dishes on the table.

For afters there were often starchy and cereal based puddings. Steamed syrup and jam sponges and plum duff were favourites and quick bread and butter ones. Jam tarts along with stewed plums, apple turnovers, or Mary's specialty, apple shortcake when fruit was in season and peach or rhubarb (home grown) and apple pie preserves or softened dried fruit when they weren't. We had our own figs (with ginger for jam) which were delicious uncooked and prunes were regularly eaten as they were 'good for the bowels'. All sweet hot dishes were served with the universally used 'Edmonds Custard Powder' with the 'Sure to rise' Edmonds Cook Book recipes. Edmonds was first produced in 1907 and was NZ's biggest selling book and a few years later 'Aunt Daisy's' was also on hand for new variations to food. Tapioca, sago, semolina, and rennet junket were also on offer but not really family favourites although watching milk turn into slops using the bottled Rennet Junket was fascinating. Sticky date pudding and lemon meringue pie not a family treat for us. Cream was, although it needed to be used up on the day, and was especially delicious on scones or sponges (when eggs were plentiful) with raspberry or strawberry jam for a visitor's afternoon tea.

When cream was unavailable the top of a couple of the full cream milk bottles could be purloined and whisked as a small substitute, often to complaints from Granddad. In the country (when we would sometimes have to scald milk to make it keep longer) I once watched as an elderly woman beat cream to butter by hand (reserving the butter-milk) and then using small wooden paddles, she formed perfect flat pats to fit into her special holders for storing in the cooled safe under the house. I don't recall salt being added but it was an option. Other people had small round wooden containers (butter churns) that sat on a table or bench as part of everyday kitchen utensils, suspended by struts at the sides to a flat base. A handle was attached to the container which was turned until the cooled cream formed butter. I have a vague memory of someone making their own cheese but the details escape me, although the smell has lingered longer.

Mary was a good cook and normal baking was done at least once a week, sometimes twice especially if there were visitors coming – prearranged by letter when we lived at Levonia St. in the city.

Baking would often be done with home saved dripping (fat) or lard, keeping butter for bread mainly. Quality margarine was not available and was only really used many years after when butter was considered bad health-wise. All baking was stored in bright coloured tins of various shapes and sizes, sometimes old sweets or chocolate ones, often with an exotic scene or pictures of flowers. Everything was cooked on the coal/wood range or in the oven. It would have been a tricky art gauging the baking time with their unpredictable oven temperatures. Aside from shortbread the only other things I can remember are scones (cheese, raisin, date etc.), pikelets, raisin cupcakes, Madeira & fruit cake, ginger loaf and biscuits like peanut brownies (limited by imports) and afghans but especially ANZAC biscuits during the war as they used no eggs and kept well for sending overseas to the soldiers. They had been popular since the 1920's anyway. Our neighbours baked different things which we kids sometimes sampled when playing at their place around morning or afternoon tea-time like Neenish tarts, caramel slice, coconut ice or marshmallow cakes (that were a bit rich for my taste) and rum balls – when made with real rum for adults only. Easy to get drunk on and I did once.

The war and the aftermath may also have been the reason for this limited range because of the shortage of imported ingredients. Eggs were one of the biggest baking limitations though and probably depended on how everyone's chooks laid. Eggs were always broken separately before adding to a mixture in case of finding a rotten one. (Mary would totally freak out for years if an egg got accidentally dropped and broken – they had been so precious. When we shifted into our state house in the fifties and could afford eggs again Mary had a problem with her sponges in the electric oven as it baked unevenly and she yearned for her old black coal range.)

We had our own chook run in the far corner of our grandparents' backyard in a roughly built chicken net pen, as did most people on quarter acre sections. Neighbourhood roosters competed with each other at dawn for the loudest crow, which we mainly slept through. We would preserve extra eggs by rubbing Ovaline on them and storage was in a 4 gallon kerosene drum. Kerosene tins were a handy container and a common sight used for all sorts of innovative things, even hammered till flattened out when wanted as a covering often as rudimentary roofing. I think that's what our chooks' house had.

The fruit selections were more limited than today's as were the vegetables. For instance 'avocado' was a word we never heard till around the 1980s.

It was scarce imported fruit that would sometimes be a special treat as a Christmas present. Bananas were not back in our diet until I was about 12 (1949) when we came back to live in the city again, but they had been around from about the turn of the century. An English lady once told me they didn't eat them in Britain until they were black and apparently they are at their most nutritious when at least dotted with black – the internet hails them as one of the most useful foods. Things like Chinese gooseberries (kiwi fruit), tree tomatoes (tamarillo), guavas, pears, peaches, figs, plums, quinces, feijoas, grapefruit, watermelon and occasionally other types of melon were around but not always in favour. Raspberries, strawberries, wild blackberries, passion fruit, banana passion fruit, loquats, kumquats, cape gooseberries, and especially Albany Surprise black, sweet grapes were grown by others we knew and we sometimes reaped the benefit if we happened to pop in at the right time, otherwise grapes were for hospital visits. Fig and ginger jam was Nana's favourite, fruit chutney Granddad's, both made from our own fruit. Tastes our family inherited. Later in Panmure Mary was able to indulge her love of fruit trees on our quarter acre section until mowing the lawn (with a hand mower) was an art no-one but Ralph would do as there was hardly a free space where it wasn't necessary to bend under the often laden branches of fruit. Mary grew a variety of apples, plums, peaches, nectarines and even tried apricots. I don't think they did that well in the Auckland climate. Tree tomatoes did and small guavas always covered the low shrub and were squished and strained to make a jelly-like jam.

Although often imperfect, backyard orchard fruits probably with a similar range to ours were so much more sweetly delicious than today's crops that are treated or stored with chemicals. Even the organic produce cannot match the old homegrown taste. A neighbour with a glasshouse used to sell tomatoes cheaply and the scent from displayed ones, as we passed his gate, drew us in. Like other areas in life that our grandchildren will not experience, which is a disappointment. Probably not able to raid orchards either as was done in the country. It was a boys' pastime as a rule but I was cajoled into going with them once. I only got stomach ache for my troubles from my one purloined green apple.

Earlier, in the thirties as the Depression deepened and people began to suffer, especially when children were going hungry, sharing became more common and neighbours and friends helped each other with surplus from gardens and orchards. For instance if one family had extra cabbages or apples they may offer them to neighbours or friends swapping for other vegetables or fruit if it was appropriate. We once exchanged some food for fresh comb honey from a local man who had a couple of hives in his big back yard – not uncommon. A level of trust was established this way that may have always been around but it was more obvious in those hard times. This formed the basis of the society that I grew up in.

Christmas

Christmas could be about mixed blessings. For one of our neighbours in Grey Lynn, it was painful as they had lost a 2-year-old baby girl around that time many years before from diphtheria, but the memory of the loss never seemed to lessen, like so many other families for various reasons. These were the ones who seemed to have more respect and understanding about death and the trauma that could define others' lives.

Weekends and public holidays always had to be prepared for ahead but Christmas needed more attention. Businesses and factories used to close down, not just for the statutory holidays but sometimes for weeks and this could include wholesale bakeries. Once the bread ran out it would be scones. Considering there were no fridges or freezers till the late forties (for us not till 1954) shopping ahead for everything needed to be organised with forethought and was a busy time for women, a practised and sometimes hard-learned routine. Anything special like a present or purchasing hams and other special Christmas fare made ordering mandatory, as was sending parcels and cards off early.

Other things to consider and be prepared for included sewing for the family, especially altering growing children's outdoor clothes from the previous summer's hot days or passing them down or on to others. Coping with summer ripening fruit for bottling and jam making needed to be considered around a well-timed holiday. 'A woman's work is never done' was often a wall hanging in the home.

Christmases at our grandparents' home meant Ralph and I would help with shucking the peas fresh from the garden, although more probably went into our mouths than the pot. Their sweet tenderness never forgotten and with Ralph as company everything seemed lighter. We had a large vegetable garden, not just a war effort one when people were encouraged to even plant vegetables, like tomatoes, amongst the flowers so that any available food could be sent to Britain. New season potatoes, only one variety that I know of, were always ready by Christmas for boiling and were served with mint. Older ones were roasted with kumara, pumpkin, parsnips, and carrots. There was a choice of cabbage, cauliflower, Brussel sprouts (for Granddad), broad beans, leeks, silver and spinach beet for variety with lettuces, tomatoes, cucumber, onions (for pickling, roasting, frying and soups) spring onions, celery, radishes and beetroot in the summer. Swedes were not that popular with us and capsicum and courgettes not familiar. We had wide flat mushrooms occasionally after country rambles and a vigorous examination, but no fresh herbs come to mind except parsley and mint. I think the last year we lived with our grandparents in 1943, the garden wasn't sown as the creeping pumpkin trailers amongst the weeds went under the wooden fence into the neighbours', the netting for the peas and the stakes for the beans were falling over and there was the strong smell of onion flowers. I also didn't have to eat silver-beet. No matter what I was told about 'Popeye' the cartoon character, who got strong on it, it still makes me sick and causes bad dreams.

English-based heavy Christmas lunch was all so inappropriate in Auckland's heat, even if electricity or gas was available for cooking. It was not just our English Granddad who always wanted it either. Most families followed that tradition as did we children for many years, encouraged to use our own NZ nutritious primary products of full cream milk, butter, and refined wheat. Although Christmases evolved and eventually a trifle and fresh fruit salad and Pavlova were included for those who preferred that to a rich Christmas (plum) pudding and cake. Ours were both made from a favourite special recipe only used for that time of the year or the cake one for a birthday, made weeks before the day, and moistened up with alcohol nearer eating time. It was baked in a large square tin that often needed cleaning as the rust would have set in from its sparse previous use. Mary or Nana would line it with layers of newspaper (to prevent the cake catching on the bottom) and cover that with greaseproof paper, filling it with the cake mixture after whisking or using a hand beater to cream the butter and sugar and a wooden spoon (good licking) to stir the heavy dried fruit and flour through, often with help from Granddad. (No cake mixers or non-stick tins/baking paper.) The Christmas pudding, which could also be made earlier, was spooned into a suitable rag tied at the top then dropped into a large pot of boiling water and covered with a secured lid (God help anyone who took that off. Wooden spoons were for things other than baking) and after being cooked was hung on a string from the wash-house ceiling.

Nana would sometimes make extra ones and cook them in the copper with the heavy wooden lid on as she sometimes did a ham. Her secret recipe was more in the fruit treatment than in the other ingredients and those family recipe specialties we still use today including the small dried fruit pies. I haven't tasted anything more to my liking since.

In the times we had the money, real silver threepences, or sixpences, previously boiled, could be found in the pudding that was covered by brandy sauce and custard when served up. If a child missed out, one coin at least would mysteriously turn up on his or her plate, just before it was collected for washing up. The small mince pies were on offer to go with a later cup of tea if they could be fitted in. Standard festive Christmas fare – a feast.

During the war coupon books allowed each person per week: 6oz. butter, 6oz. sugar, 2oz. tea and a limited meat ration. Because of all the restrictions many family standard routines were lost and women scrambled to make the best of what they could with what was on offer. Mutton and beef were sent to Britain from 1944 to 1948 until they got back on their feet but there was plenty of oxtail, heart, liver, kidneys, brains, tripe, assorted hocks, flaps, cheek bones, mince and sausages – not sure what would have been in the latter then. Brains (sweetbreads) were boiled first and then frittered in batter, kidney went into a pie with shin meat, tongues were boiled then peeled and usually served cold (not unlike corned beef). Tripe needed a long cooking time but when it was served in a white sauce with parsley, it was quite delicious. Not much of this food would be appreciated today.

When we lived in the country for some of those years if we were near the bush, meat was often easier to come by, as it was on a farm too when pigs were fed from the leftover milk products after the cream was separated. There were usually ducks, chooks, and sometimes geese around although not necessarily fenced in and at one friend's place, she often had hens pecking away in the kitchen. Easy pickings. The ducks weren't quite so cheeky but they would quack noisily on the porch near the kitchen door until shooed off so there were options. Pheasants were a treat and sometimes other animals were farmed as well, although most farmers were traditional. Until rationing ceased in 1950 'making do' was just a part of growing up.

Hard Times

Although I don't remember feeling that we starved really, when we lived on Waiheke for a while, during the late 1940's, Mary was on a Sickness Benefit so our accommodation and food were pretty basic. We often could not heat or cook food so Weetbix, bread and butter and milk were staples. Sometimes porridge at breakfast if there was wood for the coal range when Veronica and I went scrounging in the bush (a safe place) or we had kerosene for the Primus. Later in the evening, custard made from Edmonds Custard powder. Perhaps also luncheon sausage or cheese for protein and the odd fish meal if someone at the beach had a surplus. The tank water I definitely remember as when we turned the one indoor tap on, the water was busy with wriggly things which we had no option but to drink – in the summer at least. During the winter we put old buckets out to catch the rain. Mary would not have let on to anyone about our situation.

Home Meals

When we left the city and Ralph went boarding, he would come home for his holidays and the first meal he used to ask for was a treat of 'mincies'. Mary would combine mince, breadcrumbs, egg, salt, pepper, chopped onion, Marmite, sauces, fresh parsley and dried herbs, and roll the mixture into little balls with a coating of flour, then fry and dish them up with gravy and vegetables. He regretted telling one of the 'foreign' ladies he boarded with about how much he loved his mincies when she afterwards regularly cooked him 'frigoletties', thinking she was giving him a treat. I'm not sure if her version was her own adaption or a national dish. Ralph was forced to move on eventually as he couldn't handle the strong garlic addition.

As an adult myself in the sixties I once served our traditional Christmas lunch (cooked on an electric stove) at a time when we were very occupied running our own business and also had young children to see to. The whole meal was a special treat for a retired sheep farmer friend, so lamb was the meat. He had travelled extensively and had come back to NZ again with his new English wife. He was very grateful to her as he had waited so long to find someone – as they both had. I felt quite proud of what I had achieved with the pressure and time constraints of our life especially in the busy run up to the annual holidays. Our farmer friend was really appreciative and said so but when I offered the dish of roasted vegetables to his wife, she commented quite loudly in her cultured, sophisticated voice, "At home most of those vegetables would only be served to the pigs." Not even a 'no thank you'.

I felt really sorry for our kind friend knowing how much he loved his vege garden and enjoyed coming up to our land to help with ours. I wondered what he did with his produce – I wouldn't think he fed it to any pigs. He was always kind and never said a bad word about anyone and didn't comment that day. He was the sort of guy who would offer a helping hand whenever it was needed, especially in his rural community when he was younger, including building the school pool even though he never had any children.

Keeping fit was not a chore but part of living and although we certainly walked or biked more whenever we could – it also saved the price of a tram fare in the city anyway – and given what I have described were the basic foods and probably normal for most families around us, not many people were excessively fat that I remember. Especially during the Depression or the war as questions would have probably been asked. There were buxom women and beer-bellied men but real obesity would have been very noticeable and I think the meals were larger if anything then, especially on farms, and we certainly ate more times a day.

Eating out

There were places for lunching and morning and afternoon teas in small tearooms or like the Farmers and Smith & Caughey's (and probably other city stores) had a dining room on the top floor for a midday meal and Friday night dinner, all silver settings and Persil-white table cloths, which were for refined people with (to us) serious money. At Smith & Caughey's men's business lunches were at a specially arranged large, top table, set up on a platform at the back of the high-ceilinged airy room. People spoke quietly and tall windows added to the resplendent décor giving the feeling of opulence. A pianist would ripple accompanying background music on the piano.

Mary talked nostalgically about the elegant 'High Teas' in town as part of growing up and into the thirties, an indulgence in a time it would not have been approved of by all. It was always in glamorous and socially acceptable surroundings and in Auckland would probably have been at the top floor of one of the several department stores with a view. Tea was brought out on a shiny chrome tea-trolley with a delicate and probably embroidered tea-shower covering the food and the expensive silver service and bone china tea cups, saucers and side dishes. The centrepiece a silver 3-tiered stand, with tiny fresh sandwiches and exquisite cakes, laid out with ceremony by the white uniformed waitress on the crisp, exemplary, white linen tablecloth, serviettes to match, usually with a small vase of flowers as well. Mary and her friends wore elegantly fashionable clothing and played ladies, out to be seen, but as Mary said, giggles were never far away. There were slight overtones of reverence in the telling of that regular ritual which was with the friend Mary had indulged with most often. (Sadly I found out later, she had died in her twenties after having twins in childbirth. I think Mary really missed that friend, perhaps more than any other. My second name Ellanore is spelt that way in honour of her – Ella.

The first takeaway place about 1953 or 54 that I knew about was a chip bar on a corner by the Britomart Bus Station at the bottom of town, around the corner from where Arnold's, my father's place had been. Customers stood on the pavement and waited to be served at a high counter, not unlike the food caravans of today.

Hamburgers were served by individual shops as I remember an innovative owner in Manukau Rd. Greenlane that cooked a thick, delicious, homemade, herbed meat patty covered in tomato sauce accompanied by a salad with lettuce, beetroot, cheese, fried onions, tomatoes, and salad dressing. An egg on request for a little extra. I don't remember there being any seating in the shop. There was the 'White Lady' pie-cart in Queen St. too but Chinese and other take-out food types were not on the agenda for a long time and the takeaway food giants didn't arrive in NZ until the 1970's.

If I were in town on Friday evening for a late tea, bistros were an eating out option (meat & two veggies) but were a more formal option with males wearing a tie at least and some places risked fines and served alcohol. A fish and chips place by the Town Hall, where you could eat on the premises, offered loads of free, fresh, buttered white bread with the meal. There were local seafood shops for fish and chips, wrapped in white or unused newspaper, sometimes with a greaseproof lining. My 20 pence treat on the 20th of the month after working late in the city, was eaten on the walk home as the food would have been cold otherwise. In the dark I would tear a small hole in the top of the parcel and I remember once on a chilly winter evening while trying to find a chip, I found a piece of hot fish instead and burned my fingers and mouth. I sucked my sore salty finger to relieve the pain.

Later when cars became more available and affordable many families had fish and chips on a Friday night. They knew it would be fresh as it was the night Catholics always had it (no meat on a Friday), so shops would have had to stock up. A big family order would be taken home and often eaten straight from the paper spread on the floor in front of the fire in the winter. They are still the most popular takeaway meal apparently.

A hotel restaurant was the place to go for a special outing like an anniversary or birthday. There would probably have been some common soup offered first, the main course plain foods we had at home like a roast and veggies, sometimes not as good, although the battered fish and chips were usually better. A choice of sweets were perhaps a boiled pudding and custard, trifle with sponge and fruit salad out of a tin with a drop or two of wine and perhaps with ice-cream if it were available. (Pavlova was not on the menu and the only ones we ate were home-made, which would not have been that often during the lean years. Mary didn't make them but a girlfriend of mine did later and we always had it for dessert with strawberries and cream if I went over for tea in the summer, which would have been in the sixties.)

Hotels had a monopoly and all meals were served specifically between six and seven or seven-thirty. This was strictly enforced by the uniformed staff (for their own sakes) and only hotel guests and acceptable customers who had passed the inspection of a required dress standard and a sobriety test by a severe, controlling hostess – not even a pretty one – and dressed in black in one hotel at least. Drinks could be had with a meal, although often limited and not usually wine until 1961 when it was allowed for the first time. It was illegal to serve alcohol with a meal anywhere else before that. Opposed of course by hoteliers who subsequently watched their profits shift to the new restaurants, although quite slowly. Auckland received 4 of the licences granted and could serve wine, beer, and stout. At that time, what we accepted as normal, overseas visitors considered bizarre.

> Quote: 'NZ was considered a cultural backwater that harboured institutionalised barbarism and was a compliant, conformist society, hateful of privilege and had a passion for social justice and a wish for the eradication of poverty.' Wow.

Licensed restaurants as we know them today did not come into existence until about the early sixties (in Auckland). Otto Groen had the first liquor licence in 1961 (*NZ Herald* 21/08/10). Dine and dance ones became popular where white tablecloths and silver service were offered and food such as Toheroa soup, Chicken Maryland and a Carpetbag Steak were served and, as quoted by Orsini's, chicken at twenty two shillings and sixpence was more expensive than crayfish at nineteen shillings and sixpence. The El Rey in Hillsborough was a bit far out for most of us but if you ever made it you were considered to be moving in a 'fast circle' and had a taste for t-bone steaks and plenty of alcohol. For most it would be a once or twice a year anniversary type outing.

Chapter 27 Our Summers

Holidays

Like thousands of New Zealanders of the 40's & 50's, in a time (in my memory anyway) of reasonably predictable fine Christmas weather, for several years from when I was about 7 or 8 at the end of school term, we joined the mini migration to our favourite retreat by the beach. Sometimes we would have stayed overnight at Uncle Ross' in Mt. Eden to make travelling simpler, all going together.

A caravan always appealed to me. I admired their clever compact designs and wondered what it would be like to be on the road permanently, (like some of the baby-boomer generation are now) and I imagine that Mary would definitely have loved that life. Like us however, camping under canvas was the way most people could afford a break.

Waiheke Is., Hauraki Gulf

We would leave the city behind, lugging everything we needed to catch the boat at Auckland's Kings Wharf, (not far along from the Britomart bus station) joining the holiday crowd. There would be taxis, (we sometimes had that luxury) cars, trucks and vans manoeuvring among people everywhere, all heading in the same direction for the 9 am departure of the 'Baroona' or 'Tangaroa', whichever boat was scheduled that day. Walkers from the bus terminal struggled between the railway tracks, then in Quay St., with all their paraphernalia, with even the youngest having to carry something. Parents would count exuberant children's heads trying at the same time to control wayward animals and track precious gear. On arrival at the wharf, someone would be given the job of watching the crew roughly load it on board, every piece a necessity.

A jumbled stack of tents (basic style only – different sizes) stretchers, bedding, fishing lines, food, suitcases, mysterious shaped Christmas parcels and stacked goods for the local shops, were on the top deck open to the elements. We didn't worry about thieving in those days. Large silver aluminium farm milk cans (with a pint measure inside) were set in the covered middle of the boat out of the sun and away from the funnel and engine room. There was so much to take as Waiheke did not have electricity and only a few stores where meat was delivered from Auckland 3 times a week and bread and milk Monday to Friday I think. Most of us took food too because of the higher shop prices of the Island but there were so many bits and pieces needed for camping or baching it took hours of thought and preparation.

The crew would give as good as they got if there was any criticism as they were usually scrambling to get everything on board in time for cast-off.

With 12 months between visits, it was difficult to remember everything, but the basics would have been taken care of. Uncle was lucky that a neighbour by our holiday site, Mr. Jones, an old bachelor and permanent resident on the Island, allowed us to store much of our fishing and camping equipment under his house. We made do over the things we had forgotten.

The waiting crowd were mostly tolerant, the holiday spirit catchy, with the odd person frustratedly annoyed with someone but the queue would have its quota of yahoos and comedians, often including Uni students who liked Waiheke for its freedom and behaviour indulgence. They kept us entertained. For the adults, who may not have seen each other for a year, it would be catch-up mode.

The boat engine fumes and the sun-liberated scent of caged cats and birds, impatient dogs, spoiling food and sweaty people mixed with the salted air drifting across the harbour on a light breeze, evoking thoughts of past holidays, creating a happy atmosphere for the crowd on the cusp of a carefree break. Our clothes were light and bright, like the day and hopefully others to come. Standard shorts and tops mostly with brown Roman sandals, the latter shucked as soon as possible, often going unused despite the large stones on the Island's unsealed dusty roads. (No such thing as a t-shirt or jandals nor portable radios and long before TV. If you were lucky, someone might have a hand-wound turntable to play records on for music.)

For the children, the wait for purchasing tickets and boarding added to our anticipation and excitement was often too much to contain. We would tear around chasing each other, tripping over things, hanging precariously out over the water from the edge of the unfenced wharf to see what was floating around the piles and underneath, with yells from adults of, "Be careful" and "Keep away from the edge". Granddad had told me that he once rowed a dinghy under the wharves and further uptown under Queen St., as far as the Civic Theatre at the Wellesley St. intersection. I don't know what year and it always intrigued me to think about it when I was on an Auckland wharf. Queen St. had been called Ligar Canal before it had been drained, cleaned out and covered in and the road built over it.

Often the eldest child in a family would be sent ahead onto the boat to grab seats in the family's favourite spot, or at least somewhere pets or small children might not fall overboard. The bustle and noise would reach a peak about 10 minutes before departure and I don't think we ever left without someone racing up at the last minute.

The engine noise would change at 9 am, shore ropes would be lifted and thrown loose for the crew to catch, and there would be flapping bundles and red faces struggling up the gangplank at the last possible moment to the crowd's cheers. Often a guy on his own or with a mate would even leap on as the boat was moving away from land to the shouts of, "Jump, jump!" and laughter from helping hands as they were tugged unceremoniously on board. The crew never seemed to take anything too seriously and would watch with casual forbearance at what they called "idiots". It added to the already festive atmosphere.

There was always someone who just missed the boat though – disappointment and frustration clear on their faces – they would know from experience the captain would not stop. A long wait for the next trip. The wharf would seem to move away as the old boat swung ponderously out into the harbour, seagulls swirling languidly above while relatives and friends waved and yelled goodbye as they, the buildings, vehicles and cranes imperceptibly grew smaller until downtown Auckland amalgamated into an uneven cluster of buildings on the skyline.

Once the adults were seated and settled we kids would race to the front of the boat to watch for the Navy boatyard, North Head and then Bean Rock, the strange wooden light-house on stilts with a veranda. It looked so much like a real house just sitting in the middle of all the passing water traffic that I used to yell out thinking some lonely child might come out and at least wave back. Then came each island landmark we named as we passed; Browns Is., Rangitoto, Motutapu, Motuihe until we could see Waiheke itself. In between, we'd wave enthusiastically at passing boats, looking down on big yachts sliding gracefully through the waves; sometimes baby ones racing in the distance and little fizz boats, many of them going faster than us. We would find secret niches to play 'hide and seek' and 'touch' especially on the full decks and explore our favourite places, always peeking around the corner to where it said, "Crew only – no admittance" or where the beguiling steps at the top of the dark hole of the engine room stairs led to the heart of the boat where noise and heat erupted and there was always a 'No Entry' sign across them. Temptation, but the diesel smell was overpowering, so we wouldn't stay long. Sometimes just standing dreamily in the scented sea sprayed wind was enough, with the sun's heat, repetitive engine and water noises creating a meditative lulling of thought.

The later, faster Fairmiles, ex-American Patrol Boats built in NZ for submarine hunting, the Motonui and Iris Moana, did not quite have the same charm and useful hiding places. Most things were transported by boat to the island as there were no helicopters or planes though later a novel experience was exhorting everyone to get off the beach if a small plane wanted to land when the tide was out. There was a vehicular ferry which left from further around the isthmus and the city and earlier a scow – a flat-bottomed boat with a blunt bow used for hauling bulk freight. There was loss of life once when that one went down in a storm in the gulf which seemed unbelievable so near to land. A girlfriend's father had been on it and she said that someone had survived holding onto a wooden beam with one hand and a bottle of whisky to keep him warm in the other, but tales like that often surfaced after disasters.

Adults wound down to a sea-induced trance, others nearer the engines were numbed to sleep from their constant hum. The change of lifestyle was incredible. Embarking on the boat brought a sense of freedom from the usual day-to-day responsibilities, worries sloughing off like the boat's bow waves, the further we were from home – part of the joy of an island holiday and its relative inaccessibility – especially with very few phones around.

Some passed the boat trip by reading or playing board games or cards and lovers canoodled in quiet spots. You could line up for a cuppa at the mini shop but it was hardly worth the effort of queuing. People were aroused to attention after an hour or so, depending where they were headed, by the cries of children calling, 'We're nearly there, we're nearly there!' For us it was Ostend, the third port of call after Blackpool and Surfdale, and the boat used to pass really close to the headland rocks of Kennedy Point on the way into the bay, where we could see seaweed like mermaids' hair, flowing lazily in the wash from the boat and sometimes the flick of an elusive fish tail.

Everyone scrambled to collect bags, kids and animals, counting frantically in the queuing crowd around the gang-plank's chained opening with the boat noisily docking, engines labouring, and white water gushing around crusty old piles. Young guys leapt over the side to be first off, encouraged by the crowd, drowning out the warning yells to 'Wait' from the crew. Unloading was a good-natured noisy bustling affair although sometimes a dog or even a person fell in the water, the rescue the most exciting part of the trip, everyone yelling encouragement, not to be taken too seriously although people had died, but not often enough to stop anyone jumping.

The first passengers off the boat were guaranteed a bus seat but some just walked up the narrow metal road with their baggage to local destinations. Amongst the exodus, friends would call out a greeting to identify themselves to local residents or visitors and vice versa. There was normally a small crowd at the wharf for various reasons, some for the brief excitement as it was often the only interesting thing to break up their day, residents perhaps for pick-ups, so there would be someone to catch a rope from the crew and tie to a groaning, creaking pile. Others came for the return journey to the mainland and there were sometimes children showing off, jumping from the wharf where the water was quite deep.

Dusty and obsolete rattly buses, open carrier trucks and the odd beat-up private car or taxi awaiting passengers were parked at the end of the wharf to take packages and people for the quarter-hour trip to Onetangi on the ocean side of the island. I don't recall anyone losing anything, except perhaps temporarily from the carriers delivering things and that was mainly from lack of directions. No street numbers just, 'It's going to so & so's place' in Onetangi, Surfdale, Ostend, Oneroa or Palm Beach. Ours always arrived not long after we did. (Matiatia was not the boat's main stop then and I don't know if it even had a wharf or a road to it.)

Onetangi

On the drive to Onetangi, once the ancient labouring bus ground up the hill from the wharf and out of Ostend, we began identifying familiar spots like the hill that to us seemed shaped like a crouching lion, the weird-looking tree struck by lightning and the old rusty, red wool-shed, until we rounded a corner and saw the open sea again – nothing quite like that view to confirm our holiday had begun. Little Barrier was framed in the two points of headland 2 to 3 kilometres apart that formed the curved bay off the beach and after that nothing but miles and miles of blue-green open ocean.

It was late morning and usually quite warm by the time the bus dropped us off about three quarters of a mile from our campsite. We loaded up our gear again, whatever the carrier wasn't bringing, and walked downhill at first on a grassy side track, smelling the sea and feeling the different heat of the sun. As we started up the hill we spread out more in a winding snake-like column on what was to eventually be a proper road. With Veronica being the youngest and dragging her feet, we hung back with her and took turns sometimes carrying her bag and/or her too, resting now and then. Houses or baches were scattered anywhere, usually with scrub or trees around them, with very few having close neighbours except perhaps for properties right on the beach front or sometimes those higher up with a view. Their isolation and the Island's slow pace probably the biggest attraction along with rock or boat fishing, horses for hire and native bush rambles, but most people were happy with lying on the pristine beach, often in big pools left by the tide, swimming, fooling in the warm water and lazing about. (No wineries then.)

Mary and Uncle Ross had pooled resources and I think Mary's contribution would have been from the sale of one of Nana's family sections in Australia. Our rough mini paradise was an empty unfenced – so no boundaries or neighbours – one acre of tea-tree scrubland set on the crest of a hill near the point of a small steep peninsula that formed the land periphery of Onetangi Bay. There was only the odd building around but they were below the level of the headland so we had a 360 degree, sharp, uncluttered (and at the time probably unappreciated) amazing view of the glittering sea, distant small heat-hazy islands and undulating miles of rugged open country where the grass grew long and untouched. It was a continuous flow of gentle golden movement, which the ocean mimicked in blue when we turned in the other direction. Closer we glimpsed large and small steeply scalloped bays with gleaming green bush valleys running inland and upward from the sometimes crumbling coastline. It compared to any Mediterranean island and in our ignorant, untravelled eyes was the better, and that feeling still holds with those of us who actually went to some later.

Once we had a rest after the hot winding walk and the carrier had delivered what we couldn't carry, our first job was to collect water. The daily walk with our buckets, even Veronica had a little one, was back down to a lush bush reserve. Ralph and Mark (Uncle's son) would fly ahead to inspect the struggling creek that wound down erratically among exposed roots and rocks, originating from a small spring starting part way up the steep escarpment which could have been contaminated overnight by dead animals. Trying to follow its route up through the dense bush of mature natives and choking lancewood and other cutting or prickly species was a pain to check out but luckily there were also supplejacks and Nikau palms, one to swing from the other to use the curved fronds to slide down on in the clearer patches. Tarzan, a hero at that time, would have been proud of us.

The boys would look for likely fishing spots too, as the stream course could change slightly from year to year, depending on the rain intensity. Meanwhile the rest of us dawdled along with Veronica, our bare feet pushing through the bracken, feeling the soft fallen leaves and undergrowth, and jumping sideways with a squeal when we felt something moving. Following the narrow track down to a grove where a small pool had formed, we first checked for wisely hiding eels near the banks, and then rested in the sheltered coolness. For entertainment till we got the all clear we listened to the birds, trying to identify their calls, and then feeling the squishy mossed rocks between our toes we would kneel to fill our buckets.

Going back to camp was slower and although the Kauris, Puriris and other trees sheltered us from the sun, the gradient was steep in parts and the ferns and creepers caught at the carefully hoarded water and the heat dragged at us as well. We had forgotten the work side of the holiday so the water trek was accomplished to the accompaniment of some groans.

We would have a brief rest then the boys and Uncle (he could not make me go later after an incident) would retrieve our tents, tea-tree stretchers, tables and chairs from under our neighbour Mr. Jones's bach. It was built on sloping bush high enough to get a sea view, so there was plenty of storage room underneath. It was also exposed to some winds so we had to check the primitive hammocks were still okay and tighten the stretched sacking if needed. They were quite comfortable unless the boys had apple-pied them with wetas or other interesting insects like tea-tree jacks or huhu bugs or praying mantis.

The roughly-made loo was always a scary place too and was a pain when we had to shift it from its previous year's site to over a new deeply dug hole. With its homemade tea-tree seat and surrounding staked brush wall, through which anything could and often did crawl or was placed strategically, visiting the toilet was scary. Nonchalantly lounging boys close by, whose summers were for teasing, waiting to hear the screams of terror was a good indication to leave going there till some-one else had been. Never, but never, wait till the last minute to go though, as a careful inspection was required and at night we girls always went in the bush instead to the accompaniment of the resident morepork. I don't know how much difference that would have actually made but the chances were less frightening getting your bottom tickled by grass than something else unimaginable. To this day wetas freak me out.

We'd set out the handmade rough tables and chairs and bench for washing up and ablutions, erect tents (the boys had their own pup tent), throw blankets over our makeshift beds, store food (our safe like the ones in the bush hanging on a branch) put up a makeshift clothesline between trees (disturbing the noisy cicadas and avoiding the stick figures of tea tree jacks) and collect tea tree for firewood. According to Mark's sister Jill, one year Mary had brought her own couch down (that I would think was a bed-settee) which she said had looked incongruous in the tent.

The old trenches, like mini-moats for collecting and draining off the rain water preventing it from flooding the inside of the tents, were cleared out and the tea-tree windbreak from previous years was repaired. Tents were erected in their shelter and the ropes and pegs tested for strength. The ground was often cracked from erosion and sun. The kitchen tent was the biggest one where excess odd bowls, pots and bone-handled cutlery etc. from home were washed in a basin and stacked on the bench. Also a smaller one rinsed and used for ablutions. An open fire was set into a dug-out slight rise with a make-do grate across it in an area near the kitchen tent entrance. Not a proper BBQ but a rudimentary one. A heavy old frying pan, a Dutch oven and a pot did us for cooking the main meal of the day and porridge for breakfast sometimes – instead of Weetbix – probably when Mary was there. They were some of the best meals I've ever tasted.

Uncle Ross regularly caught fish near a blowhole amongst the rocks at the bottom of the steep hill near our tent site. There was a huge rock with a flattish top that had split away from the surrounding land. If we went with him, we used to slide down on our backsides then make the required leap across the wide gap, the blowhole way below, where the magic fishing spot was. (No hair would curl on Uncle's nearly bald head, as it would have on mine thinking about it later when I had my own children.) We did this with no sense of fear as the roaring of the sea breaking against the wall cavities dulled our senses and we couldn't wait to watch the fish. They swam in the steep crevice of deep blue water where all sorts would dart or laze, as the mood took them, effortlessly navigating the sea as it rose against the sheer cliffs, unfazed by the blow-hole roaring close by. Uncle caught snapper there regularly but one day he snared a wily old Kingfish he'd been after for years and the taste was worth his patience and it lasted for several meals. My palate for shop-bought fish was spoiled forever.

The beach, whatever the weather, was where we spent the best part of our days. The years we were there, there was only one really big storm. A strong windy easterly, the worst for us and our tents in our exposed cliff-top position. But even then the waves were great for body surfing (before surf boards were invented, that we knew of anyway) and we'd often be tossed ashore and caught in the undertow until we didn't know which way was up, crashing onto the rough seabed and grazing ourselves before being beached.

Waiheke had its own hotter microclimate where the heat seemed different as well, usually a bit warmer than the city but with less of its oppressive humidity and the temperature fairly constant. If it did rain lightly it was never cold or for long, so it didn't really bother us. We woke nearly every morning of the 6 weeks summer holidays to clear, sweet air after initially acclimatising from Auckland. We all reconciled ourselves to getting the routine chores over with quickly each day, especially the water collection, straight after our breakfast. Shopping was more fun. Carol, (Uncle's daughter – a year younger than me) and I and sometimes Veronica later, went mostly every day for milk. It was sold to us straight from the silver dairy cans, ladled carefully into our billies. On the way back to camp, we would gleefully swing the lidless containers in a full circle daring each other to spill a drop. We were pretty adept so there were no accidents which would have been just as well with money very scarce. It's a wonder the milk didn't turn to curds and whey though.

If we were lucky we could buy a bottle of orange cordial to flavour our water or an extreme treat would be broken chocolate biscuits, which would have already half melted before we got back. Woe to us if we opened that brown bag. Biscuits came unpacked in those days, needing to be weighed as they were delivered to shops stacked but unwrapped in large square tins, about the size of an old computer monitor with a picture on the front of a boy holding the same tin with Bycroft Biscuits written on it. It was repeated over and over infinitum. That always fascinated us. Occasionally we would be given a free broken biscuit by the grocer to our delight. Once at that local store an old man was curing bacon. As I seemed interested he told me the way of it as I watched him work. He obviously loved his job and I'm sure others loved his tasty bacon.

When at last we were free to be off to the beach for a swim we'd go down the steep sloping hill via the zig-zag with towels and feet flying. The boys would have already found old Nikau palm tree husks they used as natural toboggans, seated in the curved bowl and steering with the stem. The quickest way to the bottom was to go straight down, bumping over the slippery dry grass, ignoring the intermittent bumpy breaks formed by the zig-zag path on its angled side to side route. Picking up speed on their mad ride until diverting to the safety of the regular path using their heels to slow the speed the last couple of laps at the bottom (sometimes desperately). Although they were always aiming for the soft cushioning sand of the beach at the exit it didn't always work as planned. The next best thing was to simply fall off or continue to fly on through the last of the earth and coastal plants lightly covering the built up rough rocks below that marked the end of Onetangi Beach. I never heard or saw anyone do it but sometimes the boys would be moaning about something to themselves but no-one ever admitted to it so perhaps they saved each other before anything too serious happened. (I only tried it a couple of times when one of their husks was at the zigzag top but I didn't have enough strength for control.) Uncle Ross would never had said much anyway but Mary would have been totally freaked out if she had known.

We would race barefoot along the sand, leaping real or imagined obstacles, dodging the bigger waves and all the while scanning for anything of interest. If we hadn't already changed, it was done discreetly behind a towel among the sand-hills, usually to smart remarks from the boys, who of course were in the water first. That first dip would seem cold and maybe it was, if full summer heat hadn't quite arrived, but we never noticed much after that. Boys dived, girls squealed, birds flew, waves crashed. We'd be in the water as often as possible, at least 2 swims a day, and soak after in the warmth of huge pools that had formed on the beach, depending whether it was the outgoing tide. When we had Veronica she particularly loved that and we never had to worry about her. She would be happy there for hours. (No thoughts then of exposure to later skin cancer which in fact did happen to Veronica, Ralph and me, painfully but not fatally.)

The beach, whatever the weather, was where we spent the best part of our days. Waiheke had its own microclimate with the temperature fairly constant, usually a bit warmer than the city but with less of its oppressive humidity and if it did rain lightly it was never cold for long, so it didn't really bother us. The years we were there, there was only one really big storm, a strong windy easterly, the worst for us and our tents in our exposed cliff-top position, but even then the waves were great for body surfing (before surf boards were invented, that we knew of anyway) and we'd often be tossed ashore and caught in the undertow until we didn't know which way was up, crashing onto the rough seabed and grazing ourselves before being beached.

Adults may have been around but not our families and I don't think any of us had swimming lessons, we just learnt as we went. There may have been drownings, although I don't remember any, and the beach at Onetangi at least was considered safe. I do remember my Nana saying 'learn to float, it can save your life' so I did. A friend of hers had been the only survivor of a boat wreck years before, because she could float. I didn't fear the water and would often spend hours floating and diving in it alone when the others had had enough.

Once, and only once, I talked my way into going eeling with Ralph and Mark and we arrived much more quietly down at the creek where we filled our water buckets, so as not to disturb the fish. It was a magical place then. The trees felt silent, strong, and patient, their age unimaginable. Birds sang but the sound was muted by the trees' height and the little valley seemed like a tranquil retreat, even the familiar sound of chirping cicadas hushed in the sluggish, heated peace.

We used a bent pin and worm to fish and I had had the first bite and to my surprise and dismay really, caught a large eel and struggled to pull it in to the laughter and teasing of the boys. It gave me such a fright when I got it out; I dropped the wet wriggly thing. As the boys hadn't had any luck with their hook and worm they were envious and covering it with derogatory remarks and leaping around in laughter at my squeamishness when the slimy slithery eel came towards me and then slipped back to the water so fast the boys missed it. It became a much-reminded teasing holiday episode.

Back at the camp site on a particular knob of the headland, my special peaceful citadel, the dried out slippery grass dropped away nearly vertically down a treeless bumpy slope for hundreds of metres to the ocean below. I would watch whales spout and undulate in the distance, wavy gliding stingrays, drifting and accelerating snapper, kingfish, and dolphins playing, sometimes close to the breakers where fearless swimmers frolicked in the day's warmth. Except for one occasion in those innocent days when I thought it might be different, even the odd shark seemed more placid and were only usually ever seen from steeper cliffs in deeper water further around in a smaller bay.

Sharks

One morning I was out looking for Uncle Ross for some reason. I knew he had gone fishing off the rocks but not quite where, as he wasn't in any of his usual places. Standing at my favourite viewing spot to be able to see him I thought, 'He is missing out today,' as there seemed to be unusual movement at the blow hole rocks. Shading my eyes against the sea sparkle to see better into the swelling incoming tide I realised to my horror I was looking at the shapes of smoothly weaving sharks making their way around the headland toward Onetangi Beach where the boys would be body surfing.

The shark shapes seemed sinister and sleek, their swiftness in abeyance though as they cruised strung out for about a hundred metres eventually positioning themselves just out beyond the line of white water breaking into waves for the Onetangi beach.

I ran to the top of the zigzag to get a better view of the scintillating blue sea parting easily as a lethal fin occasionally broke the surface – which no-one else appeared to see. No people were leaving the water. I was suddenly more aware of the noise of the waves crashing, gulls screeching and children yelling in play as the sounds wafted up to me through the heat, humidity and strong sea scents. It all seemed unreal and incredible. My horror and fear had by then shocked me to frozen stillness in the sultriness of midday, my hand pathetically across my mouth.

I suddenly came to life though and screamed a primal warning, so loud and high thinking they must hear me, but knowing really it wasn't possible. The boys were barely distinguishable from others in the water at the distance and height I was up and waving my arms and jumping around would make no difference, although I did it anyway.

The beauty and the unbearable terror of the scene continued to mesmerise me. In the glaring light I shielded my eyes again, watching the sharks' deadly fins, a signal that no-one even saw. The dozen svelte shark shapes swerved in and out, serenely gliding along their parallel path to the beach. I expected that any moment the lighter blue water would erupt and change to red – but it didn't happen. People were still contentedly floating, swimming and paddling in the warm water and summer sun, oblivious to any threat to their bodies being potential food, and I stood there feeling absolutely useless, impotent with fear but nothing changed.

The sharks did eventually nearly reach the other end of the beach still in line, then about a kilometre along they casually peeled away uninterestedly where the bay curved, and went looking for a more appealing meal in deeper water. From the headland arms of the bay the vast ocean opened out to an endless infinity horizon, the next land thousands of miles away where I hoped the sharks would go.

I gradually collapsed down onto the warm, comforting dry grass, legs weak, heart still racing, until my panicked breathing slowed and a reasonable near normality returned. In future, I thought as I lay there, others may not notice when swimming but I would always be looking for shark signs although their elegant, dangerous beauty was what really mesmerised me and was seared into my memory. So portentously alluring. An unforgettable sight.

Fish

Sometimes at a high tide, in the early evening after a lovely day, a couple of fit young guys would anchor one end of a net in the sand and tow the other end out through the water with a dinghy and form a half moon by rowing into shore again. Within minutes the quiet empty beach would be crowded with people. Help yourself time to a free sea harvest! Yapping dogs and sometimes a cat on the periphery, kids trying to find treasures from what the sea may have yielded, dodging amongst the adults who were concentrating on finding their favourite fish. Octopus, starfish, miniature squid, flapping fish in all colours, shapes and sizes and even stingrays (don't touch) and once a little shark. Small boys with long sticks poked and prodded it while it moved but lost interest when it didn't, its teeth not big enough to be interesting.

We would trudge back up the zigzag to camp in the lustre-less evening light with our booty, to get candles and lamps lit before full dark, Uncle probably gutting and perhaps putting the fish in the smoker before he went to bed. We would always be so exhausted that the familiar night sounds would quickly blend into our dreams and we wouldn't even remember to check for wetas.

Rooster Point

Once each year we would go off for our little adventure and pack a lunch for a trek to what we called Rooster Point, befitting its shape. It was a long walk and we had many rests, the first at nearby Piemelon Bay, which, like most of the rest of that part of the island, had no habitation of any kind and we never heard or came across anyone else ever.

At the top of the hill overlooking Piemelon Bay, we would first see Rooster Point in the distance forming as it did the end of the curved land, like a right arm embracing us, before we dropped down the steep, dry, grassy incline to the white beach of the bay, sliding, slipping and clambering – noisy and happy. At times sheep would have been left to range so the side of the hill was covered with horizontal ridged narrow paths that helped control our momentum. We would roll onto the beach where the dead plants mingled with the often pristine sand giving a sense of rediscovery each time. We would race along the empty beckoning scene yelling, laughing and fooling, watching each other's footprints disappear in the warm waves until we were so wet we swam, often in our clothes or we'd sometimes throw them off. It didn't matter with no-one else around.

Our lunch would be augmented by the gathering of pipis and mussels, some of which were so huge one would be a meal in itself, eating them raw or roasting them succulently over a fire amongst the rocks or in a sheltered cave if it was a bit windy. (Today's mussels in shops seem to be mere embryos to me.) After a rest we would explore the tiny island that was just part of the land when the tide was out. It always seemed slightly mysterious to us and, I anyway, would weave it into imaginary stories later before going to sleep after our long day.

From the end of the beach we would make our way along the foreshore as far as we could, exploring rock pools and searching for caves or anything interesting and when we couldn't get around the rocks any longer because of crevasses or the steepness of the cliffs, we'd divert up bush-lined gullies, often glad to be out of the heat for a while, onto the undulating land.

Standing in cliff-top winds, arms open to the world, the land behind reaching off into waving, wind-brushed dried growth, and the sea in front of us so sharply reflecting the sun that we had to squint at its shining silver vista to see the distant line of the horizon. It gave us that feeling of 'freedom forever' probably not often experienced except perhaps by people living in open isolated areas and sailors. We must have reached Rooster Point but it is the journey that leaves the most vivid picture.

Sunday Sermon

On Sundays, lacking a formal church, there would often be an interdenominational religious service held in a marquee on a spare section across the road from the beach, about halfway along it. A no fuss place; no 'Sunday best' outfit with hats, gloves, high heels, purses, stockings or hat, suit and tie. All sorts of clothing including shorts and Roman sandals were acceptable wear or just bare feet and tops too sometimes for guys.

I think many people were glad of the opportunity to worship, around Christmas especially, the subject uplifting and more joyful on that day. Other Sundays there would be an old fashioned 'Your sins will find you out and the Devil will get you if you don't' sort of sermon – which seemed quite popular too with some. Due to my varied existence and no fear of 'the Devil', that sort of rhetoric went over my head, as it seemed to, I think, with most of the other children too although maybe not Carol. We often snuck out of the rolled-up side flaps of the marquee, more interested in the brilliant wet sand display someone made on the beach every Sunday. It was usually a huge sculptured open bible with a seaweed book-mark trailing down between the top two sculptured raised pages which sloped out to the edge. Other pages showed their edges underneath too, all perfectly separated out just like a real flat open book but on a giant scale. It was set under a flowering Pohutakawa tree still growing there today, spotted with celebration crimson, like Christmas decorations. The clusters of disintegrating, hair-fine needles from the flowers covered the whitish sand in a light, windblown layer like red decoration on a white iced cake.

The bible would show the psalm for the day, beautifully and proportionately indented in even, old English biblical text, the first capital letter scrolled all the way down the page and decorated like Nana's very old bible. The wide embellished borders often had seaweed for emphasis. Scenes depicted what the words represented on the facing page and these pictures were outlined and filled with beautifully shaped and coloured shells, real leaves and flowers from the Pohutakawa and succulents that grew in the sand, all thoughtfully selected and placed and always the nativity scene at the Christmas meeting.

We might not have understood the meaning of the words of the sand book but we all appreciated the skill of the person who sculpted such a spectacular creation, especially when we were encouraged to duplicate it ourselves later when the younger members of the congregation would eventually come with a teacher. We would all sit or lie among the lupines that grew in the warm, sliding sand dunes; singing hymns to the rhythm of the gentle waves beat and smell of the summer scents. We listened to the old bible stories mesmerised by the seas open before us – not necessarily following the message of what we were hearing but showing respect by keeping quiet. No land to be seen over the water except Little Barrier – just two shades of blue where the sky made an incredibly straight line meeting the sea in the distance.

Sometimes we could track the watery shadow of an odd white cloud on the water straying leisurely overhead until we lost its darker colour as it headed to the horizon, slowly changing shape into whatever our imagination conjured before it dissipated in the heat. Later, we'd go swimming and exploring rock pools and caves or sometimes just run and dance along on the firm dark sand on the edge of the water in sheer exhilaration and the joy of innocence. One of my very best ever memories.

Holidays Over

Time was not a consideration for us children, so it always came as a shock when Mary would come down for the last weekend. The adults would say we'd be going home on Sunday. The last few years Mary would have been working in the city during the week. I think to us the holidays had seemed to last for months not weeks and in fact if Polio was around they did. No matter how long though, it was a prolonged stretch of amazing time that was still never enough.

One year, near dusk on the last evening, Ralph and I had been sent down to buy something at the shop and on the way back, because we were so going to miss our temporary island home, we slowed down and eventually stopped for a rest. We sat at first but after a while leaned back on the dry, bumpy slope, nearly at the top of the hill, picking at the grass to chew the stalky roots that *had a bit of moisture in them. There were scrappy low flowering tea-tree (Manuka) bushes around and the air smelt as if it had been purified and deliberately scented for our pleasure. It was still warm with no wind and the humidity was low so the sky was clear with the bright intensity of contrast between night and light and there were no planes or satellites to confuse us. There were a lot of stars to choose from and they seemed huge and different seeing them from the island as it was much darker at night than in the city and the lights of Auckland weren't visible (not so many then).*

We just gazed up at the extraordinary panorama trying to remember where to look to identify the constellations we knew, the ones Mary had first told us about in Mokai, the Evening star the brightest. Ralph seemed to know more than me but they all seemed so close it felt that if our arms could stretch like rubber we could reach them and gather them in. We dreamily marvelled about how they were used by people to find their way around the globe on land and sea. We could faintly hear the latter, but this night, it was only lazily lapping and smoothing up the sand in its constant way adding to the serenity of our special spot. We touched on eternity and what it meant for a moment but it was too vast a stretch for our tiring minds and although we talked about it being an ideal night to sleep outside, we wouldn't have been allowed.

I also thought about the next day – we would all head off for last long walks alone, exploring the bush and finding our own favourite areas, usually in a secluded place, mine not too different from this, for a final rumination and later take lingering swims and relax in the big tidal pools that seemed warmer than ever. Afterwards, we would run madly along the shore, kicking the waves as they reached us, yahooing to the heavens with our arms thrust out to the sea, exhilarating until we came to the rocks and rest, finding it unbelievable we were having to go and leave the joy of our summer freedom behind for another year to the business of the city.

Re-reading this holiday reminiscing I was thinking how grateful I am for what we experienced. How amazing is New Zealand and how lucky are we all to live here?

Chapter 28 Personal Pen Portraits

Our Mother – Frances Mary Beal

Married names:

Mary Simpson (1st Marriage)

Mary McDonald (2nd Marriage)

Frances or Mary Connolly (3rd Marriage. This the longest Mary used a married name)

Francis Mary Beal was born in Rotorua on the 10th June 1906 – the 20th anniversary of the eruption of Mt. Tarawera, so still a living memory. According to her mother, there was a string of 'blackberries' around Mary's neck, which I presume were joined blood-clots and she did not breathe straight away. This may have affected her for life as oxygen loss did my own first daughter later, only much more seriously.

Mary was an only child and grew up without other white children around her till much later on. There were Maori children in the local 'Taheke Pa' at Okere Falls, who she was forbidden to play with. When she and her mother went into town at Rotorua to visit, Mary was so desperate for young company, she would run up their front paths and knock on people's doors and ask if they had any children she could befriend. Her mum would just keep walking along the road until Mary was forced to chase after her in case she got lost. A family friend said that people remarked that Mary was one of the most beautiful children they had ever seen.

By the time she grew up and left school at 14, the leaving age then and especially for girls, the family were living in Rotorua where Mary worked for a time in one of her mother's millinery shops. Hers was the perfect look for the twenties era. Thick, long, dark, wavy hair, which she later had cut to the bobbed style of the times, often wearing a head band above her widow's peak (all her husbands died before her), smooth open face with wide-set light blue eyes and the current movie star cupid's bow mouth.

Slim, graceful, coquettish and appealing and always beautifully dressed, a fashion icon, she was crowned a Rotorua beauty queen. (Mary always wore gloves, a hat and high heels and carried a handbag when she went out, right up until she was incapacitated in her early eighties. She was the generation of the late Queen Mother Mary so it would have felt proper to her.)

There was an incident when Mary was 17 and became engaged, that probably set the pattern for the rest of her life as she left home not long afterwards and went up to Auckland to live on her own. One of her first independent moves and pretty unusual for the times and also a precursor to how Mary handled problems – she left. I don't know what else she could have done though really. Rotorua was a small town and gossip and innuendo would have been rife. Whatever had happened, probably rape, she would have been disgraced.

Mary did go back to be married to my father Arnold when she was 24 in 1930, 8 years later. Ralph was their first child born on the 11th June 1934, just after Mary's 28th birthday. She had me in December, 1937 and later another daughter, Veronica to her second husband in April, 1944. We were all born after operations to her uterus for cysts on her one good ovary. She'd had an accident in her teens when the other ovary had her bicycle handle jammed into it.

I think Mary liked the idea of having children and had probably felt left out with friends around her all having families much younger including her best friend Ella who had twins but died not long after. Also what else did you do when you married then, if not have children? I'm not sure Mary ever really understood about loving a child though and what it encompassed. I don't know if she was alone in that as it is difficult to assess when thinking about other generations and their expectations of parenthood and of children's behaviour. It was also not long since the Victorian/Edwardian ethos of 'children shall be seen and not heard'.

My brother Ralph and I called her Mary from when I was about 16 and our family were all living together again for the first time in years and with no husband about. She hadn't really seemed like a mother to me anyway, partly because she wasn't around that often. She also used my brother and myself as confidantes, merging boundaries with co-dependence, a common enough survival technique and we got used to trying to deal with her problems as well as our own. Especially anything concerning blood. Later, when my own problems were really serious, Mary wasn't the one to go to. Although she did make an effort.

I got used to experiencing her as other people did, seeing her fondly as a flitty, often tastily flamboyant but always fashionable friend that turned up now and again and whose melodramas seemed fanciful, even when they were not, but entertaining anyway at a time when perhaps there was little else to look forward to and when women were mainly confined to their homes by husbands, housework and children.

Mary was compassionate, vivacious, pretty and engaging. Most people liked her and many I think loved her, not really knowing her in the way we children did, or understanding there was a very determined, self-willed Mary beneath the soft, caring, genteel, ladylike exterior. Mary had grown up in the ongoing generations of women who had very little actual power or choices in life (unless they had their own money) aside from persuasion and manipulation, so they had learned to find some control over their lives their own way, often devious from necessity, so her behaviour was not unusual. According to some older men this approach is still as pervasive today and maybe it is the attitude of those men that makes it a necessary option for women, as they can feel they have a right to happiness too. I see there are husbands who are kinder and more malleable or fairer than others were/are and the women who chose them were/are lucky or they in fact made their choice very carefully having had good examples in their childhood. Lucky you, lucky ladies. Mary wasn't one of them. Nor was I.

It wasn't until I learnt a bit more about life I realised in fact I mothered my mother most of my life. I said it half in jest once and although it had been apparent to my grown daughters, Kerry and Jenny, they were amazed I hadn't known and astonished I had only just thought about it.

Like many things in our lives, obvious to others but not ourselves, especially when we are so set in patterns that have evolved from our childhoods. As we had only lived with my own father a short time, I hadn't even known that most people had authoritarian figures in their lives either and often resented them.

In my slightly superior, pseudo-adult way, I remember situations where I thought some children in my age group pampered and spoilt and that they needed a mother like mine so that they had to sort things out on their own. I felt they should be more independent and look after themselves. Isn't that what you were supposed to do? And many in fact did, more so country children I think, often having to do farm work and take on responsibilities much earlier as did children from large families.

When I was a bit older I found that city adults, particularly, spoke to me in the condescending way they did then to children and ignored me when speaking to Mary. It puzzled me when they failed to recognise I would follow their conversation and understand it (because of Mary sharing most things, although secretive of course when it suited her). I could tell I often used to know more about some things in life than these adults, especially some women that Mary cultivated occasionally who had been brought up like her with prosperous parents but, unlike Mary, had married men with 'good prospects'. I would sometimes have my say too, which they found appalling. As they would!

At the mill settlements, Mary spent what spare time she had on creative things like writing, millinery, knitting, crocheting and sewing, putting clothes together in attractive ways, knowing her colour combinations and styles to make herself and us girls as fashionable as possible. Mary could draw well, although seldom did. She had played piano and had sung in a choir and my half-sister Veronica, and later my daughters inherited her singing ability.

Mary also wrote a novel called '*The Twa McDonalds*' about the making of the main trunk line from Auckland to Wellington which included the famous Raurimu Spiral. Her father, being an engineer himself, had known some of the men and engineers involved and was very interested in its development, as was the rest of the world. Mary would have understood the significance of the feat of engineering that line was. She eventually sent the novel off to some book competition back in Auckland because I remember her saying that the judges were impressed with it but it was outside the subject they were appraising. Their comments were all they could offer. She never pursued other publishers.

The book would have had an interesting background and made good historical reading. Mary had a clear memory and her long-time friend Ross' son, Mark, said years later although it read well it wasn't his sort of book and he doesn't remember much about it. It must have got lost in our travels as I only ever saw it the once. Perhaps a shame as I think Mary could have made a career as a writer – she would have had enough experiences to call on and a vivid imagination and would have fitted into that society niche. People loved her letters and she wrote to friends extensively.

Mary had been religious although not practising, for short periods of her life I think, at least since we had lived with Nana in Levonia St. Grey Lynn till I was 6, where our next-door neighbour, Mrs. Gibson, had introduced her to a small select set of people with their very restricted culture. They seemed to me not to be too unlike Quakers, except for their specialised clothing. Part of their creed was not to be 'followers of fashion'. Their constraining beliefs didn't really fit into the society we were becoming. They followed biblical teachings interpreted by the male church elders (apparently originally from South Africa) and included rejection of many modern things. They chose to not be ostentatious in any way, not attend any sort of entertainment, hair to be left long and put up in a bun (not dyed), not wear make-up or embellish their looks in any way, which at that time and for years would definitely not have suited Mary.

Mary had found another near neighbour in Panmure, where we did eventually settle, who was involved in the same religious group as the Grey Lynn one. This church's protocols obviously drew Mary and that must have been meant to be, as it was a very small group of people, so meeting another near neighbour was fate or whatever. There was no official building, I understand, people just met in each other's homes or rented halls and although there were religious elders to control things, everyone was free to speak at meetings. This religion sustained Mary in later years when she needed it, but to me, another less extreme church could have done the same. I have since envied both my sister Veronica and Mary finding comfort in their God as, given my childhood experiences and later relationships, having faith in or trusting a man in any form did not particularly appeal to me. Later on the men involved in that church were caught up in a scandal that dated back to their roots in Africa.

Because all our lives we had understood that appearances were everything we were all pretty amazed when Mary let her hair go white in her fifties, after she had re-embraced her religious faith. No matter how poor we were or how difficult it may have been to obtain hair products in some of the most remote places in NZ that we had lived, after 10 years of fastidiously dyeing it, very few people knew Mary's hair was dead white from in her early thirties. (It had lost its entire colour when she was very ill after my half-sister was born.) Not only her religion would have been against it, in the early 1940's and 50's it was not commonplace to dye hair anyway, it was something vaguely associated with movie stars but more often blonde street girls.

The one thing Mary did want was to live to see Halley's Comet for the second time. I think the 1986 one was a bit of a fizzer to her after the first viewing in 1910. Her mother had woken her up from sleep to see it when she was nearly 4 years old. Mary said it was absolutely, terrifyingly beautiful and seemed to fill the whole Rotorua sky. She thought to herself it was the end of the world, but as more and more people came to watch the display and were so excited and happy she eventually enjoyed it too.

Two Swallows in the Morning

Two swallows came to see me when my mother died.

Mourning on the balcony, I stood alone outside.

They flew up in unison, each chirping to its mate,

round my stillness in the sun, they formed a figure eight.

The beauty of their swooping in graceful lifts and dives,

created a sweet healing, a soothing bond survives

When I slowly moved inside, they followed me there too

love envoys, they signified, two spirits rendezvous.

Mary's father – Dupair Edward Burrell/Beal

Granddad was an Englishman born in London on 15th June, 1867. He was eventually brought up somewhat indulgently, thanks to two maiden aunts who took him in after his mother died and the family split. He was the youngest boy and they were probably pleased to have him with no family of their own. They were seamstresses for the late nineteenth century landowners, and I understand lived on estates for months at a time, employed to make clothes for all the family members, no doubt sewn by hand although I inherited a very old hand-turned Singer sewing machine from my Nana, so machines may have been around then. Granddad was often allowed to join the sisters' employer's children when they were being tutored, so received a good education. Luckily he was bright, so I would think a pleasure to teach.

He did well and eventually entered Oxford University, the details of which are elusive, but according to Mary, he became a court lawyer. Records from the *'Cyclopedia of NZ'* say he was also trained in London as an engineer and was with a firm of engineers and later at the Government Constructing Dept. and an electrical company where he was employed in connection with various installations in England, including the City of London.

Granddad developed a chest ailment and was advised by a specialist to leave London's aggravating smog for fear of it taking his life. Although he didn't actually die till 1952, he had been thought to be dead several times. Granddad would sometimes go into a rigid trancelike state at night, everything in his body closing down like death for some health reason, which was never diagnosed. As was the custom in England in the late 1800's (where he lived anyway), he was laid out in the parlour on the kitchen tabletop. His pre-burial wake would proceed until he would suddenly come back from wherever his brain had been, no doubt with all the noise, and terrify friends and relatives by sitting up demanding a drink and wanting to know whose party it was.

The relations, who were aware of this after the couple of near burials, had looked out for him, but later living in NZ away from them (and anyway most of them would have been dead) he had a horror of being buried alive, as many were once, their nail marks on exhumed coffin lids to prove they had needed to escape. (No-one suggested he give up his pipe and anyway his lungs never seemed to be affected nor his mouth, unlike a friend who had smoked a pipe since 15 and had died of mouth cancer).

Charcot-Marie-Tooth Disease (CMT) is an inherited disorder which I think is what Granddad may have suffered from. Although it possibly did not have any relation to his penchant for near-death experiences, it affects the nerves that carry information to and from the spinal cord. It causes symptoms of weakness and loss of sensation in the limbs. The peroneal muscles in the lower legs are often affected in the early stages of the disease. Granddad's case had been serious and Mary less so but she had a slight club foot and had to be encouraged to walk as well. I may have inherited it too as I need to walk every day now or I'm not able to, just like Granddad.

Encouraged by his aunts, in his home city of London, Granddad always walked for miles across London, Mary said, and knew all the streets and alleys as the city was then, enjoying watching human nature, often retrospectively making wickedly witty and perceptive observations. I imagined him striding along in his purposeful way, tall straight figure heightened by a top hat, swinging his cane casually, a 19th century man about town, observing city life. He could do imitations and we have a photo of him standing on a box (it may have been in Hyde Park) with a parson's collar on, convincingly looking the part with an open bible and sanctimonious expression on his face.

Perhaps on the suggestion of an older brother after hearing about his health problem, probably Thomas who was a marine engineer, Granddad left London eventually in his middle thirties, travelling out to Australia arriving in Sydney in 1893. He may have taken passage on a boat with Thomas, as he too later lived in NZ. The only indication of what Granddad saw in his travels was comments Mary said he made about India and he must have been in the Middle East also as I have inherited a gorgeous vase with an oasis scene in the foreground and a pyramid in the background. The colours are in soft iridescent pinks, greens, mauves and purples with a touch of gold and black. It was on display in the lounge of our Levonia St. home which I always associate with Granddad. His old steamer trunk made all our shifts with Mary until she moved into a pensioner's flat in Orewa, her last real home.

Grandad married Jean Tymms of Ryde, Sydney (father W.C. Tymmes), in 1893 and in February 1900 he travelled across to Auckland NZ. He was employed with the NZ branch of the Brush Electrical Co. (whom he had worked for in England) as foreman of works on contract for supplying electric light and power to Rotorua, a government town at the time.

The Spanish Flu Pandemic or Typhoid or Enteric Fever similar to the 1918 one took his wife on the second of March 1901, and Granddad also suffered from the effects of the flu for the rest of his life with the shakes, his stomach ailments and his childhood physical disability affecting his limbs.

Granddad's name change from Burrell (his ancestry was French from around the time of the French Revolution when the family had moved to England) to Beal in NZ may have been for snobbish reasons, Beal being his mother's maiden name. He had not approved of his marine brother Thomas' behaviour, who had left a wife and children to go off and live with another woman, I think a Maori. Maori were, in his era anyway, not generally accepted into local English social circles so he wouldn't see his brother again although he did see his children and the son became very fond of him, his feelings returned. Also I don't think the rest of his family were as well educated as Granddad.

Widowed Granddad, described as an elegant Englishman, met and married our grandmother, Alice Maud Hayter, when she was 30 in 1903, while she was visiting Rotorua from Kyogle Australia, seeing the 'Geothermal Wonders' and taking the 'healing waters' at Rotorua known in the British Empire for their curative powers.

On the completion of this work with the Brush Electrical Co. he received his appointment as 'Engineer in Charge of Rotorua Electric Lighting and Sewerage Plant' and he was also responsible for the hot pools. As part of his job he often used to have a large plank thrown over the smaller pools which he would then walk fearlessly across to the middle for testing. He took the depth of Lake Rotorua too and near Mokoia Island, in the middle, it appeared to be bottomless. He had a theory that, because the Rotorua lake level lowered when there was a corresponding rise in Lake Pupuke in Takapuna Auckland, he surmised they were connected by underground water, as did an Auckland engineering friend.

Granddad and Nana moved out to a large, Australian-looking government-owned house at Okere Falls. A white picket fence surrounded the large grounds – not far out of Rotorua today, but it would have been quite a journey then, possibly by stage coach but by horse anyway. To build the power station for Rotorua, Maori labourers were hired from the nearby Te Kaha Pa. Apparently the Okere Falls power station was the only one in New Zealand to service a town, although there were others privately owned including for mine works. Okere Falls Station is referenced in the history of the town at the Museum and Granddad's name is on the Okere Falls information sign. There is a photo of Granddad in the '*Rotorua Electricity – A brief History of Power in the Rotorua District*' produced by D.M. Stafford in March 1988 and also one of Mary at about 4 years old, with her long hair covered by a hat, standing in the unsealed country roadway outside their house, watching the huge power station turbine being delivered by horse and dray to Okere Falls. We also have a photo of the Okere Falls house with Granddad, Nana and Mary standing at the gate to their home, dressed in their best, Mary with a white frilly frock, all with hats, looking as if they were out of an English garden scene.

Contemporary description of Okere Falls from '*Riding the White-water with Ali Smith*'.

'*Evidence of the Okere Falls' early days as a power station, east of Rotorua, lend a mysterious feel to the beauty of the jade waters and native bush with its hidden folds of moss-covered caves, accessed by steep steps. The station was built in 1901. Suitably impressed locals described their town as "fairyland", but the station soon struggled to meet the community's needs and was finally closed in 1939. The now rusted iron skeleton of the station became a terrain park for Ben on his journey down the falls.'* (Edited)

The steps at Okere leading down the river were discovered by Granddad on, the story goes, the day that Mary was born. He was too busy to immediately come and see his daughter. The Maori labourers had not known the steps were there so were very pleased to find them. They had been overgrown quite heavily and the caves were filled with debris, which Granddad organised to be cleared, history perhaps not so treasured then.

Rotorua has always been a Mecca for tourists, often famous ones even then in the early twenties, and our family met many of them as well as royalty. Mary (14) saw Edward, the Prince of Wales, who visited in 1920, and was impressed with him, saying she couldn't believe how beautiful his colouring was with his blue eyes, fair golden hair and clear skin. To honour the royal visitors, Granddad had the Rotorua Gardens festooned with lights including a specially made welcome archway and Mary had her frock made in England that Granddad had attached tiny lights to. He may have devised some sort of battery system as there is also a sepia print of the family and friends having a picnic in their bushy garden with an electric kettle in the foreground which may have been the same for Mary's frock. However I think perhaps the kettle was close enough to the house to have had a long lead to it so I am not sure how Mary's frock was lit and she never said.

I would think Granddad met Sir George Bernard Shaw on his visit as he often spoke of him familiarly but it wouldn't have occurred to me at the time that he could have actually seen him, and he also wrote letters to many engineers all over the world. It would account for GBS' photo being above his bed in hospital. There was a definite likeness between the two of them although beards cover profiles. Granddad survived till he was 85 with his amazing retentive memory clearly intact.

Although hard for me to conceive of in New Zealand, it was comforting to know Granddad came from a city where, although change continues, there is a place in the world where my ancestors lived, where buildings have stood for centuries, where the Thames has always run and a person could stand there and think of continuity. Roots that gave me a sense of belonging. Difficult to do in a new country with a mixed heritage and also our transient lifestyle. Many immigrants can probably relate to that too.

Mary's mother, Alice Maud Hayter/Beal

The maternal side of our family, named Hayter, was from Australia and were originally from Camden Town near Sydney where there is a street named after the Hayters. The family grew prize produce for the Sydney Agricultural Show, consistently winning many firsts, becoming part of the management until they eventually decided to shift to a warmer and more challenging farm in Kyogle. It is on the border of Queensland and N.S.W. My Nana's father was buried not far from it and when he died; his monument was built and displayed in Kyogle's main street.

My maternal Nana had been her father's right-hand (wo)man on their farm in Kyogle, Australia when she grew up. The outdoor girl of the family of 6 sisters and 2 younger brothers. Although she was short of 5 feet, she was the one who helped with the farm labouring, riding a horse astride, not side-saddle which would have been the accepted norm, working as hard as any male. She broke the backs of dangerous snakes while the other sisters quaked and being a crack shot, could shoot them from a distance if necessary. I think Nana would have been pleased to use her practical brain – more use outside the house to her than women's work inside. The family farm was very successful and there are also many descendants of the family who carried on establishing businesses and continue to sustain rural and city lifestyles in Australia.

There is a Hayter psychic ability as well which none of our generation purposely pursue, only flirting with it occasionally usually by choice although things happen which we have no control over and as a family we accepted just knowing things – often that we didn't want to know – like someone's approaching death. Mary used to know that by a person's nose somehow and she was never wrong. The Hayter family had many weird stories, some about precognition and true dreams and also Nana's dad's ability to levitate things like sacks of flour and chairs and tables, the standard party trick, all accepted by locals and probably not seen in the light it is today. Nana and her sisters also regularly used a Ouija board from when they were young, until at the turn of the 19th century, when something really frightening happened, never referred to again, and their mother forbad its use. Mary said she hadn't found out what had occurred, but it must have been pretty scary as whenever she asked, everyone went quiet.

In her late twenties, and unmarried still, Nana developed difficulty with movement in her limbs from an inherited disease, then called 'Creeping Paralysis' (possibly Spinal Stenosis, a genetic based back problem) which brought an end to that farm lifestyle. She came over to NZ for a course of treatment in the Rotorua mud and hot pools. I've seen the gloomy, low-ceilinged, damp basement rooms and the special treatment tables and chairs of the time (in the museum where they were still on display) and it must have been a torturous workout. The system did work though as her eventual remission lasted most of her life. However like many who contracted similar conditions such as Infantile Paralysis, it did come back on her when she got older, but luckily only a short while before. Unlike Mary, who could touch her toes till a few years before she died.

Nana, although short, was a person you would treat with respect, with her strong, even facial features and thick, fine, dark hair worn up in a soft topknot in her twenties, she was very capable and forthright. A person with a great deal of courage. The only thing she really feared was someone with a mental problem. Her strength of mind was probably shared by many in those generations descended from people who had the staunchness and resolution to leave their countries, travel half way around the world, and have the tenacity and health to survive the hardships, harshness and strangeness of a new raw land. Her Australian family feared for her living in 'Maoriland'. They were always appalled that she would choose to stay on and live in the 'shaky isles', especially after the Napier earthquakes.

Nana met and married our Granddad, Dupair Beal, while in NZ and never went back to live in Australia although she crossed the Tasman Sea many times by liner on visits to her ever-expanding family at home taking Mary with her, who thought nothing of travel as a child. (Perhaps it gave her a mind-set for moving, as she was always restless. With money I have no doubt she would have travelled everywhere.) Mary had favourite aunts, uncles and cousins and went and saw them on her own for years after Nana had gone. There were so many of them by then, living up and down the coast, it took her weeks to see them all.

Granddad and Nana had visiting cards for their friends in Rotorua and Nana used to have teacup readings (tea leaves from a teapot not a tea bag), which Mary carried on intermittently and she also read ordinary cards (but used them like Tarot ones) which was looked on as a bit of joke until the reading came true. It was not a big part of our lives and done mostly as a form of weekend entertainment when someone was bored or wanted to know about their future love life or how many children they would have – a favourite for the ladies.

One of NZ's first postmistresses, Nana was in charge of and worked the exchange at the Okere Post Office just out of Rotorua. It was part of their government-owned house as many post offices were then. Granddad had needed a phone by the bed for emergencies relating to the power station anyway. It was a luxury when very few had a phone at all.

They were cumbersome ones mounted on heavy timber and attached to a wall, together with their large batteries and two bells on top. The phone instrument itself usually hung hooked to one side and had a handle to turn to ring the exchange for a connection on the other. A caller would lift their receiver and wait for the operator at the PO switchboard (Nana) to respond. Nana would ask what number they were calling for and connect them. These were party line numbers so they each had their own individual ring to distinguish them as the sound could be heard in everyone's place who shared the same line. Morse code keys sat beneath the wall switch board at the back of a desk and were used to identify the letter allocated to a home or business. I think it would have been a fairly small phone exchange. Nana could recite everyone's code for years afterwards as I found older Post Office employees could too.

Nana and her family often met famous people like Dame Nellie Melba, and when Alexander Graham Bell came to Rotorua, Granddad, Nana and Mary were introduced to him as part of Granddad's job. When Nana mentioned she sometimes had problems as an operator, like dialling up Tauranga and instead getting Whakatane, he answered; "Someday there won't be any lines to cross, as they won't be used and everyone will have their own personal phone," which seemed an amazing statement for that time, which Mary did not live to see come true. Bell obviously had incredible vision and knowledge.

Beside the two millinery shops in Rotorua which Nana opened when they returned from Okere Falls to live there, she also owned a couple of houses. Because of the successful family farm in Australia, and her own work, it had always been Nana's money which bought any family luxuries. She seemed to work at a time when it wasn't particularly acceptable for a married woman to do so, but I don't think it bothered her. Mary and I and my daughters followed on.

Nana

Do you know how precious you are to me,
my grandmother of my own mother's kin?
From the first time you sat me on your knee,
I've loved you and felt a rapport within.

Even before from my dark warm cocoon,
your gentle presence could be clearly felt,
I always knew when you came in the room,
later accompanied by how you smelt.

No other fragrance could ever replace,
the fresh warmth when nestling into your neck
and the consolation of your embrace,
while I gave you a wet nibbling peck.

A poignant memory of our forty winks,
the slow soothing rock on your narrow bed,
falling asleep losing count of the blinks
you sang to me softly, cradling my head.

Your tranquil answers to every 'why'
or your immersion in some short-lived game.
Your patient encouragement when I was shy
allowing yourself to be a child again.

You accepting me as a worthwhile being
my kind comfort when all else seemed forfeit,
Your common sense way of quiet listening
and nurturing my unfolding spirit.

Though puzzled by some contemporary phase
my anchor, my rock, my validity,
you never changed your established ways
your love was my freedom to just be me.

Mary's second husband John McDonald

My first stepfather was a bizarre mixture of a man. He had been conceived 'out of wedlock' as it was referred to in those days. His father, with a well-rounded education, was a creative and intelligent man both an engineer and inventor. When John was conceived in a brief encounter his father had with an uneducated Irish woman, his father was already engaged to a society miss in Sydney. However he did the 'right thing' and married John's mother instead.

The family story says she tried to abort herself and failed, perhaps damaging the developing embryo which would become John and perhaps partly accounting for who he grew up to be. If it had been in today's world it would have been interesting to do a DNA test, as physically and mentally there were no likenesses that I could perceive between John and his father.

John's parents appeared to have lived separate lives as he was raised in a bach in the bush with his mother when young and had little schooling or companionship. His punishment for misbehaviour was to be banished to a small shed on the property, even to sleep there. This from very early on, which must have been terrifying and lonely for a little boy. Not surprisingly he remained a loner for the rest of his life, except for those few years spent with Mary and us (traumatising for us because of the violent relationship) and towards the end of his life, when he was in another relationship for a few months.

When John's mother died, his father took over his upbringing and struggled to relate to his less astute son who had an intense manner and no sense of humour (I don't remember him ever smiling or laughing but he would lighten up at times around Mary when they were first married). He was often self-absorbed and had an uncontrollable, violent temper. An extremely physically powerful man, and tall compared to most men of that time anyway. John was well-proportioned except for his hands and feet which were massive (shoes had to be especially made for him), but a handsome man, aside from what I always thought of as 'livery lips' that were a strange, slightly mottled purpley colour. His deep-set haunted eyes were overhung by a heavy cro-magnon brow and dark longish eyebrows. They sometimes looked lost and puzzled in reverie when he sat smoking alone by the fire.

His wavy hair and regular strong-boned facial features relieved the sense of difference about him and gave him a distinctive appearance and although John had some superficial cultural training and possibly enough vanity to dress appropriately for social acceptance (he always wore braces), he was inept in company with no self-awareness and was also a Communist. Not the most popular choice of political beliefs, and he would rant for hours on this subject as he did with other things, isolating himself from most people very quickly. Male companions did not last long after they discovered he had no sense of humour – including bosses.

A rough, simple man who constantly swore (although not in company) confused in a world that often must have seemed alien to him, he was still the nearest man to a father to me of Mary's husbands and male friends (seldom lovers – not her way). In the evenings if he was not at work living in his bush hut, he would sit smoking by the open fire with me on his knee and sometimes sing in a deep bass voice, teaching me the words to rustic songs. Mary and John had a daughter but I doubt John loved any other woman than my mother, who would have been his antithesis in many ways, having grown up in Rotorua society with her well-off intelligent and civilised parents.

The Old Bushman

Resting forward, body slack,
Happy by his bushman's shack.
He sits serenely, on a log,
Eyes half open, like his dog,
Focused on the trees and glade,
As the light begins to fade.
Cigarettes rolled by his side,
Another on his lips has died.

All around soft sounds of dusk,
Mingles with the bush's musk.
Shallow stream on mossy stones,
Gurgles muted undertones.
A pigeon's whoosh from somewhere near,
A morepork motionless with fear,
Its halted sound, prelude to flight,
A stiff-legged kiwi waits for night.

A tui's ritualistic song,
Echoes back but not as strong.
Fantails flit, a white-eye stares.
Settling noises everywhere.

Slowly, kindly, stars and spheres
lightly smooths, the old man's years,
Then, like the day gone with the sun,
His spirit left, life gently done.

Colleen Aitken, cousin

John's first cousin, Colleen, is one person who had known me nearly all my life – from about 3 years old. It was very comforting to have someone like her for the length of time she was around when so many others had come and gone. She never said a hurtful word to me that I can remember and still offered innocent insights into our life until the end. She would have been appalled if she had known what really happened when she talked about her memories of our family and John. I left her with them intact.

Colleen's mother, May, was fond of John, he being her Australian brother's son and often took our family in, sometimes just my mother, sister Veronica and myself, with John usually off looking for another job. They had a rented bungalow in Herne Bay for years. Uncle Charlie was a Scotsman, a builder by trade, and didn't believe in buying a house, even if they could have afforded it on his wage as a carpenter at the old Otahuhu Railway Workshops. He regularly sent money home to his sister in Scotland so maybe they simply couldn't afford to buy.

Their place had huge rooms and Mary, Veronica and I would all sleep together in a double bed. The soft electric hall light would be left on for us children, but with the street light as well as the moving shadows from the trees outside, it was a very scary place to us. The villa ceilings were much more distant than we were used to as well and the reflected constant flitting movements often looked like weird figures – so Veronica and I never settled properly till Mary came to bed. We were used to no foliage (people never stayed long enough to bother planting shrubs or trees in a garden that belonged to the mill companies in the country settlements we were used to) and unless it was a moonlit night, our comfort was the dense darkness of the bush settings.

I used to lie there trying to distract myself by thinking about Colleen's beautiful dolls that were kept in the drawers beneath the heavy Victorian wardrobe that was positioned across the corner of the large room, though I did not look at its mirrored door. These dolls were intricately dressed in delicate lace and silk clothing, every layer a replica of old-fashioned attire down to the frilled pantaloons. Their hats were spectacular – decorated in miniature flowers, feathers and beads, all matching in colours, including real leather boots that fitted on the life-like feet and limbs. The whole outfit a Victorian couturier's dream. The dainty little lady faces, that each had a personality of its own, were smooth to touch, and framed with implanted natural hair, beautifully coiffed. Veronica and I were only allowed to see them under constant supervision and when we had been 'good girls'.

Colleen would sometimes play the piano in the lounge in the evening and some nights Veronica and I would eventually fall asleep to classics like the haunting 'Rustle of Spring'. She went on to get a music degree but I don't think she really enjoyed it as she only played for the adults and would put us off if we ever asked her for a tune. She became a very skilful seamstress though, which suited her nature, as she was a careful and particular person.

Colleen often came for the weekends and longer in the summer holidays from when I was about 11 and we were first living down at Waiheke in baches. She always brought food and although it was pretty basic, homemade baking with things like pies, even meat ones, it was a delight to us as we had little to live on around then.

When we went for walks along the beach, just to shock me, Colleen would sometimes bizarrely wolf whistle if we saw someone we fancied, but not before sussing out a hiding place first. On a wet day we'd all join in a giggling session, although Veronica probably didn't get the jokes, but after a while just holding up my finger was all it took for her to collapse. We would egg each other on by going one better with some story until someone would cry out to stop to get relief from our aching sides or wet our pants in helpless laughter if we couldn't make the outside toilet in time. Colleen and Veronica both had infectious laughs and also had their family colouring of fair skin, blue eyes and dark hair although Colleen had a more prominent nose, but a lovely smile and good teeth. Her build was average as was her height and she always dressed well, enjoying making and wearing her own beautifully sewn fashionable clothes. Although Colleen was 12 years older she never talked down to me and we enjoyed each other's company as I got into my teens. I would have been fairly responsible by then too having often to look after Veronica especially when Mary did her disappearing acts and, given our life, my short irresponsible childhood with my Nana would have been a distant memory.

Colleen was intermittently in our lives right up until I married and then at odd times over the years. She was engaged at least 3 times, once for 3 years, but never lost her virginity and I think her mother, May, had a hand in breaking up any relationships. May always had nicknames for the boyfriends – she had a quirky Oz sense of humour and would laugh silently with her full round tummy vibrating with the effort of restraining it, while her glasses glinted as her head bobbed. One slightly pathetic suitor of Colleen's she called 'Mouse's bum' as his mouth was so small and tight and a particularly aggressive one she called 'The Wolf'.

May had had Colleen late in life and was a friend as much as a mother so as well as probably not finding any man good enough for her daughter, May would have also missed her companionship had she married. They slept in twin beds in the same big warm north facing bedroom at the front of their home, watching over the street and sharing everything. Colleen's Dad, Uncle Charlie, was always in the background including his south facing bedroom, but seemingly contented, involved in the Labour Party and work unions – a thoroughly good Scotsman.

Colleen did finally find her man in her late fifties when she would have been called an 'old maid' in the terms of the day and he was very good to her. May approved as she was ill by then, dying of cancer not long after, happy that Colleen had found someone to take care of her. Henry was an Australian too which was in his favour, and had been married before and was older but he and Colleen got on well. He bought a house and they were doing it up before getting married, still living apart meantime. The night before their wedding he had a heart attack and ended up in hospital but he was not daunted. He'd already changed his will leaving everything to Colleen, and suggested they get married in hospital the next day. It never happened as he died that night. Poor Colleen.

All I can think is that Colleen wasn't meant to marry. She did go on to have another 'boyfriend', much younger, who she met when she joined a church. I don't think he considered her his girlfriend, although he was fond of her, but he never asked her to marry him – just hung around really when it suited him. She once asked me if she was missing anything by not having had a sexual relationship, but as most of the time she lived in a fantasy world of romance, I think the reality may have been too much for her to cope with. She was a fairly simple person.

Colleen had her cat Boris for many years who was her precious companion. When he died, she kept his ashes in a special box on a lounge seat next to the fire, not to be moved for anyone, no matter how cold it was. Colleen used to sit opposite, watching TV. By 2006 she had slowly developed Alzheimer's and at 80 years old, as often happens when you live long enough, old friends and relations had died or moved on so it was left to me to have her established in a residential home nearby so I could easily visit her regularly until she died. That was seven years later. We played the haunting 'Rustle of Spring' on repetition at the women's run funeral parlour for her.

Cousin Colleen

Her hand will always grasp at mine,
response an automatic sign
somewhere her mind remembers when
she had control – but won't again.

The inert stillness quietly claims
her body's movement that remains.
Obedient, her silent soul,
lost to the old disease that stole
the essence of her very being,
empty eyes not comprehending.

Her gentle manners still persist,
brain defiant but can't resist,
a powerless wait for closing breath
slow dissolution unto death.

Uncle Ross Turner

Uncle Ross was not a real uncle. Ralph and I always called him that though for the sake of courtesy and a lack of a more appropriate title. Mr., Mrs. or Miss were the usual respectful way to address adults (can't remember Ms or Sir much, unless perhaps at school for the latter) but often too formal for some relationships so families had many people they called Aunty and Uncle, unrelated by blood or marriage.

Uncle had survived Gallipoli but had been injured in the leg. He was hospitalised in Egypt and was granted a war pension when he returned home. He was slightly deaf but it was strange how he always heard the things we didn't want him to, and didn't hear the things we did. Uncle married a childhood friend of Mary's, although she was about six years older than her, and she and Uncle had five children. I don't remember her so she had probably already left with their youngest boy by the time I was old enough to think about it. Uncle had agreed to her taking that son but wanted to keep the other children along with their baby daughter Carol, of around my own age. Not a common thing to do. Left on his own, he brought up the four children with the help of his older daughters.

Uncle Ross had a chook run too, ordinary fowls as well as a variety of others with peculiar names and distinct colours which we had never had at home so I only remember the name of the little Bantams. They were housed in a makeshift run surrounded with chicken wire and set at the back of his large city section of straggly old fruit trees, with a haphazard garden and long grass to the back boundary by the old wooden fence which had vegetation rubbish piled against it. The high pear tree was full of Codling moth and the other mature trees weren't much better but as there was heaps of fruit there was usually enough for family use if selected carefully and bits cut out. The chooks would have their choice of anything they fancied.

Uncle Ross would have singled out pre-Christmas dinner (real Christmas would have been on Waiheke) ahead of time and on the appointed day would line Carol and me up with a bucket of hot water to be ready to pluck the unfortunate chosen chook, which probably would not have been a good layer. His idea of entertainment would then be to ceremoniously bring out his axe, waving it around in anticipation, open the rickety gate to the chook run and begin his chase of the victim.

I would think it was all staged for our girlish squeals of horror and revulsion as he never seemed to be able to kill it efficiently as it would mysteriously escape, and Uncle would spend ages hilariously chasing it all around the back yard yelling and swearing away like a demented leprechaun. The chook would hide anywhere its terrified wings would take it with Uncle performing enough to frighten the poor thing to death anyway. He would eventually corner it and chop off its head with relish and then pretend again to be unable to catch the still running, gory headless body.

Eventually Uncle would triumphantly open the old wooden gate, where we had been intermittently peering through the handle hole, holding onto the chook by its legs, blood everywhere, saying, "Here you are girls, get that dipped and plucked for dinner!" I can't believe we did it really, feeling so horrible about the whole performance but you did as you were told in those days. Everything Uncle did was tongue in cheek and even when he apparently told you the truth about something, you were never sure it really was.

We always seemed to spend summer holidays together camping down at Onetangi on Waiheke Island. In the times Mary had to work back in Auckland, Uncle dominated our days, usually in a casual way, unless he was in one of his moods in the morning or the boys, Ralph and Mark (his son of a similar age to Ralph) had been up to something. Uncle's sense of devilment was always to be wary of and any lovers around were never safe. His glee at later teasing brought embarrassment and retaliation too, so he needed to be ahead of the play in case anyone got the better of him. We all considered it a good victory if we did as it didn't happen very often. I'm not sure who was the bigger kid.

We also often stayed with his family in the big front bedroom of their old Mt. Eden villa, between Mary's husbands or quick trips to the city from country settlements, and I did too when I was older and on my own at times. Uncle was in our lives right up to my teens. There were only Carol and Mark left at home by then – his elder daughters Dorothy and Jill married and gone.

Uncle was a radio buff. Unable to sleep at night, we would vaguely hear him in the lounge, hunched up closely to the big short wave radio, picking up programmes from all over the world, finely fiddling to tune it until a clear BBC English voice would suddenly erupt through the wavy, crackling static. He knew all sorts about interesting things, and Mark commented to me that he learned from him that, "It helps in life to know a bit about everything." Mark had got so used to us being around he hadn't known for years we were not actual family.

Uncle had a series of strokes toward the end of his life which left him in a wheelchair. After I was married, I visited once with Mary and my children Shanla and Bevan, who were both quite small. We saw him as we came through the street gate onto the rising house pathway. He appeared through the trees to us on his villa's front porch, about four feet (just over a metre) or so off the ground appearing as if he were perched there on a bough. He seemed like a wizened weird old bird, all shrunken and bent forward, crouching patiently waiting for attention. By the time we became close enough to speak, and he saw us, I'd recovered enough to be cheerful.

Uncle was completely paralysed, his clever tongue silenced forever. The only spark of life was in his eyes which twinkled when he saw us. Surprisingly, his ex-wife had come back to look after him at the end. No doubt he would have had some witticism for that too, could he have spoken.

Auntie Alice Tyson

Ralph and I often ended up with our Auntie Alice in Rotorua, usually separately. She was not a real aunt either, just a long-time older tolerant friend of Mary's, who had not had children and hadn't married till quite late. She said to me after her second husband had died, "Oh dear! Oh dear! I never thought I would ever marry, never mind have two husbands."

Uncle Henry, Auntie Alice's first husband, had died not long before from a heart attack as they wouldn't have a doctor attend him, being Christian Scientists. Aunty had a close woman friend who died not long after too, so her husband became Auntie's second one.

Ralph and I must have been there together for a short time once. When Veronica was born Mary was in Auckland Public hospital for 6 months afterward. Ralph was about 10 and I was nearly 7. Auntie was good to us both, but very strict. Not what I was used to, so I often felt rebellious. Sundays were the worst, as following an afternoon rest which used to really frustrate me; we walked from their place to the church, which seemed quite a long way into downtown Rotorua. They were strictly religious and sermons were read by Uncle and other men sitting at a table in the front of the meeting room. They only once caught my attention as Uncle somewhat subtly referred to the previous week, when I had been meeting him after work. I had ridden ahead of him on Auntie's bike. He'd had to force me off the road with his front wheel on my back one, to stop me crossing in front of a car whose speed I had underestimated. I think it was his way of telling Auntie without repercussions. After the boring service, I would skip and dance all the way home glad to be outside again, Auntie's cat meeting us at the top of the road, about half a kilometre from the house. (Ralph had found a way to avoid this religious torture and would be off doing his own thing with his mates.)

Once on a weekend Ralph took me to the Blue Baths, without an adult, not unusual then. On the way we stopped and both had a milk shake, my first. I was very impressed that Ralph had money and the drink was such a novelty I probably drank it too quickly. At the pool, Ralph met his mates and they competed with one another to see who could dive from the highest board. I watched from the shallower pool on my own for a while, enjoying the warm water and holding on to the sides at the deeper end as I couldn't swim, not really noticing the sulphuric smell of Rotorua, as we didn't after a while living there.

Getting bored, I decided to have a dive too like the boys in the big pool and stood on the side of it looking down, thinking, 'that's not far' and jumped in. It was a belly flop and I lost my breath and sat on the bottom of the pool for a second or two before thinking of getting back to the surface. Ralph luckily had seen me and as I struggled to the side to pull myself up, he swam down and grabbed me by the hair. Once out of the water at the pool's edge, I promptly brought up the milk shake I'd so enjoyed. This little outing did not impress Ralph so that's about the last time he ever took me on one.

Auntie and I often went to visit a friend of hers who, although her house was not far from the town centre, had dozens of birds living in the nearby trees. Auntie took old bread or food left-overs with us so that we could go out and feed them before our morning or afternoon tea. The birds, mostly sparrows, were used to being looked after and around the feeding time they all squeaked, squawked and fluttered around, jostling to find the best position. They would come tantalisingly close, pecking, and eyeing us with quick side head movements, ready to flit off if we moved too near. Others would watch from afar and whip down and back when they thought they were safe. I always believed my aunt after visiting this friend when I asked how the friend had known about something that was going to happen. She said, "A little bird told her." (No phone for messages)

Auntie had a wicked sense of humour, belied by her firm, no-nonsense attitude and her longish serious face, short cropped hair and tall thin body (although she seemed to shrink as I got older). She and uncle worked daily out in the beautiful quarter-acre garden that they both prized, planting and weeding amongst the flowers that were good enough for a florist to come and pick every week day for her shop, and sometimes vegetables or fruit in season was bartered at the local shops. Being on the pension it was an income boost for their little luxuries.

People seldom used front doors so for callers coming down the side path from the more formal area with shrubs and trees, turning the corner to the back of the house was like walking into a garden lover's dream. Scents were overwhelming in the spring and summer and the glorious massed show of colour was good enough for any Monet painting. Aunt's raspberry jam, made from the side fence climber, was to die for and she gave small samples of it to friends. If we were visiting when the raspberries were ripening, each person was allowed one jar only.

Aunty had come across an old-fashioned boot from the late 1800's once when Uncle had turned the turf at the back of their property for an extra piece of garden. The leather boot fascinated her as it wasn't in too bad a condition, so she cleaned it up and had it as a door stop for a while. Not long after, she and Uncle were invited to a fairly formal wedding and a present was discussed for some time before Auntie made a decision.

She wrapped the boot in layers and layers of newspaper and packed it in the bottom of a huge box with covering tissue and also impressively decorated the box with a billowing blue material bow on top with tufts of net entwined to keep it firm. Everyone was trying to guess what was in it (and no doubt a few of the men had put wagers on it) and some had tried picking it up but it was awkward and heavy, so they were eager to see it opened. When the bridesmaid removed the decorations and eventually worked her way through the top layers of tissue and papers, nearly disappearing into the box, she finally found the grungy old boot and struggling out with it, held it up so the guests could all see. There was a slightly embarrassed silence until Aunty popped up and said, "Tip it".

To everyone's delight out poured ten shilling ($1) notes, which had been weighted down with stones. They were dropping around people's feet, some floating near children who raced to grab them amidst the laughter of their parents and the rest of the guests.

A lot of money then, so it went down well with all, lightening the atmosphere of old fashioned formality. Aunty was happy with her gift and it became a family story, to be retold to others with chuckles.

THE END

Home

Comfort from familiar things
my own haven from the world.
My own bed with its soft springs
waking to delight, uncurled.

And the scents, the sounds, the feel
of things cherished and well-known.
Those worn places that reveal
unique patterns of my own.

Tranquil colours merged to soothe
spirit's quest for calm and peace,
keeping rhythms of life smooth
for resistance all to cease.

Background trees of privacy
nature's lovely natural screen
and sure source of constancy
sun-fed cells all shades of green.

A bright bird's brilliant flaunting flash.
A fluttering squawk behind dense leaves.
A hopeful cat's brief thwarted dash,
nearby a placid spider weaves.

Hanging baskets flow with flowers
where dainty butterflies alight.
Bees validate their droning whirr
and seem somnambulant in flight.

Life is good and full of pleasure
and I am grateful to be free,
for the options and the power
of my own choices to be me.

Made in the USA
Columbia, SC
03 July 2022